ELECTRONIC PUBLISHING
ON
CD-ROM

ELECTRONIC PUBLISHING
ON
CD-ROM

Steve Cunningham & Judson Rosebush

O'REILLY™

BONN • CAMBRIDGE • PARIS • SEBASTOPOL • TOKYO

Electronic Publishing on CD-ROM
by Steve Cunningham and Judson Rosebush

Published by O'Reilly & Associates, Inc., 101 Morris Street, Sebastopol, CA 95472

Editor: Deborah Russell

Production Editor: Clairemarie Fisher O'Leary

CD-ROM: Steve Cunningham

Printing History:

July 1996:   First Edition

This book is printed on acid-free paper with 85% recycled content, 15% post-consumer waste. O'Reilly & Associates is committed to using paper with the highest recycled content available consistent with high quality.

ISBN: 1-56592-209-3

Table of Contents

Preface

This book describes the stages of publishing an electronic title on CD-ROM—from an author's initial idea, through detailed design and authoring, to manufacturing, marketing, and distribution. The book has grown directly out of the authors' own experience in creating electronic publications. The two of us have very different kinds of experience: Judson heads up his own production company, a company that produces professional educational, informational, and entertainment titles. Steve has published a number of technical titles based on the annual Association of Computing Machinery (ACM) SIGGRAPH conference. Our different backgrounds in CD-ROM publishing complement each other, and they've allowed us to experience much of the spectrum of the current CD-ROM publishing world.

In this book, we try to share our experiences with other people who are considering publishing CD-ROMs, or those who have begun that process—what is easy and what is difficult, what is inexpensive and what is costly, what works and what doesn't. We want to provide an outline of the issues and problems you'll have to deal with at each stage of publishing an electronic title on CD-ROM. Some of these are common to every CD-ROM publishing project; because these have well-developed answers, we try to cover them quite comprehensively. Other issues and problems are unique to each disc project you might undertake; for those, we can do no more than discuss options and point to some relevant examples from particular projects.

About CD-ROMs

The CD-ROM market is growing at a fast pace, and there are many different types of CD-ROM titles available today. These titles can be roughly divided into the following major categories:

- **Informational CD-ROMs.** The main function of these discs is to present a volume of information to the reader. Informational CD-ROMs include historical titles that shed light on a historical period or subject; technical titles that present state-of-the-art information to a particular user audience; and how-to-do-it discs that serve as handyman's helpers.

- **Educational CD-ROMs.** The main function of these discs is to engage the student in learning about process as well as content. Educational CD-ROMs include classroom topics for schools and simulations that allow a student to experiment with scientific principles.

- **Entertainment CD-ROMs.** These discs are designed to engage both the user's emotions and his intellect with the material on the disc. Entertainment CD-ROMs include movie discs, games and entertaining simulations, and stories with illustrations or movie clips.

In fact, these are not clear-cut categories because simulations can be both entertaining and educational, while technical subjects can also be educational. The CD-ROM publishing enterprise is as broad as the whole concept of publishing itself. The main concerns in publishing all of these CD-ROMs are much the same: developing the concepts to be presented to the disc's audience; acquiring, creating, and preparing the contents of the disc; choosing appropriate technologies for the disc and its contents; testing the operation and suitability of the disc's contents; mastering and manufacturing the disc; and marketing and distributing the disc to your audience.

About CD-ROM Publishing

Electronic publishing does far more than provide a way to store and present large quantities of information in electronic form. Beyond that obvious benefit, it has the potential to change the very nature of information: what it is, how it is organized, and how it is communicated to others. As we gain fluency in this broader kind of communication, electronic publishing also has the potential to change the publishing world as we now know it. This book explores this potential, describes many kinds of electronic documents, and discusses a range of specific issues involved in making electronic documents usable. Although we try to be complete and up-to-date, be aware that electronic publishing is a dynamic and fast-growing field; authors, developers, and publishers need to keep an eye on developments that can change the electronic publishing environment—seemingly overnight.

Publishing Media

At present, there are only two viable media for electronic publications: CD-ROM and the networks (both the Internet and the various commercial networks, such as America Online and CompuServe). So many people are now using CD-ROM and/or the networks that they have become worthwhile ways to reach an audience. CD-ROM and the networks are alike in the kinds of information they can present to their users, but they differ in their stability, their information access rate, their costs, and the ways in which products based on them can be marketed to an audience. As an author or publisher, you need to understand the strengths and weaknesses of both publishing media before committing to one or the other for a particular product or an overall publishing program.

The CD-ROM Publishing Process

The information in this book is organized roughly in the order in which a CD-ROM title is developed and manufactured. This section briefly outlines that process.

Developing the content

As we've mentioned, electronic documents often expand the way we think about information and how it is presented. An electronic title can contain text, graphics, sound, digital video, and simulations, and this content must be organized through an interface that is itself part of the content. In this book we describe different approaches to developing the content for a CD-ROM. Although we emphasize the facilities, staff, and stages needed to develop professional-quality content, we also describe production approaches that will help you create your own CD-ROM and assemble other authors' work onto a CD-ROM.

One critical question you'll need to ask when you produce any kind of electronic publication is which target systems readers will be using to access the publication. Different systems have different resources and behaviors, and it's often difficult to create a title that can be used on all or even most platforms. Some genuine cross-platform systems are becoming available, however, and we discuss them in this book.

Organizing and budgeting the production process

Producing an electronic publication involves significant organizational work. You must take a worthwhile idea and put financial and staff resources behind it. You need to develop specifications for implementing the concept, as well as define the roles and responsibilities of everyone working on the project. You need to acquire and develop content and then integrate it into the product so it's usable and engaging to your audience. Throughout development, you must rigorously test the product to make sure that it is technically seamless and that it transmits your vision to your audience. Finally, you need to put the product into its delivery medium, and deliver that master to a manufacturer or network provider.

All of the development work we've described requires the skilled work of one or more people, and it may also involve the intellectual property of others. It also requires financial backing. Contributors to the process may include directors, editors, writers, artists, video specialists, programmers, and others. A CD-ROM might be made for as little as a few thousand dollars or as much as several hundred thousand dollars. Regardless of the size of the budget, any CD-ROM publication must be taken seriously in terms of both time and money. For most projects, electronic publication is not a cottage industry.

Designing the publication

In some ways, the design properties of electronic publications are similar to other types of two-dimensional publications; in other ways, they are quite different. In the simplest case, information is presented on a screen and is laid out with familiar grid and template techniques (although the screen's properties limit some of the design options of other media). However, since electronic publications are also interactive, navigation and interaction design are critical to a successful publication, and a successful CD-ROM designer must be able to work in these areas as well.

Preparing the contents with an authoring system

In this stage, you create the overall content and organization of your title so it can be put onto the appropriate electronic media for testing. You'll usually need to use one or more authoring systems (or other tools) to translate the CD-ROM contents into an appropriate form for publication. An authoring system helps you create the set of digital components and integrate them into a coherent whole. This stage may require the following:

- Collaborating with craft professionals to create your title's various components

- Applying high-level translation tools to move the components into your distribution format

- Programming to build the framework for your components

Bringing the components into an assembly system is similar to the way you'd bring text and images into a prepress system, except that it also involves bringing together interaction and navigation functionalities. In addition, it involves a variety of cross-platform authoring issues.

Testing

Before you publish any electronic document, you must make sure that it works correctly for your users. With electronic documents, particularly with multimedia ones, you can't assume that assembling and translating the content to fit your delivery system will create a product that works. It must be tested thoroughly to:

- Ensure that all materials have been assembled in their proper places and that they are correctly spelled, labeled, captioned, and edited

- Verify that the navigation works as you intended it

- Ensure that your audience reacts to and interacts with your materials as easily as possible

- Check that the product operates on all appropriate system configurations

- Ensure that the product works on an actual CD-ROM or Web server, as appropriate

There are established methodologies for all of these tests, and each will help you improve your product in a different way. There is one fundamental principle in testing: you can never test your CD-ROM too much. Never cut testing short, because once you manufacture the discs you cannot go back and change anything.

Mastering

Creating the master CD-ROM for distribution involves a number of issues. You must first decide what format of disc you want to create (ISO 9660, Macintosh HFS, dual-directory, etc.) and recognize how that choice will affect your publication. You may create your disc master on CD-R, DAT, or some other medium yourself, or you may have a contractor or your disc manufacturer create it for you. In general, if you are going to be doing a large amount of CD-ROM publishing, you'll save money and be able to produce test discs more quickly if you buy your own mastering system.

Manufacturing

There are a number of steps in the mastering and production of your finished CD-ROMs and their packaging, including:

- Selecting the appropriate CD-ROM standard

- Determining the packaging you need for the disc

- Determining the content and design for the artwork on the disc label

- Getting bids and choosing the manufacturer who will do your disc duplication

- Determining the timelines for the packaging and disc manufacturing steps so you can meet your completion dates

- Preparing any print pieces that will accompany the disc

- Shipping the print pieces, the design of the disc label, and the master disc or tape to the disc manufacturer

- Arranging for the manufacturer to ship the finished discs to your site

None of these steps is difficult, but they do require various types of writing and graphic design, and they must be planned in advance.

Marketing and distribution

Marketing (promoting and selling your product) and distribution (moving your product to the market) are broad activities, and in this book we don't try to explore them in detail. We touch only on the special characteristics of marketing and distributing electronic titles on CD-ROM. Issues include whether to sell discs through an established publisher or through retail and catalog channels, as well as setting the price and determining quantities. Disc marketing has become more difficult in recent years, as the overall flow of products has grown broader and deeper. Distribution is a full-fledged business issue that deserves careful study. We describe some models for CD-ROM marketing and distribution activities; it's likely that one or more of these models will be appropriate for any particular title that you'll be developing.

About This Book

This book is divided into four parts:

Part I, Overview of Electronic Publishing

- Chapter 1, *Electronic Publications*, describes what electronic publications are and why they have become so popular. It discusses the special qualities of electronic documents, touches on a number of emerging technologies, and looks briefly at intellectual property issues for electronic publishing.

- Chapter 2, *CD-ROM and Online Publishing*, examines the pros and cons of publishing on CD-ROM and on the Internet. It also looks at hybrid products that take advantage of both publishing models.

- Chapter 3, *Two Electronic Titles*, profiles two very different kinds of CD-ROM titles. *Isaac Asimov's The Ultimate Robot* is a professionally produced, mass market "edutainment" product, which blends education and entertainment. The electronic version of the Association of Computing Machinery's (ACM's) SIGGRAPH group's conference proceedings is a volunteer-produced technical title.

Part II, CD-ROM Development

- Chapter 4, *Developing a CD-ROM*, provides an overview of the CD-ROM development process, from initial product planning through final production of the CD-ROM image. It discusses the staffing that is required for most development projects, and provides cost estimates for several different types of projects.

- Chapter 5, *Designing Electronic Documents*, discusses a variety of design issues for CD-ROMs, in areas of overall title navigation, graphics, user interface, sound, digital video, and software.

- Chapter 6, *Authoring Systems*, examines what makes a good authoring system for electronic documents and looks at a number of examples of systems being used today, including Director, HyperCard, Acrobat, Gain*Momentum*, Media Tool, and HTML.

- Chapter 7, *Electronic Document Standards*, summarizes a variety of standards for electronic documents, in areas of text (e.g., SGML, HTML), page description (e.g., PostScript, PDF), network (e.g., Java, VRML), image (e.g., formats such as BMP and TGA, and compression methods such as RLE and JPEG), digital video (e.g., QuickTime, MPEG), and sound (e.g., MIDI).

- Chapter 8, *CD-ROM Disc Standards*, describes the various CD-ROM standards, focusing on the ISO 9660 and HFS specifications.

Part III, CD-ROM Manufacturing, Marketing, and Distribution

- Chapter 9, *Manufacturing CD-ROMs*, describes the process of manufacturing CD-ROMs, including production timelines, preparing data for manufacturing, and all of the production steps.

- Chapter 10, *CD-ROM Publishing Costs*, provides concrete examples of CD-ROM publishing projects and the costs of developing, licensing, producing, testing, printing, mastering, manufacturing, shipping, and marketing.

- Chapter 11, *CD-ROM Marketing and Distribution*, provides an overview of approaches to marketing titles to various audiences, and different distribution models for CD-ROMs.

Part IV, Appendixes

- Appendix A, *Resources*, lists resources for organizations that provide CD-ROM hardware, software, and services.

- The *Glossary* defines the terms used in this book and in the electronic publishing business.

- The *Bibliography* provides references for further reading.

About the CD-ROM

This book is accompanied by a CD-ROM containing a variety of resources that will help you learn more about CD-ROM publishing. You'll find some software tools; detailed technical reports on CD-ROM technology; frequently asked questions (FAQ) listings of topics related to CD-ROM publishing (e.g., JPEG, MPEG, graphics file formats, data compression, etc.); and several QuickTime movies. You'll also find parts of the book (summaries, Appendix A, Glossary, Bibliography, color figures), with links to additional resources on the CD-ROM and the Internet. See "Using the CD-ROM" on the page facing the actual disc at the back of this book for more information.

There's More to Learn About CD-ROM...

There is much more for you to learn about CD-ROM publishing than we can fit into this book. Not only is there a great deal of information, the information is changing very rapidly. We recommend that you look at the many references provided in the Bibliography, that you contact some of the organizations listed in Appendix A, and that you check out the additional resources included on the CD-ROM provided with this book. You'll find email addresses and URLs (Uniform Resource Locators) for these resources, so you can check periodically for updates to the information provided here.

People sometimes ask us to suggest a reading list of "ideal CD-ROMs" for prospective disc authors. That's a good challenge, but we can't begin to do it; such a list wouldn't suit everyone, and in this changing world, any list would be almost immediately out of date. Instead, we recommend that you look at a lot of different kinds of titles to see what discs can do—we suggest about 20 different discs, for starters. Pick titles that represent a broad range of prices, capabilities, and functions. Look at some of the inexpensive discs in the plastic-bag bundles. Look at reference materials, a bestseller or two, and a few that simply interest you because of their content. Look at a variety of topics—Supreme Court decisions, conference proceedings, discs of technical data, educational and cultural experiences, and even games. Check them out for ideas and examples. Just as writers must be readers, CD-ROM authors must be disc consumers; they must know what others are saying in the medium. And be sure to look at both good discs and bad discs, because bad ones will show you what *not* to do. The discs will show you new ways of conveying ideas and information; for example:

- How different kinds of pictures look in a document

- How movies can be presented

- What happens when you use different kinds of scrolling

- How using text in different fonts or sizes makes it more or less readable

- How sounds on the disc affect your perception of a presentation

After you get a lot of experience with actual CD-ROMs (and particularly after you create some discs of your own), you'll be more discriminating. You'll be able to look at a new CD-ROM and pick out the fine points and the features that are new to you. For example, you'll notice when the user moves the mouse into a new field and something happens that's handled very well, or how a particular shading effect makes a screen look richer. At that point, you'll be well on your way to a personal vocabulary of effective communication in electronic media.

Acknowledgments

The existence of the book is due largely to Mike Bailey of the San Diego Supercomputer Center, who encouraged us to do the SIGGRAPH 94 course that was the genesis of this project. Steve Langer and Breck Rowell of Disc Manufacturing, Inc., participated in that course and contributed to the notes. As we wrote this book, Steve and Breck also helped us by providing technical reports and a number of detailed pieces of information. The full set of DMI technical reports listed in the Bibliography is included on the CD-ROM accompanying this book; you can get future technical reports and a CD-ROM containing further information from DMI at:

Disc Manufacturing, Inc.
1409 Foulk Road, Suite 102
Wilmington, DE 19804
800-433-disc, 302-479-2500; fax 302-479-2527
Applelink: DMI.CD

We would like to thank a number of people who have helped with particular items in this book. Christine M. Shostack of the Judson Rosebush Company assisted with a number of examples and was very helpful in supporting the collaboration of the authors. Richard Bowers of the Optical Publishing Association, and Katherine Cochrane of The CD-Info Company both provided a number of resources included in the Bibliography. Christopher Warnock of Adobe Systems helped ACM SIGGRAPH get started with Acrobat for their conference publications and thus has had an influence on Steve's work; he also provided additional material for the included CD-ROM.

We are grateful to the people who reviewed the manuscript at different stages, and especially to the following reviewers, many of whom went out of their way to provide extremely valuable help: Judith R. Brown of Advanced Computing Research Services at the University of Iowa; Joan Huntley of Second Look Computing at the University of Iowa; Lynn Pocock of Pratt Institute; Jeff Moskow of Ready-to-Run Software; and Stephen Spencer of the Advanced Computing Center for Art and Design at the Ohio State University.

We also want to thank the following individuals and companies for permissions to use their work as examples in this book: Dick Phillips, Andrew Glassner, Tom Volotta, Pat Hanrahan, Tom Lane, Peter Schröder, Arthur van Hoff, Jamie Siglar, Jean-loup Gailly, James Murray, Frank Gadegast, Norm Walsh, Bob Hathaway, Charles A. Poynton, Electronic Book Technologies, Inc., Disc Manufacturing, Inc., and ACM SIGGRAPH.

Finally, thanks to the many people at O'Reilly & Associates who have helped shape this book into its final form: Debby Russell, our editor; Lunaea Hougland, our copyeditor; Mike Sierra, who converted and formatted files and solved technical problems; Clairemarie Fisher O'Leary, who managed the production process; Michael Deutsch, who edited the files; Jane Ellin, who checked the final manuscript; Chris Reilley, who did the figures; Seth Maislin, who wrote and produced the index; Edie Freedman and Hanna Dyer, who created the cover design; and Nancy Priest, who designed the interior format.

PART

I

Overview of
Electronic Publishing

This part of the book contains the following:

- Chapter 1, *Electronic Publications*, describes what electronic publications are and why they have become so popular. It discusses the special qualities of electronic documents, touches on a number of emerging technologies, and looks briefly at intellectual property issues for electronic publishing.

- Chapter 2, *CD-ROM and Online Publishing*, examines the pros and cons of publishing on CD-ROM and on the Internet. It also looks at hybrid products that take advantage of both publishing models.

- Chapter 3, *Two Electronic Titles*, profiles two very different kinds of CD-ROM titles. *Isaac Asimov's The Ultimate Robot* is a professionally produced, mass market "edutainment" product, which blends education and entertainment. The electronic version of the Association of Computing Machinery's (ACM's) SIGGRAPH group's conference proceedings is a volunteer-produced technical title.

I

Electronic Publications

Electronic publishing is the publication of any kind of information on any form of electronic media. Although the medium may be any type of computer storage or communication, by far the dominant types are CD-ROM and the computer networks (e.g., the Internet and networks such as America Online and CompuServe). In this book, we focus on CD-ROM publishing (and, where appropriate, look ahead to the changes that DVD (Digital Video Disc) technology will bring). However, we also spend some time examining the potential for online publishing, particularly on the Internet, and discuss how that model of publishing may differ from the CD-ROM model. Together, the technologies of electronic documents and the delivery media of CD-ROM and the networks offer authors, publishers, and users exciting and challenging ways of thinking about teaching, learning, and communicating with broad and diverse audiences. Before plunging into a detailed discussion of how to publish, this chapter spends a little time exploring what this new world of publishing might look like.

What's an Electronic Publication?

There are many, many kinds of things that can be called electronic publications— information resources of all kinds, educational aids, and games and other entertainment products.

Once they've been made machine-readable, reference materials such as encyclopedias, census data, legal decisions, and telephone directories can all be considered electronic publications. So can plays (e.g., the works of Shakespeare), music (from Beethoven to the Beatles), and great books (the Bible, the Greek and Roman epics, the novels of Dickens and Balzac, and more modern works) that have been put into digital form for any electronic medium; we call these works, originally developed for a nonelectronic medium, *legacy products*.

Many other electronic publications have been specifically developed for the digital age. These include digital magazines such as *HotWired*, *Nautilus*, or *Blender*; adult trade titles such as Microsoft's *Musical Instruments* and *Isaac Asimov's The Ultimate Robot*; games such as *Myst* or *Gahan Wilson's The Ultimate Haunted House*; and electronic archives such as clip media and even digital erotica. Anyone who publishes these materials—or any titles like them—on the Internet, on CD-ROM, or on diskette is doing what we call electronic publishing.

In this book we focus primarily on what the publishing world calls *titles*, that is, works that have a significant individual scope and an individual market. Because of their complexity and individuality, these works are the rough equivalent of books in the print world. Although this focus does color our discussions—particularly our presentation of publishing and distribution models—the information we provide should also be useful to people who are doing more limited kinds of electronic publishing. Publishing, remember, involves both an author and an audience.

Who's Using Electronic Publications?

The professional and consumer markets for electronic publications are continuing to grow. Just a few years ago, only the academic and research communities had access to large-capacity storage on disk or to high-speed network capability. Today, these resources, like CD-ROM and the Internet, are available to all kinds of businesses, to professionals at all levels, and, most importantly, to consumers at large. Many local libraries now offer network access at no cost.

People in the technical professions have surprisingly good access to electronic media. A survey of technical program attendees at a recent major conference on computer graphics showed that 93 percent of those surveyed had CD-ROMs and 94 percent had full network access. Although these individuals are admittedly hardly typical of the general public, overall we are seeing explosive growth in both the number of people who now have online network access and the number of CD-ROM players in the home. The CD-ROM player has become a routine computer peripheral (and we expect that the DVD disc will be hard on its heels).

How do these new electronic consumers want to get their information? One option is to use the Internet and the other global electronic networks. Network access and capability have certainly increased to the point where there is an audience of appreciable size on the Internet and other networks, and all of the networks are becoming more and more international. Indeed, network and online growth have been rapid, and sometimes exceed their capacity. (We look at network publishing in some detail in Chapter 2, *CD-ROM and Online Publishing*.)

We are optimistic about the future of publishing on the Internet, and interested in the capabilities and challenges it offers. For today, however, we believe that CD-ROM is the key electronic publishing vehicle for consumers, professionals, and businesses. There are many reasons for this, including the CD-ROM's large capacity, ability to store diverse types of information, familiar editorial and publishing models, and low cost of manufacturing. The CD-ROM has been slow, however, in living up to its promise in true mass-market entertainment. And here we believe that the coming DVD disc, with its huge capacity, will fill the needs of the market. We'll look carefully at the advantages of the CD-ROM medium in Chapter 2.

Why Electronic Publications?

Electronic publishing offers a number of excellent opportunities for information publishers, including:

- Greatly decreased publication costs

- A way to publish information that can't be put into traditional media formats

- The ability to greatly increase the amount of information in a single publication

- A way to move into new approaches to organizing and presenting information

Perhaps most fundamentally, electronic publishing allows an author or publisher to integrate text, sound, pictures, video, animation, and interactive computing into a common paradigm and a common medium. Currently, documents that integrate all these capabilities are called *multimedia documents*, but we feel that "multimedia" is a temporary term that emphasizes the novelty of such documents. All media and all processes, both computing and communication, are fused into a common digital domain. This section expands on these themes.

A New Publishing Culture

Electronic publishing may most certainly be done by a large organization. But today, we're in a revolutionary period in which technology allows a single individual to own the basic means of publishing. By lowering the cost of entry into the publishing world, electronic publishing gives dedicated people, who love the things they do and want to share them with others, new opportunities to publish unique and individual works. These opportunities can create a kind of electronic *samizdat* culture—a self-publishing or personal vanity press—which has the potential to revolutionize publishing in the same way that electronic prepress revolutionized the production of print and democratized design. One young person with an idea and a PC or a Macintosh can now publish a title on his own; all he needs is creativity, insight into an audience, a lot of hard work, and (by finding his own distribution sources) a small amount of money.

This new world of electronic self-publishing is already thriving. Many individuals have developed CD-ROM titles containing their own work, collections of others' work, and work they've obtained from the Internet and other networks. They've then marketed these CD-ROMs to specialized communities using electronic word-of-mouth marketing on the networks. Other individuals have created World Wide Web (WWW) sites on which they post materials that are of personal interest to themselves. Today, for example, someone who writes short stories can create a simple HTML (HyperText Markup Language) document as his personal Web home page, and link it to files containing each of his short stories, enhanced with images or digital video. With inexpensive CD-ROM mastering systems, our author can also create his own CD-ROM containing the text of his short stories, along with the accompanying images and/or video. The figures below show two examples of home pages—an individual page for Andrew Glassner, a computer graphics researcher (Figure 1-1) and a corporate page for the Judson Rosebush Company (Figure 1-2).*

Courtesy of Andrew Glassner, Microsoft Corporation

Figure 1-1.   Part of the home page of Andrew Glassner (screen capture). Images Copyright © 1996, Andrew Glassner. (see the color version in the center insert)

---

*Be aware that, because of the dynamic nature of the Web, these pages may have changed dramatically, or even disappeared altogether, by the time you read this.

Figure I-2. The home page of the Judson Rosebush Company (see the color version in the center insert)

Some of the people who started with home pages and a passion for sharing their work have already formed small businesses and created successful mass media titles, and some of these small businesses may one day evolve into major publishing houses. But don't be deluded by the apparent simplicity of it all. Although a dedicated author can create a title on a desktop with relative ease, developing that title into a full-fledged product and bringing the product to the attention of millions of people is a challenging task. The competition for consumer dollars is fierce and the market is filled with players from many industries. The multibillion-dollar media conglomerates that dot the face of America, Europe, and Japan have already made their first forays into electronic publishing, and they fully expect to remain there. So do a lot of smaller (million-dollar size) companies.

We expect that the education and academic communities will be among the greatest beneficiaries of the new opportunities in electronic publishing. For those communities, there are four key attributes of electronic publications, particularly for textbooks and the kinds of technical journals that university communities need:

- **The ability to include material that can't be represented in print alone.** Unlike paper textbooks and journals, online and CD-ROM publications are able to include simulations and experiments, as well as full-color figures and digital video. Simulations and experiments can be performed on large-scale real-world data sets that are easily provided on disc.

- **Their low cost**. The cost of paper textbooks and journals makes it difficult for university libraries to find the funds to maintain their collections.

- **Time to market**. Electronic publications can move from submission to distribution much more quickly than is possible with paper documents, so universities more quickly get access to new material.

- **Ease of updating**. An online title can be kept up to date by updating its files, and a CD-ROM title can include links to publishers' Web sites where up-to-date information may be maintained. This strategy alleviates the burden of trying to keep the information in paper documents current.

Like the gold rush years of the last century, the next few years are going to be full of both promise and heartache. There are going to be winners and losers, rich and poor, lucky and unlucky. Successes and shake-outs are occurring at all levels. Amateur publications across the board will have to raise their standards as people's tastes and expectations in electronic products mature, and as professional editorial processes begin to provide higher and more consistent quality. Advertisers will make their demands, too—for consistency, image, and content. Large media conglomerates may find that their size inhibits the kind of light-footed innovation required by the new medium. It's possible that these large organizations will hemorrhage cash and market position, trying to do things through traditional methods. It's going to be a very interesting period.

Diverse Kinds of Information

As we've mentioned, electronic publications lend themselves to the publication of many kinds of information, and to the intermixing of those kinds, as we describe below.

Textual and numeric information

What kinds of information are most appropriately represented in electronic titles? At the most elementary end of the spectrum are very large databases and archives of primarily technical data, in textual and numeric form. This type of publishing accounts for the majority of the electronic titles currently being manufactured. Here are only a few of the examples in this category:

- Census information

- Amalgamations of stock market and other exchange transactions

- National telephone directories

- Legal decisions, laws, and regulations
- Streams of scientific data from satellite sensing
- Parts catalogs for computer, hardware, and auto parts stores
- Archives of government documents
- Major newspaper morgues

The information in this category is often timely (in many cases, it's used for analysis and decision-making), and it's often already in usable machine-readable form. This type of information can be easily formatted into an electronic document, and can be distributed both cost-effectively and in a timely manner. Putting this information online is a natural development, and CD-ROM is a good medium as well, particularly if it is important to keep archival copies of the information. CD-ROM titles based on textual and numeric information are typically manufactured in pressing runs that are small and subscription-based (i.e., an updated set of data on disc comes out monthly or quarterly).

Pictorial information

Many CD-ROMs containing pictorial information are also being manufactured today, and there are many archives of image information on the Internet. In some ways, these archives are similar to the text-oriented titles described above. They contain collections of information; examples include clip art, font collections, and photography portfolios. However, the economic model for images is somewhat different from that of text. In fact, there seem to be many more models for pictorial CD-ROMs than there are for text-based products. Image titles may be distributed as shareware, as royalty-free images, as stock libraries that can be reused on a fee basis, or as stock libraries that can be used only by the end user.

Sound information

Sound is available for both online and CD-ROM publications. In many respects, sound is the godfather of CD-ROM, since present-day CD-ROMs have inherited their physical layout and characteristics from audio CDs. Virtually all CD-ROM players can also play audio CDs, and information in audio CD format can be intermixed with information in CD-ROM format. CD-ROMs can be manufactured containing audio tracks that play only on audio CDs, as well as text, picture, and video information that play only on the more advanced CD-ROM players. Some recording artists are already beginning to create CD-ROMs that supplement their music with pictures or videos included on the discs themselves, and some artists are publishing their music through the World Wide Web.

Digital video information

Digital video is another kind of information that may be provided either online or on a CD-ROM. Until now, video has been limited to small windows (generally postage-stamp size to baseball-card size) on the computer monitor, and to frame rates below 15 fps (frames per second). However, newer compression technologies and faster playback hardware have recently raised this threshold to full-screen, 30 fps video—achieving a quality equal to, or better than, the home VHS video cassette recorder. Video can already be played back from a CD-ROM onto an ordinary TV set or computer screen. (At present, there is some competition among available formats and playback technologies, but we expect these to resolve in the near future.)

The Changing Nature of Information

The previous section described a number of different kinds of information that lend themselves well to electronic publishing. But such publishing allows us to do more than simply present and intermix existing types of information in electronic fashion. Electronic publishing challenges us to take advantage of their new opportunities to expand our notions of both technical and popular communication. Eventually, this type of publishing may change the very relationship between information and the document that conveys that information. Let's explore this further.

Expanding communication opportunities

In the technical area, opportunities are relatively straightforward, but still challenging. Putting technical materials online or on CD-ROM means we can publish longer papers and incorporate additional information that may have too limited an appeal to be included in printed journals. This additional information includes not only text, but also data sets, color images, video clips, and research notes. For example, in recent SIGGRAPH conference proceedings CD-ROMs, authors' papers have included source code, multimedia versions of papers, data sets, movies, and high-resolution images. (We describe the proceedings CD-ROM in detail in Chapter 3, *Two Electronic Titles.*) We expect that as authors become more familiar with electronic media, they'll go beyond even these multimedia frontiers. As publishers are realizing that there is important information they can't convey in paper form, they are including floppy disks and CD-ROMs as companions to their books. Perhaps authors and publishers will come up with a convenient way to allow readers to interact with the author's work, thereby helping them understand it more deeply and allowing them to draw their own conclusions from it.

In the consumer area, we see similar, but even more wide-open opportunities to reshape the nature of presenting information—especially by having users interact

The Vocabulary of Interactive Publications

We don't yet know everything about communicating in the new world of computer media, but it should not take very long to figure out most of the techniques and vocabulary to do so. After all, motion picture film, camera, and projector were perfected about 1894, and by 1903 the essentially complete vocabulary of modern film was established, including parallel action, the close-up, the matte shot, the feature film, and the short. To take another example, television was introduced in the late 1940s and, again, all the basic vocabulary of the medium was established within about 10 years. These included real-time broadcasting, multiple cameras, and a cooler line of pacing. Like the movies, with sound and color, television has also had late bloomers, such as instant replay and the paint system.

Electronic titles and multimedia are only a very few years old, and the audience is only now becoming significant. Multimedia is a parallel medium to movies and television, and we expect that the medium will unfold in a similar way. Thus, the fundamental vocabulary of multimedia and electronic documents will be established during the next few years. We expect that we will be surprised by some of the things we find. We know that users can quickly become used to button palettes and to navigation arrows; that they readily take to text searches; that some sounds reinforce actions and support the user's model of how a title works while other sounds only annoy most users; and that users will attempt to click on everything in a picture to see what each does. But these are only a limited set of things an author may need to know about how users work with a title. We do know that multimedia computing is an amalgamation of many different things, and in order for a title to be really successful in this new medium, there has to be an integration of the many different components these technologies allow an author or creator to bring to the product.

In the same way that the movie audience needed to learn to understand the new ways films were being presented, the multimedia audience also needs to learn to work with information that is structured differently from single-focus media. Skills such as keeping track of your location and recognizing the options that are available at any point in a document are not necessarily easy for people who come to electronic media from books or television, as most users do.

At this time, most writing about multimedia (and most events on multimedia) are product-based, that is, they deal with how to make a certain product provide a certain set of functions. This, however, is not the long-term issue. The significant question is how an author can create a working multimedia vocabulary with which to communicate the author's vision of information or experience. This will take time.

with that information. We expect this to be true for entertainment CD-ROMs, as well as self-improvement (education) titles. Many existing titles have already broken away from text- and picture-centered information to incorporate sound, animation, video, and clickable activities that set up two-way communication and actively engage the user in the content. Why not provide a dictionary that actually pronounces a word for you, rather than requiring you to figure it out from a phonetic alphabet? Or an atlas of the body such as *The Visible Human*, distributed via both networks and CD-ROM, which lets users layer the body and explore hot (clickable) regions that expand out to let users trace anatomical features? And why not extend this idea to movies? The Mars Navigator project, produced by Volotta Interactive Video in collaboration with Apple Computer,[*] enables a user not only to fly over the surface of the planet, but also to click on the screen during the fly-by animation and get information about what she's seeing. Two examples of such screens are shown in Figures 1-3 and 1-4. Popular CD-ROM games like *Myst* and *Doom 2* also popularize virtual navigation.

The advent of electronic publishing gives us the opportunity to change the fundamental relationship between information and the document that conveys that information. In traditional publishing, information must take the shape of the publication—we have to prepare the information for that particular medium, whether it's paper, photography, or television. With electronic publishing, we can actually make the publication take the shape of the information it is to hold. This revolution is already beginning, and soon we expect to go far beyond this model. Inverting the historical relationship between information and document has powerful implications!

Compound and smart documents

The new relationship between documents and information suggests that the future electronic document will be a *compound* one, a document that is capable of holding structured text, sound, images, animations, simulations, links, and any content that we could envision as being "executed"[†] on a wide range of platforms by very interactive and flexible presentation systems. We also believe that future titles will be designed to be *smart*—that is, they'll be able to take advantage of the flexibility offered by electronic documents.

---

[*] Like all complex projects, Mars Navigator (presented at the San Jose CA Technology Museum of Innovation) involved many people in many different capacities, including Robert S. Wolff, Apple (project manager), Peter Hughes, Apple (3-D animation), Gary Rydstrom, Skywalker Sound (sound design), Pacific Video Resources (online editing), Karl Anderson, VIV (computer programming), and Tom Volotta, VIV (producer), with special help from NASA/Jet Propulsion Laboratory, MassMicro Systems, Pioneer Electronics, and Del Yocum, Apple (the patron saint of the project).

[†] In this context, saying that a document is simply "displayed" seems much too limited.

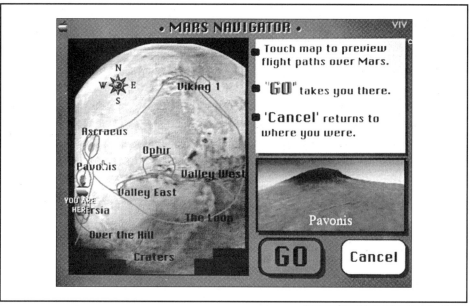

Courtesy of Tom Volotta, Volotta Interactive Video

Figure 1-3.   A screen from Mars Navigator (orienting the user to the map and controls)
(see the color version in the center insert)

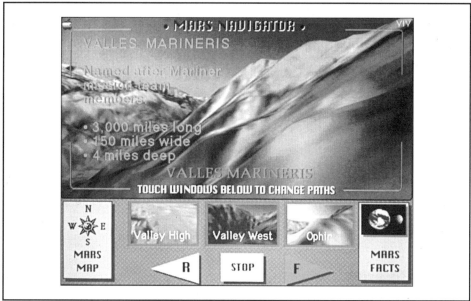

Courtesy of Tom Volotta, Volotta Interactive Video

Figure 1-4.   A screen from Mars Navigator (user has stopped the fly-by at Valles
Marineris) (see the color version in the center insert)

One very important characteristic of compound documents is their ability to present their information in more than one way. For example, any of several media could be the organizing factor for a title. Perhaps the user will be able to choose which medium he wants; the title will then adapt to the user's choice by changing the interface. Depending on the preferences and needs of the reader, a document may be seen as text with figures, as a movie with a text supplement, as a set of images with hot spots for visual browsing or to pull up explanatory text, or as a business graphic. The document may support browsing tools, outlining/summarizing tools, and a number of additional ways to personalize the way the user works with the document. A reader may be able to customize the size of the type, the width of the column, the size of the pictures, the speed of instant replays, the filtering of sound, and even the language. This ability to customize is valuable because people have a vast diversity of learning experiences and browsing styles. With experience and more capable authoring systems, we expect to learn more about the potential of electronic publishing and learning.

There are some multimedia document creation systems today, and others are emerging. Systems like Macromedia Director and Adobe Acrobat already allow authors to create powerful and capable products. Other new compound document architectures to support applications in electronic documents include Sybase's Gain*Momentum*, Microsoft's Object Linking and Embedding (OLE) and Apple's OpenDoc architectures, Authorware, and HTML. We're not sure yet what true compound documents will look like in the long term. In the short term, document standards will continue to evolve and some industry shakeout and consolidation will occur. The systems already in the market, as well as those under development, are already forcing us take a long look at the digital analogs to traditional publishing and document concepts, whether they are print, video, sound, or software. (Chapter 6, *Authoring Systems*, describes authoring systems, and Chapter 7, *Electronic Document Standards*, discusses document standards.)

NOTE

If you are creating electronic documents, you will have to closely follow developments in this changing world. The survival of your organization may well depend on knowing how to take advantage of changes—not only to keep up in the market, but also to avoid chasing down fads and transient technologies.

Digital Libraries

Traditional libraries serve their patrons in a number of ways: by building collections of materials for readers, by providing them with catalogs and indexes to these collections, by preserving a historical record, and by guiding the reader who has specialized needs. Digital libraries—shared collections of digital materials that may be widely distributed geographically—have the same goals. But these new libraries also have access to new document formats and new technologies to support access, catalogs, indexes, and expert assistance. By supporting new kinds of materials, they also broaden the concept of what a collection can contain.

These days, there is quite a lot of activity in investigating and building digital libraries at universities, businesses, and government agencies. The idea is to build focused collections of digitized legacy documents, formal and informal reports, multimedia documents, and even data sets so that researchers and others can access and use these collections in unified ways with powerful tools. Such digital libraries are expected to provide a much broader and deeper kind of collection than any but the wealthiest library could ever dream of building. The research efforts now underway are expected to expand to support educational work and, ultimately, use by the general public.

Naturally, digital libraries are expensive to build and maintain, and there is active discussion going on about how they can be supported once the initial research funding is gone. The two most common schemes are:

- The "pay per use" approach in which every user will pay a very small amount (microdollars) each time he accesses a document

- The "subscription" approach in which the user will subscribe to a particular library or collection and will then have full access to its contents for a period of time

We expect that these competing models, like so many business models in the electronic publishing arena, will eventually sort themselves out. Whatever the outcome, the digital library is likely to significantly enrich our lives and our work.

Materials That Can't be Handled in Print

One of the most attractive features of electronic publications is that they allow us to achieve a common medium that can integrate many very different information types in flexible and highly interactive ways. As such integrated publications become commonplace, we'll come to accept compound documents as the normal way to publish electronic information.

The new media landscape involves combining interactive functionality and navigation with elements such as text, images, sounds, and video—elements that have historically been passive and noninteractive. In other words, we'll be publishing not only information, but also dynamic solutions—programs, simulations, and other things that are interactive and with which a person is able to work directly. It is the difference between publishing a multiplication table and providing a true virtual pocket calculator on the desktop. Much of the new world of publishing will involve building virtual representations of physical tools, and then using these tools from the desktop.*

A good example of a system that explores this media landscape is MediaView, developed by Dick Phillips at Los Alamos National Laboratory for the NeXT computer. MediaView provides a good template of the way we think that electronic documents, authoring systems, and delivery systems should be developing. One of the key pieces provided by MediaView (but often absent in the current multimedia world) is the interactive simulation. The following figures demonstrate two screens containing such simulations. Figure 1-5 shows a technical paper—in this case, on medicine—accompanied by a data set that can be explored by the user. Figure 1-6 shows several examples of technical and nontechnical animations the user can control. Such an interactive facility allows users to work with data or other resources to create their own ways to understand or express information. Facilities of this kind may allow the user to visualize scientific data, to create (or recreate) historical or cultural experiences, or to create artistic expressions within the disc's context. A simple example of this third function is the robot construction kit on the *Isaac Asimov's The Ultimate Robot* CD-ROM (described in Chapter 3).

We believe that simulations of the kind shown here are as important as video in giving users a full experience in an electronic title. Simulation allows users to explore their own strategies in solving problems. For example, in the popular title SimCity, a user lays out a city infrastructure and makes the city grow and stay alive. Unfortunately, with most current authoring systems it can be very difficult to provide these kinds of simulations. Standards for interaction will ultimately allow authors to integrate simulations easily into their titles across multiple platforms. Authors will also need to learn how to use these simulations in their documents so they can reinforce or extend the range of experiences they offer their users.

What would a truly integrated electronic document look like? Let's suppose you were designing an astronomy CD-ROM and want to provide the concept of a space voyage. You could include a textual atlas of all the stars; pictures of the planets; animations of the planets moving around the sun and of the stars and galaxies moving relative to each other; planetary fly-by computer animations; and sounds from a radio telescope. You might also want to provide the user with a three-dimensional database of the location of all the nearby stars so she could position herself on any star, look out into space, and see what it looks like from

---

* On discs that run on two or more platforms, the authors obviously must include two or more different compiled versions of these functionalities, one for each different machine, or they must compose these applications using a language that can be interpreted on various platforms.

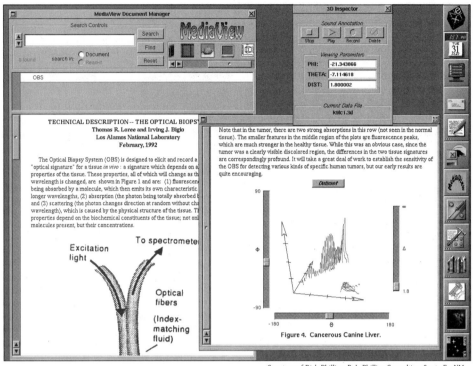

Courtesy of Dick Phillips, R. L. Phillips Consulting, Santa Fe, NM

Figure 1-5.   MediaView screen (showing a 3-D medical data set that can be manipulated interactively) (see the color version in the center insert)

there. Or you might want to let the user navigate to any planet, maneuver into orbit, and experiment with the nature of living on that planet's surface.

Using this type of CD-ROM would be fundamentally different from simply following a path laid out in a book or videotape. Simulations add a dimension well beyond what can be accomplished with conventional media (text, sound, television). Simulation tools, combined with traditional outlines, texts, and pictures, are critically important in textbook and educational publishing because they can allow users to explore and test relationships from their own individual points of view. Because this kind of simulation is an enabling technology, we believe that it's one of the places where the real revolution is going to occur in this industry.

Features of a Good Electronic Title

What facilities should a good electronic title offer its readers? One way to answer this question is to look at all the ways that people use printed documents. Another is to think creatively about the special opportunities offered by electronic

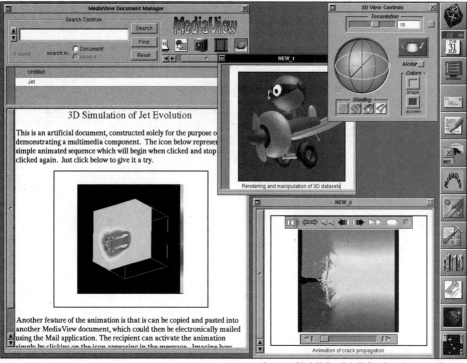

Courtesy of Dick Phillips, R. L. Phillips Consulting, Santa Fe, NM

Figure 1-6.   MediaView screen (showing both technical and nontechnical animations that can be controlled by the user) (see the color version in the center insert)

documents. The following list is only a starting point. (Note that some facilities might be appropriate for certain kinds of titles, and not for others.)

A good electronic title should:

- Support a full index and table of contents, at least as thorough as those usually found in print

- Support many kinds of browsing (including graphical thumbnails as well as text searching capabilities) so the reader can skim documents quickly

- Allow the reader to set individual access points—something like dog-earing pages in print or putting slips of paper in the pages of a book

- Allow the reader to extract information and save it separately, that is, take notes and compile a "clip file" from different titles

- Allow the reader to move around the document naturally, while always keeping track of where he is and what his navigation options are at that point.

- Help the reader clearly understand what his choices are, and how to execute any option easily and intuitively

- Not require the reader to wait an undue time for the results of a choice to be presented by the system

This is a fairly natural set of requirements, but not all of these facilities are easy to achieve with today's authoring systems. (Chapter 6 looks at those systems in some detail.)

Indexing

Indexing (a table of contents or a button palette is just another kind of index) is achieved by defining an information space and then creating selections that can be chosen easily, often by clicking a mouse on a selection. The author or designer of a title needs to determine just what indexing is helpful and appropriate, and he needs to be cautioned that indexing is often a manual process that requires keen editorial judgment.

Browsing

Browsing a paper document means leafing through it, letting things catch your eye so you can follow up on them as you wish. It's difficult to have an exact analogy of this kind of browsing for electronic documents, because sometimes an authoring system prepares things the reader sees on the fly. But it is possible to include outlines, picture and page thumbnails, abstracts, keyword lists, short examples, expanding and collapsing outlines, and other extracts or summaries that a reader can scan quickly in order to make choices for more thorough examination.

Access Points

Setting access points such as hyperlinks can be relatively easy for the publisher of an electronic document, because this is much like a table of contents function. Allowing a user to set access points can also be straightforward if the medium and the delivery system allow the creation of a set of custom links. But neither CD-ROM nor networks allow writing to the original document. It is necessary to create an external set of links on the user's hard drive and save the experience locally. These link files can also be shared on the nets. This capability must be supported by the document retrieval system, however, and is not common.

Ability to Extract Information

Extracting information from the document means that a reader may copy material from the document onto separate media for separate use. This has implications for copyright, but if the author gives good notice of appropriate copyright, the onus for respecting the copyright is with the user. Except for the quality of the copy, these copies are not all that different from photocopying, scanning, or retyping a document's contents. The user's right to copy for his or her own use is protected by the copyright law. Extracts should be in the original digital form; the reader should be able to clip out a piece of text, an image, a movie, a soundtrack, or any other part of the document. We must also be aware that many documents, such as games, may not function correctly if they are copied in part.

User Interface and Navigation

The document's user interface and navigation capabilities are extremely important issues. This is true whether the document is a dry Internet paper or a snazzy video game. The document interface must quickly show the user where he is, what he can do next, and where he can go. This must be done in a way that engages the user and makes using the document an enjoyable and positive experience. Creating this kind of interface and navigation is a task for an expert. The interface developer needs the support of authoring tools that give the author and designer easy access to a rich range of interface objects. Authoring tools that allow an author to integrate both media and interface objects in customized and flexible ways are only now beginning to become available.

Performance

Performance quickly becomes an issue with any kind of computer system, and a multimedia electronic document system is one of the most demanding in terms of both information transfer and computation. Users want to have all the components of a document delivered to their screen with no significant delay and in the highest possible quality. They do not care about the demands of sound, images, and movies; they want to have the materials in real time at higher resolution. High-speed hard disks are barely capable of providing everything the user wants, and CD-ROM drives are often slower than users expect. Downloading documents over networks is fun for the technophile who really enjoys using the technology, but for the average user it seems slow and clumsy. Network speeds vary widely, from high-speed networks inside institutions and businesses[*] to slow-speed networks that utilize telephone lines. Networks will have to be improved significantly before they can provide a satisfactory interactive medium for a mass audience. Most people will not be satisfied to wait several seconds for the next page of an online magazine to come up on the screen, let alone wait for animation, but this wait is inevitable with current technology.

---

[*]The current buzzword here is "intranets."

Using Authoring Systems

As we've mentioned, the real value of CD-ROM publishing is not that text, pictures, sound, video, games, or software can be published on a CD—it is that any blend of these media can be combined within a single electronic title on disc. These media may be integrated into what we've previously described as compound documents, which seamlessly merge the various kinds of media needed by the document. This is done using an *authoring system*. An authoring system allows the author to build a user interface (probably a graphical one that runs on the desktop) that helps the user navigate around the product. Providing such an interface is one of the requirements of an authoring system. Documents must also have content, something to navigate to or to unfold at a given location, and the authoring system also allows the author to create content through media integration.

In Chapter 6, we describe a number of different types of authoring systems. Here, we provide a very brief summary of how one authoring system, Adobe Acrobat, supports a user reading a document from a CD-ROM. Although authoring systems differ from each other in many ways, all share many similar characteristics.

Acrobat presents a document on the computer screen as if it were a paper document. This presentation is done with a *document reader*. The document you view incorporates full design, including color figures, fonts, and styled text. Acrobat provides browsing through thumbnails and outlines, and supports text searching and copying. Acrobat allows nonlinear documents to be created through links to provide alternate paths through documents, and it allows authors to provide document support such as tables of contents. Acrobat supports full indexing, in-line video and sound within a document, access to Web browsers to allow an Acrobat user to get Internet resources, and the ability to present an Acrobat document within the Web browser context. All of these capabilities extend the functionality of a printed document and make the Acrobat version more valuable than the original in many ways. The general electronic reader provides the document with navigation, searching, sound, and, in some cases, gaming and simulations.

Electronic Titles vs. Electronic Resources

Although electronic publications all have similar characteristics, there are two basic categories that deserve to be treated separately: the electronic title and the electronic resource.

- An *electronic title* has much in common with familiar types of media from traditional publishing—books, videocassettes, or music recordings. A title is complete when it's shipped to the customer.

- An *electronic resource* is a window on a dynamic, changing body of information. The growing access to networks and the increasing capabilities offered by the World Wide Web have led many people to create online resources. In some cases, these resources are intended for special audiences; in other cases, they are potentially useful to anyone who has Internet access. A resource must be kept up to date if it is to remain useful; an aging or out-of-date resource quickly loses its value.

As we've said, this book focuses particular attention on fully finished titles, especially on CD-ROM, but the information provided here is in most cases just as relevant to electronic resources. The discussion in Chapter 2 of hybrid disc/online products is especially germane here, since a hybrid product is typically released on CD-ROM, but is provided with current information through online connections.

The issue of updating is fundamentally different for titles and electronic resources. Creating any kind of publication—electronic or traditional—is something like participating in a birth. If you create a title, your role is similar to that of the physician; when the title is released, you're finished. If you create a resource, however, your role is much more similar to that of the parent; you must care for the child throughout your (or its) lifetime. An online resource must be kept updated because, like yesterday's newspaper, an outdated resource quickly loses its value.

It's possible to publish electronic resources either on CD-ROM or on the Internet. However, keeping that resource updated takes a different form for online resources than it does for resources on disc. Given an encyclopedia on a Web site and an encyclopedia on CD-ROM, the one on the Web site can be more topical.[*] Online resources are always accessible to the person who manages the resource, and he can provide updates to users at any time. Some people use the word "fine-grained" to describe this kind of control over the resource. On the other hand, updates for CD-ROM resources can only be made by releasing a new version of the disc. The word "coarse-grained" describes this kind of control of the resource. Given a CD-ROM encyclopedia and a Web site encyclopedia, the Web version can obviously be more topical.

Intellectual Property Issues for Electronic Publishing

Intellectual property is an important issue in electronic publishing, and it's one that is very much in flux. Authors, users, lawyers, and advocates on all sides of the issue have a variety of opinions about who owns what in the electronic

---

[*] In our culture, a lot of valuable information is now topical.

world. Electronic intellectual property issues are complicated, and deserve far more discussion than we can provide in this book. Here, we only touch on the topic.

Copyright

Many people in the electronic community have the attitude that all information should be free. Although this is philosophically an attractive notion, it's one that could keep electronic publishing from being financially viable. Historically, copyright has served as the fundamental intellectual property protection for authors and publishers. In theory, copyright provides incentive to publish; it ensures that the investment authors and publishers make in creating and distributing information will be repaid by the community that uses that information. But publishing on the Internet, or some other network, has the potential for breaking the historical bond between the author and publisher on the one hand, and the reader on the other. What should the nature of protection be in the electronic world? Should electronic works be copyrighted? How can copyright be enforced? These are issues that have yet to be resolved.[*]

Should Information Be Free?

The idea that information should be free is an attractive one, and one that some people—especially many in the computing milieu—espouse with great fervor. On the Internet, we see a constant stream of questions along the lines of, "Does anyone know of a site from which I can download this document?"

There is an old economics acronym, however, that's relevant here: TAN-STAAFL (There Ain't No Such Thing As A Free Lunch). There are, inevitably, costs associated with preparing, producing, and distributing information. The people who take responsibility for preparing and distributing that information must be compensated for providing something that has value to the user. If they receive no financial return, these information providers will eventually cease to operate—and no more information will come from them. An important part of our discussion in this book is how to ensure a reasonable return on your investment in electronic publications.

---

[*] Pamela Samuelson's article, referenced in the Bibliography, contains an excellent discussion of intellectual property issues in electronic publications.

To provide protection of intellectual property, the most fundamental need is that it be possible to identify an original document and to know when another document has been derived from it. This can be difficult to keep track of for some electronic media (for example, for documents distributed by direct network downloading—especially since some people set up mirror sites that may not always be known to the original author or publisher). In terms of intellectual property, publishing on CD-ROM may be somewhat less problematic than publishing on the Internet. With CD-ROM, there is a physical artifact, and it requires a clear action for someone to move a document from the disc to another medium. The clear nature of this action offers at least minimal protection from copyright violation and unintentional copyright infringement.

Even if the individual items on a CD-ROM are not owned by the publisher, it is usually possible to apply copyright to the CD-ROM itself as a collection. If you are a publisher, be sure to make clear copyright statements and to pursue possible violations (e.g., mounting a copyrighted CD-ROM on a networked server).

NOTE

There is another characteristic of CD-ROM publishing that provides implicit protection of intellectual property. The economics of CD-ROMs are such that it is usually cheaper for a consumer to buy a CD-ROM than to copy and steal its contents.

Detecting Unauthorized Use

At the individual document level, there are two related intellectual property issues to consider:

- Electronic documents do not suffer from degradation after generations of copying. As a result, it's almost impossible to tell whether a document has been obtained through valid channels unless the document is associated with a physical artifact. A CD-ROM can provide the artifact that effectively validates someone's right to possess a document.

- Electronic documents can be changed without showing evidence of change. As a result, a document might be downloaded from the CD-ROM and changed, but someone might assert that this modified (and unauthorized) version is, in fact, the original document. From an intellectual property point of view, it would be preferable if the original document itself were read-only. Many kinds of documents, such as Acrobat and Director titles, are read-only documents; they can't be changed once they are fully developed or integrated.

Obtaining Licenses and Permissions

When you publish a title on a CD-ROM or online (as when you publish any other materials), you are responsible for making sure that you're not violating anyone's rights.

If you are the author or original creator of the materials, and if you have not assigned ownership to someone else in a contract, you own these rights and can use the material in any way that you please. If you are not the author or creator, you may have to get permission to use any of those materials in your title. These include reprints, pictures, video clips, songs, and so on. You may need to obtain written permission for the materials (text reprints, pictures, video clips, sound, games, etc.), or you may need to arrange to license them. A license usually involves paying a flat fee, but a license for a CD-ROM title might involve a royalty on each disc distributed.

Obtaining permissions and proper licenses can be time-consuming, and may well involve much more than simply asking how much the rights would cost. Because rights involve negotiations, don't assume that you can include materials until there is an actual signed contract for their use. Be sure to have all these arrangements lined up early enough so that if they fall through you haven't wasted a lot of time working on a project. Because permissions and licenses are legal documents, be sure they are all handled on paper so there will be no misunderstanding after the project is published.*

We discuss permissions and licensing in greater detail in Chapter 4, *Developing a CD-ROM*, and Chapter 6.

Obtaining Copyright

Don't forget to obtain your own copyrights on your work. When you develop a title, even one that contains a good deal of somebody else's work, you will surely be adding a great deal of value—text, images, video, sounds, etc., that can be copyrighted on their own. In addition, a collection of materials may be copyrightable even if you don't control the copyright of all of the individual pieces. By copyrighting the title or its original contents, you assert your rights to control its further uses and to receive whatever financial return is generated by the work.

---

*Many lawyers do not believe that an email permission is adequate, and a verbal permission is almost never adequate.

Emerging Technologies

If CD-ROM and the World Wide Web are the present, what's the future? This section takes a somewhat speculative look at some technologies that are on the way.

Digital Video Disc (DVD)

Digital Video Disc (DVD) is a new disc format (created from at least two competing laboratory developments in the early 1990s) that is expected to be very important to the future of digital video. DVD will come in several varieties (single-sided, single-layer; single-sided, double-layer; and double-sided, double-layer). The maximum capacity of a disc will be about eight times the capacity of today's CD-ROMs for the low-end DVD, and 32 times its capacity for the high-end DVD. The enormous capacity of these devices will make them prime candidates for mass-market entertainment products. Throughout this book, we note where the use of DVD, rather than CD-ROM, may be relevant to our discussion; for example, because of the different capacity and manufacturing of these devices, some analyses may differ for DVD.

DVD-capable players are expected to be available very soon. However, because of the time needed for prototyping and development of equipment and titles, we don't expect to see real market penetration until about the year 2000, and we anticipate that DVD will be a fully viable market about four to five years after that date.

For more detailed technical information about DVD, see Chapter 8, *CD-ROM Disc Standards*.

Portable Media Machine

We expect to see CD-ROM consumer technology during the next five to ten years include portable *multimedia machines* with a solid-state liquid-crystal screen, a built-in CD-ROM or DVD drive, stereo speakers, and a game pad that includes a mouse, direction arrows and possibly a keyboard, all priced well under $500. We expect these systems to present digital video at 30 frames per second from broadcast or disc sources, to have CD-audio sound or better, to be highly interactive, and to provide high-resolution text. Basically, we expect to see machines that have everything we now see in a color flat-screen multimedia portable computer—but these will be small enough to be worn on your belt!

Our vision isn't unique. People in such consumer products industries as records, movies, TV, games, and software all recognize that this kind of machine is coming—and they're all scrambling to produce content for it. The companies building these products are, in many cases, staffed with uniquely multigenerational development teams: young people who have been raised on video games and who are comfortable with the multimedia aspects of products designed for this kind of device, as well as older people who are experienced in marketing and distributing hundreds of millions of dollars of products into stores. The result of all these efforts will be not only a new type of portable machine, but also a new breed of electronic title that takes advantage of its capabilities.

Network Computer

Another variation on the media machine is the *network computer,* a device that provides all the capabilities of the media machine, but that depends on the networks (instead of disc drives) to get its content. Recent developments on the Internet—Java, in particular—offer the vision of getting all the applications for these computers from the networks so their owners will never need to purchase software directly. Emerging standards such as VRML offer the possibility of including full 3-D graphics with the network content and sharing processing between the client and the server. (We briefly describe Java in Chapter 6 and VRML in Chapter 7.)

The network computer is being actively developed by a number of companies in the computing industry, and it seems evident that such a device will be available soon. This may change the paradigm of computing so dramatically that we can't yet predict how it will play out, but the opportunity is clearly an intriguing one. Before such a machine could work, however, we'll need to strengthen network capacity to serve the additional users and traffic required by the new network computers.

Television Set-Top Box

Another emerging technology, similar to the network terminal but perhaps farther in the future, is a smarter, more encompassing *television set-top box*, the interface between a cable provider and a TV set. Current set-top boxes include cable service boxes as well as video game boxes. Future set-top boxes are likely to integrate not only these two functions, but also services such as:

- Home shopping (even taking your credit card numbers)

- Access to online networks (including the Internet), serving the function of a network computer

- Interactive networked gaming with many simultaneous players

- Video dial tone—broadband services that would be provided by the phone companies

Major software and computer firms such as Microsoft and Silicon Graphics, telephone companies such as Bell Atlantic and NYNEX, and cable companies such as Time Warner are already developing software systems for these devices. We expect that the set-top boxes will merge entertainment and information technologies in ways we can't yet appreciate. It's clear, though, that they will have a major impact on how information and entertainment are organized and delivered. The leading systems for this are CD-I from Philips and 3DO from the 3DO Company.

CD-I and 3DO are interesting technologies, but there is a major gap between multimedia that runs on a television set and multimedia that runs on a computer. This will probably continue to be the case as long as we have NTSC (National Television Standards Committee) television, because of its low resolution and uncertain color properties. Because of the fundamentally different engineering of computer and TV screens, what works well on one is very different from what works well on the other.

To create a document for a television screen, you must make the type much larger than you would on a computer screen, and you must deal with much lower-resolution images. Basically, the graphic design for the entire title, front to back, must be completely redone. As long as the TV set is not a very good reading device, the CD-I and 3DO world will not completely commingle with the Macintosh and Windows world.

When it arrives in quantity, HDTV (High Definition Television) is expected to overcome the resolution and color problems of the consumer TV set. Since HDTV has resolution not too different from the larger desktop monitors, and since computers are likely to adopt HDTV screens for their monitors, we will see a tighter blending of television and computing technologies when this arrives. Other emerging technologies will also contribute to drawing these technologies together. MPEG (the Motion Picture Experts Group standard) will likely dominate video in both worlds, the DVD will provide full digital video on a CD-ROM-like disc, and we will see the expansion of networks that work with data that is remote from the box, whether it's a TV box or a computer box.

Goodbye to Print?

With all the emphasis we see on electronic publishing, some people ask if print is on its way out. We don't think so.

Just because electronic document technology is available doesn't mean that it should be used indiscriminately. The book is one of the triumphs of human culture: books are well understood by authors, readers, publishers, distributors, and institutions. Publishing books is a major international industry. Writing books conveys status and credibility to the author. Acquiring books is an indication of culture. Developing habits of reading books is one of the major goals of public education. In fact, even though the authors are very involved with digital documents, we have chosen to communicate with you through a book (although one about electronic media).

Books and magazines are "user friendly" in different ways than documents that must be read from a screen. A book or magazine fits in a tourist's waist pouch, a vacationer's beach bag, or a bathroom's reading rack. Moreover, a book or magazine requires no electrical outlet or batteries. You don't have to buy special equipment to read a book, and you don't need to have voltage converters when you're traveling. A publisher doesn't need to create different versions of the book for people who happen to have different reading equipment.

For all their highly touted benefits, electronic documents don't stack up very well in comparison to books. To a large extent, it's a matter of how convenient reading is; most reading is done in the "three Bs" of books and magazines: bed, bath, and bus. Ultimately, any truly universal publishing technology will have to support all three of these. At this point, electronic publishing doesn't support any of them very well. Indeed, we don't see how even highly portable computing devices will be able to offer all the advantages of the humblest printed publication.

At this point, it seems unlikely that electronic documents, whatever their format, will truly displace the book or magazine as a major medium for information and entertainment. That doesn't mean electronic publishing is doomed. There are things that electronic documents do better than print, such as search large volumes of text or data. It simply means that we need to learn the appropriate position for electronic publications in the overall information and entertainment world. Instead of going head to head with existing book models, we need to focus on creating titles that take advantage of the unique opportunities provided by this medium.

We are familiar with many ways to use print documents that take advantage of their physical properties, but electronic documents aren't physical artifacts. You can browse a book or magazine by flipping pages, looking for headings, pictures, or sidebars that attract your attention. Pages can be marked by dog-earing, by inking page edges, or by inserting scraps of paper. Once you've marked a paper page, you can easily go back to that spot to read in more detail. You can rip out a page from a magazine, and you can easily photocopy it. But you cannot do any of these things with an electronic document.

Electronic documents have some browsing capabilities today, and their developers are working on making browsing work a lot better. Later in this book, we'll show some of the ways Adobe Acrobat allows browsing (and other authoring systems provide similar capabilities). In general, though, a document that requires extensive browsing may not be the best candidate for electronic publishing.

Electronic publishing seems to work best in situations where the reader can navigate by some sort of index or contents, or by paths laid out by the author. Electronic documents also excel when different media are combined—for example, text with sound or video, text with executable programs, and so on.

CHAPTER

2

CD-ROM and Online Publishing

As we've described in Chapter 1, *Electronic Publications*, electronic publishing includes two primary types of publishing: publishing on CD-ROM and publishing online (either on the Internet or on some other network). In this book, we focus mostly on CD-ROM publishing, both because of our own experience and because of our conviction that the CD-ROM medium is a successful way to publish. This success can be measured in terms of both providing satisfying content to the reader and providing opportunities for rewarding business ventures. However, the Internet and other networks provide another publishing world, and any wise publisher should evaluate both the CD-ROM and online publishing models before committing to either. In this chapter, we look at these two publishing worlds and assess the benefits and present-day limitations of each. We also suggest a number of ways that hybrid products can combine the best characteristics of the CD-ROM and online worlds. We have a strong belief that CD-ROM and online publishing can coexist to their mutual benefit. After all, the real revolution in the publishing world today is the multi-faceted change to all digital media, which encompasses publishing tangible package goods as well as broadcast models.

The Current CD-ROM/Online Debate

Our commitment to CD-ROM publishing, both in this book and in our own work, doesn't keep us from understanding the role of online publishing. Publishing on the Internet will have an important impact on the world of electronic publishing—if not the world of publishing in general. At present, though, there are both technical and business challenges that need to be met before this promise can be realized. We describe these in later sections.

Right now, online publishing works better with certain kinds of information and business situations than with others. The best online publications seem to be those that work with small, encapsulated information as opposed to larger pieces, and with constantly updated information as opposed to less volatile experiences. The Internet is a very good resource for research requiring up-to-the-minute findings, such as looking up child pornography cases from the last 15 to 18 months, or looking for the latest versions of computing technology. The Internet can also be a good resource for library archives (when they are put into digital form, as is the case with the Library of Congress and some university libraries). On the other hand, the Internet isn't a very good place to get massive quantities of information, to find analysis, or to examine libraries of maps, films, or sound recordings. The Internet has a definite grassroots nature and one that's fresh and open; we hope it retains this spirit as it develops. The Internet also has the potential to provide a multitiered distribution structure which will allow garage publishers, as well as billion-dollar publishers such as Time Warner and Disney, to flourish.

CD-ROM publishers have been concerned about the headlong plunge into Internet publishing, which sometimes has been at the expense of CD-ROM publishing efforts. One of the problems is that investors are often fickle and run with trends. The CD-ROM was hot until the Internet caught the eye of the media, at least somewhat replacing CD-ROM, and a lot of the speculation in CD-ROM publishing flew to the Internet. We're not talking only about a shift of capital, such as the capitalization of Netscape, but a shift in the efforts of some publishing and entertainment companies. Several companies started CD-ROM publishing ventures, spent 12 to 18 months of effort, incurred $5 to $10 million in expenses, and have now retreated without earning significant returns.

Some pundits predict that the Internet will undergo a similar retrenchment as the speculation bursts. The good news is that both technologies—CD-ROM and the Internet—are fundamental parts of tomorrow's landscape. There is tremendous confusion among content providers. Many of them read that the Internet is hot and think they're missing out; they hire a vice president or two and set up a group to figure out what to do with the Internet. The problem is that only a few people have figured out how to make big money publishing on the Internet. Not too many people are making big money yet publishing on CD-ROM either, although a lot of them are now spending money in both areas (many not quite knowing the territory). But they learn.

Overall, we're in a period of economic and cultural confusion about what is and what should be happening in electronic publishing. People are uncertain about many things: whether to use CD-ROM or the networks or both; the cost of bandwidth; and the rate of deployment of CD-ROM players, network users, and network capacity. Other people worry about the cost of information and copyright issues. Actually achieving anything approaching the goal of universal information access through the networks (a Global Information Infrastructure) still requires building a new large delivery system—and the costs of that system must be borne by the consumer, either by purchase or taxation.

We believe that simple absolutes are wrong. There's a symbiosis between free networked media and media that people pay for. When the radio first became widely available, people said it would destroy recorded music and that "free" music would completely replace music people had to pay for. For a period of time, musicians went on strike and refused to have any of their music played on the radio. We now know what the musicians discovered: that free radio generated more record sales. Paid-for music, in albums and music CDs, has remained a viable business, worth many billions of dollars. Hollywood was similarly reticent about having movies shown on TV, and was resistant to videocassette rentals and sales. The movie industry has also learned that it's the combination of these media that makes a movie property successful. A movie producer now structures distribution by including first-run movie theaters, TV rights, and videocassette sales and rentals to create a profitable structure for a film. We expect that as the electronic publishing field matures, similar relationships will grow between information available online and information available on CD-ROM. The section later in this chapter on "Hybrid CD-ROM/Online Products" explores some of these relationships.

Why CD-ROM?

In most of the discussion so far, we've been looking at electronic publishing in a general way. In theory, the features and benefits we've discussed are characteristic of publications both on CD-ROM and on the Internet. In this section, we look more specifically at CD-ROM. What attributes make the CD-ROM an attractive medium for publishing electronic titles? The major qualities are:

- A large and growing market

- The large capacity of the disc

- Familiar editorial and publishing models (similar to those of other businesses that publish tangible property)

- Low cost of manufacturing

- Durability and stability

Acceptance in the Market

The CD-ROM market has grown tremendously in the past few years, and there is now wide acceptance of CD-ROM as a medium. More and more computer systems have CD-ROM players, and the public is becoming accustomed to purchasing discs for education and entertainment. How large is the CD-ROM audience? Because CD-ROM drives are sold through so many channels, it's difficult to get hard data on the number of drives sold and the number in use. Market surveys return a wide variety of estimates. In this book we tend toward fairly conservative estimates of CD-ROM numbers.

The rate of increase in the installed base of CD-ROM players has grown from about one million units per year in 1992, to six million or more a year by 1996. At least 80 percent of these drives are used for multimedia applications. The *Wall Street Journal* estimates that there will be an installed base of more than 22 million CD-ROM units in 1997 and 80 million by 2000. The Digital Video Disc (DVD) system (which will be compatible with CD-ROMs) was launched in 1996, and will be seeing significant sales by the end of the decade.

NOTE

The estimates presented for DVD use are, by necessity, rather speculative. Some key participants in DVD development believe that it will be 2000 before significant numbers of DVD consumer titles and players are sold. So take any estimates you hear for DVDs with a grain of salt.

The dominant market for CD-ROM is now in the United States; we believe (without too much supporting research) that 75 percent of the world's CD-ROM drives are currently in the U.S. However, Japan's purchase of CD-ROM technology is very close to that of the U.S. Although Europe is three or four years behind the U.S. growth curve, sales there are proceeding on a parallel path; 2.7 million units were sold in 1994, and projections are that there will be 36 million units in place by 1998. Most European PCs are in the home, and in 1994, 60 percent of new European PCs had CD-ROM drives. In general, we expect numbers outside the United States to grow quickly, as CD-ROM and DVD devices reach the same proportion of computer desktops currently seen in the United States.

Large Capacity

A CD-ROM provides a very large capacity—654.7 megabytes (MB). This capacity can be freely divided into any combination of text, sound, pictures, video, and software needed for a particular title. What actually can fit into this much space?

First, let's consider some comparisons with ordinary printed books:

- A 300-page book, with an average of 300 words per page and an average word length of 6 characters, contains 1800 bytes per page, or 540,000 bytes total. We could store about 1,000 such books in ASCII text format on a single CD-ROM.

- The same book containing monochrome (black and white) figures requires about one MB in a standard word-processor format. We could store about 600 books in word processing format on a single CD-ROM.

- The same book, with the same figures, requires about 20 MB in PostScript format, giving us a capacity of about 30 such books in PostScript on a disc.

- The same book in a format such as Acrobat PDF requires about 2.4 MB, giving us a capacity of more than 250 books on a single disc.

What happens if you add color images to the book? Your space requirements increase dramatically. A single 1K x 1K 24-bit color image (a worst case) could require as much as 3 MB all by itself (although there are excellent ways of compressing such images and keeping the size down through the use of JPEG or other image compression technologies). Even with color images, a CD-ROM remains very competitive. With print books, there is a high cost of separating and printing high-quality color figures, and their quality still falls short of the quality of the digital originals on a CD-ROM.

Line drawings and 3-D graphics databases can be stored in compact form on a CD-ROM. There are several reasons: only the vertex points really need be stored, and data in many different formats can be converted and saved either in binary form or in an expanded ASCII representation such as PostScript. For example, a single rectangle in three-dimensional space, complete with surface descriptions, stored in binary form can be engineered with 28 bytes (12 bytes for the coordinates, 4 bytes for a name, and 3 bytes each for the color, transparency, specular reflection, and diffuse reflection). The same data stored in ASCII format requires about 80 bytes. Thus a single CD-ROM is able to store a database in excess of 20 million rectangles in binary format, or 8 million rectangles in ASCII format.

Note that these estimates assume that every rectangle contains not only a geometry, but also a surface description; obviously, if the surface properties are applied to many rectangles, we can easily store even more rectangles.

Image storage is directly proportional to the size and color depth of the image. The total storage for an uncompressed image is equal to:

```
Horizontal resolution x vertical resolution x
number of bytes of color per pixel
```

A gray-scale image has only one "color" channel, usually 8 bits (one byte) deep. Thus, a full-screen gray-scale image has 640 x 480 x 1 bytes, or about 300 kilobytes (KB). Color images either use a single color channel with a reduced color space, or three channels (one each for red, green, and blue). Thus, a full-screen color image might contain either 300 or 900 KB. These sizes can be reduced significantly with compression techniques (we describe some of these in Chapter 7,

Electronic Document Standards); many images can be compressed into one-tenth their size with little perceptible loss of quality. Even without compression, a single CD-ROM can hold about 2,000 full-screen two-color (including black and white) pictures, or 600 full-screen full-color images. A CD-ROM can also store images of higher resolution; the Kodak PhotoCD format, for example, can store about 115 images at 2,000 x 3,000 pixels each on a single disc.

Additional Capacity of DVD

The DVD provides even larger disc capacity. In its simplest form, a DVD can contain 4.7 GB of material, almost eight times the capacity of a CD-ROM. Other formats hold 8.5 GB and 17 GB. DVD technology represents a phenomenal increase in disc capacity. However, it will probably be the case that few DVD discs will use all this capacity, except for those using full-screen, full-motion video. At present, most music CDs use only about half their disc's capacity, and most CD-ROMs use well under their full capacity. With DVD, the developer will have available to him additional capacity beyond the current capacity of traditional CD-ROMs, but it remains to be seen how fully that capacity will actually be used.

Especially Appropriate Types of Information

Although CD-ROM is an excellent medium for storing virtually any kind of data, it's particularly effective for software, video games, sound, and video.

Software

CD-ROM provides a good medium for software because of its capacity and economy. A single CD costs about the same to manufacture as a single floppy disk, but it provides a much larger capacity.

Not long ago, virtually all popular application programs could be stored and distributed on one or two low-density (800 K) floppy disks. Although the newer versions of many software packages have grown in size, even today few of the popular graphics or office applications exceed 4,000 KB. Most utility programs are much smaller, ranging in size from a single KB to a few tens of KB. You can fit hundreds, or even thousands, of standard programs and software utilities on a single CD-ROM, and this represents quite an economy. For very large software systems, CD-ROM is a positive godsend. Some software systems, such as high-end graphics and animation systems, may require as many as eight or more CD-ROMs.

Many of the larger present-day software systems also require special installers to copy the product onto the user's hard disk, making the product harder and more cumbersome to deal with. CD-ROM comes to the rescue here: the entire product can usually be located on one disc; the user cannot accidentally erase one of the discs in the series; and there are plenty of bytes left over for style sheets, tutorials, manuals, plug-ins, pictures, and even video demonstrations.

Video games

CD-ROM also lends itself well to the distribution of video games. Historically, such games have been distributed on floppy disks or cartridges, but the CD-ROM enables much bigger and more complicated games to be manufactured at a much lower cost. The extra disc space, or "real estate," may be devoted to richer sound, better quality video, and more and better graphics.

Actually, there are two different flavors of CD-ROM-based video games—those that play on computers and those that play in set-top boxes that connect to the television. (Nintendo, Sega, and 3DO are examples of the latter technology; we described set-top boxes briefly in the previous chapter.)

Sound

Sound may be stored on the CD at several different fidelities. The standard audio CD can store 74 minutes, 30 seconds of high-fidelity stereo sound (the kind used in music recordings), or up to 20 hours of monophonic sound (the kind used in speech recordings). Sound may be stored in digital files at several different data rates.* Data rates of 18,900 4-bit samples per second (Level C) are fine for spoken words; data rates of 44,100 16-bit samples per second (Level A), which exceed the capabilities of human hearing, are used for high-fidelity sound; this latter type is the data rate for music discs.

Video

Video can also be stored at many different resolutions. The amount of video that can be stored on a disc depends on a number of factors:

- Size of the video window

- Number of frames per second

- Compression ratio—that is, how much information is expunged out of the video signal

Compression can also reduce the color space, as well as the spatial detail inside the frame. Although it is quite possible to store high-resolution video on a CD-

---

* These data rates are defined by the Adaptive Differential Pulse Code Modulation (ADPCM) standard, a standard for encoding sound.

ROM, in practice, the challenge with video is to play it back from a CD-ROM so it looks like a moving picture, and not occasional frames that jerk by.

The limiting factor is the data transfer rate of the CD-ROM to the host system. The first generation of CD-ROMs had a theoretical maximum data transfer rate of 150 KB per second; in practice, many systems were unable to sustain data rates much above 90 KB per second. Double-speed drives, now the minimal standard for disc performance, have data transfer rates up to 300 KB per second; triple-speed drives transfer data up to 450 KB per second; and quad-speed drives transfer data up to 600 KB per second. Even higher-speed drives are available, with ratings up to 8x (8 times the first generation rate), but these drives seem to be unable to offer sustained data transfer values higher than 800 or 900 KB per second.

In 1993, the single-speed CD-ROM standard for performance was flawless 160 x 140 compressed movies. By 1994, better compression technologies raised this standard to 240 x 160 movies that run flawlessly on a single-speed drive. If the video is compressed so that it can run at 90 KB/second, then a minute of video consumes 5.4 MB of disc space; thus a 650 MB disk can hold 120 minutes of video (and nothing else). But a double-speed drive can play back a 320 x 240 movie at a sustained data rate of 300 KB per second, and although this is a bigger picture, the video requires 18 MB of disk space per minute, giving you a total of only 36 minutes of video. For higher-speed drives, such as the 4x, 6x, or 8x drives, taking advantage of the extra bandwidth for video continues on the same path. While increased bandwidth offers larger movie frames and better frame rates, it continues to decrease the amount of video you can put on the disc. In other words, the bigger the video, the less of it one can put on a disc.

NOTE

If you are considering developing a video-only disc, you should look into the newer DVD technology or the White Book standard, which specifies MPEG video compression and audio/video data interleaving. See Chapter 8, *CD-ROM Disc Standards*, for details.

Video is best approached as a bandwidth problem. Once the bandwidth is determined through various key characteristics (screen size, color space, and frames/second), then to make the product work, you will have to determine a compression ratio. Note that many different video formats can play back at a bandwidth of 90 KB/second.

Familiar Editorial and Publishing Models

Despite the rapid growth in publishing on the Internet, we expect that the publishing of personal tangible property will continue to be a prosperous growth industry. Currently, the business model for CD-ROM publishing is very viable, both for products that are large consumer hits (those selling in excess of 100,000 to 150,000 units) and for more modest products (those selling 3,000 to 10,000 units). We see three main reasons for this viability.

Cultural commitment

The world has already made a cultural commitment to CD-ROM. The vast majority of computers now on the market come with CD-ROM drives; we expect that within a few years, every computer sold will have one.

Why? Because CD-ROM has become the preferred distribution medium for anything over a few megabytes in size. CD-ROM is preferred over floppy disks because it doesn't get erased or damaged, and because it's cheaper than floppies to manufacture in quantity. It's preferred over online distribution because it doesn't take time and connection cost to download, and because your original copy can be kept offline without your having to worry about accidental erasure. It's preferred over rotating memory because nobody is selling such memory for anything like the 70 cents for a half-gigabyte that a CD-ROM costs. If you need to store 100 or 1,000 pictures, you'll very quickly run out of disk space, but you can put thousands of photos on CD-ROM for much less than the cost of the hard drives it would take to hold them.

Aftermarket

Another major reason why we believe that CD-ROM publishing will continue to be a viable industry is the existence of an aftermarket for discs. Every other successful medium—music, books, videos, and videogames—has an aftermarket. So do CD-ROMs. What does it mean to have an aftermarket? It means that there is a secondary market for *artifacts*, or things; there simply isn't such a market for purely electronic media. The Carmen Sandiego CD-ROM you buy for your 10-year-old can readily go to your next child, to a niece or nephew, to a neighbor's child, to your child's school, or to a garage sale.

Editorial control

The third reason why we believe in CD-ROM publishing is that CD-ROMs have editorial control applied to their contents. Some people tell us that the ease of publishing on the Internet spells the doom of traditional publishing; after all, since there are no filters on the Internet, anyone can publish anything. We disagree. Let's look at a historical parallel. When the Xerox photocopier first came out, they said the same thing. All you'd have to do is copy 300 sheets of paper, bind them, and you'd have a book. You could be the author and the publisher, all in one. But the advent of the photocopier hasn't put book publishers out of business. While the photocopier has allowed people to "publish" books, it hasn't cut into the book publishing business, because publishers do more than copy and bind books. They provide a complete editorial construct by thinking about content, picking the material, filtering what's going to be presented, and making the presentation the best it can be.

Consider what it means to publish material about a topic such as World War II, and think about the difference between raw and filtered material. The raw material would include all kinds of Allied and Axis records:

- All personnel files for each serviceman

- All purchase orders and manufacturing specifications and blueprints

- All shipping orders for materials

- All medical records and burial records

- All original stories filed by war correspondents, and all the original photos and films taken

- All position and deployment maps for all armies in all battles

- All public relations files of all the armies, air forces, and navies

The sheer volume of data would require thousands of lifetimes to digest. We'd have all the documentation on the war, all the raw material of history—but we would not have *history*. We don't have history until we apply historical filters, points of view, and analyses. History gives us the five volumes of Churchill on the war, based on carefully selected cables and personal recollections; the Harrison Salisbury book *The 900 Days,* which records the siege of Leningrad, based on his experience and contacts as a war correspondent; the *Life* magazine picture history of the war, based on photos from *Life*'s war correspondents; and even Leni Riefenstal's film *Triumph of the Will*, based on the Nazi propaganda view of the prewar period. History is not raw material; it's the material carefully filtered to distill important ideas and actions from all the others.

Or look at the publishing of CD-ROMs today. The Judson Rosebush Company's *The Vietnam War* disc, for example, is a collection of previously published material, but with an authentication and an editorial filter that shape the product. This CD-ROM represents a lot of thinking, planning, and design, not only about the selection of the materials, but also about how these different parts relate. Someone has decided what the content should look like, picked the most appropriate material, and performed the filtering process for you.

The same editorial control applies to magazines. If you're interested in muscle and fitness, in sailing boats, or in cat breeding, the magazines for these industries let you find products that are interesting to you. They provide a packaged way to enter into that world.

The filtering and editorial control we've described is very valuable to customers of books, magazines, and CD-ROMs. There isn't much Internet publishing yet that provides the same control (though some of the new online magazines are starting to provide such value). All in all, though, we don't believe that free-for-all online publishing is going to cut into the desire of most people to continue to buy editorially sound CD-ROM products.

Low Cost of Manufacturing

One of the remarkable things about CD-ROMs is how inexpensive it is to manufacture them. For a small run (about 1,000 copies) the total production cost (including mastering, replication, and packaging) for a disc in a jewel box might well be less than $2.00 per disc. More elaborate kinds of packaging (e.g., printed boxes) can add another $1.50 to this cost. Printing and binding a book, on the other hand, is likely to run more like $10 or $12 in these quantities. Although shifting to DVD manufacturing is expected to increase these costs (if double-layer or double-sided discs are needed), CD-ROM manufacturing costs remain a modest component of the overall publishing budget. The shipping and storage of finished discs is also much cheaper than for books. By far the greatest cost for the CD-ROM is creating, integrating, and testing the content in the first place.

Another characteristic of CD-ROM costs is that you don't see the economies of scale that are common in the book publishing business. The per-disc cost is likely to be almost the same in small quantities as in larger ones. This situation is the result of the fact that CD manufacturing has a very low setup cost. The advantages to publishers are obvious: they can manufacture discs in only the quantities needed and maintain small inventories. By contrast, in book publishing (especially for books with color plates), the setup and make-ready cost is so high that most publishers are forced to manufacture larger quantities at one time and maintain larger inventories.

Durability and Stability

CD-ROM is a remarkably robust storage medium. A disc suffers no physical wear while it is being played, and it's difficult to actually damage the reflective surface on which the information is stored. The polycarbonate plastic through which the laser passes is extraordinarily transparent and is not damaged by the laser or other light, including sunlight or ultraviolet light. In fact, the only way to damage a disc in normal use is by scratching the disc surface. You can avoid this danger by carefully handling the disc. Even if the surface is scratched, we've heard that discs can be repaired by polishing them with a jeweler's compound.

What's Wrong With CD-ROM Publishing?

While we believe strongly in CD-ROM publishing, we must acknowledge that there are some disadvantages to the medium, as we describe in the following sections.

Limited Capacity

We've just talked about how large the capacity of a CD-ROM is. But the size of the medium is a matter of perspective. If you're used to working with diskettes, and if your computer has a total disk capacity that's smaller than a CD-ROM, you won't identify with this problem. The fact is, however, the growing sophistication and size of electronic titles means that even the 654.7 MB capacity of a CD-ROM falls short of the visions of many authors. Fortunately, DVD discs are expected to provide a much larger disc capacity than the present-day CD-ROM can offer.

Restrictions on File and Directory Naming

Another disadvantage of today's CD-ROMs is that the ISO 9660 disc standard (the primary one for CD-ROMs, as we describe in Chapter 8) imposes a rather limited directory and naming structure. It's not clear when this situation will change for standard CD-ROMs, but we expect the ISO 13490 disc standard for DVD discs to offer improved file and directory name handling—in part, so the new discs will be able to accommodate the larger set of files on the disc. And CD-ROM drivers will quickly adapt to the new standard so they can be compatible with the DVD discs.

Slow Access and Transfer Times

Still another disadvantage of today's CD-ROMs is that the access and transfer times of most CD-ROM drives are much slower than those of hard drives, and are much slower than the capabilities of even today's entry-level home computers. As a consequence of this relatively slow speed, users often have to wait for data, which impairs the performance of video, graphics, and video games.

Present-day CD-ROM drives are starting to reach their speed potential. The drives for the emerging DVD discs will have at least the speed of the fastest current CD-ROM drives, fast enough to allow full-screen video playback.

Obsolescence

Another serious concern some people have about CD-ROM is the potential for the physical medium of the disc to become obsolete. Some pundits worry that CDs will eventually become as obsolete as the wax cylinder, 78 and 45 rpm records, the LP, and 4-track and 8-track tapes. The history of media suggests they are right to be concerned—although we're quite sure that the DVD will extend the life of the molded disc for a number of years.

Nevertheless, the problem with this argument is that it confuses the content with the delivery medium. Any medium can become obsolete, but that doesn't mean the content will die. Today, great movies are shown in theaters on 35 mm film, in schools on 16 mm film, and on television. They are also transferred to videotape, and some will even end up on CD-ROM. Benny Goodman recorded on wax masters, and the Beatles recorded on quarter-inch audio tape; their work was released on 78s, 45s, and LPs, and now millions enjoy their work on digital CDs. Electronic documents are similarly independent of their physical medium. As long as a medium provides enough capabilities to replay the document, many of the documents being published on CD-ROM today will enjoy lifetimes far beyond the expected life of the CD-ROM medium.

Alternative Media

Are there other kinds of physical media that could be used for electronic publications? Besides CD-ROM, the only other media with anything like comparable data capacity are large magneto-optical (MO) discs or digital-audio tapes (DAT). But there are currently some major problems with both of these media. Magneto-optical discs are relatively expensive, and they are not nearly as reliable as CD-ROM. Digital tape is not random-access, and it requires search times that are unacceptable to most users. In the short term, we do not see other physical media as being a replacement for CD-ROM. In the long run, many of us may live to enjoy sugar-cube-sized, solid-state media containing thousands of gigabytes of data. If we're fortunate, though, we'll still be able to enjoy our old favorites and greatest hits on CD-ROM.

Why Online Publishing?

The vision of online publishing is that readers will have immediate access, from their homes or workplaces, to a body of knowledge that is being constantly updated by its authors. There are some very exciting opportunities to shape the nature of electronic publishing on the Internet, and some real challenges for authors and readers alike. This whole area is still evolving, so the vision is not yet a reality, except in certain limited cases. In this section, we'll assess where we are today, and where we're going in online publishing. We'll also contrast online and CD-ROM publishing where we can.

NOTE

Although we refer mainly to the Internet in the following sections, in fact most of the discussion is also applicable to publishing on the private networks, such as America Online, CompuServe, and others.

Who Needs Online Publishing?

The number of people now using the Internet, and the other networks, is hard to get a handle on, but we certainly know that the numbers are increasing at a rapid rate. Here are some statistics from published results from the Network Wizards at *http://www.nw.com/* (they are accepted as authoritative on these matters). According to these estimates, the Internet has grown from approximately a couple of hundred hosts in 1981 to 4,000 in 1986 to 500,000 in 1991 and to almost 10 million at the start of 1996. Figure 2-1 graphically shows this growth. The number of Internet users is also growing very rapidly, and some projections suggest that there will be as many as 200 million people using the Internet by the year 2000. Clearly, this rate of growth cannot continue indefinitely.

The United States is by far the largest user of Internet services, with more than 60 percent of the hosts as of the middle 1990s. Most of the rest of the world (especially Europe) is on the same growth path as the U.S. Japan, however, has fewer than 2 percent of the overall number of Internet hosts—apparently because there is no government agency promoting networking in Japan.

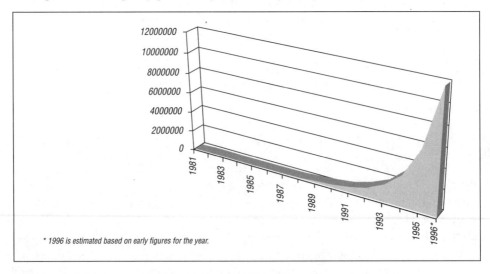

Figure 2-1. Growth in actual numbers of Internet hosts, 1981—1996

Let's look at some interesting comparisons; for convenience, these are based on July 1994 numbers. At that time:

- Germany was the largest user of Internet services in Europe, with more than 64,000 sites.

- The United Kingdom, Canada, and Australia (and Massachusetts, Texas, and Ohio) each had more than 32,000 sites.

- Austria (and Oregon, Utah, and Arizona) had more than 8,000 sites.

- Portugal, Singapore, and New Zealand (and North and South Dakota) each had more than 1,000 sites.

In general, the U.S. states we've mentioned have a sites-per-capita figure that is at least double that of the corresponding countries, except for Australia, which is about even with Texas in both population and sites.

The growth of the Internet has also led to an explosion in Internet traffic. As the number of online users continues to expand, data transfer rates are slowing down, and it's becoming increasingly difficult to distribute large documents on the Internet, as we'll discuss in "Bandwidth Problems" later in this chapter.

Low Cost of Online Distribution

If you are a publisher, you are likely to be quite concerned about the cost of developing, manufacturing, distributing, and warehousing your products. If you compare printed books, CD-ROM titles, and online publications, you'll see that certain costs are dramatically different while other costs are very similar.

As we discuss in Chapter 9, *Manufacturing CD-ROMs*, the manufacturing, distribution, and warehousing costs are far more for books than they are for CD-ROMs. Still, for CD-ROMs, these costs are a noticeable component in the overall cost of a title. For online publications, the distributing of a single document costs only the price of the network transaction. This is what makes online publishing so attractive to potential publishers. Before you plunge into this world, however, realize that there are costs beyond distribution that must be considered.

If you're publishing in a low-volume academic environment, your university may take care of putting your materials online. However, in any other environment, you'll have to take care of this process yourself. One way to do this is to set up your own Web site. Remember that the cost of setting up a site includes the cost of equipment, network access, and a system administrator to keep the site running. These costs are not negligible, and yet many people are so eager to get online that they overlook them.

There are various ways to set up business on the Web:

- You can set up a small site on a personal computer and do all the work your-self, but you will have to pay in excess of $500 per month on telecommunications.

- You can develop a full commercial Web site whose focus is on providing content. Be aware, though, that the site for a real publishing concern could cost $100,000 to $1 million or more.[*]

- You can choose to put your content on someone else's site and pay them for your storage and download usage. This can be done for only a few thousand dollars.

The upshot is that, while the Web can be cracked by a garage publisher, moving into real online publishing is not free.

Distribution is probably the only place where the cost of publishing online differs from the cost of publishing on CD-ROM. The cost of developing the content for a Web title is much the same as the cost of developing the content for a CD-ROM. Indeed, costs for the online content can actually be significantly higher than for discs. If you take advantage of the opportunity to keep your content constantly updated, then somebody has to pay for keeping it up to date. After all, online is all about timeliness! By contrast, once a disc is finished, you incur no further content costs. You (or your publisher) will, however, need to maintain a user help line for it.

Setting Up Your Own "Publishing House"

Historically, one of the traditional barriers to authors is the need to go through standard commercial publishers to get work published and marketed. Because it's usually hard to persuade large publishers to publish them, authors who want to get their word out have had to turn to other approaches. Self-publishing and the use of specialty publishers are the most common approaches, but these usually don't result in access to large audiences.

The Internet provides a new arena for publishing. Authors now have the potential to reach a much broader audience by putting their materials online. Most such authors have only a few titles, so they can generally afford to set up shop with a personal computer kind of Web site. They can put their novels, short stories, or multimedia works up for the world to see, and, if they make their sites attractive

---

[*] And these are 1996 figures. They're expected to rise rapidly as user expectations increase.

enough, may be able to get a modest financial return by attracting purchasers to download the materials.

Authors need to realize, however, that no matter how attractive their material may be, it is commingled with all the other material on the Web, and has to compete with it for attention. It has equal access opportunities with the other material, but it still lacks the marketing dollars that a major publisher can put behind a Web site.

Reaching Specialized Audiences

Some authors and publishers publish for a very small market, one in which it's hard to identify the person who is likely to want particular information, or where it's difficult to justify the cost of manufacturing paper publications. For such people, electronic publications are an attractive option. However, you need to look carefully at the differences between CD-ROM and online distribution for these audiences.

If the content is minimal or if the author has created the content, it's possible to manufacture even 500 to 1,000 CD-ROMs for a very moderate price. While it's also possible to make this kind of information available on the Internet, it's a very large commitment to maintain a Web site with significant information content, even when the amount isn't huge, and even when it isn't constantly changing. It's also difficult to make a commitment to provide a significant set of information to the whole world forever. The system management can certainly be done by an eager and energetic volunteer, but to provide a long-term resource on which others can rely, you will eventually need to have staff for this job.

Suppose you're a graduate student who wants to put the complete English translations of Molière's plays online, along with a collection of critical essays. In all, we may be talking about only 10 to 20 MB of data. But this data resides on a spindle that must be kept running, and the system that runs the site must be kept up and connected. This may be a manageable task while you're allowed to put information up on your university server, but it becomes much more complicated after you graduate. Your university probably won't be able to maintain your specialized material online for long. Unfortunately, once it's gone, scholars who have begun to rely on your material won't be able to find it and probably won't even know if it's been moved to another site. Yours will become another "ghost site," a site that no longer exists or a site whose content has aged and whose pointers go nowhere. Your publishing efforts will have failed because there won't be another way for such scholars to get this material.

Timeliness of Information

There are a few useful rules of thumb regarding which information is better distributed online, and which is better distributed on CD-ROM. In general, information that's more timely is more useful on the Internet, and information that's less timely is more useful in a book or on a CD-ROM. (On a CD-ROM, the lead time to market may be months or even years, and the information on the disc is static once published.) Useful information on the Internet is also media-lean, that is, it does not contain large media components such as movies or large pictures that must be downloaded. This distinction may become less important as the network infrastructure is reinvented to provide everyone with high-bandwidth bidirectional communication. This extra capacity may come from telephone companies, from cable television, or from utility companies; until it does happen, however, the networks will suffer from the current and worsening strangulation of too much data and too little bandwidth which we discuss later in this chapter.

In order to have timely information on your Web site, someone must track the information on the site and must regularly integrate new information into it. The new information may come from regular sources, such as news wire services; in such cases, the person managing the site information will select items of interest to the patrons of the site and will place it in an appropriate place within the structure of the site's information. Alternatively, the new information may come from people who specifically create reports or other information for the site; in such cases, the information will come to the site manager only to be integrated. At sites that continually update information, it's common practice for the site manager to first put new information in a "What's New?" section on the site, and then, some time later, move it into the usual information areas. The site manager will also need to remove out-of-date information, such as announcements of events or opportunities that are past their useful dates; in addition to the information itself, the manager must be sure to remove any references to it.

NOTE

There are books related specifically to managing Web sites, so we won't attempt to go into more detail here. We do want to point out, though, that managing a Web site is a significant effort. Don't take it lightly!

Because timeliness is such a unique and attractive feature of Web information, a publisher could choose to make timeliness a key part of a site's editorial makeup. For example, there are now sites where current weather information and weather satellite photographs are online. Keeping up-to-the-hour information on the status of pending legislation could provide a significant service to site users, as could current sports scores. Of course, the more important timeliness is to your particular site, the more time you're going to need to expend to keep the information up to date.

Some online publishers have recently taken timeliness one step further—almost into real time—and are now generating ongoing information for an audience to follow. Examples are online drama or situation comedy, online "talk" shows, online stock quotes, and play-by-play sports. In effect, these publishers are creating a parallel between broadcasting on computer networks and television or radio broadcasting. A nice attribute of broadcasting on computer networks, however, in contrast to radio or television, is that things can be set up so that anyone checking in on a given day or week can see at any time what's happening and what's new.

Growth of Business Models for the Internet

There is a great deal of interest in conducting business over the Internet, and a number of different kinds of business models people envision. Most of these businesses involve making sales of products or services; here, the main concern is that the Internet provide a secure means of transmitting credit card numbers or debit card numbers, verifying them, and fulfilling the sale. Sometimes, the product sold is information. Nevertheless, the ability to sell information or products online is growing, and as online publishing increases, this area will increase in importance. There are now reliable access controls that allow a user to verify that he's a valid subscriber or purchaser through the use of an access key—a kind of password into the publisher's domain.

There are currently several distinct types of income streams from Internet sales, which we describe below.

Metering Content

There are some places on the Internet that you have to pay to get into. Sites now using this model include sellers of adult material, multiple-user game systems, and online services, but some news, financial, and sports sites are starting to charge for their material as well. Sites charge in a variety of ways for access:

- Some charge a flat fee (usually a monthly charge) for access

- Some charge for each individual item you access or download

- Some charge for the time you spend in the space

When people talk about Internet publishing, they usually refer to this business model. We're not convinced, however, that it will be possible to build a real publishing business using this model.

Advertising Other People's Products

Another way to make money from Internet publishing is through advertising. Most people using this model create a site that's full of content, attractive to a large audience, and free to users. They then sell advertising to vendors who want to reach this audience. Yahoo and a number of other organizations are now generating revenue in this way.

Selling advertising can be an effective way to make money through your site. Both the appeal (a targeted audience) and the metric (demonstrating circulation) are familiar to advertisers from print and broadcast media. As with other types of advertising, you can provide advertisers with the cost-per-thousand numbers they understand. Although simply counting hits (the number of times people visit your site) is the simplest metric, Web software provides more sophisticated ways of tracking usage as well.

As with targeted print magazines and radio and TV shows, advertisers want to show their goods to people who are disposed to buy them. Since many Web sites are highly specialized, there is often a very good match. For example, suppose that your Web site publishes articles about skiing. If you can offer a good cost-per-thousand rate to someone who manufactures a new line of ski clothes or equipment, your Web site will be a good place for an ad because its audience is so carefully screened.

Advertising Related Products

Another business model is to give away your content, but use your Web site to advertise your own products. We are starting to see companies such as Time Warner (who have properties like *Superman*) create Web sites that try, with their content, to build a following of people who will then buy comic books, T-shirts, movie tickets, and similar franchised material. Or consider the idea of creating home pages for movies. Disney pioneered this idea with the *Toy Story* site, and many movie studios and broadcast and cable programs (e.g., CBS and the Discovery Channel) have followed. The idea is to build a Web site that contains movie- or program-related content that's fun for people to play with. Word of the movie or program gets out; more and more people visit the site; and the product eventually acquires a kind of currency, getting into daily conversation and taking on a life of its own.

A record producer for a large music company has this to say about this phenomenon, "I never sold a million copies of a record in my life—I sold a half-million copies, and the next half million, they sold themselves." It's a lot of work to get a product to the critical mass, but once it's at critical mass and the ball is rolling, it takes off. All you have to do from there on in is keep feeding the public's interest.

Through this model, there are opportunities for people to become involved in creating electronic advertising messages. Those who know about and are successful at marketing will tend to do these things better than people who know only technology. In the long run, we believe that advertising on the Web will be dominated by seasoned, saddle-weary Madison Avenue professional types who understand the human psyche at some gut level and who have enough money to make enough mistakes to finally understand what they are doing and effectively deliver their messages.

The Web serves other publicity purposes as well. It can be an effective, alternative way of dealing with the press. The press can use the Internet to download press releases, promotional material, and pictures without having to be sent this material..

Selling Links

At present, links on Web pages are free, but we predict this won't necessarily be the case for too much longer. Think about it: you can't find anything on the Web unless you already know explicitly about it, or unless somebody sends you there. Services like Yahoo now get their income from advertising, and they provide links for free, but other companies are already charging for links. Paying for links may sound outrageous, but it's really no different from paying for classified advertising in traditional industries. For example, the Judson Rosebush Company routinely pays an annual fee for being listed in the New York Film Guide.

What's Wrong With Online Publishing?

Although publishing on the Internet offers a lot of benefits—and some real future promise—there are also a number of serious obstacles to online publishing today.

Bandwidth Problems

When the Internet was new, people discovered that it was a pleasure to be able to browse and look at media-rich content. Movies and large images gave the Net a visual richness not found in most areas of computing. Similarly, the power to navigate widely (both physically and via links) provided Net users with an interactivity not found in most media—not TV, not film, not theater, not music, and not books. The increased popularity of the Internet has resulted in a great deal more traffic, and with it a corresponding sluggishness of downloads and transfers. Expectations are still high, but movies take many times as long to download as they do to view. Many people feel that the Internet is almost at the point of saturation.[*]

Although the theoretical capacity of networks promises quick access to online files, the reality of current networks is that information transfer is currently quite slow. Lately, all classes of users (from research institutions to private homes) have been complaining that data transfer rates are often slow enough to frustrate their use of the Internet and the other networks. Even with high-speed networks and nonstandard phone lines, pictures and video can take many minutes to transfer. Movies can take many times as long to download as they do to view. It's not uncommon for files to move at a rate of less than one KB/sec. At that rate, it can literally take hours to download documents of any significant size. Unfortunately, in the world of electronic publishing, a delay means more than just a few extra minutes here and there. It can cause the user to lose all the eloquence of concept and production built into the electronic document in the first place. Some partial solutions exist, but so far they only address relatively local networks.

The Hacker's Dictionary on Bandwidth

On the topic of Internet bandwidth, the *Hacker's Dictionary* has this to say: "Nothing beats the bandwidth of a Boeing 747 full of CD-ROMs!"

Bandwidth is an important issue. At the present time, we feel it's too risky to base a significant publishing enterprise on network distribution, especially if it involves high-resolution pictures and video. We expect that the current problems of Internet capacity are likely to improve if there is enough pressure from enough people to support the development of significant network growth. Things are changing rapidly on the Internet. Significant new technological solutions (such as the new IP scheme) and new capacity (as cable, telephone, and utility companies provide online services) will be needed to manage the current and still-increasing long-distance volume that is now present and that will grow in the future. In the United States, the National Science Foundation is passing control of the U.S. network backbone to commercial communications companies, and the consequences can't yet be determined. For now, the research community is dealing

---

[*] An example of the saturation is the fact that the original IP (Internet Protocol) addresses are becoming scarce, and that it has become necessary to develop a new, extended addressing scheme.

with the problem of excessive traffic by developing its own separate new network—one that won't be available to the general public.

If the Internet and other networks can solve the problem of providing enough bandwidth to allow users to acquire electronic materials comfortably and quickly, we're sure that online publishing will become an important business. Until then, we'll continue to espouse electronic publishing on CD-ROM, as well as the hybrid models we discuss in the next section. Those models have the nice quality of combining up-to-the-minute timeliness with stable contents.

Unstructured and Ever-Changing Information

In some ways, the Internet has become a nightmare. The sheer volume and lack of structure of information on the Web make it difficult to find anything (and maybe even harder to find it twice). First, you search—often for a long time—to find what you're looking for (or anything available that seems to fit your criteria). Next, it takes a potentially long time to download the long-sought material and assess whether it's actually what you want. But then, if you try to go back to the site tomorrow for another look, you may not be able to find it. As someone said, "I love the Net. It's constantly changing and it's never the same two nights in a row!"

The Internet is like Times Square. You can spend hours there watching what happens in front of you. If you enjoy immersing yourself in an ever-changing milieu, this quality of the Internet is great. From a publisher's point of view, though, this changeability is not a good quality—this isn't the kind of stability we want in a published product. The increasing number of "ghost sites" on the Web makes users wary about relying heavily on them. In fact, estimates are that as many as 20 percent of corporate sites will become ghost sites in 1996—usually because the content is simply not updated.

Even established online sources, such as Lexus, Nexus, *Newsweek*, and the *New York Times,* include only short synopses of articles. If you want to obtain something that isn't current (six months or a year is old on the Internet), or something that's a little bit oblique or out of the way, you're going to have a hard time finding it.

Some people talk about putting "the whole world," or at least a good deal of our history, online. What does this really mean? We're looking at 1,000 years of books, 100 years of recorded music, 100 years of cinema and television, and 100 years of radio. Are you really going to be able to digitize all that, and put it on a file server or set of servers somewhere? If you look realistically at this mountain of data, and do a little arithmetic, you'll see that the idea simply doesn't work. In North America alone, we accumulate information at the annual rate of two billion pictures, thousands of monthly magazines, and thousands of daily newspapers. Do you genuinely believe that all of this material is going to go online? If you do, then we highly recommend that you buy stock in disk drive companies and memory companies—enormous amounts of disk and memory will be needed to support true online content. Realistically, though, this goal is something of a fantasy; there is some value in working toward the goal, but we believe that, as a reality, it may well be 25 to 50 years away.

A Different Model

As one author said, "The publishers don't get it. They think this is a top-down technology, like newspapers or TV. It's not. It's bottom up, like the telephone."

Lack of Editorial Control

In addition to the huge quantity and the ever-changing nature of the material on the Internet, another key shortcoming of the online publishing medium is the lack of editorial control there. There are few ways to distinguish high-quality materials from mere noise. This situation may change as publishers begin doing serious work on the Internet. At present, though, CD-ROM publishing provides a model of editorial control that is much closer than online publishing to that of traditional publishing, as we described in "Editorial control" earlier in this chapter.

Censorship

We are also worried that censors are beginning to exert their influence upon the content of message traffic, and are citing local community standards to regulate the content of publishing in distant cities. Network censorship is becoming law or common practice in several countries. If the network is to be useful, it must incorporate a free flow of ideas. The effect of recent policies restricting certain kinds of traffic is not yet known, although we hope that freedom of speech will prevail.

Passive Nature of Information

The Internet differs from standard publishing practice in another key way. If you subscribe to a newspaper or magazine, or get a newsletter from your favorite affinity group, that subscription or membership keeps you informed about things of interest to you without any additional work on your part. Book and record publishers and video stores keep you informed about their material by sending you catalogs and by advertising, again without your initiative. Libraries stock "newly arrived" titles on special shelves where you see what's new whenever you visit. All of these information sources reach out to you and actively compete for your attention. But material on the Internet is *not* active. It's extraordinarily passive, and you must make an effort to start up your Web browser and visit each site of potential interest in order to find out whether anything new is available there. It's as if you had to place a phone call to each publisher and ask them what they've published every time you are thinking about reading a novel. As a publisher on the Internet, you have to realize that your potential audience has to cope with the flood of materials on the networks before they can hope to find yours; that's not an effective way to reach an audience. Cynics say, "The Internet belongs to people who can list their Web addresses on the side of a bus."

Cost for Storage

If you get content off the Web and want to keep it around, you're going to have to pay for the media on which you store it. While prices have been falling rapidly, rotating media is still about $200 per gigabyte in high-volume disk drives, and writable high-volume media is close to $100 per gigabyte plus the cost of the drive. By contrast, the CD-ROM manufacturing cost is so low that you get the storage itself essentially free; all the cost goes into developing the content. It seems hardly worthwhile to pay as much for the rotating storage or high-volume media to hold a set of content as you would pay to purchase the content itself on a medium that is not subject to crashes and failure.

Hybrid CD-ROM/Online Products

Up to this point, we've been treating CD-ROM and online publishing as if they are two completely separate alternatives. To some extent they are, but an intriguing new type of product is emerging that shows promise of combining the best features of both types of publishing in a single product:

- The CD-ROM's ability to hold large volumes of carefully crafted archival information

- The Internet's ability to maintain timely, up-to-the-minute information

A number of publishers are starting to explore the concept of developing tangible discs that come with an online, updateable source of information. There are a number of different models for these hybrid products, as we describe in the following sections.

"Secret Door" Products

One approach to developing hybrid products that has caught many people's attention is to build a "secret door" to the Internet into the CD-ROM. Users spend most of their time working with the CD-ROM; however, in some situations, a user can make a choice that leads to a Web connection. The product might automatically dial a modem and connect you to an online service that serves a Web site, for example. Once this happens, you now have access to the functionality and user interface of the Web site or the online service (not the physical disc).

The technical advantage of a hybrid product is that product developers can update the online part of the content on a very timely basis. Users can enjoy a consistent interface and access to a lot of data on the CD, yet a piece of the product can indeed be live. Depending on your product and your development approach, the ratio between the content on the CD and the online component can be whatever you wish—one disc might provide only 1 percent of the content on the disc, and the other 99 percent online. Another disc might contain most of the content, and offer only a small amount of online updating.

The business advantage of a hybrid product is that it enables publishers to get some income from their online content, since users must buy the CD-ROM in order to get access to the online content. It also facilitates access to information that may need additional formatting or processing.

Providing an online component also gives publishers a way to enhance the contents of the CD-ROM. For example, suppose you're offering a disc that contains images of all of Vermeer's paintings, along with a list of the owners and most recent sales price of each. The paintings won't change with time, but the owners will. Putting sales information online lets you update this information as needed.

There are many ways to implement the links from a CD-ROM to its associated online information. They may range from elegant (the user may not even know that a link has been made) to abrupt (your program has to pause while the connection is visibly made). In general, live links are difficult to do properly because they have a number of technical requirements:

- The computer must have an Internet connection, such as a modem and a phone line.

- The Internet connection must be defined in advance or be configured to your system.

- The Web site or online service must actually be up when you make the link.

- The product must be able to handle all kinds of exception problems, such as what to do if the phone line goes dead. In this case, you want to make sure that the CD-ROM doesn't quit and that the local processor doesn't crash.

Several current products use the "secret door" model of hybrid publishing with the primary content on the disc, augmented by updated material on a maintained Web site. The Microsoft *Baseball* CD-ROM contains a wealth of baseball history, including scores and team statistics from the earliest days of the sport up to 1994. To keep this archive up to date, the CD-ROM links to an online source which supplies scores from the seasons since 1994 as well.

O'Reilly & Associates recently released a combined book/CD-ROM/Internet title, the second edition of the *Encyclopedia of Graphics File Formats* (GFF). The GFF CD-ROM contains an electronic copy of the book, as well as the original vendor specifications (some of them very large) for most formats, sample images, and code examples. The disc also contains nearly 100 public domain, shareware, and demo versions of programs that may be used to convert, display, or compress graphics files. A copy of Enhanced Mosaic is provided as a browser.

To supplement this static information, users who have Internet connections can click on an "Internet" button (see Figure 2-2) to go to the O'Reilly GFF Web Center, where new information is constantly being added and maintained by one of the book's authors. At that site, users can find new format descriptions and specifications; additional software packages and images; links to other vendor and archival sites; and a "What's New" section. Figure 2-3 shows the Web Center home page. O'Reilly has made a commitment to maintain the Web Center to provide continuing information to this book's audience, a commitment that is critical to making a hybrid title work.

Posting Modules for Downloading

Another hybrid option is to post part of a product online. This is a nice marketing approach. You can make the online part available free, and after people have downloaded it and gotten a taste of the product, encourage them to buy the full product on CD-ROM. This approach can work well for both games and information products.

One version of this approach is to make some fully functioning parts of the product available online at no cost. In this case, the customer can acquire content by downloading modules on demand, or can buy the CD-ROM to get all the modules at once. There are actually advantages to both the online and CD-ROM options in this setup. The advantage to the customer of downloading the modules is the cost savings. Because individual modules may be small (a few megabytes or less), downloading them would not be too time-consuming. Still, it isn't trivial, the

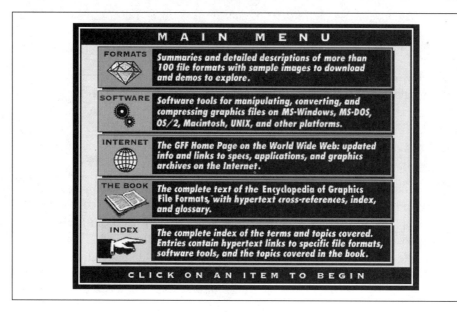

Figure 2-2.   GFF CD-ROM Main Menu

Figure 2-3.   GFF Web Center

customer does not get the full product, and the customer also needs to be able to pay for the real estate (disk space) to store them. (Not too many have an extra 600 MB of free space around.) The advantage to the customer of buying the CD-ROM is that he can get all of the modules at once, without waiting, paying connection and phone charges, and having to find the space to store them.

Another variation is to put the entire product online and to charge customers to download modules, one by one, through the online service. This variation is a purely onlein publishing scheme; however, it provides interesting marketing options, such as a "module of the week" subscription.

A third variation available for both games and software is to provide a main resource (e.g., a game) on CD-ROM and allow users to download additional parts of it. The additional parts might come either from the developers of the original content or from third parties. The idea of building a product so that parts can be added to it (to give the product more options, to provide an afterlife for the product that keeps it fresh after the sale, to allow others to become authors of new capabilities, or to provide "Easter eggs" of new and cool functions) makes it more robust and viable.

Downloading doesn't have to be an integral part of the product. The interface can be a very ordinary download, provided by a Web browser or an ordinary FTP connection.

Uploading Files From Users

Another, somewhat different type of hybrid model is a CD-ROM product that allows the user to upload or save files created by it. For example, note cards or game parts that fit into templates may be created by one player, uploaded to a common area on the Internet, and then downloaded by a second player. Or consider a slightly more complicated product, such as a CD-ROM that includes aircraft flight simulations. Using a tool for building aircraft, a user could build an aircraft and upload it; another user could then download that aircraft to use in his own simulation. Or consider the idea of a library of aircraft sitting on a Web site, possibly supported by the people who built the original product. This could be expanded into a shareware resource, where people could upload contributed aircraft, and download other aircraft for use in their individual simulations.

One interesting thing about this model is that the information that's uploaded and downloaded is more or less meaningless without the CD-ROM at either end. Essentially, you're providing not only a product but a facility with that product. You can embed the download and upload in the product, or can simply imple-ment them as writes to disk, where the uploading and downloading are done in one of a variety of ways—with an ordinary browser, by standard network techniques, by "sneakernet" (i.e., carrying diskettes around to give to others), or even by ordinary postal services. The business advantage of this model is that you must have two retail sales, one on each end, in order to make the process work. You might consider distributing the CD-ROM with some of these data sets on it to begin with. This way, not only does the user get the CD-ROM, but he also gets a base library, plus the ability to go to the Web or to swap diskettes and select from an even larger library.

NOTE

The hybrid models we've just discussed can be summarized easily. In one model there are CD-ROMs that have a portal into the Web through an online service. In a second model, there are CD-ROMs that read and write files that can be moved over the Web. In another model, there are online modules used as a disc pre-sell and as alternate distribution, possibly with some modules you can only get from the Web and/or some modules you can only get from the CD.

Filters and Browsers

A final, interesting type of hybrid model we've seen involves CD-ROMs that are basically shells (perhaps containing only five or 10 MB of content in them), functioning only as filters and browsers that work on information that's located on the Web. This is a very different type of purpose for a CD-ROM—it has little content itself, but it provides a way to better use content that comes from someplace else.

Although at first glance this may not seem to be a useful product, consider some examples. We would be interested in buying a CD-ROM from the *New York Times*, for example, that doesn't contain any information per se, but that does contain a collection of sorters, filters, and tools to be used to access the large library (probably 50 or 60 GB overall) of *New York Times* contents. It's true that the same type of filtering and browsing functions could simply run on the server, but it would be difficult to make a product out of them. Such products would definitely have a place in the market. But it does presume that you are buying stock in the *New York Times* company, because if they go out of business, then this CD-ROM that you've paid money for is no longer useful. (The Microsoft *Baseball* CD-ROM, on the other hand, is at least still useful up to its 1994 information.)

The Idea of Value Added

Products such as the Microsoft *Baseball* disc, which as far as we know was the first disc to provide a back door to online information, get a significant extra value from having up-to-date information online that complements the content on the disc. This is a good example of the way hybrid discs allow a publisher to blend content from different sources into a title.

Blending content into different publishing channels and media, as these models suggest, is a common practice in traditional areas of publishing as well. For example, consider *Sports Illustrated*, a magazine that covers sports, but that also publishes a swimsuit issue each February which attracts a lot of attention. The magazine also produces television specials that have footage of swimsuit photo shoots and in-depth material on the models, photographers, and locations. If *SI* were to publish a book called *50 Years of Swimsuit Photography in Sports Illustrated*, it could contain every swimsuit photo that ever ran in *Sports Illustrated,* as well as other never-before published pictures, together with some stories and the video in the TV specials.

When you take content from one area and present it in another, you want to be sure you are adding some value that you don't get in another way. Consider the *Sports Illustrated* example again: in order to blend your editorial content on your prime media asset (e.g., the swimsuit photos) and on your secondary assets (e.g., video of the photo shoots or background on the models, photographers, and locales), it is important that you have some sort of value added (e.g., each gives you some information about the other). This requires that you use your marketing ideas to make decisions about how you manage and control your content.

Problems With Hybrid CD-ROMs

Despite its many benefits, the hybrid approach is not without its hazards. As we've mentioned, Web sites have a habit of turning into ghosts if they're not maintained, and publishing a CD-ROM that relies on a ghost Web site is pretty useless. We're also concerned about just how much we ought to depend on diversified technologies: the more you diversify your technology base, the more unreliable it could become as time goes on. Unfortunately, as society builds more complex technologics, they become much more fragile, and their longer-term utility (their value for five years or more, for example) becomes increasingly suspect.

At this point, we're confident that CD-ROM itself is a relatively stable technology. However, as publishers start to add network connections to a distant Web site to a CD-ROM product, we're taking a real chance that our technology commitment may fail. How serious a chance this is depends on the details of your technical and business models. In the case of the Microsoft *Baseball* CD-ROM, you're not taking a very big chance. If Microsoft goes bankrupt and you can't get the current year's baseball scores any more, your product still has historical value. On the other hand, if for some reason the CD-ROM locks up so you can't access the past 100 years of baseball scores provided on the disc, that situation is devastating to the product.

What do these comments mean in terms of the various hybrid strategies we've been discussing? In general, we advocate locating information as close as possible to the user. With this goal, we believe that the preferred approach for such information as the baseball scores is to put as much information as possible on the CD-ROM, and then to provide access to information that is more up-to-date than the disc.

Other people have different opinions. Some advocate putting the information on a remote server and making the communication "transparent" to the product. They view this notion that users might want information within a couple of yards of them, physically, as something of an old-world idea—an unfortunate result of growing up in an era of tangible personal property! We believe (as do a lot of users) that even having to get information through a computer screen is something of a barrier to the information. If your computer has to be hooked up to a cable or telephone, that's an additional barrier. Today, it's often possible to carry a computer from place to place, but it's often not possible to carry the connection around. That secondary barrier, even if it's only 5 percent of the cost of the first barrier, is an equally complicated one.

CHAPTER

3

Two Electronic Titles

So far in this book we've discussed electronic publishing in a general way; but the problem with being general is that there are tremendous differences among the various kinds of titles currently being published on CD-ROM. Different publications have many different goals, and there are different ways to produce these publications for many different kinds of budgets. When we lump all of these publications together, we feel almost as if we're trying to write about producing films in a way that addresses Hollywood feature films, documentaries, and home movies—all in the same book.

Our goal in this chapter is to be specific, rather than general. Here we describe two very different (and somewhat representative) kinds of electronic publications we've developed that are currently being distributed on CD-ROM:

- *Isaac Asimov's The Ultimate Robot*. This CD/ROM falls into the category of what's now being called an *edutainment* product—one that blends education and entertainment. It has high production values and very creative contents. It's produced by media professionals and corresponds, in many respects, fairly closely to the Hollywood feature film concept.

- *SIGGRAPH Technical Proceedings*. By contrast, this CD-ROM is a technical publication. This product also has relatively high production values. However, instead of being produced by media professionals, it's produced by volunteers, using a very straightforward production process based on original electronic materials that have been submitted by a large number of individual authors. In contrast to the *Ultimate Robot* product, this product corresponds more closely to a documentary film.

By looking closely at these two very different products, we hope to demonstrate the range of capabilities available in CD-ROM products today, and to examine some of the development choices that need to be made.

Example 1: Isaac Asimov's The Ultimate Robot

The first of our two examples is a CD-ROM named *Isaac Asimov's The Ultimate Robot*. This product was created by the Judson Rosebush Company (a company owned by one of this book's authors), in conjunction with Byron Preiss Multimedia and Microsoft.

NOTE

The background of the group that published this product is characteristic of the CD-ROM publishing world. The Judson Rosebush Company is a production firm grounded in commercial computer graphics, computer animation, software, and film and video production. Preiss's background is that of a book packager. Microsoft is most noted for its operating systems and applications software; however, Microsoft also publishes books, and in the 1990s the company has moved aggressively into publishing CD-ROMs.

Goals of the Product

The original concept of the *Ultimate Robot* was an electronic book built around a collection of short stories Byron Preiss had licensed from the estate of the late science fiction writer, Isaac Asimov. We wanted to add value to the original stories in several ways:

- **Media format.** Many different kinds of media were brought into the product, including video, book covers, photographs, animated illustrations, pop-ups, and even an interactive, build-it-yourself robot toolkit.

- **Intellectual perspectives.** We broadened the product in several axes revolving around the theme of robots. In addition to narrative fiction, Asimov's short stories provide a philosophical discussion of the role of robots today and in the future. In the product, we augment the stories with a chronology of robotic developments, treatments of robots in feature films, computer-animated robots, a section of robot mechanics, a collection of industrial robots and their uses, and a glossary of robotic terms.

Multimedia CD-ROMs are most often produced by teams, as we describe in Chapter 4, *Developing a CD-ROM*. This CD-ROM is somewhat unusual in that one of this book's authors wrote virtually all of the copy for the disc (except, of course, for the actual Asimov stories), programmed the disc, and processed most of the graphics and video. Once Preiss began to see the overall vision for the project, however, he accelerated this process by financing an art director, illustrator, and assistant. By the time the CD-ROM came out of quality control testing at Microsoft, a year had elapsed from the project's inception.

Design Decisions

The production of any type of media involves extensive planning and design; the production of a CD-ROM title is no exception to this general rule, as we'll describe throughout this chapter. Even the installation and opening credits of the product require careful crafting.

Installation

When you first insert the *Ultimate Robot* disc in your CD-ROM drive, its design manifests itself with the display of a custom-made disk icon on the desktop. The CD-ROM opens automatically and presents a second (also custom-made) program icon. This is the icon for the product, and it is presented to the user to click on, as shown in Figure 3-1.

Figure 3-1.   Main Ultimate Robot program icon

Once you click on the program icon, the title launches and comes up in full-screen fashion. As natural as this opening may seem to be, it is neither accidental nor casual—it is by design, as we'll see.

There are two main techniques for launching a program:

Running from the hard disk

Many CD-ROMs require the user to run an installer—a program on the disc that copies certain software and files from the CD-ROM onto the hard disk. In some cases, the installer also tailors the files it installs to the configuration of the system. When this task is completed, the user can launch and run the product from the hard disk. The advantage of installing files onto the user's hard drive is that it improves the performance of many applications.

Running from the CD-ROM

The *Ultimate Robot* disc does not run from the hard disk; it runs entirely off the CD-ROM. The advantage of this approach is that it is very simple for the user to run; he won't end up with a collection of mysterious files left behind after he removes the CD-ROM from the drive. At best, such files take up space on the hard drive; at worst, they interfere with other applications.

Both techniques have merit and, in fact, it is even possible to engineer CD-ROMs that can work either way.

Logos, opening action, and credits

Once the *Ultimate Robot* is launched, the user is presented a series of company logos, shown in Figure 3-2. *Ultimate Robot* follows the cinema style with regard to this sequence: The first logo is the distributor (in this case, Microsoft); the second is the publisher (Byron Preiss Multimedia). The next screen, the title screen, contains the name of the product and the copyright notice. (This is not the only copyright notice in the product, but it is the most important one because it is obvious, unambiguous, and not buried in the product.)

Figure 3-2.   Ultimate Robot company logos

The title screen is followed by an opening animation and a listing of the main credits, which end with the credit of the director, Judson Rosebush. (See the sidebar, "The Theory of Credits" in Chapter 4.)

Main Menu

The opening action and credits lead to the main menu, shown in Figure 3-3. This is the most important screen in the product, and is the home base for users. It provides them with a location from which they can quickly and easily venture out

Figure 3-3.   Ultimate Robot main menu (see the color version in the center insert)

into any corner of the product. Conversely, it's a place to which users can quickly and easily return and regain their bearings.

NOTE

Although it's easy to get back to the main menu, most products do not allow the user to replay the opening logos, animation, and main credits; this is also the case in *Ultimate Robot.*

The main menu in the *Ultimate Robot* consists of eight icons surrounding a central illustration. The eight icons represent eight different sections; clicking on any one of them takes the user to that section. In this discussion, we are loosely defining a section to be a part of the disc that has similar purpose and/or format. In some respects, a section is analogous to a chapter. However, whereas "chapter" often implies a serial, one-after-the-other, sequence, the essential random-access nature of the CD-ROM suggests that sections are not serially related. In fact, sections are often thought of as structures that are orthogonal to each other and that represent radically different ways of delving into a subject matter. For example, in *Ultimate Robot* the sections include the following:

- The Asimov short stories

- A chronology

- Picture galleries

- Asimov speaking

- Robot videos

- Robot mechanics

- A robot toolkit

- Help

Each of the sections has a common graphical format.

The purpose of the main menu is functionality, but it must also have a strong graphic design. Clicking on one of the eight icons in *Ultimate Robot* plays a sound, and then jumps the user to the section represented by the icon. Although the user can return to the main menu, the icons for the eight sections appear everywhere in the product (except that they are represented as a menu on the right side of the screen, and the active section has a green bar next to it, as shown in Figure 3-4). Our way of presenting this menu involves an interface design issue, not a graphics design issue. It concerns how the user may navigate the product—not simply how it looks.

There is often debate in the world of CD-ROM publishing about what exactly should appear on the main menu. As with so many characteristics of product design, there is no single right answer. Here are some of the choices, along with the arguments for or against their implementation:

Only icons
Icons alone are graphically clean, and their meaning is obvious after repeated usage, but may not be obvious at the onset.

Only text
Text alone is obvious at the onset, but it is not very graphic or appealing.

Both icons and text
Icons with text combine the best of both icons and text, but are redundant; one argument is to use them together on the main menu, but to use only icons later on.

Figure 3-4.   Icons for the CD-ROM sections

Icons with audio rollovers

With this approach, the subject is spoken when the mouse is positioned over the icon. Icons with audio rollovers preserve graphic purity (with the rollover providing the expanded definition), but they become annoying with repeated usage. One solution is to delay the audio by a second or two, so the user can click the button before it starts talking to you.

Icons with textual rollovers

With this approach, text boxes pop up when the mouse is rolled over the icon. Like icons with audio rollovers, icons with text rollovers may become annoying with repeated usage. One solution is to delay the text display by a second or two, so the user can click the button before it starts sprouting text definitions in little balloons.

Section and Subsection Menus

In addition to the *Ultimate Robot* main menu, there are eight section menus, each of which contains several subsection menus and several hundred leaf cards; this organization is shown in Figure 3-5.

A leaf card is a terminal location in the product, akin to a page in a book or a frame in a movie. Although a leaf card may consist of one or more media

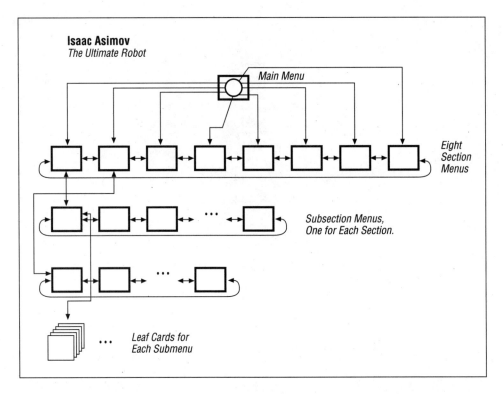

Figure 3-5.   Ultimate Robot structure of subsections and leaf cards

elements (e.g., a headline, text, or picture and caption), these elements are presented as an integrated unit, and there is no way for the user to access them outside the page context. (We'll describe these cards in more detail in "Leaf Cards" later in this chapter.)

The navigation of the section and subsection menus is very compact; it utilizes a schema initially conceived by Jeff Hixon, the art director on the project, in which the section and subsection menus share a common screen, shown in Figure 3-6.

The left side of the section menu contains the list of subsections. Clicking on one of them displays a list of the leaf cards that make up the section on the right. Clicking on one of the names on the right takes the user to a leaf card, such as the ones shown in Figures 3-7 and 3-8. Although a leaf card may consist of one or more media elements (e.g., a headline, text, or picture and caption), these elements are presented as an integrated unit, and there is no way for the user to access them outside the page context.

The next three sections describe some special characteristics of the overall product structure.

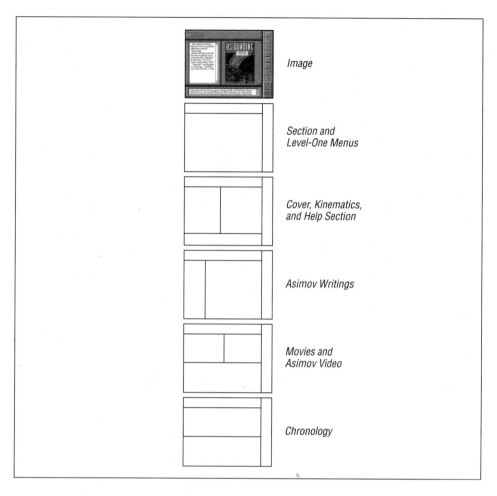

Image

Section and
Level-One Menus

Cover, Kinematics,
and Help Section

Asimov Writings

Movies and
Asimov Video

Chronology

Figure 3-6.   Ultimate Robot overall screen design

Levels

The *Ultimate Robot* product includes multiple levels of cards. The depth of the product is measured in the number of levels of indexing. In *Ultimate Robot* there are four levels (counting the main menu).* As we've mentioned, the main menu points to sections; each section points to several subsections; and each subsection points to several (or many) leaf cards.

---

*Some people would argue that the main menu does not count as a level, and that *Ultimate Robot* contains only three levels.

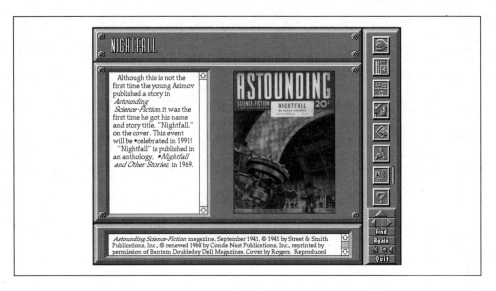

Figure 3-7.   One Ultimate Robot sample leaf card (see the color version in the center insert)

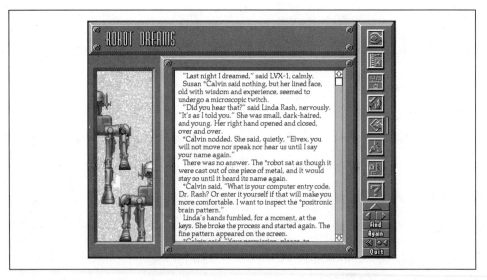

Figure 3-8.   Another Ultimate Robot sample leaf card (see the color version in the center insert)

The choice of how many levels, and how many leaves, to incorporate into a product is a design issue—one that is driven somewhat by the amount and nature of the content. In fact, a product with only a couple of hundred leaf cards would probably only require three levels; in such a product, the sections might point directly to the leaf cards.

In general, it's desirable to create as few levels as necessary, since the user has to click his or her way down through them, and this is more work.

Hierarchical tree design

Ultimate Robot is designed as a hierarchical tree in which the selections fan out and expand as the user goes more deeply into the disc content.

A hierarchical tree is only one way to structure information; rings and networks are also possible approaches. The tree is an extremely familiar kind of organization, however, and one that deserves serious consideration. Such a tree structure is not only the organizing principle of a typical book, encyclopedia, and atlas, it's also how we organize our understanding of natural structures—those as diverse as our solar system (star, planets, moons), river systems, and the family relationships of plants and animals. One of the powerful aspects of multimedia is that it allows an information designer to provide multiple frameworks of access to information in the same product; you will find that, very frequently, one of these frameworks is going to be a hierarchical tree.

In this particular product, you will notice that the contents of each subsection are unique; leaf cards that are addressed in one subsection are not addressed in any other subsection. This does not mean that there are no other ways to get to these cards, but it does mean that there is only one way to get to them when traversing the hierarchy.

NOTE

Again, it's not necessary to impose this restriction; an alternative design might support the addressing of a single leaf card by many different subsections.

Ragged information organization

The information organization in *Ultimate Robot* is what we call *ragged*, which simply means that different sections contain different numbers of subsections, and that different subsections contain different numbers of leaf cards. If the product were designed so that each section contained an equal number of subsections, and if each subsection contained an equal number of leaf cards, we would say that the information organization was *uniform*.

Leaf Cards

In *Ultimate Robot,* the subsection menu presents the user with a list of leaf cards. When you click on one of the card names, you jump to it. The structure of the leaf card varies from section to section (again, see Figure 3-6); generally, however, you will see these components:

- A title at the top

- A major piece of text

- A control panel

- A picture or video

- A caption or credit

The control panel facilitates navigation within the product. The series of eight buttons at the top right represents a compact form of the main menu, and jumps the user directly to the individual section menus. A bar to the right of one of the buttons indicates the current section.

Navigation is also facilitated by a series of tactical controls at the bottom right of the panel:

Up arrow
   Moves you up one level.

Left and right arrows
   Take you to the previous (left) or next (right) leaf card. Alternatively, if you're on the section level, the arrows take you to the previous or next section.

Find
   Opens a dialog box that prompts you for a word or string of words. Once you've entered the word or string, it searches for the next occurrence of the string in the leaf cards.

Again
   Repeats the Find operation.

Double-left arrow
   Retraces your steps back through all the previously viewed screens.

Bullet-back arrow
   Retraces your steps through hyperlinks (explained in the next section).

Quit
   Exits the document.

Text Features

Two different kinds of *hyperlinking*—words that can be clicked on to make an action occur—are built into the text. One set is prefixed by a degree symbol (°), the other by a bullet (•).

An example of the first set of hyperlinks, the *degree words*, is shown in Figure 3-9. Clicking on a degree word causes an annotated definition to pop up. In *Ultimate Robot*, the definition box is dynamically positioned adjacent to the word, but within the text field.

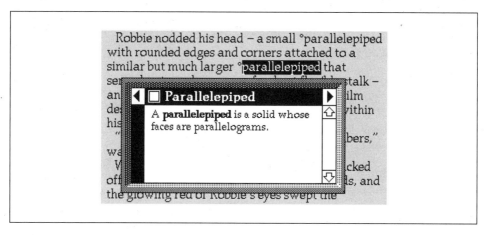

Figure 3-9. A glossary definition pops up adjacent to a word

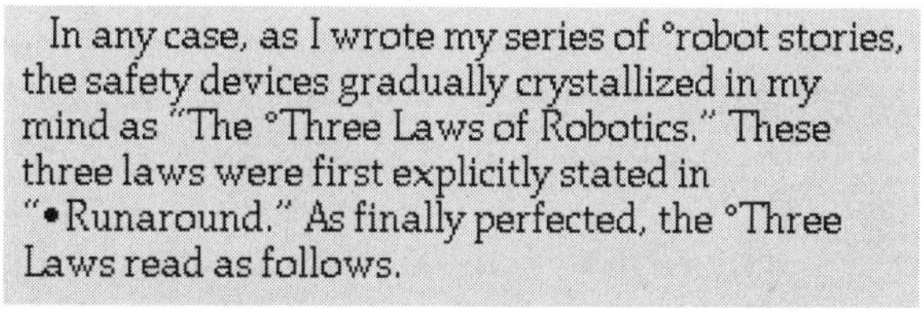

Figure 3-10. A bullet word hyperlinks the user to a new location

An example of the second set of hyperlinks, the *bullet words*, is shown in Figure 3-10. Clicking on a bullet word jumps the user through the information space to a new location. For example, clicking on a date jumps to the chronology; clicking on a book may jump to a picture of the cover; and clicking on a concept may jump to an illustrative movie. In a programming sense, you might think of the bullet words as *buttons*—something the user may click on which performs an action. In fact, the bullet word can be programmed to perform any action, but in the *Ultimate Robot* those actions consist only of going to another point in the document.

The Robotoid Assembly Toolkit

Earlier in this book, we said that the CD-ROM experience should exploit all five axes of multimedia—text, pictures, moving pictures, sound, and interactivity. The last of these, interactivity, tacitly implies that there is a computer inside the system, and it covers all actions that occur as the result of striking a key or moving a cursor, including mouse movements and button clicks. Interactivity can be simple and straightforward (such as clicking a button and going to a section), or it can be complex and sophisticated (such as flying a virtual airplane in a virtual flight-simulator world).

In *Ultimate Robot* we wanted to introduce a level of interactivity that was more engaging than a simple click and jump navigation. Toward this end, Byron Preiss, illustrator Ralph McQuarrie, programmer Matt Schlanger, and director Judson Rosebush came up with the idea of a build-it-yourself Robotoid Assembly Toolkit, shown in Figure 3-11.

The toolkit consists of a button palette of different robot parts, an assembly slab, and some control buttons. You're given a variety of heads, arms, legs, and other parts to choose from; once you've assembled a robot, you can rotate it from side to side, as well as rotate the arms around the individual joints. The toolkit also allows you to drag pieces of five different robots together to build a unique model, and then to animate the arms and legs of the newly constructed robot.

In business/editorial terms, the purpose of the toolkit is to extend the age demographic of the title downward (in other words, to give kids something to play with). In intellectual terms, the toolkit is very much in the spirit of the product because it allows you to experiment directly with robotic mechanisms. This capability—to build and explore interactively—is one of the critical differences between multimedia and more passive media such as television. In order to justify publishing a title on CD-ROM, you must be able to do something with a disc that you *can't* do with a book or with television. You have to bring extra value to it; you have to make it multimedia and multimodal; and you have to make it useful.

Production Issues

Our publisher was concerned about the costs of using video in the product. Licensing the rights to the movie *2001* was very expensive, and we licensed five or six other movies as well. At that point, we decided that we couldn't afford to pay any more license fees. So we brought in a researcher, Gwen Sylvan, and set her the task of finding footage about robots that would be engaging, interesting, and informational—but that we could use without fees. We sought out national

Figure 3-11.   Robotoid Assembly Toolkit (see the color version in the center insert)

laboratories that were doing research on robotics, companies that sell robots, and computer animation companies. We soon had more robot footage than we knew what to do with—wonderful footage of robots painting cars, running milling machines, defusing bombs, and working in hospitals, as well as footage of robotic vehicles, and even virtual reality robots. We also transcribed all the narration in these pieces so that users could read and search that narration in addition to the original Asimov stories provided in the product.

Does the Product Fulfill Its Goals?

In the end, we think that the *Ultimate Robot* product has been a big success. The product was designed to focus on a specific market that's clustered around Asimov and robotics, and it provides a rich spectrum of "edutainment." For a niche product, *Ultimate Robot* has done well in the market. We hope it has provided many people with information, entertainment, and thought-provoking ideas.

Example 2: SIGGRAPH Electronic Conference Proceedings

ACM SIGGRAPH is the largest professional society in the field of computer graphics and interactive techniques. It prides itself on the quality of its annual conference and its publications, and it makes a conscious effort to stay as close as possible to the leading edge of technology in its field. Its publication goals involve gathering and distributing state-of-the-art information in strongly technical areas, and its conference proceedings are eagerly anticipated by the computer graphics technical community as a primary resource in the field. The electronic version of these conference proceedings is intended to carry all of the content of the printed version, and to add as much electronic document functionality as possible (within, naturally, the time and cost constraints that always accompany a volunteer-prepared conference proceedings).

One of this book's authors (Steve) was deeply involved in designing the CD-ROM version of the SIGGRAPH electronic conference proceedings and was its production editor for its first few years.

Goals of the Product

The SIGGRAPH conference proceedings is a highly technical title consisting of between 50 and 60 research papers and a significant amount of other material. Like most technical research papers, the SIGGRAPH papers are text-intensive with a large number of formulas and tables. Since these are papers on computer graphics, however, they also include many high-quality color figures critical to illustrating the work described in the papers. The printed proceedings are created from authors' camera-ready copy, with hardcopy images in place as flat art, and SIGGRAPH takes great care to reproduce the authors' color and image details as accurately as possible, utilizing the color separation tools available for print.

SIGGRAPH has published CD-ROM versions of its conference proceedings since 1993. These discs are given to the people who register for the conference's technical program, and are also sent to regular SIGGRAPH members. The electronic proceedings have three distinct goals:

- To provide an electronic version of SIGGRAPH's most important publication.

- To allow authors to present information that cannot be fully represented on paper. Examples of such information include animations, code, and data for the systems that are described in the book; interactive examples of the authors' work; and additional text that could not be accommodated within the page limits of the printed book.

- As the electronic publishing field matures, to serve as ongoing testbeds for electronic publishing and the distribution of documents for technical subjects.

Design Decisions

Two important decisions dictated our approach to developing the SIGGRAPH CD-ROM. First, the nature of the electronic conference proceedings dictated that we needed a CD-ROM that was basically an electronic version of the printed proceedings book. Because of time limitations, authors could not be asked to create two versions of their work. Moreover, the production staff (one volunteer) could not work directly with either the papers' text or design. Thus, we decided to keep the format of the printed book. As a result, there were few layout design decisions that needed to be made on the project.

Second, we decided that the electronic proceedings needed to include the papers' figures in their original digital form, and to support other electronic contents as the authors provided them.

In thinking about developing the electronic proceedings, we asked the following major design questions:

- Which authoring system should we use for the documents?

- What electronic formats should we use on the disc?

- What document reader system should we use for the documents?

We chose simply to make the best use possible of whatever functionality the authoring and delivery systems gave us.

Choosing an authoring system

In examining and evaluating authoring systems, we used a number of criteria:

- The electronic documents produced by the system must retain the production quality of the printed proceedings.

- Volunteers must be able to create our electronic documents quickly and with a reasonable amount of effort.

- The documents must be readable on as many platforms as possible.

- The cost of having document readers on our CD-ROMs must be as low as possible.

- The finished documents must be able to contain at least as much information as was in the printed papers.

Acrobat

SIGGRAPH had created an experimental CD-ROM in 1992 based on presenting scanned pages, but that disc received a lukewarm evaluation so we abandoned that approach. Initially, it seemed that no electronic document systems truly met our needs, and we were tentatively planning to build our own simple file system that contained documents in raw formats: ASCII, RTF, and/or PostScript for the papers, TIFF for images, and QuickTime for animations. Luckily, we heard about Adobe Acrobat before it was released, and an evaluation team visited Adobe to look at the product. While the original version of Acrobat did not provide everything we wanted for the conference papers, it clearly met most of our needs. We ultimately chose Acrobat as the primary authoring system for the CD-ROM.

We've successfully used Acrobat to present electronic versions of the conference papers. Although we mainly use TIFF and QuickTime for images and movies, respectively, we've sometimes used other file types as well. As we originally planned, there is a file system on the disc with Acrobat (and sometimes PostScript as well) files of the papers, as well as files in appropriate formats for image and movie materials. The disc also contains installation packages for the Acrobat reader and for QuickTime for Macintosh and Windows.

We've maintained this overall information architecture in more recent versions of the proceedings disc, and we've used it for other proceedings discs from other groups. Ultimately, we may choose to change the title's file structure, or we may move to another authoring and delivery system—for now, however, our approach does the job well.

Production Issues

Acrobat takes PostScript as its primary input source in producing the PDF (Portable Document Format) files the product displays. This characteristic turns out to be an excellent fit between Acrobat's design and the particular needs of SIGGRAPH authors. Almost all of these authors can easily produce PostScript versions of their papers; to assist them, SIGGRAPH has developed a set of template documents that give authors good document formats to work from. Further, almost all SIGGRAPH authors are connected to the Internet, so they can transfer their PostScript, image, movie, and other files to SIGGRAPH's electronic communications site.

The overall production process for the disc is illustrated in Figure 3-12. Authors send their files to the Internet site, from which they are downloaded to the SIGGRAPH production editor's desktop system. (Materials come in over a period of about two weeks.) If a file is in PostScript, it is sent to the Acrobat Distiller for translation into PDF format, and the editor checks the file to be sure that it works with a standard set of viewers. (Chapter 6, *Authoring Systems* describes the

Distiller and other Acrobat features in greater detail.) If a file is a movie, the editor simply checks it. Prepared and checked files are stored on a hard disk for later processing.

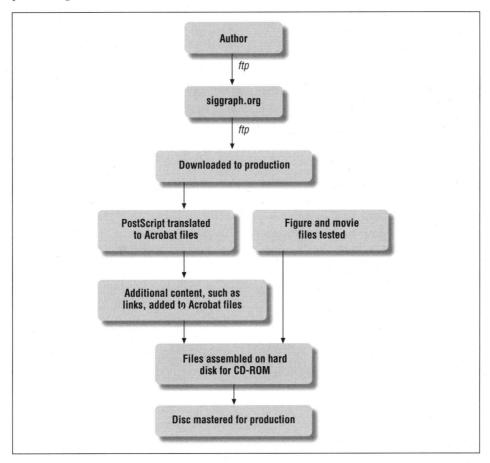

Figure 3-12.   Information flow in SIGGRAPH CD-ROM production process

NOTE

It has been something of a surprise to find out how many things can go wrong with PostScript files! Our primary problems have been the use of bitmapped fonts instead of outline fonts (particularly when the documents come from TEX and LATEX systems) and problems with margins in documents originally designed for A4 (international) printing. With experience, we've learned to readily handle most of these problems, though, and we're now prepared with solutions to most of them.

Once the files have been translated and checked, the production editor uses Acrobat's Exchange and Catalog applications to add features to the files (e.g., links and indices) and to prepare them to become the final proceedings document. In addition, he creates the front and back materials for the conference proceedings.

At the end of this process, we assemble an electronic "book" from the authors' individual electronic "chapters." The book has actually had different characteristics in different years of publication. In 1994, it consisted of all the individual papers assembled into one file (as shown in Figure 3-13). In 1995, the book consisted of a set of index materials that linked to papers as separate files (to take advantage of additional linking capabilities in Acrobat).

The additional content we add to the authors' materials is of two types:

- **Textual information.** Notes with copyright information and some overall directions.

- **A significant amount of navigation support.** A large number of links between navigation tools such as the table of contents and the author index, and the actual papers in the electronic proceedings.

Ongoing developments in Acrobat allow authors (and, if time permits, the production group as well) to embed movies, sound clips, and Web links into the papers. In 1996 we are embedding movies in the proceedings as well. We intend to take further advantage of authoring system developments as time goes on.

CD-ROM Organization

There are many ways to organize the contents of a CD-ROM. In Figure 3-13, we illustrate the organization used for the 1994 electronic proceedings. We expect both the contents and the organization to evolve as our experience develops and changes in authoring systems occur, and, in fact, the 1995 proceedings aren't exactly like this.

The file system on the CD-ROM contains three top-level directories:

apps—the application directory
> Directories containing the Acrobat and QuickTime software, along with READ_ME text files describing the packages. These applications are necessary to allow users to read the papers (via the Acrobat Reader) and view the movies (via the QuickTime application).

Papers—the papers directory

One file or directory for each of the individual papers on the disc. If only PostScript is provided by the paper's author, there will only be a single file. If the author has provided additional materials (e.g., images, movies, datasets), each of these will also appear in its own file within the paper directory. (See the Azuma directory in Figure 3-13 for an example.)

Procs—the overall proceedings directory

One consolidated file (in viewable PDF format) containing all of the papers, along with a file containing title information and a set of READ_ME files.

This CD-ROM layout may not seem as sophisticated as one in which there is an overall navigator document from which the reader can move among the papers and other content. However, it's appropriate for the technical nature of the information. Because the CD-ROM must be usable across all possible computer systems, it's impossible to have a single navigator document, and it's too much work to create a separate navigator document for each possible computer system.

This CD-ROM is produced in a dual-directory structure—that is, in most cases, it contains one copy of each file that is referred to by both an ISO 9660 directory (for use by DOS/Windows and UNIX), and an HFS directory (for use by the Macintosh); we describe the purpose of this structure in detail in Chapter 8, *CD-ROM Disc Standards*. Basically, structuring the disc in this way allows it to be read on as many platforms as possible, and avoids a variety of issues that arise for multiplatform CD-ROMs. However, this doesn't work for some files, such as text files. As we describe in Chapter 8, text files aren't easily interchanged between platforms because the characters used to terminate lines differ. (PC, Macintosh, and UNIX systems all use different conventions.) In some cases on the CD-ROM, you will see multiple versions of the same text file; thus, READ_ME.DOS files on the CD-ROM are for use on PCs, READ_ME files are for the Mac, and READ_ME.txt files are for UNIX. (Chapter 9, *Manufacturing CD-ROMs*, describes other platform-dependent issues.)

Navigation Options and Facilitation

This section shows how the Acrobat Reader works for the SIGGRAPH CD-ROM, and what tools it provides for the user.

Cover page

When the user opens the overall proceedings document, the cover page comes up, as shown in Figure 3-14. This screen has two live link areas: if you click on the title, the reader jumps to the table of contents; if you click on the image, the reader jumps to the image credits. These are explained by the note at the top right of the cover.

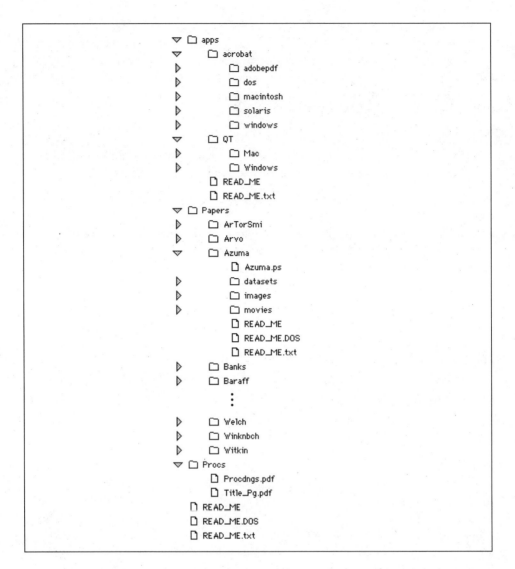

Figure 3-13.   SIGGRAPH CD-ROM directory structure

Table of contents

Most readers will want to go to the table of contents. Figure 3-15 shows basically what the user will see; however, here we've outlined the links to show you the active areas. On the user's actual screen, these outlines are invisible.

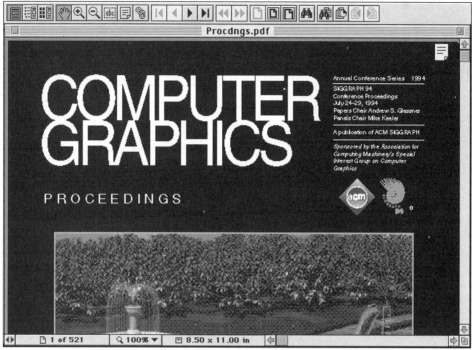

Courtesy of ACM SIGGRAPH

Figure 3-14.   SIGGRAPH 94 cover page (see the color version in the center insert)

Papers and thumbnails

When you click on a paper's title, the reader jumps to the first page of that paper. Because the paper was designed originally for reading in print, the form factor of the page does not fit the screen especially well, but a thumbnail view allows the reader to see several pages' thumbnails at once. Figure 3-16 illustrates the first page of one paper, with thumbnails.

Formulas, tables, and figures

If the author includes formulas, tables, or figures in the PostScript version of the paper, they are included in the Acrobat document as they were in the original; Figure 3-17 shows pages zoomed into a formula, and Figure 3-18 shows a figure in place.

Text searches and other features

Acrobat offers a number of additional features. For example, you can search for a text string, using the kind of search dialog box shown in Figure 3-19; the results of the search are shown in Figure 3-20.

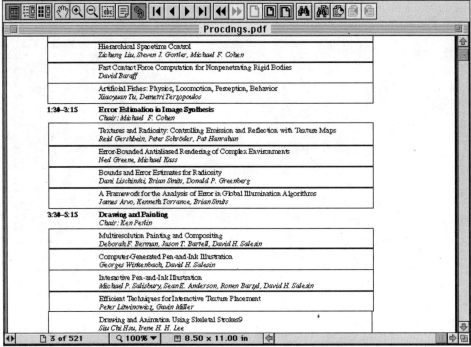

Courtesy of ACM SIGGRAPH

Figure 3-15.   SIGGRAPH 94 table of contents

New versions of Acrobat allow inline movies and Web links (links to documents on the World Wide Web), but these features were not available for use in the conference proceedings shown in these examples.

Does the Product Fulfill Its Goals?

The electronic version of the SIGGRAPH conference proceedings offers three basic features:

- A copy of the information that appears in the printed book. As we've mentioned, the Acrobat reader displays the electronic proceedings in an "electronic paper" format—the screen display duplicates the printed pages as they appear in the traditional printed proceedings.

- As much functionality for the electronic papers as Acrobat and the production process will allow; such functionality includes links, indices, and so on.

- Both extra content and extra functionality that can be provided only by electronic media. In addition to the papers, the disc includes additional material that is not available in paper form—either because there wasn't room there, or because the paper medium did not support the material. For example, on

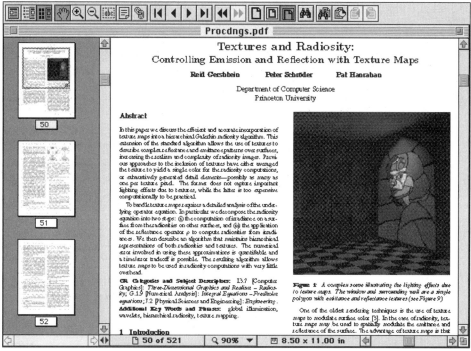

Figure 3-16.   A first page of a paper with thumbnails shown

the CD-ROM are image files for most of the color (and some of the line art and halftone) figures in the papers; movies in QuickTime or MPEG format from many of the papers; papers in alternate formats such as HTML, as provided by the authors; and additional material, such as source code for graphics systems and datasets for some of the models or experimental results in the papers.

The best measure of an information product such as these electronic proceedings is the response of the people who receive it. The response of SIGGRAPH's members and conference attendees has been very positive. An overwhelming number of SIGGRAPH members have ready access to systems with CD-ROMs. Although they want to continue to receive the printed proceedings, they are happy with the electronic one and the additional functions it provides. For example, they can read the papers, search them for text strings, and print individual ones if they need to; they can also examine the original digital images provided by the authors; they can run the movies and see them presented as the authors intended; and they can use the software that's on the disc.

Authors have also welcomed the opportunity provided by the CD-ROM proceedings; they often create their own PDF files and other documents for the disc, and

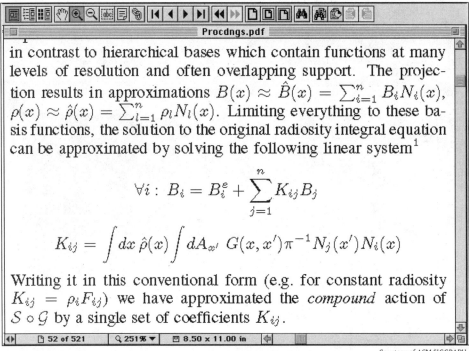

Figure 3-17.   An Acrobat document zoomed in to display a detailed formula

they are happy to be able to provide materials (e.g., movies) that could not be included in the printed version.

The electronic proceedings are also successful in another way that may not be evident to the reader, but certainly is to the organization. They provide SIGGRAPH with a testbed for ideas in electronic publishing, and they allow authors to experiment with different document formats. For example:

- The 1993 proceedings include a paper presented as a Voyager electronic book.

- The 1994 proceedings include two papers as HTML file sets.

- The 1995 proceedings include a great increase in the number of movies, as well as an index that allows rapid searching of all the papers.

- The 1996 proceedings include movies linked to the papers.

With electronic publishing technologies still changing rapidly, this project represents an important capability for the SIGGRAPH organization. Both the organization and the conference are expanding their electronic publishing

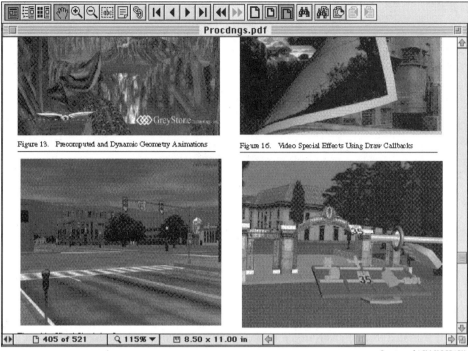

Courtesy of ACM SIGGRAPH

Figure 3-18.   A set of figures in an Acrobat document (see the color version in the center insert)

Figure 3-19.   An Acrobat search dialog box

programs based on this experience and on some other online publishing experiments.

The main problem we see with the SIGGRAPH CD-ROMs is with the document formats we provide. Acrobat gave us a good initial electronic publishing capability, and has now been ported to enough platforms to satisfy the community. However, the display of a document is determined by the author's print-oriented

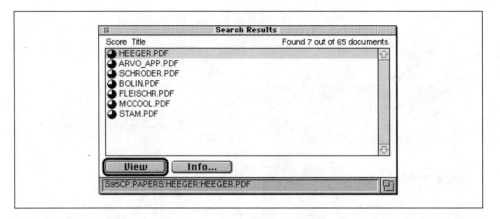

Figure 3-20. Result of the search (with all matches and an indication of the quality of the match)

Synergy: The Printed and Electronic Versions

Some people have asked why we continue to distribute the printed version of the SIGGRAPH conference proceedings, since the electronic version has been so well-received.

All along, we've viewed the CD-ROM version of the SIGGRAPH conference proceedings as a supplement to, not a replacement for, the printed proceedings. Why? Mainly because our members have told us so. Although they appreciate the special capabilities of the CD-ROM (searching for particular text, cutting and pasting text and images into their own work, comparing different presentations, etc.), they don't want to give up print.

Clearly, the electronic version offers greater capacity and the ability to provide content that can't be included in print (such as movies and datasets, as well as automatic links between material). The quality of the images is clearly better; the reader is able to directly examine the images provided by authors, instead of having to rely on printed copies (created by printing separations).

But there is a special and familiar quality to print that readers don't want to give up—the ability to carry the text from place to place (office, home, train, beach) without special preparation, the familiarity of nonelectronic access methods (sticking a Post-it on a page and handing the book to a colleague), and even the intangible sense of value provided by the physical heft of the book. These are qualities of print we've grown up with, and many people aren't ready to give them up.

layout and does not adapt itself to the layout of a screen or, better yet, a window on that screen. If we were to have Acrobat papers that fit the shape of standard screens, authors would need to be asked to provide reshaped papers, and we have not been willing to make that extra demand on them.

As opportunity and experiences permit, SIGGRAPH plans to extend its work on the proceedings CD-ROMs to provide additional electronic publications. In addition to proceedings discs, SIGGRAPH also produces a disc version of its conference course notes (again, primarily using Acrobat). CD-ROMs emphasizing the arts and technologies programs at the SIGGRAPH conference are now being developed, and discs from specialized conference programs and from other conferences are under consideration.

As authoring and delivery systems for electronic documents rapidly become more sophisticated and powerful, SIGGRAPH, like any publisher, must keep aware of changes and be ready to respond to the availability of additional tools. SIGGRAPH is currently looking at several other publishing options. One would involve the use of HTML and World Wide Web browsers, as we describe in Chapter 6. Another would use an intermediate SGML approach, translating authors' original documents and using a document viewer such as *Dyna*Text from Electronic Book Technologies.

II

CD-ROM Development

This part of the book contains the following:

- Chapter 4, *Developing a CD-ROM*, provides an overview of the CD-ROM development process, from initial product planning through final production of the CD-ROM image. It discusses the staffing that is required for most development projects, and provides cost estimates for several different types of projects.

- Chapter 5, *Designing Electronic Documents*, discusses a variety of design issues for CD-ROMs, in areas of overall title navigation, graphics, user interface, sound, digital video, and software.

- Chapter 6, *Authoring Systems*, examines what makes a good authoring system for electronic documents and looks at a number of examples of systems being used today, including Director, HyperCard, Acrobat, Gain*Momentum*, Media Tool, and HTML.

- Chapter 7, *Electronic Document Standards*, summarizes a variety of standards for electronic documents, in areas of text (e.g., SGML, HTML), page description (e.g., PostScript, PDF), network (e.g., Java, VRML), image (e.g., formats such as BMP and TGA, and compression methods such as RLE and JPEG), digital video (e.g., QuickTime, MPEG), and sound (e.g., MIDI).

- Chapter 8, *CD-ROM Disc Standards*, describes the various CD-ROM standards, focusing on the ISO 9660 and HFS specifications.

4

Developing a CD-ROM

This chapter provides an overview of the process of developing a CD-ROM title. Development extends from initial product conception and staffing of the development team, all the way through the final preparation of the CD-ROM image, which is then sent off to the plant for manufacturing. We focus here on the various phases of development, and how those are performed by the various staff members of the development team. We've broken out two special components of CD-ROM development into their own chapters: Chapter 5, *Designing Electronic Documents*, describes product design, and Chapter 6, *Authoring Systems*, describes the use of authoring systems. Manufacturing is described in detail in Chapter 9, *Manufacturing CD-ROMs*.

A CD-ROM title can be developed in a number of different ways:

- Production by media specialists in a multimedia production facility. This is the approach you're most likely to take if you're developing a full-feature, commercial title. Since most media is now developed in this way, this chapter emphasizes this professional approach.

- Production by assembling electronic content that is received from authors and translated and assembled as needed. If you're developing a technical title, this may be the approach you'll take.

- Production by preparing all the materials for a title yourself.

We also describe a variant form of production from legacy paper archives and techniques.

Your choice of approach depends mainly on the nature of your contents and on how much you want to do your own work.

Although many of the sections that follow assume development by a professional production team, it is certainly possible for you to successfully produce your own CD-ROM titles. Definitions of success vary, of course. Some successes are technical—a successful CD-ROM might be one that clearly conveys its information to the user. Some successes are artistic—another successful disc might be one that embodies certain desirable effects, or has a certain impact on the viewer. And some successes are financial—a third successful disc might be one that returns its development costs and a surplus to the parties involved. The first two definitions measure success subjectively, but the third is quantifiable.

What's Involved in Creating a CD-ROM?

Although it's possible to create an economically successful CD-ROM from your own efforts and investment, it's not as easy as you may think. The CD-ROM world is evolving into a true publishing industry—one that includes both business and media technology. It's becoming much more like making movies, records, or books than it is like writing in your diary, creating technical documents, or making home movies.

Required Skills

Whether you create a CD-ROM on your own, or have the facilities of a full-service production facility, you must pull together the right set of skills. The set of skillls needed for CD-ROM publishing is broad. You have to know how to:

- Write, edit, and proofread

- Take pictures, scan them, color-correct them, and crop them

- Record or even compose music, lay it down on tape, and digitize it into the computer

- Shoot videotape, edit it, and direct actors

- Create animations

- Program a computer

- Design user interfaces, buttons, and navigation

- Act as a psychologist, able to understand how people use and relate to media

- Market and package the title, and get shelf space for it

- Figure out all the money and time involved

What resources will you need to accomplish all this? You will need words, so get a word processor. You will need pictures, so get a good still camera. You will need video, so get a good video camera and a video digitizer. You will need animations, so get some good animation software. You will need music, so get a MIDI board for your computer, or get a MIDI keyboard. You will need to assemble all of these components into a title, so get a good authoring system.

But electronic publishing is more than the sum of its parts. It's not just words or pictures or video or games or simulations—it's something that blends all of them together into a larger whole. In a professional environment, electronic publishing involves assembling a team of craft-oriented professionals who work together, often for a period of months, to create a title. Although it's possible to perform most CD-ROM activities yourself—as the authors of *Myst* did—you must be particularly multitalented to make it work. A successful CD-ROM title requires a complex mix of creative, technical, and business talents. It can also take a very long time for one person to do all this work.

Who's Who in Publishing?

Creating a CD-ROM combines the experience of people who have ideas, people who build products, people who finance those products, people who market and sell the products, and, ultimately, people who buy them. These are the main players:

Author
   The person who writes and develops content.

Developer
   An individual or company who actually creates a CD-ROM title for publication, and who produces and integrates the contents of the disc (up to the point of manufacturing).

Publisher
   An individual or, more typically, a company who is in the business of investing in, manufacturing, and marketing titles. Usually, a publisher produces many titles, and enters into contracts with authors, developers, and distributors.

Distributor
   Also called a wholesaler. A company that ships titles from the publisher to stores. The distributor acts as a go-between linking retail stores, which carry many titles, and publishers.

Retailer
   A store that sells to end users or customers.

In general, this is the model in the industry. However, in some cases, these roles are blended, rather than being completely distinct. For example, large publishing companies may also circumvent the wholesaler and sell directly to the large retail chains or catalog companies—something an upstart publisher cannot do.

Publishing Models

Publishing is the process of handling the financing, packaging, manufacturing, and marketing of a CD-ROM title. In some cases, the publisher may also be responsible for creating and/or acquiring content. There are several different publishing models for publishing your CD-ROM: self-publishing, acting as a developer, and acting as a publishing company.

Self-publishing

Self-publishing means that you create, produce, and manufacture the CD-ROMs yourself. In this scenario, if you don't self-finance the venture, you must find other investors—either limited partners for a single disc, or stockholders in a corporation. As your own publisher, you must also distribute and retail your product yourself, or at least make your own distribution arrangements.

The developer

One alternative to self-publishing is to work as a CD-ROM developer. In this scenario, you take responsibility for creating and producing the disk, but your involvement ends with the creation of the gold master. The master is delivered to a publishing company, which then packages and manufactures the CD-ROM, and makes the distribution arrangements for it. Functioning as a developer allows a small company to focus its strength on the creative and the product development tasks, while leaving the marketing and distribution to the professionals.

The developer-publisher relationship is not unique to the CD-ROM business—it's very common in book publishing, in the music business, and in the movie industry. This relationship can make a good marriage, because developers tend to be strong in creative areas and weak in marketing, while publishers, conversely, tend to be weak in creative areas and strong in marketing. As a developer, you don't have to put up all of the money; the publishing company typically pays you an advance against royalties on some or all of your development costs. However, the publisher may want a significant financial stake in the product in return for the company's participation and contributions.

The publishing company

A third alternative is to function as a publishing company. In this scenario, you acquire or develop the concept, produce the disk (or hire a developer to produce it), arrange all of the necessary financing (often out of your cash flow), create the packaging, devise a marketing strategy, and arrange distribution.

A CD-ROM publishing company works in much the same way as a book company (e.g., Random House, Simon and Schuster), a record company (e.g., Atlantic Records, Epic), or a movie company (e.g., Paramount, 20th Century Fox). Although each of these companies publishes very different media, they all do much the same thing. In each scenario the publishing company acquires concepts, develops them into finished products and then markets those products into the "channel." The publishing company itself rarely does the distribution or the retailing (although some publishers do sell through catalog sales, as we'll describe below). For example, the retailing of books is done by thousands of bookstores; the retailing of records is done by thousands of record stores; and the retailing of movies is done by thousands of movie theaters. And each of these industries has distributors who move the product from the producer to the retailers.

Becoming your own publisher is very difficult because it requires considerable capital, a broad range of craft skills, extensive knowledge of your market, significant marketing savvy, and access to wholesalers. The larger publishing companies in the CD-ROM business have sales in excess of tens of millions of dollars annually. Several companies even have sales in the hundreds of millions of dollars each year. It is difficult—though not impossible—to compete in this world with sales below a few million dollars. That's why, as we've mentioned, smaller companies typically function as developers, rather than full-fledged publishers.

The manufacturer

Just as few book publishers actually own their own printing presses, and few movie studios actually have their own film laboratories, few CD-ROM publishers actually manufacture their own discs. Authors and publishers typically make a master computer tape or CD-R disc (write-once CD-ROM) containing the disc contents, ready for duplication, and then send it out for manufacturing. Disc manufacturing is a very specialized business that requires significant capital and know-how. There is little reason for authors and publishers to become experts.

Chapter 9 describes the disc manufacturing process in enough detail to allow you to discuss it with your manufacturer.

Development by a Production Studio

As we mentioned at the beginning of this chapter, there are several different approaches to developing CD-ROMs. This section describes the most common method—development by multimedia specialists in a production studio. We describe the basic steps in the production cycle and the typical ways of staffing such a project, including cost estimates.

Career Options in CD-ROM Publishing

There are many options open to people who are considering a career in the CD-ROM development or publication business.

Some people prefer to work as individual artists, or in a small partnership, and these models should continue to work well in the CD-ROM business. However, if you want to develop a reliable career, and ensure that you'll regularly earn a good salary, we advise you to specialize—to become an expert in some facet of the business, and to develop a connection with a development or publishing group. As small CD-ROM development or publishing companies grow and get to the level of employing five to seven people, employees tend to start specializing in performing certain tasks. As the industry matures, many mature professionals who know how to provide the various craft disciplines will flow into it and find ready employment; all they will need to do is to make slight adjustments to reorient their careers. For example:

- A color-correction expert from the print industry can learn how to color-correct for CD-ROMs in a day or so.

- Video editors from advertising or television can quickly learn how to edit video for CD-ROM.

- Writers, photographers, graphic artists, and sound technicians are all craft professionals who should be able to adapt quickly to the CD-ROM industry.

If you are planning to work in the development or publishing business, you need to make contact with these professionals and start using their skills. You also need to work with younger people who have fresh visions and the creativity to use the craft skills in new ways.

In general, these are the steps you'll follow in developing a CD-ROM product:

- **Initial product planning.** During this stage, you'll develop the concept, treatment, and possibly a rigged demo. You'll also obtain financing and work out all the necessary contracts.

- **Detailed design.** During this stage, you'll develop a functional specification and a technical specification for the product. We describe much of this stage in this chapter, and Chapter 5 contains additional details.

- **Content development.** During this stage, you'll acquire existing content (and associated rights) and/or develop new content.

- **Integration of content into the product.** During this stage, you'll pull together all the individual content and integrate it into a coherent whole, usually via an authoring system (see Chapter 6 for details). This stage culminates in the release of a preliminary product—first in an alpha release, and then in a beta.

  An alpha release is a working shell of the product with minimal content (perhaps only five or six screens, one or two movies, and a half-dozen pictures). The goal of an alpha is to illustrate the look and feel of the product, so that it can be tested in a preliminary way.

  The beta release, in contrast, is a complete product with full contents in it, which is ready for detailed testing.

- **Testing.** During this stage (which actually occurs at different points during the project), you'll test all content and system functions.

- **Output.** During this stage, you prepare the final files and associated artwork for delivery to the manufacturing plant.

Development completes with the production of the final CD-ROM image. We'll discuss later stages of manufacturing, marketing, and distribution of the CD-ROM in Chapters 9 through 11.

Planning and Designing the Product

This section briefly describes initial product planning and product design. Although these are logically two separate stages, in many ways they occur in tandem, and staffing for these stages overlaps. Basically, the work we describe here must all be completed before you plunge into detailed content development. The planning process has two main purposes: it should help you produce tangible design documents, and it should also help you understand how you envision the product, and how you can better communicate your ideas to others. This section covers the design process, and Chapter 5 goes into more detail on actual document design.

Not every step listed in this section has to be performed in a formal way. For example, although we describe such written documents as a treatment, a functional specification, and a technical specification, you don't absolutely have to write these documents, as long as you have the design clearly in mind.

Be aware, though, that if you aren't able to specify each of the components described below, at least for yourself, you probably don't have a good enough handle on your CD-ROM's concept and contents to be really successful in developing it.

NOTE

In focusing on the professional type of development process in this book, we don't want to dissuade you from just jumping into CD-ROM design and "doing it," if that pleases you. But we owe you the responsibility of suggesting that there *is* a formal design process that most products undergo. In all probability, publishers or other professionals in the business won't take you seriously unless you work through this design process— that's simply how the real world does things! Some people haven't made this discovery yet, but the CD-ROM publishing community is learning very quickly about real-world expectations and constraints.

The concept

The first step in the planning process is to come up with the idea, called a *concept* in the media business. If you talk to anyone about your plans for a CD-ROM, they'll ask "What's the concept?" You must have an answer in 25 to 30 well-chosen words. You have to know quite precisely what the concept is, and if the concept is much bigger than this description, it's probably too big for a CD-ROM. The concept may be very small or it may be grandiose. It may be to present an old product in a new way ("Let's put the encyclopedia on CD-ROM"), or it may be a new idea ("Let's make a CD-ROM where you can go on tour with the Rolling Stones—you can even play on stage with them").

A concept that is going to become the basis for a CD-ROM must be nurtured and developed. It must be examined to see if it is a good idea, a useful idea, and a practical idea. Its scope and focus need to be explored, and the idea may need to be shifted, expanded, or constrained. In the end, the idea must be able to be translated into a product that fits into 650 MB of digital storage, to be assembled by a few or several people using tools that more or less already exist, and to be finished in a finite amount of time for a finite amount of money. That's all!

It's particularly important that the concept have a *hook* in it. The hook makes the concept special and compelling, and provides a rationale for why you're doing a CD-ROM, rather than a book, magazine, photograph, film, Broadway play, or marching band drill. Creating a CD-ROM of Shakespeare's plays is a sweet idea, but unless the disc is going to contain something other than text, it has no hook, no reason to use the special capabilities of CD-ROM. But what if you include a virtual reconstruction of the Globe Theatre? What if you incorporate clips of famous performances? What if you allow the user to participate somehow in a performance? Now you have a hook—you're making the CD-ROM into something more than a book could ever be.

You can go through the same exercise with any number of other ideas. How about a CD-ROM containing a collection of photographs from the space shuttle? By itself, this concept isn't enough for a real CD-ROM product. Can you come up with a hook for that concept?

The treatment

After you have a well-developed concept with a good hook, the next step is to write a *treatment*. A treatment is a three- or four-page document that contains the following, in concise terms:

- Concept and hook

- Contents

- Target audience

- One-page budget

- One-page schedule

- Description of key staff

- One page of special features of the disc; for example, be sure to mention it if you have an exclusive contract with Steven Spielberg!

- Marketing strategy, which may include a return-on-investment analysis (i.e., how many units you need to sell at what price to recover your development investment)

The treatment for a disc on how to play golf, for example, might describe interviews with great golfers, hole diagrams for 25 famous golf courses, the rules of the game, and a special virtual reality golf game (one that includes a whiffle ball that plugs into your mouse port and that you can whack with your golf club, coupled to a program that shows the ball lofting down the fairway and then advances you to your next position).

Ironically, the key technology for making CD-ROMs is the written word, because that's almost entirely what we work from in creating the treatment and in almost everything that follows up to creating the actual electronic components of the title.

The rigged demo

It's sometimes necessary to take the treatment a little further and make what's called a *rigged demo* of the project. This demo differs from a prototype, which is designed to test out ideas for the product. A rigged demo is simply designed to give a potential publisher or distributor a sense of what the project will be like when it's finished. It shows what the title will contain and what it will do, and it demonstrates the look and feel of the product on the computer screen.

The rigged demo doesn't showcase the entire product, only a small piece that shows the concept and hook. You can think of the demo as being a carefully scripted tour of the product you intend to create. Feel free to develop the demo using whatever language is convenient for doing quick work. It doesn't have to really work—it just has to look as if it works. In fact, if the demo really does work, you're doing too much. What you want is simply a mockup, a fake, a dummy.

A rigged demo isn't always necessary. With a sophisticated audience, paper storyboards may do the trick. Most people, though, need to see a rigged demo before they can actually understand the idea you're demonstrating.

Be sure to listen carefully to what people tell you when you describe your concept and show them your rigged demo. Often, people will tell you things you don't want to hear, or things that indicate that they don't understand your concept the same way you do. Although you may end up dismissing some of what they say (perhaps they're reacting to what they want to see), you do have to process everything they say—ultimately, your success or failure rests on their ability to understand you. Sometime, somewhere in people's reactions may lie the one thing that will make your audience accept or reject the product.

Financing

Let's move from the technical to the practical. Before you get any more deeply into product planning, you need to secure *financing*. Your financing may come from your own pocket, from your employer, from a limited partner (one who finances the property for a percentage of the return), from a publisher, or from a distributor. We won't discuss these sources in any detail here; each approach to financing is a complete subject in its own right. Whatever the method of financing, this step embodies the commitment of resources.

Unless you are self-financing the project, this financing phase of production is concluded with a contract—a legal agreement between you (the owner of the idea) and the financier (the owner of the money). This contract can be as short as a few pages or as long as 25 pages. If the amount of money involved, or the amount of money you expect to make, is more than a few thousand dollars, you will need to retain a lawyer who has experience in intellectual property law.

This contract is only one of the contracts you'll have to negotiate. You'll also need a contract with your publisher (assuming that you are not self-publishing) as well as with any staff you employ. For additional information about contracts, see "Contracts" later in this chapter.

Assembling the design team

Every project has its own characteristics. In general, during the earliest stages of product planning, only a few people will be involved—primarily the producer and director of the product. During these early days, the idea for the product is evolving, and usually there are financial issues to be worked out.

As soon as the project is solid enough to require a functional specification (see the next section), a larger design team begins to collaborate on the detailed design of the product. This team is mainly responsible for the functional specification and, in general, for the formulation of the product. In medium- to large-scale productions, the design team consists of:

- The director, who shapes the product as a whole

- The editor-in-chief, who shapes the textual content

- The art director, who shapes the look of the product

- The interface designer, who shapes the feel of the product

- The sound designer, who shapes the sound of the product

- The software designer (very likely the author of the technical specification we describe below), who creates the "engineering" of the product

- The instructional designer (for educational titles), who ensures the educational quality of the design

We'll describe these functions in greater detail in the staffing sections below, and will present a series of tables showing some actual cost estimates for the time spent by the members of the team.

Resonance between all the different roles of the design team members is critical; none is really superior to any other, and each influences all the others. It is this resonance that makes it so valuable to create and keep a good production team, as we describe later in this chapter.

Usually, the design team plays a critical role up to the time of the alpha release of the product. After that milestone, the role of the design team in setting direction ordinarily diminishes. (They are responsible for setting policy—not for processing volumes of work.) Although all of these people need to remain involved throughout the project, their involvement should, in almost all cases, be to ensure quality control. They take responsibility for focusing the work of the creative people who actually develop content, and for making sure that the content comes together according to the product design. (Exceptions are the director and/or editor-in-chief, who work throughout the entire project. In some environments, the art director may stay involved because he or she is also the one who makes all the art; even if this is the case, however, that person's role is not different.)

For more information about staff, see "Staffing a Multimedia Project," later in this chapter.

Functional specification

Once you've secured financing and assembled the design team, your project is really off the ground. Now you'll need to develop a detailed *functional specification.* This is a document of approximately 40 to 80 pages that itemizes every single element that goes into the disc. As we've mentioned, everyone on the design team contributes to this document. You can think of the functional spec as being a design document, an architecture, and a plan, all rolled into one. It contains a summary of every single screen, function, and section of the CD-ROM, along with the design and interface rules that specify how the CD-ROM is to look and feel, and several budgets. The functional spec is essential to figuring out what staff you need to work on the project.

If you have done media architecture before—as a book editor, movie producer, TV show producer, software developer, or record company executive—you should find this specification process to be a somewhat familiar one. A book publisher might specify a book in terms of the number of pages and the quantity of color figures and line drawings. A movie producer might specify that a movie is to be 90 minutes long, is to have 211 shots in it, is to have three starring roles and 25 supporting bit parts, is to use 300 extras, and will need a crew of 15 for a shoot of four weeks. The budget lines and items are different, but the mechanics are basically the same from industry to industry.

Example 4-1 shows a heavily abbreviated version of the functional specification for the SIGGRAPH conference proceedings CD-ROM described in Chapter 3, *Two Electronic Titles.*

Example 4-1.   Abbreviated SIGGRAPH functional specification

```
The disc consists of the annual SIGGRAPH conference
proceedings on CD-ROM. It is created as a dual-directory disc
for both ISO 9660 systems and Macintosh HFS systems. When the
disc is mounted in either system it will show a top-level view
of the files and directories.

The disc contains a number of files that come from the papers
in the conference. The central feature of the disc is an Adobe
Acrobat document that is a page-by-page replication of the
printed proceedings. Each page contains whatever text,
diagrams, and color pictures are found in the printed
conference proceedings. There is an index in this document
that lists each paper, and there are thumbnails that show the
```

Example 4-1.   Abbreviated SIGGRAPH functional specification (Continued)

```
overall shape of each page. There are hyperlinks so when you
click on the linked areas you will see the appropriate area of
the proceedings. The disc contains three particular link
areas: a table of contents, an author index, and cover image
credits.

The table of contents is the printed version and will contain
hyperlinks whose linked areas include the title and author
list for each paper; they are set up so that if you click on a
title the first page of the chosen paper will appear. ...

    ...

Besides the overall Adobe Acrobat document, there is a
directory for tools that are needed to view the contents of
the disc. ...

There is also a directory for each paper in the proceedings.
This directory contains additional material provided by the
author. For each paper there is a READ_ME file in formats that
work for UNIX, DOS, and Macintosh, a full PostScript version
of the paper with whatever figures are provided by the author,
original versions of figures as provided by the author
(preferably in TIFF format), digital movies as provided by the
author (preferably in QuickTime or MPEG format), and
additional material such as appendices, datasets, or source
code as provided by the author. ...
```

Design rules. Design rules are important to achieving a consistent and workable interface for the user. Although we discuss design in detail in Chapter 5, let's look at one typical example of a design issue that the functional specification might need to address. In any CD-ROM product, there will need to be "hot spots" on the screen—places you can click on. There are several potential designs that might work for these hot spots:

- One design might have no visual indication of the hot spots, but rely on content context to help you find the hot spots.

- Another design might show some visual indicator on the screen to give the locations of the hot spots.

- Another design might have the cursor change its shape when you roll over a hot spot; that's less obvious than a visual indicator, and has less effect on the screen design, but you must learn to watch for the change.

- Yet another rule might specify that, when you roll the mouse over a hot spot, the hot spot lights up so you'll know it's clickable.

The functional specification needs to spell out these kinds of details.

Interface. The functional specification also identifies what the interface will look like. The *Ultimate Robot* CD-ROM described in Chapter 3 has an interface with only five components on the screen: a title field, a text field, a button palette, a picture, and a background. Details of these items would be part of the functional specification. Here are some examples of what you might specify:

- **Title field**. Set in Helvetica medium bold, 32 points (or a certain number of pixels) tall.

- **Text field**. Each piece of body copy is not to exceed 150 words, set in 12-point Helvetica, and paragraphs are indented three spaces.

- **Button palette**. The palette will consist of *Previous, Next, Back*, and *Go To Contents* buttons; the functionality of each button is also described in the functional specification.

- **Video**. The video in the title will be 240 x 160 pixel QuickTime movies using Cinepak compression methods, placed in a video window, and the amount of video on the disc will not exceed one hour.

- **Picture**. Each picture is an 8-bit PICT file, 121 x 327 pixels, uncompressed.

Captions or credit. Text is formatted as in the text field, but is associated with the video or picture.

Sound. The functional specification must also specify all the sound required for the CD-ROM. This includes sounds that play when you click buttons, when you transit between different sections, sounds that accompany video or animation, and sounds that play at the opening.

Opening and closing. The functional specification should also specify whether the disc is to contain an opening animation and/or closing credits; these are the bookends for the product.

Budgets. The functional specification should contain two budgets: a money budget and a CD-ROM real estate budget. The CD-ROM real estate budget will describe the components and the amount of disc memory each takes. For example, consider a sample disc with 100 pictures, 200 text blocks, and 50 Quick-Time movies. Suppose each picture takes 127 KB, each text block takes 1 KB, and each movie takes 10 MB. For this disc, the total space for pictures is 127K x 100 pictures or 127 MB; the total text allocation is 1K x 200 text blocks or 200K (which we will round up to a generous 1 MB for simplicity); and the 50 Quick-Time movies at 10 MB each consume 500 MB. The total is 628 MB. You have enough room, but just barely! If the total real estate exceeds 650 MB, you've got too much material to fit on the disc, and you must rethink the project to make it fit.

The money budget breaks the CD-ROM down in terms of costs. There are different ways to approach doing a budget, but all involve listing a series of budget lines and the costs associated with each line. One way is to itemize costs in terms of the different people and services the disc requires; another approach is to use unit costs, such as the cost for each second of video. This is described in some detail in Chapter 10, *CD-ROM Publishing Costs*.

Technical specification

Another document you'll need to prepare during the planning stage is the technical specification, which defines the technical environment for the product—such operational characteristics as:

- Target platforms (e.g., Windows, DOS, Macintosh, UNIX)

- RAM requirements

- Video display requirements

- Required system services (e.g., sound, picture, or video handling)

- All global variables, functions, objects, and their properties needed in the product

Whereas the functional specification describes behavior as seen by the user, the technical specification describes how the behavior is implemented; it details how you intend to engineer and program the disc.

Here's a somewhat imprecise, but possibly useful, analogy. Suppose that you are writing a specification for an automobile starter mechanism. The functional specification might say something like this:

> The user shall insert the key into the ignition switch and rotate the key to the right, activating the starter motor and causing the car to start.

The technical specification, on the other hand, might say:

> The ignition switch shall consist of a rotary lock with two electrical contacts. Completing an electrical circuit across the contacts shall cause an electrical current to flow to the starter motor, causing it to rotate. The starter motor shall be connected by a belt or a chain to the engine of the car, causing the crankshaft of the engine to go around, the spark plugs to fire, and the fuel in the engine to combust, and the engine to start.

The functional specification is a view from outside the hood looking in, whereas the technical specification is a view from inside the hood looking out.

Now let's look at an example of a CD-ROM design issue. The functional specification description of a button might say:

> Button *Back* takes the user to the previous page.

The technical specification description, on the other hand, might say:

> The back button functionality shall be achieved by composing handler PageBack. The handler has one argument, which is the label of the current page. The handler examines the list of labels for all pages and determines which page, if any, is the previous page. If there is a previous page the handler jumps to that location. If there is no previous page the handler returns an error code.

Contracts

We've already mentioned contracts under "Financing," above. Make sure that all of the contracts for your product are in place before you complete the planning stage.

If you're an author or developer doing business with a publisher (or if you're a publisher who is doing business with an author or developer) you'll need to develop a contract for that relationship. A contract is a written document between the parties involved in an agreement that specifies the terms of the agreement. Among other things, the contract specifies:

- What work is being performed

- What resources each party is providing

- What rights are being transferred

- How much money is being paid

- How credits are to be treated (see the sidebar, "The Theory of Credits")

- When deliveries and payments are to be made

A good contract will also define how the parties disengage in the event the project is not proceeding according to plan.

There are many subtle issues involved in contracts, and contracts vary from industry to industry. Even if you have a lot of experience negotiating book, record, or movie contracts, you would be well advised to work with an attorney who is experienced in CD-ROM publishing. Not only are there many ways to be taken advantage of if you are not careful, it's important that a contract address a range of important issues and potential pitfalls.

Lawyers are something like computer programmers; like computer programs, most contracts are mainly collections of declarations and if/then/else statements. A good contract, like a good program, may spend many more lines dealing with the exceptions than it does with the rule.

It's very easy to write a computer program for a perfect world; unfortunately, people do imperfect things. They try to run programs on computers that don't have enough memory, or have the wrong kind of video or sound card, or have the wrong size monitor. Other users have the audacity to divide by zero, or enter numbers that are too big for the machine. All of these situations require that the computer program have special code to handle the exception cases.

Contracts are no different. It's very easy to write a contract that describes what happens when everything goes right; knowing all the things that can go wrong, and how to handle them in the world of commerce, is another thing entirely. We advise you to make sure you're working with someone who has experience with these issues.

Developing contracts for your CD-ROM work will cost you anywhere between $1,000 and $10,000 to negotiate, depending on the size of the job, who you're doing business with, and the amount of negotiating you want to do. But this is money well spent. If you're doing real work, and if you believe that what you have is valuable and you want to make money on it, you need a contract that ensures your rights. A good lawyer can also help you hold onto your ownership rights, and keep you from losing your house because a clause made you responsible for someone else's mistakes or because a multimillion dollar company went bankrupt! In fact, if your lawyer is a skilled negotiator, he or she may save you more money than the contract cost—the lawyer may very well succeed in getting more money from the other party than you expected.

Creating and Integrating Content for the Product

Once product planning and design has been completed, the content development stage begins in earnest. This stage actually includes three distinct types of activities: creating new content for the CD-ROM, acquiring the rights to use existing content (when appropriate), and integrating the content into a coherent product, usually via some kind of authoring system. In this section, we'll talk briefly about the people who perform the various tasks described here; however, we'll reserve the major discussion of staffing and staff development and costs for the section called "Staffing a Multimedia Project" later in this chapter.

NOTE

Although we've placed the content discussion after the discussion of planning and design, be aware that some of the work described below should actually begin earlier in the process. For example, if you need to acquire outside rights for content, this step should begin immediately, in parallel with the various design tasks.

Assembling the content team

The actual production of a CD-ROM begins with the design and development of the *content*, often called the *assets*, that will be included on the CD-ROM. Information design involves selecting the appropriate contents and defining the relationships between them.

As we mentioned earlier, under "Planning and Designing the Product," the overall design of the product is created by a creative/design team. This team develops the functional specification and oversees the various types of content development. The team needs to resolve two key issues about the products' assets:

- **The source of the assets to be used in the product.** The contents may already exist, or they may have to be created from scratch.

- **The type of assets to be used in the product.** In broad terms, the type may be text, sound, pictures, animation, or video.

As we've mentioned, in general, the members of the design team do not do the detailed content work, but they decide precisely what content will go on the CD-ROM and they supervise the work of the actual creative staff. This creative staff includes:

- Writers

- Photographers

- Illustrators

- Videographers

- Animators

- Songwriters

- Musicians

- Actors

All of these people are creative, but for CD-ROM publishing, we want their creativity to be highly directed. Often, we do not need a photographer to shoot beautiful pictures—we need a photographer to take a picture of this barn, or of that cat, or of a certain person, or of 50 covered bridges. There may be creativity in the eye of the photographer, but the purpose at this stage of production is to shoot the specific pictures that are needed for the product. The same is true of the illustrations, video, sounds, and all the other assets for the disc.

For more information about staffing, see "Staffing a Multimedia Project," later in this chapter.

The Theory of Credits

The theory behind the order of credits (on a CD-ROM, as well as in a feature film) is that the producers are honored by going first, and the creative people (often called the *creatives*) are honored by being most adjacent to the body of the work.

Credits are a big issue in the electronic publishing industry. We have found that some producers suppress credits to people who work on a product. Their reasoning varies from a feeling that they genuinely deserve all the credit themselves to a fear that if they give credit to other people, these people will feel that they're worth more money—or worse yet, that someone else will become aware of their good work and hire them. Unfortunately, many people who fail to give credit to the creatives who make their CD-ROMs effective also fail to understand why their better creatives simply don't stick around! We advise creatives to get in writing (up front, during contract negotiations) exactly what their credit will be.

There is a flip side to our argument, however, and that is that credits should reflect what a person actually did on a project, and not be a fabrication.

Using existing assets

If the assets you plan to use already exist, they must be gathered together in an organized manner so they can be integrated into the product. This process includes not only physically locating the materials, but also acquiring the rights to use them.

Some rights are very broad, and others are very specific. For example, you might acquire the broad rights to license a character, an entire book, or a series of books so that you can build a product around this prime license. Examples are Dr. Seuss, Peanuts, Superman, etc. At the other extreme, you might be interested in licensing very specific rights, such as the right to include a specific photograph of a certain building on a travelogue CD-ROM, or a particular teapot on a disc about tea ceremonies.

Acquiring the first type of rights (very general ones) is usually the job of the CD-ROM producer, in conjunction with a business analyst and attorney, because the rights are central to the whole concept of the CD-ROM; that type of acquisition needs to take place at the very start of the project. Acquiring the second type of rights (very specific ones) is usually delegated to a researcher and may be performed throughout the project's development.

Creating new assets

If the assets you plan to use must be created, you'll undertake a production process that is unique to each medium. Writers will create text. Photographers will take pictures. Illustrators will make diagrams. Animators will create animation. Filmmakers and videographers will create film and tape. Programmers will make functions. As we've mentioned, the design team supervises this work, under the overall guidance of either the director or the editor-in-chief, who is responsible for shaping the content of the entire production.

You will derive the individual work assignments for these various creatives from the functional specification; it is the functional spec that details that there are to be 25 different teapots in the product and that, as a consequence, 25 copy blocks need to be composed, and 25 photographs of 25 different teapots need to be obtained.

The production manager usually handles the job of issuing purchase orders for these various work assignments, processing the incoming work, and developing an ongoing punch list that tracks missing pieces. This person may also take responsibility for logging program bugs and tracking their correction.

Depending upon the scope of the project and the size of the studio, much of the detailed content work may be done by freelancers and is *work for hire*, meaning that it is purchased by the production company and owned by it (see the sidebar).

Work for Hire

Making sure that freelancers do work for hire (rather than keeping the rights to their work) is almost always necessary if the production company is to be unencumbered in reselling the product. If your production company wants the work it purchases to be a work for hire, you must enter into a contract with the person who does the work; otherwise, the rights to the work will revert to the freelancer. Be sure to consult a lawyer about this issue.

Integrating assets into the product

The end result of the job of asset creation is a collection of files. You'll have some text files, image files, video files, and sound files. Now you're ready to import these individual files into the authoring system you've chosen for your product. Most of the authoring systems used for CD-ROM work, such as Adobe Acrobat, HyperCard, and Macromedia Director, offer some kind of *shell*—a programming environment in which you'll organize your files into a coherent whole. If you're a particularly adventurous developer, you might not use a ready-made authoring system, but instead write your own shell in C or some other compiler-type language. (Chapter 6 describes various alternatives.)

Whether the shell comes from an authoring system or is something you've built from scratch, it will be the place where you specify most of the functionality for your product—the look of the screens, the navigation from one part of the product to another, and so on. Depending on what system you use, you'll find that program functions like button clicks may be rather easy to install, or they may be quite difficult. Different systems also offer very different functions—features like clicking on a picture and having it zoom up, or having a picture on which you can mouse down, scroll, pan, and zoom, or having a QuickTime movie on which you can move left or right to see the movie pan to the side.

Although the specific characteristics of the authoring system will dictate much of what you are able to do during this integration stage, the various elements of product design (worked out by the design team during the planning and design stage) also are critical to the ease of the authoring work.

For example, the interface design is of key importance here. Interface design is essentially the "look and feel" of the overall product. It involves things like deciding on the functions and locations of the buttons, the look of the backgrounds of the various screens, and so on.

The graphic design is also very important to the authoring process. As we describe in Chapter 5, the graphic designer develops a "design grid" for the product. This grid is a kind of template for the various visual components of the product. Like a style book for a printed document or the format of a TV show, it sets up a format into which individual content (e.g., fields, buttons, fonts, headers, and footers) can be poured. How this grid is perceived by the user depends on the particular authoring system chosen. For example, a product using the Hyper-Card system (described in Chapter 6) would have a set of "stacks," each complete with several backgrounds consisting of fully working buttons, fields, and artwork. In a game product, the shell would include global game functionality.

Depending, again, on the authoring system and overall design, there may be a good deal of programming work that needs to be done at this point. The authoring system may not provide every function you'd like to see. The software designer is responsible for assessing what's available, and for assigning additional programming work (e.g., interactive functions, specialized control panels, simulation or game elements) to programmers on the project.

In a professional production environment, different types of content assets are integrated into the product by media-specific professionals, as we describe below.

Text. Text must be entered, spell-checked, and proofread by copy editors, proofreaders, and other types of wordsmiths. Once in the product, all text must have the proper fonts and sizes assigned. In some situations, it's possible to mark up the text before it's imported into the authoring system (using RTF or SGML coding), and have the fonting and sizing done automatically.

Pictures. Pictures must be digitized, color-corrected in various ways, and compressed by graphic artists. Prints are digitized using a flat-bed scanner; slides or transparencies are sent out for scanning. Pictures scanned from halftones have to be despeckled; almost all pictures should be scanned at a higher spatial resolution than needed, and then reduced in size. Pictures may also be cropped. Some pictures will need to be manipulated digitally to create the image needed for the title, and some will need to be created by synthetic computer graphics or by digital paint programs. The image resolution must be set to an appropriate resolution: 72 dpi for the Macintosh or an appropriate resolution for other platforms.

Pay particular attention to images that are to be used on multiple platforms, because each platform has certain resolutions that work best. For the SIGGRAPH conference proceedings, for example, we used 150 dpi to fit both Windows and Macintosh, and to allow one level of additional detail in Acrobat's image zooming.

Sound. Sound must be recorded, digitized, mixed, and edited by sound technicians.

Film and video. Film must be transferred to videotape, and videotape must be captured by video technicians using a digital video capture board. The digital video must then be color corrected, compressed, and stored. This is a nontrivial process, which requires a mixture of science and elbow grease. Some digital video may be created by synthetic animations, or by digital compositing techniques like those of movie post-production.

Programming. Programming tasks—for simulations, games, specialized control panels, and other interactive functions—are assigned to programmers. They will code the necessary functions, test them, and integrate the completed modules into the product.

Other components. Before work is complete, you'll have to construct the necessary hyperlinks, find and search engines, tables of contents, and indices. Don't forget to include main and end credits, acknowledgments, permissions and copyrights, and legal boilerplate as well.

Testing the Product

CD-ROM testing is a critical part of developing a title, and its importance shows up most clearly when it's inadequately done. In late 1995, Disney produced a CD-ROM based on its motion picture *The Lion King*, only to have thousands of copies fail to work when they were played on certain home computers. The problem apparently was that the product did not work with some PC configurations. Either earlier testing did not show up these incompatibilities or they were not spelled out adequately in the product packaging. At any rate, this problem caused the loss of a great deal of money and face from what should have been a very attractive CD-ROM property.

Although testing proceeds continually while a title is being developed, it is normally focused in two phases: the alpha delivery and the beta delivery of a project:

Alpha delivery

As we've mentioned, an alpha delivery is a working shell of the product with minimal content. It may have only five or six screens, one or two movies, and a half-dozen pictures. The goal of an alpha is to illustrate the full look and feel of the product with very little content. Its primary function is to allow testers to examine the way the content is taking shape and is being presented. Revisions based on things learned from alpha testing are made much more easily than revisions of a more fully developed version.

Beta delivery

The beta release version, by contrast, is a fully loaded product with full contents in it. By definition, code and content are complete in the beta version. The product is prepared as a one-off disc, and enters an extensive testing and final evaluation stage. This task is performed by testers, whose job it is to exercise the product, often with hostile intent, and try to drive out bugs. This phase usually lasts four to eight weeks.

Once beta testing is complete, you'll be ready to prepare the final CD-ROM image for manufacturing, which is known as the RTM (release to manufacturing) disc. See Chapter 9 for a complete discussion of the manufacturing process.

There is one fundamental tenet of CD-ROM testing: You can never test your disc too much!

Functionality testing

Testers (usually a mix of professional testers and people inside your organization) check the alpha and beta products in a variety of ways. The simplest kind of testing, functionality testing, examines the product both in terms of content (e.g., making sure the right picture is associated with the right text) and in terms of look and feel (e.g., making sure that the product behaves correctly). This type of testing is relatively routine. It needs to be performed at all levels of detail to ensure that what is present in the actual product is precisely what was defined in the technical specification.

When discrepancies are found, they are noted in bug reports. Figure 4-1 shows a sample bug report form describing an actual bug in a product.

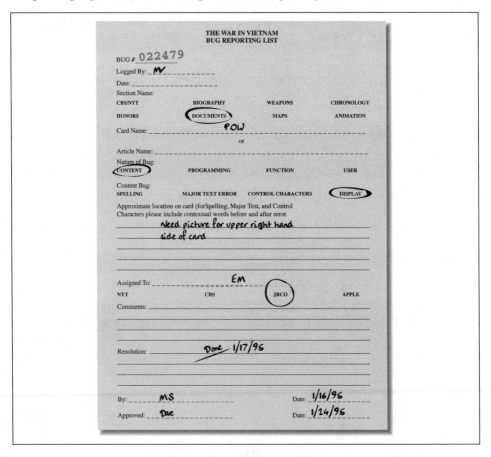

Figure 4-1.   A bug report on a test

NOTE

Some publishers do a good deal of product testing themselves, or hire professional testers to do it for them. Others expect the developer to do all testing. Chapter 10, provides some cost estimates for testing.

Environmental testing

Besides simple functionality testing, other types of more complicated testing are also required. The really tricky part is to manage to test all the things that are not supposed to happen. Here are some examples:

- Try to run the product on the smallest machine a purchaser will try to use.

- Try it out on a black-and-white machine, even though you built it in color.

- Try it out on machines of various color depths to be sure the graphics look good in all cases.

- If QuickTime or MPEG movies are used, try them on machines that do not have the right kind of movie player.

- If you built the product with a 13-inch monitor in mind, try it out on a 16-inch monitor, because the product may have some screen size dependencies. For example, the menu bar may now sit at the top of the screen while the product sits in a 13-inch window in the middle of the screen. Worse, a slick trick for menus has to be completely rethought because it used the 13-inch screen size.

Basically, in this phase testing seeks to avoid having customers buy your title expecting it to work on their system, and then calling you on the telephone, complaining about some kind of mystery error they got. To avoid such problems, if you use QuickTime, you need to test to be sure that QuickTime is on the machine. If you need 5 MB of memory free, you have to test to make sure sufficient memory is available. If you're on a multitasking machine, and the user is able to leave your product and go to something else, and come back to you afterwards, you have to be sure that you restore everything to the same system state that existed when your product was interrupted. For example, suppose users go to another application and change color tables, or they go to PhotoShop and change to 32-bit color (from the product's 8-bit color). It's simply not acceptable to have the product crash or not work correctly when it resumes.

Environmental testing is much more complex to do on the PC (with its maze of different brands of machine, video cards, and sound cards) than it is on the Macintosh. One testing lab for PC products that we have heard of has more than 30 different computer brands, similar numbers of video cards and sound cards, more than 10 kinds of mice, and eight different versions of DOS. This isn't something you're likely to be able to replicate at your own site—and that's why there are professional testers, and why professional testers are usually employed on professional products.

Testing in cycles

Testing really cannot be understood out of context. You don't create a product, test it once to try to find bugs, drive out those you find, fix those, and go to the manufacturer. Testing occurs throughout the development process; everything that is created for the product has some testing before it is integrated into the product.

Even after integration, there is a development cycle as shown in Figure 4-2—after production, the developer makes a set of one-off discs for testing; testers find errors to fix or improvements to make; and the developer fixes the problems and returns to the start of the cycle. We know of projects in which as many as 17 test cycles were needed to drive out the final problems on a disc. The only standard for a disc is the standard for all programs: if it's not perfect, it shouldn't ship.

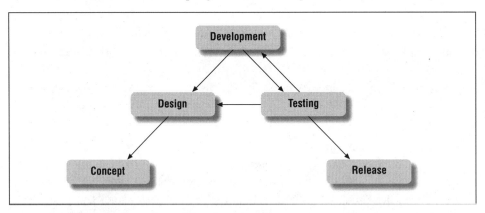

Figure 4-2.   The cycle of development and testing

Preparing the CD-ROM Output for Manufacturing

What's the final output from all of the activity we've described? Whether you develop your CD-ROM in a production studio environment, or take one of the alternative approaches we describe later in this chapter, you'll eventually end up with a set of files, reflecting all the work you've done.

If you have access to CD-ROM premastering software, you will be able to create an actual CD-ROM image from these files; the image will contain all of the data, laid out exactly as it will appear on the final CD-ROM. You can copy this image yourself to a CD-R, an MO (magneto-optical) disc, or a number of other devices.

When you send the premastered image off to the manufacturing plant, they will simply be able to duplicate this image.

If you don't have access to premastering software, you will have to send the original files to the manufacturer on a disk or tape devices of some kind. The manufacturer will first have to create a master disc from these files, and then duplicate them.

Chapter 9 describes this process in detail, along with all of the details of manufacturing. Remember to build these final output tasks into your overall product schedule and staffing. You will need to have one person be responsible for working with the manufacturer—for example, delivering the output, approving proofs of the disc and other materials, and otherwise acting as liaison. Remember as well that you must deliver more than files to the manufacturer. As Chapter 9 details, you also need to deliver a number of pieces of old-fashioned ink-on-paper artwork (mechanicals and separation negatives) to the printer (yes, that old-fashioned guy with a press, ink, and paper!). These pieces may include the disc label, brochure cover, jewel box art, shelf box art, etc.

Staffing a Multimedia Project

What staff do you need at a multimedia production facility? We've talked about the skills needed to develop a CD-ROM and some of the positions (e.g., art director) you'll find in such a facility. This section explores staffing in somewhat greater detail, and provides some time and cost estimates that should help you plan your own CD-ROM publishing projects.

To some extent, staffing at a multimedia production facility can be divided into two sets of people:

- Those who design the product and who acquire and create the content; staff in this management category are often referred to as "above the line" in classical film production terms.

- Those who integrate the content into the final product; staff in this production category, as well as associated production costs (including overhead and out-of-pocket), are often referred to as "below the line."

This division is similar to the way that production processes are staffed in traditional publishing businesses—for example, books and movies.

"Above-the-line" staff

The people who specify and design the work make up what you might call management. It is the management team that conceptualizes the product, sets the scope of content and style, and hires the creative people and the production team. The management team is coordinated by a producer, who assembles and manages the finances of the package, and by a director, who manages the creative assembly. If the CD-ROM is an educational title, you might also add an instructional designer to the team to ensure that the material fulfills its educational mission. Additional members of the creative team include individuals who specialize in one of the component media. An editor-in-chief (perhaps better called an information designer) maintains responsibility for content. An art director shapes the look of the project, a sound designer the aural space, an interface designer the feel of the product, a game designer any gaming element. A software architect specifies the technology. People who create content include researchers, writers, photographers, graphic artists and illustrators, animators, videographers, songwriters, musicians, sound effects people, actors, and video editors.

"Below-the-line" staff

The people who process the CD-ROM content into the product include copy editors, proofreaders, scanner and color-correction specialists, video editors and digitizers, sound editors, scripters, hyperlink installers, and programmers. The staff are coordinated by a production manager. Often the jobs in this category are not as clearly demarcated as are the "above-the-line" jobs, especially in smaller production houses or on smaller productions. In a tactical sense, a production manager tracks events on a day-to-day basis.

The size and scope's the thing—a staffing example

Production staffing requirements vary according to many factors, but especially in relation to the size and scope of the title's production needs. At one extreme is a title prepared by a single individual in a few weeks, with a scope of probably fewer than 500 assets, and out-of-pocket expenses of less than $5,000. At the other extreme is a project built by a team of people who have assembled perhaps more than 10,000 assets over a period of two years with a budget in excess of $2,000,000. Obviously there is a continuum between these extremes. One of the wonderful things about CD-ROM publishing is that it draws on a wide range of publishing models. It's impossible to generalize about a medium with such vast variance.

In this section, we define a sample staffing model. Our goal is to present a hypothetical production that involves a full-fledged staffing model—that is, one in which all of the various aspects of an expanded production are staffed. As you will see, this works out to a budget in the $500,000 range with a production cycle time of about one year. In general, jobs with larger budgets will simply employ more of the *same* kind of staff, not more *different* kinds of staff. Jobs with smaller budgets either will not require all the different staffing positions, or will require much more modest involvement of staff (primarily in the above-the-line category).

Table 4-1 shows hypothetical staffing for our middle-budget production. This assumes a production schedule of one year, and shows approximate annual salaries and the percentage of time devoted to the project. We assume that we're developing a high-end production with a budget of about $500,000; it contains approximately 10 different content focus areas, about 10,000 art and text assets, some 50 minutes of video and sound, and limited animation. It assumes that some materials will be licensed, but that most will be created by the production staff. The staffing is divided into two groups of people (as we discussed above): the above-the-line management team, who set the style of the piece and determine the actual contents, and the below-the-line production team, who put it all together.

About the Budget

A $500,000 budget (actually, it's $568,700 as derived from the tables) is a bit rich for many CD-ROMs that are being done today. The mainstream of the market is probably in the $250,000 to $300,000 price point. We use the larger number mainly so we can lay out the full staffing model of a project. For your own work, you may find that the sound designer doesn't just design the sound, but is also a musician who does all the music; that the art director is also the illustrator; that the editor is also the writer; and that the production manager also does the rights. In this way, by consolidating tasks you can tighten expenses. It's easier to take a high-end cost model and trim it to fit your own situation than it is to take a minimal model and understand how to expand it to fit a larger project.

By the way, if you take $250,000 and divide it by 1,000 discs, you have a unit development cost of $250 per disc. We discuss in later chapters how low the manufacturing and packaging costs for CD-ROMs are, in comparison with other types of media. This $250-per-disc figure really points out the small significance of the $4 you have to pay for the manufacturing and the box. Clearly, content and other development and marketing expenses represent the lion's share of the overall budget for a CD-ROM.

There are some obvious variables in the numbers shown in the table. Salaries, of course, are subject to challenge; those we show here reflect the cost of superior people in a major city in the United States. Projects that are interesting will often drive salaries lower, experience is a major factor, and so is the duration of employment. Certain regions at certain times will enjoy labor surpluses or shortages that will affect salaries as well, but we can assume that supply and demand will balance out quickly as schools rush to turn out candidates and as overpaid senior people begin to find competition from their juniors.

Another factor subject to challenge is the amount of time allocated to the project. You may think it's naive to suggest that a producer or director could spend only half-time managing a half-million dollar project, but in fact large projects may very well contain substantial periods where actions are set in motion and require a period of time to get done. Likewise, the commitment of an above-the-line staff person such as the art director may well be skewed upward if the project requires a sophisticated look and feel or if it has many different screens that require separate attention.

Also note that our numbers presume that we are discussing staff personnel; a freelance art director might very well cost much more than $6,000 on a half-million dollar job.

Table 4-1. Staffing of a multimedia production facility

Quantity	Staff Position	Annual Salary	% Time # Months	Total
1	Producer/account manager	$100,000	1/2 time	$50,000
1	Director	$100,000	1/2 time	$50,000
1	Editor-in-chief	$60,000	3/4 time	$45,000
1	Art director	$60,000	1/10 time	$6,000
1	Software director	$60,000	1/6 time	$10,000
1	Interface designer	$60,000	1/10 time	$6,000
1	Sound designer	$60,000	1/10 time	$6,000
Total	Above-the-line			$173,000
1	Production manager	$50,000	1/2 time	$25,000
1	Chief programmer	$60,000	3/4 time	$45,000
1	Writer	$25,000	4/5 time	$20,000
1	Artist/illustrator	$25,000	4/5 time	$20,000
1	Sound folio artist	$40,000	1/4 time	$10,000
1	Proofreader	$25,000	1/5 time	$5,000

Table 4-1.　Staffing of a multimedia production facility (Continued)

Quantity	Staff Position	Annual Salary	% Time # Months	Total
1	Content integrator/digitizer	$25,000	4/5 time	$20,000
1	Researcher/permissions	$25,000	3/5 time	$15,000
1	Production secretary	$25,000	Full-time	$25,000
Total	Below-the-line			**$185,000**
Total Labor				**$358,000**

Office overhead for the production team might look like the summary in Table 4-2.

Table 4-2.　Overhead of a multimedia production facility

Quantity	Staff Position	Annual Cost	Total
	FICA and benefits @ 15% of 358,000 labor above		$53,700
8	Person-years of hardware overhead	$1,500	$12,000
8	Person-years of office overhead, including rent, phone, photocopy, accounting, etc.	$10,000	$80,000
Total Overhead[ab]			**$145,700**

a. Office and hardware overhead per person is based on one desk and CPU with an average workstation valuation of $4,500 depreciated over three years for a value of $1,500 per year.
b. Although there are 16 people on the staff, there is only a total of almost 8 person-years to produce the product, since not everyone works full time on the production.

After staffing and overhead, the only other significant factor in our budget is rights; the cost of rights for this production is outlined in Table 4-3.

Table 4-3. Cost of rights for a multimedia title

Quantity	Item	Cost Per Item/ Minute	Total
500	Picture rights	$50	$25,000
1	Main text	$10,000	$10,000
20	Minutes of video or audio	$1000	$20,000
1	Contracts and legal	$10,000	$10,000
Total Rights			**$65,000**

Table 4-4 summarizes the total cost of production. As you can see from all this data, CD-ROM production is a labor-intensive business, and most of the cost is labor.

Table 4-4. Total cost summary for production of a multimedia title

Staff Position	Total
Design labor	$173,000
Production labor	$185,000
Labor overhead and hardware	$145,700
Rights	$65,000
Grand Total	**$568,700**

The kind of budgeting model we've chosen to present here is the one used in the Judson Rosebush Company; it may or may not be similar to that used in other media production houses. There is no industry-standard form, and we suspect that each major studio has its own blank models. You will need to give some thought to developing a budgeting model and form that will work best for your own situation.

Staff-time approach

An alternative way to approach the budget process is one based on a staff-time approach. With this approach, costs are estimated on the amount of time it takes people to do them. When you budget a project, you say "I can do this with five people in one year." Since you know that paying these people and covering their overhead is $100,000 apiece, you know that $500,000 is the total price of the project. You might want to use both approaches in doing your budgeting. Try to determine how much staffing and how many facilities are needed for the project, and how long it is going to take.

Building the production team

Actual project staffing is typically a blend of full-time employees and freelancers. Full-time people are best when there is an extended and steady flow of work, while freelancers are best when there is a small spot of work that is concentrated in a particular area of specialization. As we've mentioned, a huge range of craft skills are necessary for a multimedia production, but most of the skills are only needed in small doses. For example, almost all products must be proofread, but a company needs a very high volume of copy to employ a proofreader full time, so this job is probably best given to a freelancer. This is not to say that a good well-rounded staff cannot double up, however, so that the staff can flow into particular problems. The illustrator may also happen to be a good proofreader, for example.

There are many approaches to staffing; just be sure that you have sufficient, appropriate staff to complete all of the tasks on schedule.

The model exhibited in Tables 4-1 to 4-4 above assumes that the above-the-line people (with the exception of the producer and director) provide intermittent contact with the production staff. The production manager is an especially key hire; this day-to-day line manager tracks daily production flow, signs all purchase orders, reviews bills from freelancers, and coordinates progress to the schedule. This is a pivotal position, and one that will be familiar to people who work in other related industries, such as book and record publishing, as well.

What do you do with the staff when you're done?

What happens once production of your title is complete? When a production wraps, you'll go through a brief period of organization. All the artwork for the project must be filed away or returned; digital archives must be made of the project's working elements; you must clean up your disk drives; and the final bills for the project must be paid. This work requires only a subset of the staff. What about the rest of your people?

If your production company has a good flow of work, then the next job will be clamoring for people, and your battle-trained personnel will be able to catch only a brief rest before plunging into the next struggle. This is always good news. It's sad to lay excellent people off, and, from a practical point of view, although you cut your immediate business cash outflow, you will discover that your company's unemployment compensation rate goes up. You may also lose good people to competitors, and lose momentum in building your team next time.

Two different business models prevail about long-term commitments to staff. One model assumes that trained staff people are valuable and that such a team is the basis of developing a business. The other strives toward few long-term commitments and seeks to outsource as much work as possible; this second model also takes into account the fact that severing personnel is expensive in financial, as well as human, terms. (Unfortunately, some employers bring freelancers into their companies to work on a full-time basis, which is illegal in the United States.)

Most businesses work with a blend of the two models. Highly specialized work is often outsourced, as is work that may need a lot of creative variance from job to job—for example, a photographer who is excellent at photographing children may do a poor job of photographing fish. But personnel who do high-volume work, whether it's above or below the line, are valuable talent who are best carried on staff.

Developing a CD-ROM From Technical Content

As we said at the beginning of this chapter, there are a number of models for successful CD-ROM publishing. In the preceding section, we talked about the steps and staffing for a rather high-end consumer product developed by a multimedia production studio. Now let's look at a different model.

Consider a heavily technical title that is largely compiled from materials provided by a number of independent researchers. There are many titles in this category; in such projects, there is a set of contributions, and there may not be enough time or budget to integrate the contributions into a document with a fully smooth interface. One good model of this type of title is the SIGGRAPH conference proceedings CD-ROM that we examined in Chapter 3.

Although the process of producing a title of this kind is necessarily more streamlined, we still need to perform the same basic tasks we identified for the more professional CD-ROMs.

Selecting Content

As with any title, the first issue is the selection of contents. In the case of the SIGGRAPH conference proceedings, the content consists of the research papers chosen for presentation at the conference. Clearly, the shape and focus of the disc, as well as the primary communication with paper-authors, are provided by the selection process for the conference papers. Even though these papers come from many sources, there is still an editorial process. Just as in an authored title, there needs to be a consistent editorial point of view.

Acquiring Content

The next step in the process is to get the original contents from the authors. In the case of the SIGGRAPH CD-ROM, the production editor for the proceedings disc (an unpaid volunteer) gets electronic versions of the papers directly from authors via FTP through a computer system maintained by SIGGRAPH for its communications.

The format in which authors will be asked to provide their original contributions will depend on the authoring system used to develop the particular CD-ROM. Because this SIGGRAPH CD-ROM uses Adobe Acrobat as its primary authoring and delivery system, and because of the strong technical capabilities of the author community, we ask authors to follow these specifications:

- Provide papers (including all text and figures) in PostScript form.

- Provide figures in standard image formats such as GIF or TIFF.

- Provide movies in QuickTime or MPEG.

Chapter 3 describes the details of this process.

To help authors in the preparation of their papers, we provide them with samples in several different source formats, such as TEX, LATEX, FrameMaker, PageMaker, Microsoft Word, and Quark XPress.

Translating Content

As we discussed in Chapter 3, we chose the Acrobat authoring system for the CD-ROM proceedings largely because the product is designed to facilitate the representation of made-up pages in electronic form. In the next step of the process, we use the Acrobat Distiller module (in batch mode) to translate the authors' PostScript files. As with any other editorial process, the production editor checks the resulting files to make sure the quality of the individual papers is satisfactory; if they are not, the editor works with the author to help create appropriate sources. We create thumbnails of each page as part of this translation, so no added work is necessary to produce these pieces.

The translation work generally takes a week or two, because papers do not arrive all at once and the work must fit around the volunteer's other work.

Integrating Content

When all the separate papers have been translated, they are assembled into a single Acrobat file that contains the entire proceedings. Then, using Acrobat's various facilities, the production editor adds other pieces and navigation tools— the table of contents, author index, subject index, and credits pages, along with links from these to the individual papers. The editor also incorporates a front cover, back cover, and title page, so the electronic proceedings ends up being a very close mirror of the entire printed book. This process takes another few days of volunteer time, because most of the components have to be translated from the sections developed for the printed book.

Finally, the volunteer staff does some handwork on the completely assembled document to add functionality and value. Links, notes, outlines, sound clips, and movie files are applied by hand to the Acrobat document. There may well be ways to make this process more efficient; however, since volunteers do our production, we do not assume they have the time to become experts in this work. This final process takes approximately another two weeks. At this point, the final version of the proceedings, the figures and movies, and all of the other materials provided by the authors are assembled for testing and premastering.

Developing a CD-ROM by the Author

A third approach to developing a CD-ROM is to have authors prepare the materials in essentially their final form. A process of this kind is often attractive to authors because it gives them complete control of the final presentation of their materials. The process may also be attractive to publishers (whether they are a professional organization or a commercial publishing company) because it saves them from having to do the production themselves. In theory, the end result of going this route is that, because an author's content is more carefully organized,[*] they may have an easier time of getting it published—and also enjoy a higher royalty. At present, most CD-ROMs are produced in a studio setting, but we envision that we'll be seeing more and more situations of the kind discussed in this section—at least for portions of the market.

Developing and Integrating Content

Let's look at an example of an electronic title in which the authors want to produce a set of files for delivery through a World Wide Web browser. (We describe such a technology later in this book.)

The title is organized as a collection of individual files that are linked by having hot areas or text. When a hot area is clicked, it brings in another file identified by its URL. These files may reside on the CD-ROM, or they may be located anywhere else on the Internet or other networks. Because Web browsers operate comfort-

---

[*] Some people in the publishing business refer to this as being in a "higher energy state."

ably with local files, it's quite possible to use the Web browser to access the files on the CD-ROM independently of the networks.

What does the author do? He assembles the individual files (containing HTML tags) into a logically consistent directory structure. He then creates the links from each file to its successor detail files. The browser provides the necessary navigation and the interface. That's it—the title is complete.

As we write this section, such electronic titles are relatively scarce, but we expect them to become more common. In fact, the SIGGRAPH conference course notes and papers have been provided in this way, and other professional groups have published their entire conference proceedings as HTML-organized discs. They make solidly useful documents.

The Author/Publisher Model

Whenever a publisher works with authors directly to develop a project, everyone must put a great deal of effort into making sure that the content is coming together properly—and that they're working toward a common goal. Don't bypass proper controls simply because you're using a somewhat different publishing model.

For example, in print publishing, it is standard for a publisher to have reviewers or editors read over a completed manuscript and make comments and suggestions to the author to help focus the publication, or to identify areas that need additional coverage. Having authors do their own final preparation of the electronic title simply means that the publisher must provide an equivalent step in the electronic publishing process. Here are some other things the publisher must be sure to do:

- Develop a consistent set of styles for the authors

- Provide appropriate samples and templates for them to use in assembling the final product

- Give feedback on drafts during the authors' final development

- Give authors the tools they need to do their final preparation

Unless an author really knows what she's doing in electronic publishing, we believe that it probably doesn't save much time to have the author do the final CD-ROM development. The approach does have some advantages, however. It allows an author to move her time into earlier phases of the project, and it allows a publisher to have a final version of the title ready almost within days after the author's final edited and tested materials are received.

Developing a Title From Legacy Paper

There is one final variation on developing a CD-ROM that we want to mention briefly. Some commercial publishers have been experimenting with the publishing of materials that traditionally exist only in printed form. Examples of documents that are now being released in this form include technical journals and conference proceedings, as well as the plays and poetry of Shakespeare. Many publishers have large backlists of printed documents; they are looking for ways to get additional value out of these "legacy" paper archives and techniques. This section very briefly mentions a few approaches being taken to accomplish this publishing goal, and touches on a number of technical issues that come up when you try to adapt prepress methods to electronic documents.

The SGML Approach

Consider a system that SIGGRAPH's parent organization, the Association for Computing Machinery, has been developing. Authors' electronic submissions are put into SGML (Standard Generalized Markup Language) form—automatically where possible. The resulting structured documents can then be interpreted with appropriate DTDs (Document Type Definitions) to fit the style of a particular journal or other publication. A primary goal of this process is to create a database of electronic documents for reprints or specialized collections; this is a valuable resource for a publisher. Another goal is to streamline the process of tracking and managing papers, from their receipt from authors through the refereeing and editing process. Initially, this streamlining is intended to improve the production processes for standard journals, providing good support for the entire editorial and prepress operation. Eventually, it is intended to free other print publication processes from depending on authors to provide formatted copy in final form.

The SGML approach described here can provide the basis for genuine electronic publications (in addition to simply providing editorial and prepress support). SGML documents that come from paper publishing can be enhanced with additional media and linking tags. They can be interpreted in a number of ways to produce PostScript or other electronic document formats for use in developing CD-ROM productions. Moreover, electronic publishing systems such as the *Dyna-Text* system from Electronic Book Technologies can take the SGML as primary input.

Using SGML takes a technical publisher one step further into effective use of text in electronic publications. SGML lets you create fully structured electronic original documents that can use alternate DTDs to produce output documents that are appropriate for the screen instead of just for paper. Unfortunately, in the current market, SGML isn't a good solution for low-cost publishing environments, because it relies on text filtering and translation by relatively expensive contractors.

Independent Multimedia

Although this book is about publication on CD-ROM, the multimedia revolution is really rather independent of the delivery medium. In other words, a system for interactive documents should be able to work equally well for documents stored on a CD-ROM, a hard disk drive, a server on a network, the head-end of a cable system, or some mixture of these technologies.

The OCR Approach

We believe that another kind of legacy publication will be increasingly moved to electronic form. There is a very large backlist of material that has been published and is no longer available because of the expense of keeping slow-moving materials in print. Techniques are becoming available to scan print documents and use very intelligent OCR (Optical Character Recognition) techniques to translate them into an electronic form. Once in this form, the documents can be put onto CD-ROM for distribution.

For example, the Acrobat Capture system reads carefully created page scans and produces PDF files for use with the Acrobat Reader. This system still takes some careful handwork and does not yet deal well with color figures or equations. However, it avoids the time and costs involved in rekeying entire documents. As we describe in detail in Chapters 9 and 10, the economics of manufacturing and warehousing CD-ROMs are much more favorable than those of manufacturing and warehousing books. As a consequence, we expect that these new technologies will allow publishers to keep materials available in electronic form long after their useful printed life has ended. In this way, we'll be able to preserve, in an active form, the knowledge and information in these documents.

CHAPTER

5

Designing Electronic Documents

No matter how modest or extensive the scope of a CD-ROM title is to be, it must be designed. The design of a CD-ROM is the structural organization of the product in terms of its content, look, sound, and feel. The design process is creative, because it involves making things look attractive and work in a pleasing way, but it is also utilitarian, because it involves making things that are useful. CD-ROMs that are pretty but vapid can be fun, but they are still vapid. Content-rich disks that are ugly and hard to use can be informational, but they may turn off users before those users ever discover the value in the disc. Really successful products have both great content and great design.

In traditional publishing industries, such as book and movie publishing, the design functions are usually segregated by media. In other words, one type of designer might work with text, another with still images, and a third with movies. We think it's useful to carry this model over into the design of CD-ROMs—but there are a few differences. For one thing, traditional designers need to adapt their thinking to the vagaries of the CD-ROM medium. For another, because the contents of the CD-ROM are interactive, they require design decisions in some areas not found in traditional media.

This chapter itemizes the different design tasks that must be performed for CD-ROM publishing, and discusses what is involved in each of these areas.

The Nature of CD-ROM Design

Although design is often (and correctly) associated with the creative and artistic side, design is also a management task. It's the process of setting an agenda and enforcing—rather than executing—it. For example, a designer makes the decision that the text in a product will be colored black and will be in a 12-point Helvetica font. Many factors go into making that decision, but it is the making of the decision that distinguishes the designer (whose job it is to make such decisions) from the layout artist (who actually sets the type and installs it into the product).

The design of a CD-ROM product involves deciding all of these things:

- What information the product is going to contain

- How the information will be presented

- How the navigational structure of the product will be laid out

- How the product will look

- How the product will sound

- How the product will feel or behave

None of this process involves the integrating of the hundreds or thousands of content assets into a product, or the actual building of the product. Instead, design is the construction of the blueprints that define the architecture of the product.

The result of the design phase is a series of documents that express the rules to be followed in assembling the product. Some of this information will be included in the technical specification for a product (described in Chapter 4, *Developing a CD-ROM*); all of it must certainly be included in creating the working prototype. Because design documents will be given to the staff who actually assemble the product, they must be clearly written, unambiguous, and contain enough appropriate examples to show the intended results. It is also a good idea to test design documents by giving them to several people to review before high-volume production begins, to assure that they communicate what they should.

Let's assume that your project team is a relatively small one, consisting of five designers, each of whom assumes responsibility for one area of the overall design content. These design areas, which we describe briefly in this chapter, are

- Overall title navigation

- Graphic design

- Interface design

- Sound design

- Digital video design

- Software design

In practice, every project is different: your team may be larger or smaller than this one; certain design tasks may not be necessary; and there may be additional essential design tasks we have not included in our description.

Navigational Architecture

The first step of the design process is to decide upon the master architecture of the product. This process, part of composing the functional specification (described in Chapter 4), determines the scope and size of the world that is being created on the CD-ROM, and how the user navigates around in it.

The easiest way to illustrate this particular process is through diagrams that show the various "worlds" of the product and the navigational methods. Figure 5-1 diagrams a rather simple product that showcases six different network television programs. The product begins with an opening animation (A) that includes a title screen (B) and culminates in a main menu (C). The main menu contains six buttons, each of which takes the user to one of six similar program screens (D). The product also contains a help button which takes the user to a help screen (E), as well as a quit button that terminates the program.

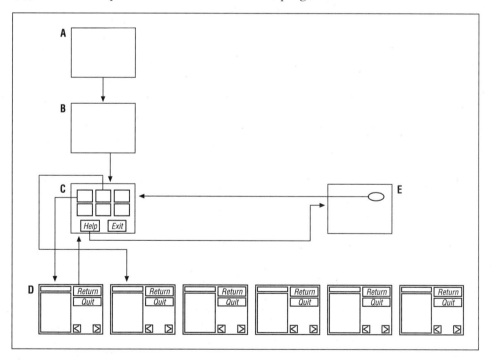

Figure 5-1.   An overall architecture for a product

The six program screens (D) all have the same format; they all contain the same three buttons: a return to menu button, a quit button, and a button that plays a movie. They are also the same in that they all contain a field showing the name of the program, a colored background picture, and a window in which the movie is played. However, each is unique in that the program name, the background graphic, and the movie played in the window is different for each of the six screens.

Although the product shown in Figure 5-1 appears to have an obvious and trivial structure, the architecture we've described is by no means the only architecture that would address the problem at hand. Let's consider some alternate architectures and suggest some of the trade-offs that are involved.

The product illustrated in Figure 5-2 is, for all practical purposes, identical to that in Figure 5-1, except that the help button has also been placed on each of the program screens. The advantage of this placement is that it allows the user to get to the help information from anywhere, not just from the main screen. The disadvantage is that each of the program screens must have an extra button. Programmers may complain that it is more difficult to write the button code for the return button on the help screen, because they must know which screen to return to. However, this is a trivial problem to solve and should not be a factor in deciding whether to design the product like Figure 5-1 or Figure 5-2.

There are other design variations as well, such as following the Figure 5-2 approach but removing the help button from the main menu screen. There is no right or wrong answer to this kind of decision; it's simply a matter of preference.

Now let's consider a third design variation, illustrated in Figure 5-3. In this variation, each of the program screens contains additional buttons that allow the user to navigate directly to the other five program screens. The advantage of this approach is that, unlike the other approaches, it doesn't require the user to return to the main menu before moving to another section of the program. This feature can make overall navigation faster. The disadvantage is, again, that more buttons are needed on each screen. And, as before, there is no right or wrong design here—it's primarily a matter of choice of how we want the user to navigate.

A subtle design issue arises if we decide to employ this third approach: should we add five buttons or six to each screen to support the navigation between the different program screens? Obviously, only five buttons are actually needed; because the user is already on one of the six program screens, he can actually move to only five other program screens. But adding only five buttons means that each program screen will have a different set of buttons from all the others. The result is that the button that takes a user to a particular screen will appear in a different place on each different screen. If, instead, we place six buttons on each

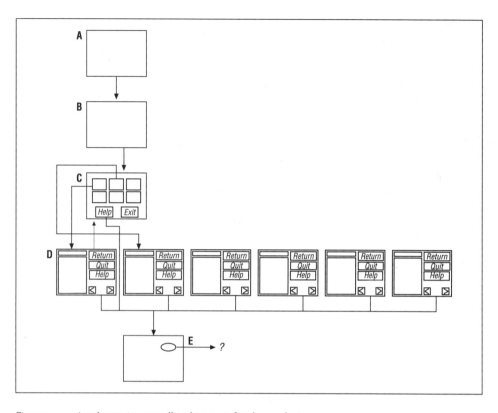

Figure 5-2.　An alternative overall architecture for the product

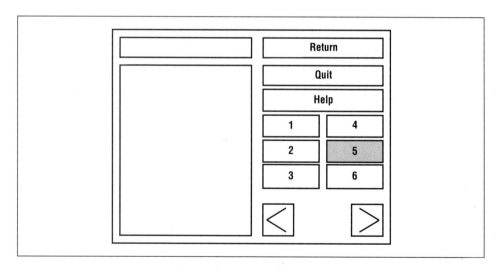

Figure 5-3.　A screen design that allows movement between separate screens

program screen, one of the buttons is for the user's current screen; obviously, this button has no real function.

So which design alternative should we select? This decision is also a design issue, as was the help button decision, but this case is somewhat different, because it has more obvious navigational consequences with only five buttons; there is a distinct risk that the user will get confused about which button goes to which screen.

There is strong consensus among designers that the right answer is to include all six buttons on each screen, but with the button for the current screen grayed out. This both implies its inoperability and tells the user his present location.

This example is a rather simple and straightforward one; other situations present greater complexity. There will frequently be more extensive information or experience requiring the user to navigate a more complex environment. The usual interface vocabulary may not be obvious or sufficient for such a title. In fact, in titles whose navigation is complex, you may want to provide a "Guided Tour" of the CD-ROM that is, in effect, a quick training tutorial in how to use the navigation tools in this environment.

The key point of our discussion here is that there is never only one way to do anything. It's critical to develop an understanding of what the choices are, and then to make decisions about exactly what the architecture is to be. Although the ultimate design you choose must certainly take technology and programming issues into account, it must focus especially on the content and how that content is organized and presented to the user of this particular product. This is the essence of the word "design"—the process of carefully reviewing the options and deciding in advance what to do on the project.

Graphic Design

Strictly speaking, the graphic design of a CD-ROM is the design of the look of the screens. This is a world of two-dimensional space, and it involves organizing the information inside the frame, or border, of the space. Graphic design is performed by the project's graphic designer or by the art director. This may also be same person who actually constructs the graphics for the product. However, as we mentioned earlier, there is a critical distinction to be made between defining the look of the product and actually fabricating it.

Design Grid

Graphic design issues encompass fonts, graphics, buttons, photography, video, and the overall grid of the product. Most CD-ROM designers use a page metaphor in designing for the CD-ROM medium; the page metaphor implies the concept of a design grid into which content is poured. A design grid is simply the organization of the frame into a series of shapes (typically rectangles) which are deployed for different kinds of content. The grid usually has some kind of border, fields with text and/or pictures, and a button palette. The button palette is a functionality palette that is consistent across many pages or screens, if not over the whole product. The design gives you a palette of pages to work from.

Using the page metaphor, you can think of a CD-ROM design in terms similar to that in other industries. Consider designs from the *New York Times*. Once you've designed a front page with a banner at the top that's seven columns wide, with text that is 10 point Times Roman on 12-point lead, and with vertical rules between the columns, you've just designed *all* the front pages of the *New York Times*. For each individual paper, you simply dump the contents into the grid.

One of the first steps in the CD-ROM graphic designer's work is to create the design grid (shown in Figure 5-4) for the product as a whole, as well as for the individual sections of the product. In this example, the frame is divided up into four different regions: a title text, a larger field, a smaller field, and a region reserved for the window's buttons.

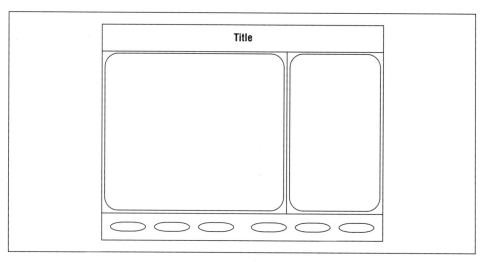

Figure 5-4.   A very simple design grid for a screen

At first glance, this design process may seem no different from the creation of a design grid for a book, magazine, newspaper, or slide show. There are, however, some special issues the CD-ROM graphic designer must consider.

The first of these special issues is that a product may very well contain different sections, and that these different sections may have different content. This isn't a novel problem for a book or magazine designer. A common solution, shown in

Figure 5-5, is to carry some of the design motifs throughout the entire product, and to allow other elements to vary. In this example, the regions reserved for the title and buttons are consistent, but the regions for information can have varying content—for example:

- The top left screen places text in the left two-thirds and a picture in the right one-third.

- The top right screen places a video window in the left two-thirds and text in the right one-third.

- The bottom left screen places three columns of text by breaking the larger field into two pieces.

- The bottom right screen places a single horizontal picture in the area of both of the fields.

This set of screens provides a consistent design theme, not only at the top and the bottom, but through the division into thirds of the central part of the screen. Enforcing such consistency keeps the content from appearing to jump around (and confuse the user) when he clicks from place to place. In fact, most of the buttons, such as return or quit, should remain static from screen to screen.

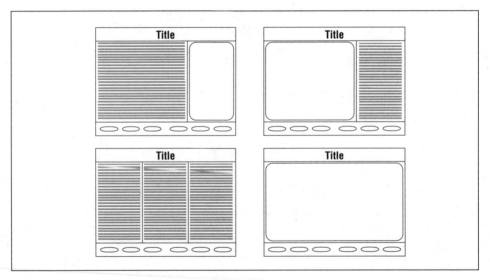

Figure 5-5.   Four different implementations of the design grid

The different sections shown in the figure do not need to have an identical presentation, but they should follow a similar theme. For example, the title bar at the top might be a different color for each section, but the colors should be thematically related. For example, they might all be neon colors, or earth tones, or pastels, or the like—but not a mixture of these palettes. You might also consider putting a designed symbol on each different section to identify it, or to create some other visual identity for the sections.

NOTE

In this section, we aren't trying to provide you with an education in graphic design; that's beyond the scope of this book. Rather, we're identifying the kinds of graphic design issues that require special consideration. For a more detailed look at graphic design issues for electronic documents, check out the design books listed in the Bibliography.

Overlays

Closely related to the design grid are issues concerning overlays on CD-ROM displays. Unlike print or television, interactive media has the ability to place one kind of information on top of another. For example, text can be displayed over an image. While this is a good idea in that it allows two different pieces of information to be displayed at once, it has the disadvantage that something gets covered up. Making either text or an image less readable may well detract from the overall impact of the display. Use overlays carefully!

Information display strategies of this kind are a key part of the overall document architecture (discussed above), but they are also graphic design issues, if only because the overlay will probably need to fit into the design grid.

Fonts

Probably the next most critical issue in graphic design, after the design grid and overlays, is the selection of fonts. The letters of the alphabet come in many shapes and sizes; some fonts are proprietary, and some are not. You must make sure that the specification of all fonts for all fields are defined and approved in advance. You must also make sure to obtain licenses for any proprietary fonts that will be used.

In CD-ROM titles, as in print media, we often categorize fonts into two classes: *headline and display fonts*, and *body copy*. In traditional typography, designers typically employ a wide variety of fonts for headlines, and a smaller set of more easily readable fonts for body copy. The same characteristic is true for electronic media, except that the designer must work with the fact that the computer screen has a much lower resolution than the printed page. The result is that the choice of fonts for both headlines and body copy is much more constrained. The choice of font sizes is also constrained; in particular, body copy must be larger on the screen than on the printed page.

Many designers try to fight against these constraints, instead of accepting the inevitable limitations of the medium. More than one good print designer has tried to force his or her favorite font and size choices into a CD-ROM product—with disastrous results.

Another issue involving fonts is the distinction between *text fonts* and *bitmap fonts*. There are two ways to represent text in an electronic document: text in fields, and text as bitmapped pictures, as we describe below.

Text fonts

Fields are multimedia objects that contain text. The text is in the original text form—that is, it is a sequence of ASCII or Unicode character bytes that represent different letters in the same way that letters are stored in a word processor. Text can be edited during the authoring process, so words and characters can be inserted and deleted. Text can also be made to flow into the field so that, if the field changes shape, the type adjusts automatically, as shown in Figure 5-6. This native text handling makes the handling of text very convenient; in fact, the electronic document can be trivially designed so that a user can search the text fields and can copy and paste text from the electronic document into his or her favorite word processor.

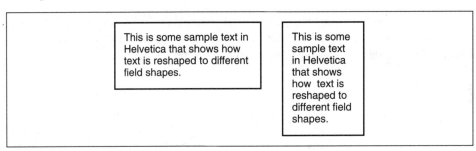

Figure 5-6.   Text adapting to the shape of the field that contains it

The fonting of text in a field is done by setting a font property for that field. Once that is done, and the font type and size of the field are defined, the field looks as shown in Figure 5-7 (a text field from a HyperCard document). It is also trivial and convenient to change the font type or size by simply changing the property; all of the letters in the text then change shape and/or size immediately.

Bitmap fonts

It's unfortunately the case that many font choices produce type that looks very bad on the screen. This is almost always because the boundaries of the letters demand more resolution than the dot matrix of the screen can provide, and

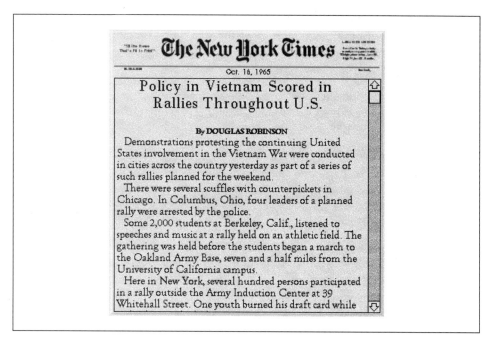

Figure 5-7.   A field from a HyperCard title with the font and size set

because quantizing the letters into black and white produces very ragged shapes. The solution is to set the type, via a program like Photoshop, so that the letters are *antialiased*, or blended, into the background. The text and its background are then saved as a picture (a *bitmap*) and are imported into the product as an picture. The differences between ordinary text and a bitmap are shown in Figure 5-8.

ordinary text   antialiased text

Figure 5-8.   Ordinary text (left) vs. antialiased text (right)

Notice that the antialiased type looks quite smooth and nice. The obvious advantage of using antialiased type is that the technique allows you to employ virtually any font with excellent results. However, there are several disadvantages:

* All type to be set in this font must go through an assembly process to convert it into images. Any edits or changes in the type must take the text back through the entire process.

- Once these pictures of the text are imported into the product, they are exactly that—pictures of type. And because pictures of type contain no ASCII characters, they can't be edited, they can't be searched using a find command, and no words can be copied out of them.

- If the text is intended to be printed—as is the case with many informational CD-ROMs—pictures of type will print slowly and won't be able to take advantage of the higher quality of traditional type on high-resolution printers.

In choosing fonts, you will need to make a choice between type that looks merely adequate but is smart, and type that looks beautiful but is stupid.

Font attributes

Most multimedia authoring systems support traditional type styles, such as bold, italic, and underlining. The choice of whether to use these styles is a design issue, but it involves broader and more sophisticated decisions—decisions that take into account the culture of electronic media. For example, bold, underlined, or colored text is often interpreted by the user as something that is clickable. (See the discussion of HTML in Chapter 6, *Authoring Systems.*)

Graphical Style

As with print graphic design, the graphic designer or art director on a CD-ROM project sets the overall graphical style of the product. He or she is responsible for ensuring that the style of the backgrounds, illustrations, photographs, animations, and video (if any) work together in a pleasing and effective manner. This responsibility also involves tactical issues, such as declaring whether lines are to be one or two pixels wide, ensuring that the direction of light for drop shadows is consistent, choosing the typography and colors used in illustration, and a myriad of other issues.

Most graphic designers and art directors are literate in electronic prepress. Be aware, though, that literacy in prepress does not necessarily carry over into literacy in the pixel-based issues of screen design—many art directors who are literate in the former are not literate in the latter. Electronic publishing is not the world of ink, trapping, and halftones that makes up electronic prepress and is oriented to the printing press. Instead, it is a world of pixels and real estate that is oriented to the screen. This is especially true when it comes to issues such as designing icons: an icon must provide a clear representation of a concept in a very small space—usually no more than 32 x 32 pixels—and designing such an image is a sizeable challenge for any designer.

Interface Design

Interface design revolves around not how the product looks, but how it behaves, and how it feels, to the user. Interface design is closely related to graphic design; as electronic media mature, it's quite likely that the same person on a development team will manage both graphic and interface design.

Although how the product behaves is often signaled to the user by how it looks (and, in many cases, how it sounds), the critical job of the interface designer is to define the feel of the product—how it interacts with the user. Interface design is an evolving area, partly because we do not yet have a standard interface vocabulary for multimedia and electronic documents. At present, the user doesn't know what actions will generate what responses, or what to look for as cues to these actions. The whole user interface area is developing rapidly, and the interface designer will need to stay current with the evolving vocabulary.

In theory, interface design concerns all kinds of system inputs and responses, from directing the computer with the mouse, to talking to it, or waving one's hands in front of a TV camera input. In this section, we'll focus only on mouse interactions because that is the most common interaction tool. Be aware, though, that this vocabulary is extensible to other interaction techniques, such as touch screens, as well.

Mouse Interaction

No one can make successful interactive electronic titles without first understanding the basics of mouse interaction. These are very simple—in fact, they're so obvious they're usually forgotten. These are the basics: a mouse can move horizontally and/or vertically, and the mouse button can be clicked down (a mouseDown event) or released (a mouseUp event).

Let's explore for a moment how mouse interaction manifests itself in button design on the screen:

1. Buttons should be designed with at least two states: the up (normal) state and a down (depressed or activated) state (shown in Figure 5-9).

2. When the cursor is placed over the button, and the mouse button is pressed (mouseDown), the button on the screen should change from the normal state to the activated state.

3. If the cursor is then moved off the button and released (mouseUp), the button should return to its up state, and *nothing else should happen*.

4. If the cursor is not moved off the button, and the mouse is released (mouseUp), the button should return to its up state, and the action associated with that particular button should be executed.

It's possible to code buttons so they work in many different ways, but the "on mouseUp" model is the most basic. Note that in this model there are always two pieces of artwork for each button. Also note that no action, other then the cosmetic action of changing the button art, occurs on mouseDown—an action occurs only on mouseUp and then only when the mouseUp is made while the cursor is still over the button. The reason for this design is that it gives the user a last chance to change his mind. If the user clicks down on the button, but then changes his mind and moves off it, nothing happens; he doesn't launch the action the button would otherwise initiate.

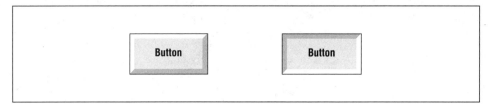

Figure 5-9.   The up (left) and down (right) enlarged views of a button

Of course, it's possible to create buttons that launch an action on mouseDown, and there may well be purposes for them in a product. Our point here is simply that button behavior is an interface design issue—the behavior doesn't just happen; it must be designed.

One example of a mouseDown activity is the behavior of an object on the screen that may be dragged by the user. Such an item works by responding to the mouseDown when the user clicks on it and holds the mouse button down. The object then becomes attached to the cursor, and the user is able to move it with the mouse. When the user releases the mouse (mouseUp), the object is released and now is placed in its new position. This is often called a "click and drag" capability.

What's Hot?

One particular issue in interface design is how to communicate to the user what is hot—in other words, what responds to user events—and how to communicate just what that response will be. There are a number of conventions to tell what's hot in text. For most World Wide Web browsers, clickable text is usually presented in color and underlined. In the *Ultimate Robot* title, clickable text is indicated by placing a tiny little symbol in front of it. Microsoft rules for Windows state that hot words are underlined, and their rules prohibit the exclusive use of color to show what is hot. There are many other possible options for showing that text is hot.

Sometimes, the user will click on an object, rather than on text or a button. This occurs quite frequently in games. Often, mouseDown on an object will cause a cyclic action to play—a functionality sometimes called "click and wiggle." It's also possible to mouseDown and animate an object while it is being dragged, a functionality sometimes called "click and wiggle and drag."

Another important mouse/cursor convention is the mouseWithin event. This event occurs when the cursor lies within the boundaries of a button or other hot region. The advantage of using this event is that the button can be designed to recognize a mouseWithin, and then perform an action of some kind. Examples of this action might be nothing more than changing the shape of the cursor—a convention that is used to indicate to the user that something is clickable or has a particular functionality, as shown in Figure 5-10. The action might also change the color of the button or otherwise highlight it. Another mouseWithin action is the display of additional information whenever the mouse is over a button, as is provided by the Macintosh balloon help facility. Again, this is an issue of interface design.

Figure 5-10.   A set of different cursor shapes

Interface Objects

An extensive vocabulary of interface objects is found throughout interactive computing. Objects used to control a program may include any of the following:

- Check boxes, which allow a user to select as many attributes as desired from a set of options

- Radio buttons, which allow a user to choose precisely one option from a set of possible options

- Pull-down and pop-up menus, which present options from which the user can choose the desired one

- Dials and sliders, which define a numeric or positional value to the program

- Buttons, which direct user navigation or selections

The control object you decide to use must be appropriate to the nature of the data and/or the options to be controlled. Figure 5-11 shows several types of objects. Choices of options typically have significant implications for how a user perceives the interaction. For example, menus are often used to select which kind of option the user wants to set; a button palette or slider in a dialog box might then be used to set the actual values for the option.

The implications of object choices can be subtle and need the benefit of someone who understands the user and the particular kind of document that is being constructed.

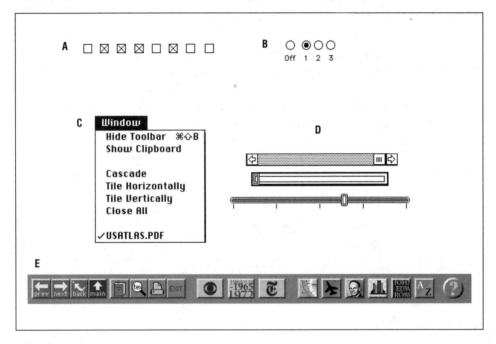

Figure 5-11. Some interface objects: (A) check boxes, (B) a set of radio buttons, (C) a menu, (D) some sliders, (E) buttons in a palette

Sound Design

For many types of titles, sound is another important part of the electronic media experience. The type of title usually determines whether you'll need sound. For some titles, sound may not be necessary, or even appropriate; for others, it may be essential.

A purely informational title may not need sound—in such titles, sound would simply take up disc real estate and users' time. Suppose you want to make a CD-ROM called "Phone Directory USA" containing every telephone number of every person in the United States, updated quarterly—you don't need a little song to play while the program searches as you type in "Rosebush" to find the 133 people with that name in the United States who have telephones. And suppose you're making a CD-ROM that comes out four times a year with the text of the decisions of the First Circuit Court of Appeals of New York—you don't need to play the "Star Spangled Banner" when the program quits.

On the other hand, if you're making consumer entertainment products, then sound plays a much larger role. And if you're truly trying to provide a multimedia experience, sound and picture become an integral part of designing that experience for the user. On a title like *Ultimate Robot,* providing sound for an introduction is important, and without that sound the product would appear spartan.

NOTE

Because sound typically is heard by others besides the person using the computer, you may want to consider providing an option to turn off the sound so the CD-ROM won't disturb others.

Like graphics, sound serves two roles: as another aspect of the interface design, and as content itself.

Sound as Interface Design

Sound may be included as part of the interface design for a variety of purposes. It can be used during transitions, especially as a bridge to cover long loading times. It can be used to set a mood. It is common to define one sound that functions like a system beep; for example, in the screen illustrated by Figure 5-3 (in which the program screen contains one button that is inactive), clicking on the inactive button would produce a null sound indicating "no action." It's also common to define individual sounds for frequently clicked buttons, such as return, quit, and go back.

When sounds are part of the interface, those sounds should be related in some way—for example, instrumentation, attack, or timbre—so the user is not jarred by any of the individual sounds.

Sound as Information Content

If sound is part of the information content, individual sounds aren't related to each other. For example, an encyclopedia may use the natural sounds of the entries to illustrate articles on various topics—whales, thunder, the gasoline engine, a violin, and so on. None of these sounds has any relationship to each other. In a product like a game disc, on the other hand, the sounds should be thematically integrated and involve similar instrumentation.

In a dramatic product, sound may be broken down into music, dialog, and effects. The music may include long thematic pieces of music (for example, accompanying the entrance of the bullfighters into the ring), as well as short dashes or themes of music (the look of the bull, the pent-up energy of the bull, the stance of the bullfighter). Obviously, you will need to think through and compose all of this music before you can record it and integrate it into the product. Similarly, you must write dialog before you can record it, and you must inventory sound effects and define them in style (e.g., comic, serious, etc.) before you can order or construct them.

Digital Video Design

Digital video may also be an important part of some CD-ROM titles. There are two approaches to video—full-screen and partial-screen.

Many people think that full-screen video is necessary for multimedia titles. We do not agree. We've seen very effective uses of video within an overall screen design, and are confident about using small pictures in a product. As a matter of fact, the small video image puts the video into context in the screen and integrates it well into the overall product, as Figure 5-12 demonstrates. The small video clips from *2001: A Space Odyssey* in the *Ultimate Robot* title fit well into the overall title concept, because they are not about *2001* itself, but rather about the relationship between *2001* and robots.

The video designer assigned to a CD-ROM project needs to understand a number of technical issues in digital video. For example, video to be used for QuickTime movies should be shot very low key—that is, with low contrast—and it needs to avoid high spatial frequency details, such as herringbone patterns on actors' costumes. There are also technical design issues having to do with making movies look good when presented on CD-ROM—a medium in which the designer must balance the size of the image, the number of frames per second that are presented, and the data transfer rate of the CD-ROM. And there are design issues associated with the size of your video files and the amount of video you can put on a CD-ROM; remember that the amount of disc real estate is limited, and that digital video tends to make large files.

The good news for the video designer is that digital video offers a considerable freedom of choice in these matters. The images in digital video may be manipulated with the same freedom as still images. The designer is free to use nonstandard screen formats and aspect ratios to make the video fit in any field needed by the graphic design. Digital video is still an evolving technology. We

Figure 5-12.   Digital video in context in a screen (see the color version in the center insert)

probably have not yet seen anything like the quality and effectiveness of digital video that we'll be seeing in the next few years.

It is very important that your video be polished, and there are many fine points that must be applied to make digital video look good. Even though it's hard to accomplish, it's possible—and it's necessary if you want to be competitive in the market.* The era of bad compressed QuickTime video on CDs should be at its end. Just remember that good video design and production will take time, and will almost always require a craft professional to do it. (You can learn it, but a one-week learning curve goes along with that.)

---

*For example, the *Ultimate Robot* product has 160-pixel-wide video, and the quality is quite good; in fact, we have yet to see a review in which anyone points out any problems about the video. Even on the worst single-speed drives, it runs continuously and flawlessly without any stuttering, burps, or jitters—and that's the minimum quality that is acceptable.

Software Design

Software design is the design of the overall software architecture of the programs used for the CD-ROM. The person who performs this design (generally the software manager) is usually also the person who writes the technical specification described in Chapter 4. This type of design involves the overall definition of the software system; you'll have to address such issues as languages, multiple platforms, elementary system functions that perform mouse and keyboard handling, and high-level functions that translate central ideas of the product into code.

Consider an example: a book simulation may include a page-turning capability, methods of performing Boolean searches on text, a facility to zoom pictures larger or smaller, a clickable index, and so on. You will need to design all of this architecture before coding begins, and to coordinate it with the rest of the design team.

NOTE

Since this book is not a textbook on programming and software engineering, we don't go into any detail about software design here. Just be aware that you must include this type of design in your overall product design.

CHAPTER

6

Authoring Systems

The choice of which authoring system to use for your application is one of the most important choices you'll make in publishing your electronic documents. In this book, we define an *authoring system* as a language and/or toolset that allows you to produce electronic and multimedia documents capable of being read by appropriate *delivery tools*. An authoring system allows the author or developer to take the assets for a title—the text, images, video, and sound—as well as the layout and interaction design for the title, and combine these components into a final product that gives the user access to the title's contents. Essentially, an authoring system integrates the work of the specialized tools you use to create the individual types of media included in your title (e.g., a word processor for text, a QuickTime player for movies, etc.).

Why is the choice of authoring system important? If such a system is rich in functionality and easy to use, authors and developers will be able to create titles more quickly and with fewer difficulties—and hence at lower cost.

Usually, the authoring system is distinct from the delivery tool—the document reader or presentation system that presents the document's contents to the user. Whereas the document reader simply exercises whatever functionality the author has created, the authoring system allows the author to create new functionality for each document. In some cases, an authoring system may provide its own document reader, along with the authoring tools; for example, both Adobe Acrobat and Macromedia Director provide readers (which are distinct from the authoring tools). The Acrobat and Director readers both allow documents created on one type of system to be used on another. In other cases, the authoring system may produce a document that can be executed as a standalone program without a separate reader application, or one that can be read by an application distinct from the authoring system.

The quality of the presentation system is also important. If the presentation system provides comfortable and natural access to the various kinds of information in the title, the user of the title will find the experience more attractive. This experience will, in turn, lead to better reviews of the title and greater acceptance of it in the market.

Authoring systems provide a wide variety of capabilities and functions. In the early days of electronic documents, one of the most important considerations in selecting an authoring system was the database and indexing tools provided to organize and retrieve text. Such tools continue to be important for many applications (especially those that publish primarily textual data), but most people now view them as being less important than the media integration and document navigation offered by complete authoring systems.

Authoring languages vary tremendously. They range from rather easy-to-use presentation graphic systems to powerful, but lower-level, compiled languages such as C, C++, Visual BASIC, and Java. This chapter examines the issues you'll need to consider in choosing an authoring language, looks at some representative systems, and explores possible motives for choosing one system over another.

Introduction to Authoring Systems

This section takes an initial look at authoring systems—whether we can do without them, and what we can do with them.

Why Use an Authoring System?

The first question we should ask about authoring systems is why we need them in the first place. In fact, it's entirely possible to create a worthwhile CD-ROM using no authoring language whatsoever. Since a computer system sees a CD-ROM as simply another mountable disk, that disc may, in its most basic form, exist as simply a collection of files. Individually these files may be text files, pictures in various formats, sound, digital video clips, or executable programs. Many such CD-ROMs have already been published. Among the most common are reprints of great books, clip art and photo collections, sound file collections, video clips, and shareware (both in ASCII source code format and as executable binaries). CD-ROMs of this kind are indeed useful, and there is no reason that they shouldn't continue to constitute a significant percentage of the total units sold. But it's a fact that such simply constructed CD-ROMs are far from the last word in electronic titles.

Consider the Bible as an example of a document you might want to publish in electronic format. You can represent the text of the Bible in one or many text files. Stored in a standard text format, these files will be easily readable on almost any computer system capable of reading a standard ISO 9660 disk. However, even such a simple presentation presupposes that CD-ROM users will have some kind of word processor on their systems able to open and read the files provided. In other words, the user has to bring some of his software to the situation. Depending upon the sophistication of the user's software, he may be able to perform text searches and other such operations. The CD-ROM author or developer might not be satisfied to have the text presented to users through a simple word processor, however, and might want to use a tool that presents the text in a more sophisticated way.

Naturally, a similar situation exists for sound, images, and video; in each case the user must bring an application utility to the table, or the CD publisher must include appropriate "reader" tools on the disc.

Beyond Informational Titles

However usable this simple type of CD-ROM may be for informational titles, it doesn't take advantage of the opportunities offered by electronic publishing. The goal of electronic publishing is not simply a random (or even clever) collection of "stuff" on the disc—rather, it's an editorially coherent presentation of material that has been carefully structured for the enjoyment and utility of the user. And once you decide to put together a work that includes many or all of the dimensions of the electronic media, you face a much more complicated technical task.

Let's look again at the example of the Bible. Suppose we want to include not only the words, but also pictures and maps of the Holy Land, histories and timelines of the region, plans and blueprints of temples, sounds of cities, singing of chants and recitations. Or perhaps we're even more ambitious: we want concordances of words, hyperlinks of the genealogies of families, comparisons of the words of Christ as they parallel each other in the different gospels, and a virtual reality walk-through of the original temple in Jerusalem or of digitally reconstructed ancient cities that are biblically significant. We want to follow the path of Moses through the wilderness on a map of the Sinai and to be able to click on the map and execute a hyperlink to the scripture; then, we want to click on the scripture and see where we are on the map. We want to see where the words were spoken, hear the sounds of the environment, and turn our heads left and right to see around us. This task can't be accomplished by simply putting a bunch of files on a CD-ROM!

Sometimes, even for academic titles—such as electronic technical books—we might have rather demanding technical requirements. Perhaps we want to allow the user to view images, to employ one or more indices or tables of contents, and to search for keywords. More and more technical titles are including video and animations; the reader supplied on the CD-ROM must be able to provide for these files as well.

One approach would be to include a set of files, along with a set of individual tools for processing them. Microsoft Word could read the text files; Adobe Photoshop could display the pictures; Apple SimplePlayer could show the QuickTime movies; and SoundEdit could play the sound files. But to get the full experience of the title, the user of the CD-ROM really needs a multimedia reader that's capable of doing all these things. Furthermore, the reader needs to do all the things a programmer can achieve with an ordinary computer language—and more. It needs to be able to use a set of variables; do conditional branching; perform arithmetic; read and write files; execute system service calls (especially those for screen actions such as putting up menus, handling events, and evaluating mouse actions, and the like); handle movies, sound, and other media objects; and quit execution cleanly.

What Makes a Good Authoring Language?

Clearly, we need a true authoring language in which we can compose documents. Authoring languages have several requirements that are a bit different from those of the classical programming languages. A good authoring language should be able to:

- Handle a full range of media

- Perform calculations and other programming operations

- Facilitate the user interface

- Provide user navigation

- Support cross-platform authoring and delivery

- Allow an author or developer to extend the built-in tools

The following sections describe these characteristics.

Handles a Full Range of Media

The ideal authoring language contains built-in commands to display pictures, play sounds, show videos, and place text on the screen. Ideally, these different media assets are not actually integrated into a single file; rather, they exist as individual files on the disk, and the authoring language fetches them and displays them when they are called upon by the application.

Traditional languages, such as FORTRAN and C, can't handle a full range of media. In fact, they have no native commands that handle media at all. Of course,

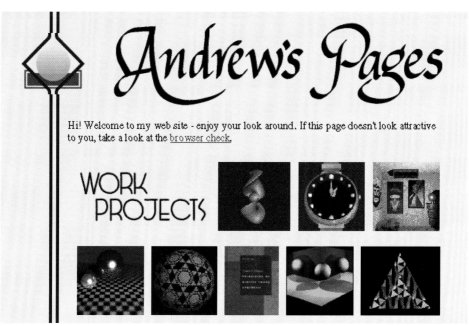

Courtesy of Andrew Glassner, Microsoft Corporation

Figure 1-1. Part of the home page of Andrew Glassner (screen capture). (Images Copyright © 1996, Andrew Glassner)

Figure 1-2. The home page of the Judson Rosebush Company

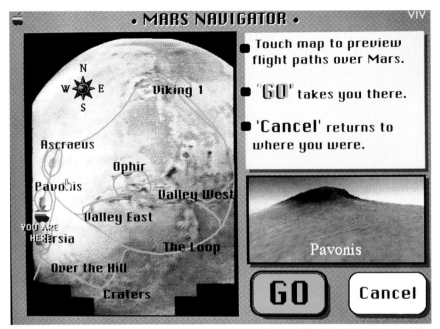

Figure 1-3. A screen from Mars Navigator (orienting the user to the map and controls)

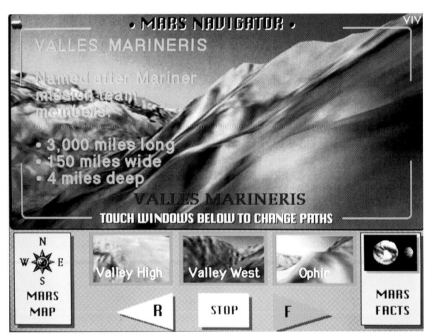

Figure 1-4. A screen from Mars Navigator (user has stopped the fly-by at Valles Marineris)

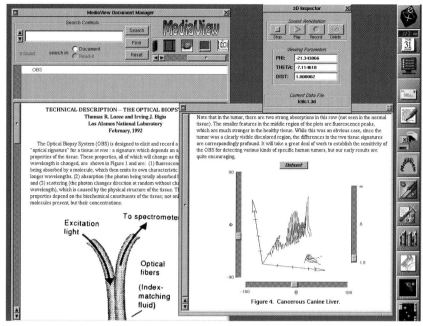

Figure 1-5. MediaView screen (showing a 3-D medical data set that can be manipulated interactively)

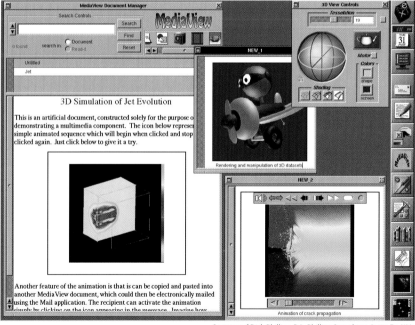

Figure 1-6. MediaView screen (showing both technical and nontechnical animations that can be controlled by the user)

Figure 3-3. *Ultimate Robot* main menu

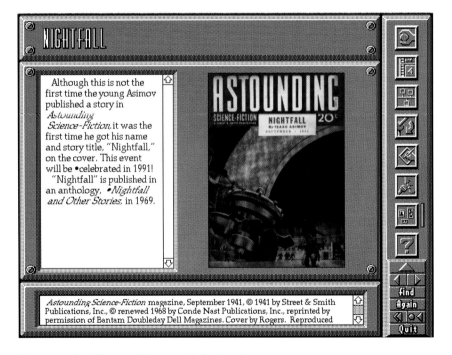

Figure 3-7. One *Ultimate Robot* sample leaf card

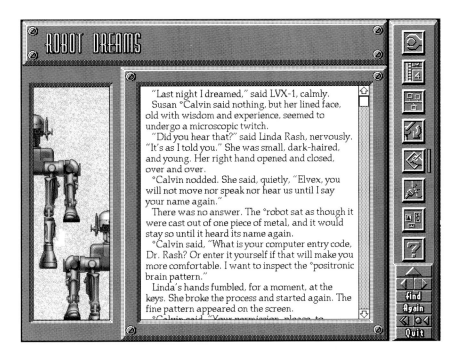

Figure 3-8. Another *Ultimate Robot* sample leaf card

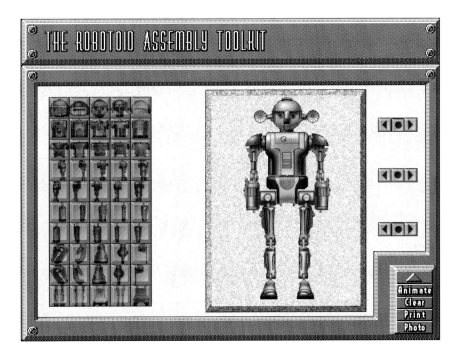

Figure 3-11. Robotoid Assembly Toolkit

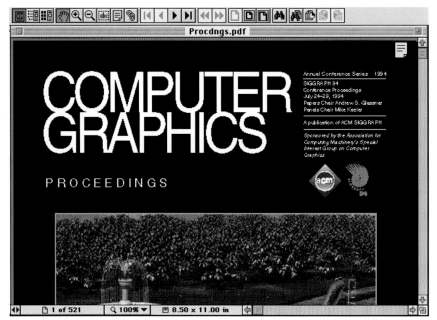

Figure 3-14. SIGGRAPH 94 cover page

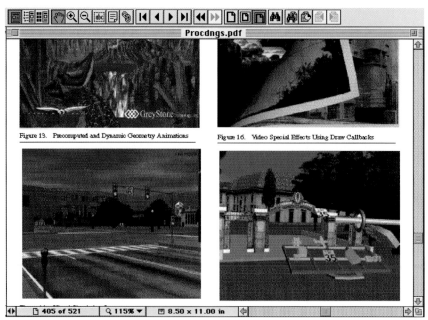

Figure 3-18. A set of figures in an Acrobat document

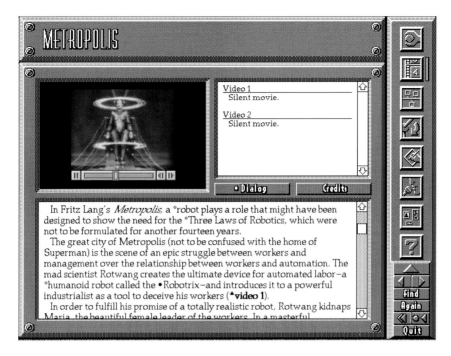

Figure 5-13. Digital video in context in a screen

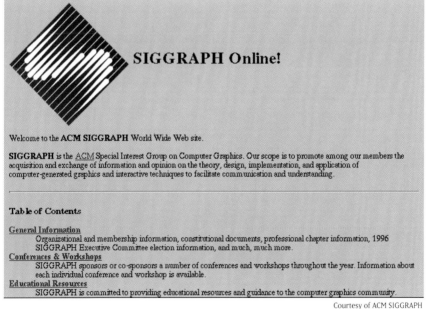

Figure 6-3. The portion of the document as played by Netscape Navigator on a Macintosh

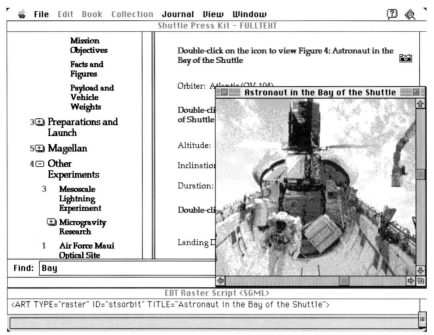

Figure 7-1. A screen from a document produced with *Dyna*Text. (Copyright © 1995 Electronic Book Technologies, Inc. All rights reserved. *Dyna*Text is a trademark of Electronic Book Technologies, Inc.)

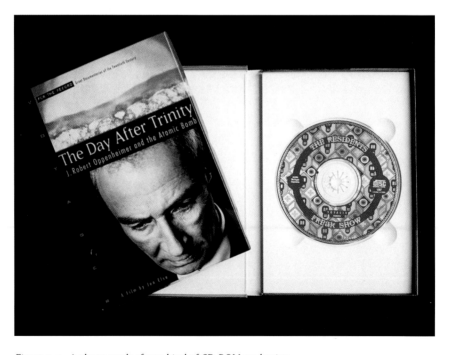

Figure 9-7. A photograph of one kind of CD-ROM packaging

Combining Visual and Textual Features in a Language

The languages we examine in this chapter include some that go beyond traditional text-based languages such as FORTRAN and C. With visual languages, an author can select title components by choosing their icons and bringing them into an assembly area. There, he can select the actions that will use the components by connecting these icons to associated action areas. Languages that allow *only* this kind of visual approach are often useful only for special kinds of titles, but combining a visual language with a textual language can produce a very powerful product. For example, Director offers a combined approach in which an author can use Lingo to specify the details of an action or behavior, and then use Director's *stage* to lay out how the components are to be presented. When a user plays the resulting title, the stage component controls how the user sees the screen, while the Lingo components control the details of the action that takes place.

---

we can write separate functionality that handles media, but this functionality doesn't come with the language out of the box. On the other hand, a language like Director's Lingo or HyperCard's HyperTalk comes out of the box able to work with the concepts of pictures, QuickTime movies, buttons, fields, and commands that manipulate them. For example, HyperTalk allows you to request specific fonts and sizes, as follows:

```
make font of card field Judson equal to Helvetica
make font of card field size equal to 26 points
```

Along with the ability to handle different kinds of media, an authoring system must be able to find the media files wherever they may reside. Ideally, the presentation software should be able to retrieve a needed file for the CD-ROM product from other disks attached to the computer on which the software is running, from the local network to which that computer is attached, or even from any network that can be reached from the computer.

To accommodate this powerful type of retrieval, a typical command to display a picture would include the picture filename (possibly as a full directory path or even as a URL), the location in the window where the picture is to be displayed, the style of the picture window, scaling, and possibly color information. It's critical that text be displayed as actual text, and not just as bitmaps of text—actual text can be searched, scrolled, highlighted, and otherwise manipulated. (The section on text standards in Chapter 7, *Electronic Document Standards*, discusses this distinction.)

NOTE

A good authoring language should also be open to adding new classes of media. For example, in the future we may see such new media object types as force-interactive data, smell information, and three-dimensional datasets.

Performs Calculations and Other Programming Operations

Some authoring tools work on the assumption that the ability to handle mouse clicks and to branch to the chosen material is adequate support for a multimedia integrator. We disagree. The tools in this category are certainly less expensive than are full-functioned authoring systems, and they'll do the job for simple titles (the table-of-contents/choose-from-a-list/branch-and-return kinds of titles). But such tools are of limited use beyond those simple titles.

Any authoring system intended for serious development use must include the calculations and other programming features available in any standard languages. These include:

- Global variables

- A variety of data types; arrays, matrices, lists (records), and other complex types of data

- Real and floating-point arithmetic

- Advanced operators such as square root, sine, and others that take parameters and return results

- Looping

- If-then-else constructs

- Subroutines, such as functions or event handlers, with parameters

- The ability to execute lines of text as if they were code statements

- A debugger

- A method of managing function libraries

- Clear rules about how execution is to be performed

Facilitates the User Interface

Almost all operating systems provide a range of services that application languages can employ by calling system functions. Authoring languages must provide basic services, as well as those that facilitate the special user interfaces required in multimedia systems.

Typical system services include disk I/O, keyboard and mouse handling, printer support, and screen support. If an authoring language is to be taken seriously as a language, it needs to provide all of these services fluently. Files need to be read and written. Keyboards need to be taken under command. Screen management and support must provide a collection of prebuilt services; some typical examples include menu creation and management, button management, text field management, sprite management, and modal dialog box management.

Sophisticated mouse handling is especially important to supporting a powerful user interface, including native language support for events such as mouseUp, mouseDown, mouseWithin, mouseExit, mouseStillDown, mouseLocation, and so on. Button and mouse behavior can be rather complex, and play an important part in the quality of the product's user interface. The content author shouldn't get distracted from his fundamental concern—figuring out what the user will see—by having to worry about the details of writing an "on MouseUp" handler (along with having to deal with functionality such as setting lookup table depth, field rectangle coordinates, or attributes of buttons or of fields).

Here are some examples of facilities that support the user interface as part of the native language:

Buttons and fields

Authors need to have support for a minimal set of functions that include buttons and fields. Buttons need to have color and icons, and fields need to support different concepts such as scrolling or nonscrolling. It should be possible to duplicate a button or field (possibly with copy and paste) and then associate appropriate new contents and actions to it.

Text capabilities

Authors need to be able to use mixed fonts with italics and other text styles; to group and select text; to click on fields or to lock on them; and to select individual words and know what words the user has clicked on.

Pictures

An author needs to be able to have pictures behind a text field or to display background through the field. He also needs pictures (both black-and-white and color) that can be dragged with the cursor, or that can respond to a mouse click.

Video

An author needs video that can be put up on the screen. The software needs to be able to respond to a click on the video window and have things happen.

Animation
> An author needs to be able to use an object that is animating and that's able to respond to clicks and be dragged while it is animating.

As far as we know, there is not a single product on the market right now that has everything on our list—and we find this frustrating.

Supports User Navigation

One of the significant differences between printed documents and electronic documents is this: paper documents are physical artifacts users can browse in physical ways, while electronic documents only present themselves on the screen. Electronic documents are thus much more abstract, and we need to make them less so by providing things that replace the physical and tactile ways in which we use printed documents.

Think of all of the ways in which individual readers use physical techniques to mark their paper documents and make them more understandable and easier to use: dog-earing pages, putting in different kinds of bookmarks, writing notes in the margins, highlighting words and phrases, and so on. Publishers provide additional physical methods to help readers find their way around in paper documents: tables of contents, indexes, and in-text footnotes and references.

Electronic documents must provide equivalents for all of these paper methods—and even more. The goal is to provide a conceptual and informational framework in which a reader can move within the document—and in this way avoid the "lost in hyperspace" phenomenon that has been reported in many hypermedia studies. Later in this chapter, we give examples of how some current authoring systems provide navigation support.

It's imperative that links, indexes, histories, and notes be supported by whatever authoring tool you select. These methods must be readily available to the author so the original document can have a prepared navigation framework. It should also be possible to create these methods automatically, so that the amount of handwork needed to create a document is as small as possible. The methods should also be available to the reader so he'll be able to create personally annotated versions of the document.

Cross-Platform Authoring

When you produce a great title with a lot of market appeal, you naturally want to be able to sell it as widely as possible—which means that you want to make it available on multiple computing platforms. Today's market is split across at least three environments (DOS, Windows, and Macintosh), and possibly more (the UNIX world, OS/2, Windows NT, and the TV set-top boxes). To reach the largest audience, most developers need to write for at least Windows and Macintosh. Most developers are not very concerned about the UNIX environment because UNIX users tend to be a significant end-user market only for discs with technical content or those with a particular kind of training orientation. These days, there seems to be greater interest in developing products for the emerging world of television set-top boxes.

Cross-platform development and delivery is a big issue in multimedia today, but unfortunately, there are no tools that have everything an author or developer needs even on a *single* platform—let alone everything an author needs on *multiple* systems.

What is the ideal cross-platform scenario? We would like to place all of our content assets in a single format on a single disc, to author in a single language, and then to produce platform-specific runtime applications (which should be quite small, so they will also be able to reside with the rest of the title on the same CD-ROM). Users would be able to pop this multiplatform CD into their drives; their CPUs would readily recognize which runtime to use, and they'd be off and running.

Is that too much to hope for? Here's an alternate strategy, one that's much like the HTML strategy or the PostScript prepress strategy. Instead of compiling different runtime applications, we would like to produce a single application that outputs a unified instruction and dataset. This instruction and dataset could then be interpreted by a platform-specific program at runtime.

Unfortunately, this strategy is a stretch as well. Because many system services are native on many different platforms and operating systems, authoring languages are often able to integrate them into a common syntax and pass them along to the user. But the set of system services is not fully uniform across platforms, nor do different authoring languages on a single platform necessarily incorporate all of the same features, or extend the same features. As a consequence, there can be quite subtle, but profound differences between two different authoring systems in the handing of something as trivial as highlighting a button on a mouseDown event. In one case, this operation may be trivial; in another case, it may be almost impossible.

Ultimately, we would like authoring tools to be able to produce high-function documents that work across the Internet and other networks. Why? Because in the next few years, we believe that the fusion between the computer and the home TV set (with HDTV and the set-top box) will allow users to run multimedia products across the network. Whether this functionality will come across the cable box or across a modem into your desktop computer isn't yet clear. In either case, though, it would be nice if a cross-platform authoring tool took care of issues dealing with servicing a user who is running across a network remotely, as opposed to having a CD simply mounted on his desk.

Extends the System's Tools

One of the most striking features of the electronic media world is how often new media types or capabilities are developed. Because any authoring system will have difficulty keeping up with these developments, it's important that your system be able to extend to support new functions.

The ability for authoring systems to support new functions is often provided through the use of software add-ons called *plug-ins* or *filters.* These components are often provided by individuals or firms other than the developer of the original authoring system, and they are sufficiently important that some sets are critical products in the electronic media world.

When you are looking for an authoring system, we advise you to choose one that is open to this kind of extension, so your system will be able to grow with the field.

Object-Oriented Paradigm

Object-oriented programming is currently the most popular and powerful programming paradigm. This type of programming is a way of thinking about software design and programming that is different from traditional programming, but it fits the concepts and activities in user interfaces and direct manipulation quite well.

NOTE

There are a number of good books on object-oriented programming, but we think that the Cox and Novobilski book referenced in the Bibliography is one of the best at introducing the dynamic possibilities in this kind of programming system.

Let's look briefly at the terminology of object-oriented programming. The central theme is the *object,* a software entity that is an instance of a *class*, from which it gets its allowable operations (called *methods*) and a template of its data. The class notion is quite analogous to the way that a data variable is an instance of its data type, except that the object gets not only the data template, but also a function template. The only way to manipulate the data in the object is through the object's methods, so the data is *encapsulated* by the object. Programs are developed by creating collections of objects that hold the data and functionality of the program, and that communicate with each other to accomplish tasks; objects communicate by sending *messages* to each other to invoke each others' methods.

Classes are constructed in a hierarchy, with each class getting data and methods by *inheritance* from its parent and ancestors.

Object-oriented languages may be compiled or interpreted. But the runtime behavior of an object-oriented system is inherently dynamic, because objects must respond to messages that are not known until the code is executed. When an object sends a message to another object, there is no way for the sender to know precisely what the receiver will do with that message. The same message, such as "MouseUp event," may be interpreted quite differently by different objects. This *polymorphism* is one of the most powerful features of object-oriented systems; each object is allowed to control how it should perform the operation that is requested of it. The most powerful kinds of object-oriented systems encourage polymorphism by dynamic binding of message to action. Some systems will even allow new objects to be imported into a running application in such a way that they will be immediately active.

In a system designed for direct manipulation—and most authoring systems for electronic titles fall into this category—the driving force is the event, and the primary event is the mouse click.

Much of the work involved in creating a title involves the development of interface objects and their behaviors. As an example, let's look at a button an author creates to launch a particular function in a title. The button will be defined as an object and will hold the data describing all of the following:

- Its color or texture

- Its screen position and size

- Any text or icon that is displayed on the button

- How the button looks before and after it is pressed

- The function that is to be called when the button's action is called for

This information can be held either by the button itself or by an ancestor of the button's class. The button's text or icon can itself be an object, because an object can contain another object as data. If you set all text as members of a text class, and you make the font a property of the class, then simply by setting the font one time in the text class, you can easily make all the text have the same font.

Let's look at how buttons might behave in this object-oriented world. The button would inherit from an ancestor (perhaps with a name such as Button-EventHandler) the methods it would use to respond to messages about events. A Screen object would display this and any other buttons, along with whatever else is shown on the screen. The Screen object's function is to accept a mouse event, to determine at what point on the screen the event happened, and to send the event message to the event queue. The system event handler would then pass the event to whatever object is displayed at that place.

If the recipient is the button object and the event in the message is MouseDown, then the button could respond by executing the ShowButtonDepressed method. If the button then gets the MouseUp event message, the button would respond by executing the ExecuteFunction method. On the other hand, if the user moves the mouse out of the button, the MouseLeave event would be generated and the button could respond by executing the ShowButtonNormal method.

These methods may be locally defined with the button (such as the function to be executed when the button is pressed) or they may be inherited from an ancestor, and thus all share a common behavior (such as the way their display is modified when they are depressed).

The object-oriented paradigm is an important one in CD-ROM development. Being able to define objects and specify their properties, class hierarchies, and message passing behavior adds another dimension to the basic authoring language properties we've discussed. Even when an authoring language simply uses object concepts, instead of the full power of object-oriented programming (as is the case with HyperCard), the concepts add a good deal to title development.

Examples of Authoring Systems

This section provides a brief overview of several important authoring systems in use today. The goal of this discussion is to illustrate the range of options available to create electronic documents for CD-ROM publications. We've selected systems from those with which we're most familiar; because of our background, the systems probably tend to be more oriented to the Macintosh than is the overall market.

NOTE

Please don't interpret the omission of any authoring system from this section as a negative statement about that system. In fact, the fast progression of technology necessarily makes any set of examples incomplete.

Comparing Authoring Systems

How can you decide which authoring system is the most appropriate one for your application? There are several ways to look at the systems we describe in the sections that follow; you can examine their technical characteristics, assess how closely their authoring models fit your specific documents, consider how hard they will be for your authors to learn to use, and figure out whether you can afford them.

Different tradeoffs and metaphors

Let's look briefly at the development of authoring systems from the point of view of the language developer. The developer is faced with several important issues:

Tradeoff between functionality and performance
> On the one hand, it's important to provide the user with a full deck of tools without having to build them from scratch. On the other hand, it's important to provide the kind of performance the user would expect from a focused application.

Authoring metaphor
> Different authoring languages provide very different authoring metaphors. Authors may find that their thinking processes fit the metaphor of one language much better than another. Examples are card-based presentations (HyperCard, SuperCard), timeline and frame-based presentations (Director's scores), presentations assembled by linking icons (Media Tool), or presentations based on printed pages (Acrobat).

Skill and focus level
> Some authoring systems require authors to have far more skill and programming experience than others. There is a significant range from the easy-to-use (Media Tool or Acrobat) to the complex (languages such as Director and Java, which require significant programming to achieve maximum effect).

Clearly, when you select an authoring language or system for a project, you will want to look carefully at the tradeoffs and choices made by the language developer, and make sure that your final choice fits your own background and requirements.

Licensing

You'll find that different authoring systems have radically different licensing fees and cost structures associated with them. Once you have some idea of which systems fit your technical and personnel requirements, look carefully at the costs of the competing systems. See the section called "Cost of Software Purchase and Licensing," in Chapter 10, *CD-ROM Publishing Costs*, for a complete discussion.

Director and Lingo

Macromedia's Director product is a widely used multimedia authoring system for both Macintosh and Windows. Over the years, Director has evolved from a simple slide-show application into a full-fledged multimedia environment.

With Director, documents can be created on a PC or a Macintosh, and then played on both systems through the runtime players provided with the product. Director can also produce standalone applications that do not need separate players. Director has a network capability, called Shockwave, that allows Director titles to be accessed and played by Web browsers. The product is able to create some media through very capable text, painting, and automated animation tools. However, its usual use is for authors or developers to create a document framework in Director, and then import high-quality multimedia content from other kinds of applications to be integrated into the Director framework.

The main power of Director lies in its scripting language, Lingo. Lingo gives users access to a powerful set of tools for describing scenes and actions. Lingo is a relatively sophisticated programming language which requires a significant learning curve. Indeed, many college media courses are really courses in Lingo programming. Lingo provides both a hypertext linking capability and access to externally programmed functions. It's one of the reasons why Director is more powerful—and more expensive, and requires more learning—than the simpler plug-and-play kinds of tools that are sometimes used for multimedia authoring. Example 6-1 shows an example of a Lingo code segment. The function shown here identifies the particular channel in which the artwork of a clicked button resides. It replaces the artwork of the button with new artwork, runs a function, and updates the screen.

Example 6-1. A code segment in Lingo

```
on mouseUp
  set chan = the clickOn
  puppetsprite chan, TRUE
  set the castnum of sprite chan = 4541
  -- put function to execute here
  updateStage
end
```

Particular strengths of Director include:

• Its color capability

• A virtual animation dopesheet for laying out action

• A draggable, clickable, animating *sprite*—a color object such as an eagle with flapping wings that can be dragged around on the screen while it is animating

• Ability to create documents on either the Macintosh or in Windows, and play them on the other platform

Director can incorporate sound and video, but its text abilities are not as strong as those of HyperCard.

Director develops multimedia documents through a theater metaphor, with action occurring on a *stage* (the display area) with a *cast* (various multimedia components and content assets) and a *score* (coordinating the location, motion, and execution of the cast elements). For example, if you develop an animation in Director, each item in each frame of the animation is a CastMember. It's possible to assemble a document by creating an overall document architecture and presentation, importing cast members by drag-and-drop, and using direct manipulation and various built-in effects to shape the final presentation. If you plan to distribute the result on both Macintosh and Windows, the media components you use need to work across both platforms, of course. For example, you can readily include digital video as QuickTime files if you move the entire movie into the data fork and remove the resource fork ("flatten" the movie). AIFF sound files are supported on both Macintosh and Windows platforms.

Director also provides tools that support the creation of documents for CD-ROM use by such aids as document compression (to reduce data transfer lags) and disc-smart file layouts.

HyperCard and HyperTalk

Apple's HyperCard product was one of the first widely available systems for creating and displaying navigable electronic documents, and it's still very popular. For some time, this Macintosh-specific product was bundled with Macintosh computers, but now it is a separate product. HyperCard has been used widely for educational and entertainment titles. It has a fervent group of supporters and has enjoyed successful use by major CD-ROM publishing companies such as Voyager. HyperCard is the basis for the *Ultimate Robot* project described in Chapter 3, *Two Electronic Titles.* It's also the engine behind the popular game *Myst.*

NOTE

HyperCard is a member of the class of hypertext and hypermedia systems that support user-directed reading of nonlinear documents. Such systems were inspired by Vannevar Bush's visionary article, "As We May Think," published in 1945, and were the subject of much research in the 1970s and 1980s. Most electronic document systems trace their lineage back to the Bush article in some way; most individual systems vary only in how they organize and present their contents, and in how an author goes about preparing the contents and integrating them into a document.

HyperCard is built around the notion of cards, fields, and buttons:

Card

A card is a logical entity corresponding to a screen, and contains a set of fields and buttons; a leaf card, which we discussed in Chapter 3, is the lowest or terminating level of card, a card from which you can't go to anything more detailed.

Fields

Fields contain content defined in the card itself, in other files displayed by the card, or in resources managed and delivered through external commands (XCMDs). Fields can be laid out individually on each card or can be organized in a way that provides a visual unity for the document (as we discussed in the section called "Graphic Design" in Chapter 5, *Designing Electronic Documents*).

Buttons

Buttons are a user's navigational resources and may be displayed either explicitly (as an image of a physical control object) or implicitly (as part of a card's content that happens to respond to a mouse event).

HyperCard does not impose any particular organization on the collection of cards in a document. There are many organizations that work:

- You could create a totally linear document by giving each card only one button, called *Next*.

- You could organize cards into a hierarchical tree structure, as we did in the *Ultimate Robot* product.

- You could organize cards in other complex (even bizarre) ways to support any kind of information design you wish.

NOTE

If an author's design is particularly idiosyncratic, the user may find Hyper-Card's history function quite useful. This function shows thumbnails of the cards visited recently, and is helpful if the user is trying to figure out just where he is in the information structure.

HyperCard authoring is supported by HyperTalk, a scripting language that has something of an object-oriented flavor. HyperTalk allows you to lay out the contents of cards and to describe the actions to be taken when users generate events such as button presses. Although HyperTalk is definitely a programming language, its syntax is quite accessible. Many people who do not consider themselves programmers have little difficulty writing simple HyperTalk scripts.

Example 6-2 shows a segment of HyperTalk code for a HyperCard function embedded in a button that functions as a toggle. The code examines the current state of the button's icon and performs one of two actions. In both cases, it sets the icon to an in-between piece of artwork, plays a sound, sets a new icon, and then runs a function.

Example 6-2. A code example in HyperTalk

```
on mouseUP
   if icon of me is 4228 then      -- is off, so turn it on
      set icon of me to 4241
      play "click"
      set icon of me to 4229       -- set "on" icon
      -- put function #1 here
   else                            -- if icon of me is 4229 then
                                   -- turn it off
      set icon of me to 4241
      play "buzzer"
      set icon of me to 4228       -- set "off" icon
      -- put function #2 here
   end if
end mouseUp
```

The particular strengths of HyperCard include:

• A very rich command set

• Excellent fluency with text

• Fluency with interface and event handling

• A close companionship with the Apple operating system

Because of the relatively primitive nature of the HyperCard system, one of the most useful capabilities of HyperTalk is its ability to execute external commands (XCMDs) to add functionality, such as color, sound, digital movies, and simulations, into a HyperCard document. XCMDs may be programmed in any language, such as C, that can provide the interface necessary to be called by HyperTalk. Most of the real media content of a high-quality HyperCard document is provided through XCMD functions.

A weakness of HyperCard is that it does not exist on the PC, although a product called ToolBook from Asymetrix carefully mimics its syntax and features on the PC side.

There are a number of excellent books and papers on HyperCard authoring. Several of these are referenced in the Bibliography; you may also want to look around for additional titles that might deal with more focused examples.

Acrobat

Adobe's Acrobat is a widely used electronic document production and delivery system. It is based on PostScript, the most important multiplatform system for print prepress and for communicating fully formatted documents containing both text and image content. Acrobat begins with a familiar page-oriented design created via familiar prepress tools, which yield PostScript output. Acrobat then translates the PostScript into PDF (Portable Document Format), a form that preserves all the design in the document and can be viewed on the screen. These pages also have considerable electronic functionality, including links, embedded movies and sound, and fast searching.

Because of its PostScript roots, Acrobat is an easy system to learn, particularly if users have experience producing traditional prepress work. As we mentioned, Acrobat is the authoring system used to build the SIGGRAPH conference proceedings CD-ROM described in Chapter 3; that chapter shows several Acrobat screens.

Creating an Acrobat file in PDF is very straightforward, as long as the underlying PostScript is sound. The standard Acrobat supports a rich variety of functions. For example, a user can:

- Select either an outline or a thumbnail view to accompany a document; outlines and thumbnails provide a particularly good facility for browsing

- Zoom into the text or figures (or anything else that has very fine detail)

- Navigate pages sequentially or retrace the sequence of pages (the history) that have been viewed

- Execute a link to move around in the document or to view an accompanying document

- Select text from the document to be pasted into another document

- Do a word search on the document

- Play a movie that is in-line in the document

- Execute a link on the Web to an online document

- Use indexes to speed up word search (if the user is reading the document with the Exchange application); such searches are quite intelligent and can be based on word stems and homonyms, as well as on the usual full word matching

Acrobat does an excellent job of maintaining the graphic design of the original document, since it presents very high-quality text and diagrams. Its use of JPEG image compression for color images represents a good tradeoff between quality and storage needs.

Acrobat's production environment is quite solid; it includes the following main tools:

Distiller

A program that translates PostScript files into PDF files in batch operations or across networks

Exchange

A program that allows the user to assemble documents and add functionality to them

Catalog

A program that creates indexes into sets of documents

PDFWriter

A pseudo-printer that creates Acrobat PDF files from other applications

Figure 6-1 illustrates the use of the Distiller, Exchange, and PDFWriter in creating an Acrobat document.

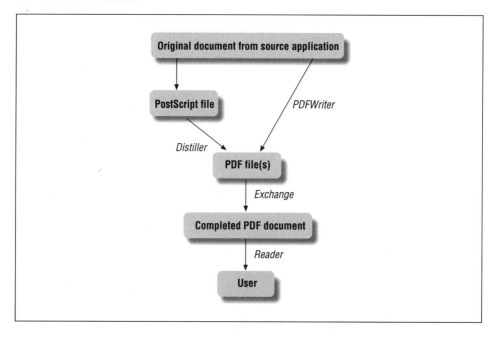

Figure 6-1.   Processes used to create a finished Acrobat document

The Acrobat reader displays the document to the user and supports the functionality in Acrobat documents. The reader can be distributed at no cost, so it can easily be put onto CD-ROMs.

Consistent Functionality

Users find that they adapt readily to the interaction techniques and functionality of Acrobat titles.   A very experienced creator of multimedia titles has commented that everything she reads created with Director works differently, whereas everything created with Acrobat looks the same. (The key is that the interfaces are different for Director, but the same for Acrobat.)

From the reader's point of view, Acrobat delivers a clean document. It preserves document design very well; gives good color representation; offers a set of controls for document viewing that are easy to understand; and adds several multimedia and Web capabilities to a document. The "look and feel" of the Acrobat reader are identical on all platforms

It your title fits the Acrobat document model, you'll find Acrobat to be a cost-effective way to create documents. There is almost no programming needed; instead, you'll simply assemble or create source documents, translate them into PDF files, and add internal and external links and other document features—that's it; you've got a finished product!

We have not worked with Acrobat in a commercial environment, so we don't feel qualified to provide detailed cost figures for developing a title with Acrobat. However, we do feel confident in stating that the work of the CD-ROM's interface designer, software director, and programmer (see the summary of their tasks in Table 4-1) would be greatly reduced—if not eliminated—if you were to use Acrobat's built-in capabilities.

Acrobat is not always an ideal choice, however. The Acrobat publishing model is very page-oriented, and does not lend itself to design options such as presenting changing information in fields within a set screen. In certain cases, though, the Acrobat model is just what you want. For example, because Acrobat documents are essentially read-only, the system is an appropriate vehicle for distributing copyrighted materials. In general, documents that are built around a text "story" are excellent candidates for Acrobat presentation, especially if those documents need to have highly designed looks to convey their full impact. Acrobat allows such documents to integrate sound and movie clips, to reach out to the Web for additional information and updates, and to support full hypertext capabilities.

GainMomentum

Sybase's Gain*Momentum* document system runs on most UNIX platforms (through the X Window system) and on Windows NT. It is specifically designed for client-server environments, and it works with applications and data distributed across networks. It offers a very helpful facility called the *canvas*, which allows a script to launch any application that can display its output in an X window; the output is displayed in the standard Gain*Momentum* display.

Although Gain*Momentum*'s lack of support for Windows 95 and the Macintosh means that it doesn't fit the main focus of this book, it serves as a good example of the functionality you might wish to find in an authoring system.

The Gain*Momentum* system meets almost all of the goals of authoring systems listed at the beginning of this chapter, and provides several nice additional features:

- It is strongly object-oriented, with the ability to work with distributed persistent object stores.

- It has a programming language, called the Gain Extension Language (GEL), that can be used to create permanent objects as well as provide runtime scripts.

- It offers a full set of integrated media editors to create, import, manipulate, and modify a full range of both static and synchronized media objects, and these can work dynamically at runtime.

- There is a full set of interface tools in the system's Visual Development Environment.

- It allows Gain*Momentum* access to corporate databases by integrating SQL calls at the GEL level, and has special features to support corporate training.

Media Tool

Apple's Media Tool is quite a different type of package. Media Tool provides an authoring environment on the Macintosh and players for both the Macintosh and the PC. Media Tool is itself a fairly simple shell program that allows multimedia specialists to work in their own area of expertise. As a consequence of its simplicity, Media Tool has a shorter learning curve than a more powerful system such as Director. The product is engineered in such a way that users can compose powerful functionalities in languages such as C or C++ and easily integrate them into a product built with Media Tool.

Media Tool lacks the richness of Director or HyperCard, but it's ideal for what is increasingly being called "electronic speaker support"—for example, applications in which CD-ROMs are deployed into the field (such as with a sales force), and there is little control over what kind of platform they will have to run on.

HTML and the World Wide Web

NCSA Mosaic was the original World Wide Web browser, although many other browsers, particularly Netscape Navigator, have become very popular.[*] Such browsers allow a user to seek out and display documents across the Internet. Browsers read HTML (HyperText Markup Language) files and provide support for text, images, movies, and sound through calls to appropriate tools on the system that's playing the reader.

Browsers are becoming very capable tools. The most important recent developments in Web browsers have been the ability to handle secure transactions across the networks, and the ability to provide more sophisticated content, such as movies and PDF files, inline in the browser window.

Documents intended for viewing through Web browsers use HTML to describe text components, and URLs (Uniform Resource Locators) to associate other documents or document components to be linked to the current one. Users can configure Web browsers to present the various tagged text components in whatever text style they desire. Compared with products such as Acrobat (which provides complete prepress capabilities), however, the amount of control a designer can exert over the appearance of HTML documents is limited. Different browsers have different capabilities, and you can't control what browser a user will use to read your document. As a consequence, you can't specify detailed fonts, sizes, and layout the way you can with many other types of authoring systems. (It's safe to say that, at the very least, almost anything presented through HTML can probably be presented more stylishly through Acrobat.)

Concepts of document style sheets and of uniform font standards for the Web are emerging, and these concepts should give Web page designers some confidence that their readers will actually see what they've designed.

Most Web browsers are thoroughly multiplatform (with players for essentially all significant computer systems) and, to some extent, multimedia. Text documents are simply displayed (and printed) through the Web browser itself. We can generally assume that a user has "helper applications," such as players for GIF image files and for QuickTime and MPEG movie files, and that there is some kind of sound support available. Although other image formats besides GIF—such as TIFF and JPEG image files—are sometimes supported, it's generally not good practice to rely on such support being available.

---

[*]In general, the comments we make in this section apply to Mosaic, Navigator, and other browsers, although specific details may vary.

Documents intended for presentation through Web browsers are usually organized as a collection of fairly small sections that are read by linking from one section to the next. Browsers also provide a history function that offers navigation through the sections that have already been read. Although Web browsers were designed for network use, they include a local mode that makes it possible to use them to view documents on a local system, including documents on a CD-ROM.

How would you create a title to be presented through a Web browser? You would design the title's contents in small pieces, and present each of these in a separate file. This is a straightforward implementation of the hypertext concept, and users seem to find working online with titles in this way quite comfortable. An example of this kind of organization is shown in Figure 6-2. The organization in small pieces makes the files transfer more quickly across the networks, and acts as an expanded outline of the title.

There are a few drawbacks, however, with this organizational approach. It can hamper a user who wants to print out the information, because the title is distributed across many files. To avoid this problem, we believe that people who design information for the Web should consider providing alternate versions that are oriented to printing.

Another problem is that because document organization emphasizes small chunks of information, there is no general way to search whole documents for particular words. Nevertheless, browsers do have standard and solid search facilities for individual files. All browsers also support standard copy operations.

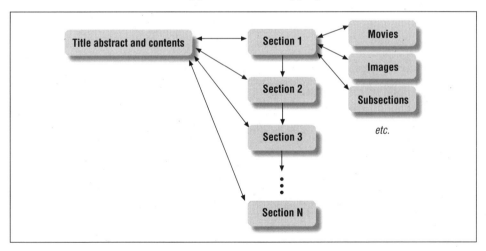

Figure 6-2.   One possible file organization for an HTML title

Let's look at another example. A portion of an HTML document is shown in Example 6-3. This document has a title, some text, and links to image files; the images are held in files such as */sig-icons/siglogo.gif* relative to the same directory. There are links to other HTML files whose paths are also given relative to the same directory, such as *conferences/conferences-and-workshops.html.* There are also links to HTML files at other sites, such as *http://info.acm.org/.* When the text document is played on the Web reader, its display is adapted to the parameters set by the user—links, headers, window size, font and size of text components, color of linked text, and the like are all adaptable.

Example 6-3.   A portion of an HTML document

```
<title>ACM SIGGRAPH Online!</title>
<body>
<h1><img align=middle src="/sig-icons/siglogo.gif">
SIGGRAPH Online!</h1>

<p>
Welcome to the <b>ACM SIGGRAPH</b> World Wide Web site.<p>
<b>SIGGRAPH</b> is the <a href="http://info.acm.org/">ACM</a>
Special Interest Group on Computer Graphics. Our scope is to
promote among our members the acquisition and exchange of
information and opinion on the theory, design, implementation,
application of computer-generated graphics and interactive
techniques to facilitate communication and understanding.

</p>

<p>
<hr>
<h3>Table of Contents</h3>
<dl>

<dt><a href="gen-info/gen-info.html"><b>General Information
</b></a>
<dd> Organizational and membership information, constitutional
    documents, professional chapter information, 1996 SIGGRAPH
    Executive Committee election information, and much, much
    more.
<dt><a href="conferences/conferences-and-
workshops.html"><b>Conferences & Workshops</b></a>

<dd> SIGGRAPH sponsors or co-sponsors a number of conferences
and workshops throughout the year.  Information about each
individual conference and workshop is available.

<dt><a href="http://www.education.siggraph.org/"><b>Educational
    Resources</b></a>
<dd> SIGGRAPH is committed to providing educational resources
and guidance to the computer graphics community.
```

Figure 6-3 shows a window on the HTML document, as played by Netscape Navigator on a Macintosh.

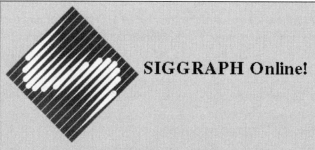

SIGGRAPH Online!

Welcome to the **ACM SIGGRAPH** World Wide Web site.

SIGGRAPH is the ACM Special Interest Group on Computer Graphics. Our scope is to promote among our members the acquisition and exchange of information and opinion on the theory, design, implementation, and application of computer-generated graphics and interactive techniques to facilitate communication and understanding.

Table of Contents

General Information
   Organizational and membership information, constitutional documents, professional chapter information, 1996
   SIGGRAPH Executive Committee election information, and much, much more.
Conferences & Workshops
   SIGGRAPH sponsors or co-sponsors a number of conferences and workshops throughout the year. Information about
   each individual conference and workshop is available.
Educational Resources
   SIGGRAPH is committed to providing educational resources and guidance to the computer graphics community.

Courtesy of ACM SIGGRAPH

Figure 6-3.   The portion of the document as played by Netscape Navigator on a Macintosh (see the color version in the center insert)

It's relatively easy to compose a basic HTML document, and the tags used to identify the various document components can be composed manually on an ordinary word processor or text editor. However, when you develop HTML documents in this way, you'll find that quite a lot of handwork is involved. A number of applications are beginning to provide a way to generate HTML automatically from page layout programs; a few examples include HoTMetaL Pro from SoftQuad, PageMill from Adobe, and Netscape Gold.

Many standard word processors can produce HTML files automatically, and can prepare fully formed file link names relatively easily. There are also some tools that will produce basic HTML files from any word processing document that uses good style sheets.

NCSA Mosaic was originally designed to be a network document reader, and it gained its early reputation by living up to that promise. Don't forget, though, that Mosaic—and its many successors—work equally well for local documents. Don't overlook the use of Web browsers as a way to provide multiplatform documents on a CD-ROM. Naturally, there are a few issues you'll have to take into account if you are going to publish HTML documents on a CD-ROM. For one thing, you'll have to follow the ISO 9660 CD-ROM file naming standards (described in Chapter 8, *CD-ROM Disc Standards*). For another, the use of HTML documents on a published CD-ROM means that users must have appropriate Web browsers for their systems; if you use features specific to a particular browser, users must have that browser to get the full benefit from your title.

Because several readers are available at no cost on the Internet, the availability of browsers has not proven to be a problem for most users. In general, HTML documents have proven to be very viable CD-ROM components.

General-Purpose Languages

Many other traditional and newer languages designed primarily for other functions can also be used to do CD-ROM authoring. This section describes a number of possibilities.

Low-level languages (FORTRAN, C, C++, Visual C)

It is possible, though more difficult, to compose electronic documents using a more traditional programming paradigm, and familiar programming languages like FORTRAN and C. If you use such languages, you will have to control things like media presentation and user interaction by explicitly writing the code to handle these functionalities. This can be extraordinarily time-consuming and detailed work, but it does allow the author a level of control missing from higher-level authoring systems.

Actually, traditional languages are used fairly often in electronic titles, but most often in the following situations:

1. When developing a special function within the authoring system (perhaps as an external command, or XMCD) that the system doesn't support directly (for example, the behavior of a certain key).

2. When developing particular types of tools that may then be used for the authoring of multimedia (for example, the ability to present a movie in-line in the title).

C and C++ are particularly popular choices for performing such functions.

The problem with using a relatively low-level language, such as C or FORTRAN, as an authoring solution is that these basic languages perform very few of the services that the media integrator needs to take for granted. Of course, C and FORTRAN are fully capable languages, and as such provide ways for you to construct all of the necessary functions. But it will take a great deal of time and expense—and any staff hired in to work on the project will have to learn the details of these extensions.

Visual C++, a relatively new language of particular interest to the multimedia community, promises—at least in theory—to complement the basic tool set of the language with a set of screen-related objects, media display functions, and an easy way to organize a calling hierarchy.

Visual BASIC

Somewhat related to the Visual C++ strategy is the Visual BASIC language, a Microsoft reincarnation into truly modern form of the old BASIC language used by thousands of students through the years. Visual BASIC retains the fundamental syntax of the language, but frames it into an object-oriented world, complete with object properties and rather facile access to the Microsoft Windows environment.

Visual BASIC allows programmers to develop multimedia titles, as well as applets (applications that can be executed across the network instead of residing on the user's machine). You should seriously consider using Visual BASIC as an authoring tool if you are working in a Windows environment.

Java

The Java language represents another, different kind of approach to programming languages. Java was developed primarily for use in networks, but it also provides very good media and interface integration. Most Web browsers are now developing Java capabilities, so the language seems to be well positioned for general media programming. The code in Example 6-4 shows how Java deals with interface objects (such as buttons) and gives a good flavor for the language in operation. It also shows how heavily Java relies on inheriting data and methods from other objects.

Java is a strongly object-oriented system with a syntax much like C++, but without some of the more baroque parts of that language. In fact, Java's complete reliance on objects allows it to operate without explicit pointer variables. Java source code is compiled into an intermediate system-independent byte code form that is compact and easy to download over the Internet and other networks. That byte code is interpreted and executed on the user's system by an interpreter that's optimized for its host.

Example 6-4. A code segment in Java

```
package app;

import awt.*;

/**
 * An applet button. You can set the label. When the
 * button is pressed it calls the action() method in
 * the AppletPanel.
 *
 * @author Arthur van Hoff
```

Example 6-4. A code segment in Java (Continued)

```
    */
    public
    class AppButton extends AppComponent {
        public String label;
        public Font font;
        boolean down;

        public AppButton(AppletPanel app, String label) {
            super(app);
            this.label = label;
            this.font = app.getFont("Helvetica", 14);
        }
        public void setLabel(String label) {
            this.label = label;
            app.touched = true;;
        }
        public void paint(Graphics g) {
            g.setForeground(down ? Color.gray : Color.lightGray);
            g.paint3DRect(0, 0, w, h, true, !down);
            g.setFont(font);
            g.setForeground(Color.black);
            g.drawString(label,
                        (w - font.stringWidth(label)) / 2,
                        ((h + font.height) / 2) - font.descent);
        }
        public void setDown(boolean down) {
            if (down != this.down) {
                app.touched = true;
                this.touched = true;
                this.down = down;
            }
        }
        public void mouseDown(int x, int y) {
            setDown(inside(x, y));
        }
        public void mouseDrag(int x, int y) {
            setDown(inside(x, y));
        }
        public void mouseUp(int x, int y) {
            if (down) {
                app.action(this);
            }
            setDown(false);
        }
    }
```

OLE and OpenDoc

In addition to the choices we've mentioned, other new solutions are emerging. For example, there are now two compound document architectures, Microsoft's OLE (Object Linking and Embedding) and Apple's OpenDoc. Both may be used as fundamental architectures for authoring systems. OpenDoc has been adopted as a standard by the OMG (Object Management Group).

The OLE and OpenDoc architectures are now being extended to support network operations. To stay on top of the evolving field of electronic publishing, you will have to actively track both fundamental document architectures, such as OLE and OpenDoc, and evolving authoring system technology.

Computing Platforms

The choice of which computer platform to use for your source development and document delivery is a very important one. Many people don't give this choice enough consideration; they assume too quickly that they'll be developing for the system they normally use. However, the choice of the document delivery system is actually a very important marketing issue and may depend largely on what type of CD-ROM you are developing. Despite your personal choice of computing platform, be sure that you are delivering your product to its natural audience. For example, the DOS/Windows world is the largest market for popular discs, with the Macintosh second. Business reference discs are mostly prepared for DOS and Windows. Discs with scientific data and simulations are usually intended for a UNIX audience.

More and more document production and delivery products recognize that they need to be able to support more than one kind of computer. As a result, we're seeing a growing number of cross-platform document systems. If you are not yet using such systems, look into them carefully, and investigate electronic media that can deliver such documents to different kinds of systems.

Chapter 8 describes a number of issues that come up when you consider developing a title for multiple platforms. If you're not careful, you'll run into problems of inconsistencies in file naming, end-of-line characters, and other problems that come up when you try to run across hardware and software platforms.

CHAPTER

7

Electronic Document Standards

There are a number of different types of standards that you need to know about when you publish a title on CD-ROM. This chapter briefly discusses the electronic document standards for text, graphic images, digital video, and sound, and it describes a number of data compression and conversion methods used for electronic documents. Such standards are essential if documents are to be placed on different media and different computing platforms. Chapter 8, *CD-ROM Disc Standards*, discusses the standards for CD-ROMs themselves.

NOTE

Although you need to be aware of the basics of the technologies underlying these standards, most readers won't need to understand all of the details. So, in the sections that follow, we provide only a summary. If you, like many readers, are more interested in content than technology, you'll find this chapter and the glossary helpful in describing buzzwords and basic concepts associated with electronic documents. If you need more comprehensive information, consult the references in the Bibliography.

Both formal and informal standards for media and compound documents are very much in flux, as we describe in the final section of this chapter, "Looking to the Future . . .". The existing standards aren't really adequate; both capabilities and expectations are growing even as we realize the limitations of some of our media and communications channels. The discussion in this chapter captures a snapshot of the state of these standards as we go to press, but it's up to you to stay up to date with the latest developments in this quickly changing area.

Text Standards

This section describes the main standards for raw text, text layout, page description languages, and documents on networks.

Text

Raw text is the most basic building block of written communication and has been used by computers since they were first invented. The description of the two basic character mappings for text—ASCII and Unicode—is a good place to start any discussion of standards for electronic documents.

ASCII

ASCII (American Standard Code for Information Interchange) is a very common character-set mapping for the part of the world that uses Roman letters and Arabic numerals (A, B, C, 1, 2, 3, etc.). The ASCII character set comes in two flavors, one with 128 characters and one with 256 characters. In both cases, each ASCII character maps to one byte. In addition to digits and both upper- and lowercase letters, ASCII also specifies punctuation marks, arithmetic symbols, a limited set of formatting controls (e.g., line feed, tab, space), and some communication control codes.

Unicode

Unicode is a relatively new 16-bit (2-byte) character set that defines the characters of most of the common languages of the world. It includes all the accent variations of the European alphabets, as well as Cyrillic, Hebrew, Arabic, and representative alphabets from India, China, and Japan. It also incorporates the definition of a number of special characters and other typographic symbols.

Text Layout

Raw text by itself is simple, but text as it as used by a design professional is anything but simple. In addition to the characters themselves, designers need to consider fonts, text size, and style, as well as creative ways to organize text. Any electronic document system must be able to handle these design characteristics.

The text layout systems described below range from the very simple (systems that simply do a good job of describing technical text) to very complex (systems that are able to describe text as it has been laid out by a designer who is using the layout to make a real impact).

troff

troff is a classic system for describing text layout. Its origins are in timeshared mainframes and minicomputers, and it developed from the original *roff* (runoff) text formatting programs for UNIX. The name "troff" actually comes from "roff for typesetters."

troff uses command lines (lines that begin with a period) to specify typesetting styles; while it is fairly awkward to use, troff has nevertheless been popular for many years, and many people still swear by it.[*] Except in a few parts of the UNIX community, though, troff is no longer a popular typesetting language.

Example 7-1 shows a fragment of a document typeset in troff.

Example 7-1. A fragment of a troff document

```
.Bh "The :set Command"
There are two types of options that can be changed with the
\f(CW:set\fR
command:  toggle options, which are either on or off, and
options that take a numeric or string value (such as the
location of a margin or the name of a file).
.LP
Toggle options may be on or off by default.
To turn a toggle option on, the command is:
.Ps
:set \f(CIoption\fP
.Pe
To turn a toggle option off, the command is:
.Ps
:set no\f(CIoption\fP
.Pe
For example, to specify that pattern searches should ignore
case, type:
.Ps
:set ic
.Pe
If you want \fIvi\fR to return to being case-sensitive in
searches, give the command:
.Ps
:set noic
.Pe
Some options have a value assigned to them.
For example, the\p \f(CWwindow\fR option sets the number of
lines shown in the screen's\p "window."
You set values for these options with an equal sign (=):
.Ps
:set window=20
.Pe
During a \fIvi\fR session, you can check which options
\fIvi\fR is using.
```

---

[*]Some O'Reilly & Associates books are still typeset in troff.

Example 7-1. A fragment of a troff document (Continued)

```
The\p command:
.Ps
:set all
.Pe
displays the complete list of options, including options that
you have set and defaults that \fIvi\fR has "chosen."
```

TEX

The TEX system and its variants (LATEX, AMSTEX, etc.) are the traditional way to lay out text in many technical environments, particularly those that use mathematics heavily. TEX offers extensive capabilities for equation formatting, as well as the ability to lay out pages and include images.

TEX is still used widely because there are well-developed tools that allow users to print TEX documents on imagesetters, as well as well-developed tools that allow users to filter TEX documents into other formats such as SGML and PostScript. Certain technical publishers (e.g., the American Mathematical Society) consider TEX to be a primary source language for papers and books.

Example 7-2 shows a fragment of a document typeset in TEX, courtesy of Pat Hanrahan and Peter Schröder of Princeton University.

Example 7-2. A fragment of a TEX document

```
\begin{document}
%**end of header
\title{On the Form Factor between Two Polygons}

\author{Peter Schr\"oder
\thanks{{\mbox{}\vrule height 0.6in width 0pt}}
\hspace{1in} Pat Hanrahan\\[8pt]
        Department of Computer Science \\
        Princeton University}

\date{}

\maketitle

\begin{abstract}
Form factors are used in radiosity to describe the fraction of
diffusely reflected light leaving one surface and arriving at
another. They are a fundamental geometric property used for
computation.  Many special configurations admit closed form
solutions.  However, the important case of the form factor
between two polygons in three space has had no known closed
form solution. We give such a  solution for the case of
general (planar, convex or concave, possibly containing holes)
polygons.
\end{abstract}

{\small
\noindent {\bf CR Categories and Subject Descriptors:} I.3.7
```

Example 7-2.   A fragment of a T_EX document (Continued)

```
[ComputerGraphics]: {\em Three-Dimensional Graphics and
Realism --Radiosity\/}; J.2 [Physical Sciences and
Engineering]: {\em Engineering\/}.

\noindent {\bf Additional Key Words and Phrases:} Closed form
solution; form factor; polygons.
```

RTF

Microsoft's RTF (Rich Text Format) is one of several text format systems that enhance ASCII by supplying a set of formatting commands. These commands specify a number of different kinds of textual properties, such as font name, font size, font color, column width, margins, leading, and so on.

Because RTF files can be generated and read by most current word processing programs on many computers, RTF is a useful resource for sharing files between platforms and between word processing systems. RTF files are stored in plain ASCII, so it is easy to share them by email, on CD-ROMs, and on other disk devices.

SGML

SGML (Standard Generalized Markup Language) is another standard that enhances ASCII text with formatting commands. SGML differs from RTF and other systems in that SGML documents describe the components of a document by name, not by specifying the direct details of the desired formatting. To allow you to print or display an SGML document, you need document type definitions (DTDs) for each of the named components; the definitions tell how the components are to be displayed. SGML documents can take on whatever look their DTDs prescribe, so a publisher can set up different DTDs for print or for electronic display and achieve two different looks with no change in the source document. It has been suggested that World Wide Web browsers may have full SGML capabilities in the near future.

Among other capabilities, SGML allows a document to have links both within the document and between documents; in this way, the language supports hypertext. SGML also allows a document to contain links to nontext documents, such as images and movies, so these nontext components can be effectively integrated into the original document.

Most text-editing and word-processing systems available on the market today do not yet produce SGML-marked output (although some are beginning to do so). It is usually necessary to take authors' materials in some other form and translate them into SGML. This translation can be done by hand, although that is a time-consuming process. To allow automatic translation, an author needs to provide files that use consistent, well-designed tagging from style sheets in a standard system such as Microsoft Word, Word Perfect, Framemaker, or even T$_{E}$X. There are a number of translators that can create good SGML when the original document uses a good style sheet consistently, and even a few that can do pretty well with poorly standardized documents. There are also editors that can clean up any remaining problems in the SGML, and can add hyperlinks and additional document components. Finally, there are some quite good document presentation systems that display SGML documents on a wide range of platforms and configurations from a CD-ROM or other sources.

A number of companies that produce these translators, editors, and document display systems are listed in Appendix A. One particularly helpful source is Electronic Book Technologies (EBT); they support not only standard SGML, but also a number of extensions. One such extension includes links, images, and movies. Another launches external programs that can display their output in a screen window. The EBT systems include tools to translate documents into SGML (*Dyna*Tag), to display the extended SGML documents on the screen (*Dyna*Text), and to translate SGML documents to HTML for use with Web browsers such as Mosaic (*Dyna*Web). *Dyna*Text runs on Windows, the Macintosh, and all major UNIX systems, making it perhaps the most universally supported of the full-function document viewers.

The SGML fragment shown in Example 7-3 includes links to several raster (bitmap) images; one of these is shown as part of a screen from a *Dyna*Text document in Figure 7-1. (Courtesy of Electronic Book Technologies, Inc.)

Example 7-3.   A fragment of an SGML document

```
<SS1><ST>Facts and Figures</ST>

<FIG ID="alaunch">
<P>Launch Date:  April 28, 1989</P>
<P>Launch Window:  2:24 p.m. - 2:42 p.m. EDT</P>

<ART TYPE="raster" ID="blaunch" TITLE="Shuttle Launch">
<P>Launch Site:  Kennedy Space Center, Fla., Pad 39B</P>
<ART TYPE="raster" ID="stsorbit" TITLE="Astronaut in the Bay
of the Shuttle">
<P>Orbiter:  Atlantis (OV-104)</P>
<ART TYPE="raster" ID="corbit" TITLE="Overhead View of Shuttle
in Orbit">
<P>Altitude:  160 nautical miles</P>

<P>Inclination:  28.85 degrees</P>
<P>Duration:  4 days, 56 minutes</P>

<ART TYPE="raster" ID="dlanding" TITLE="Shuttle Landing">

<P>Landing Date/Time:  May 2, 1989, 3:20 p.m. EDT</P>
<P>Primary Landing Site:  Edwards Air Force Base, Calif.</P>
<P>Alternate Landing Sites:</P>

<L><LI><P>Return to Launch Site ;Kennedy Space Center</P>
</LI>
```

Example 7-3.   A fragment of an SGML document (Continued)

```
<LI><P>Transatlantic Abort Landing ;Ben Guerir, Morocco</P>
</LI>

<LI><P>Abort Once Around ;Edwards AFB</P>
</LI>
</L>

<P>Crew:</P>

<L><LI><P>David M. Walker, commander</P>
</LI>

<LI><P>Ronald J. Grabe, pilot</P>
</LI>

<LI><P>Norman E. Thagard, mission specialist-1</P>
</LI>

<LI><P>Mary L. Cleave, mission specialist-2</P>
</LI>

<LI><P>Mark C. Lee, mission specialist-3</P>
</LI>
</L>

<P>Primary Payload:  Magellan</P>
<P>Secondary Payloads:</P>

<L><LI><P>Fluids Experiment Apparatus (FEA)</P>
</LI>

<LI><P>Mesoscale Lightning Experiment (MLR)</P>
</LI>
</L>
</SS1>
```

Many publishers find SGML-based systems quite attractive. For one thing, SGML documents can easily be delivered in either print or electronic format. For another, it's easy to reuse SGML documents in derived publications such as anthologies. Database systems are available that track SGML documents through the full range of editorial and production stages.

HTML

HTML (HyperText Markup Language) is the standard way to present documents on the World Wide Web. HTML provides a way to structure a document that is a special kind of SGML document.

As with SGML, the HTML markup technique uses start tags and end tags to identify portions of a document by name instead of giving them explicit formats. The tags are translated into actual formats by the standard HTML Document Type Definition (DTD). HTML documents can include links to other documents, including

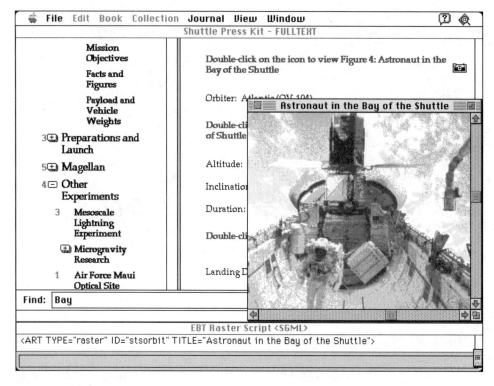

Figure 7-1.   A screen from a document produced with DynaText. Copyright © 1995
Electronic Book Technologies, Inc. All rights reserved. DynaText is a trademark of
Electronic Book Technologies, Inc. (see the color version in the center insert)

images and movies. HTML has limited document formatting capabilities, but these
are still being developed.

Tools are now available to provide automatic translation of documents from
various page layout or word-processing systems into HTML format; these tools
work in a way that's similar to the way that translations to SGML work.

Example 6-3 and Figure 6-3 provide an example of an HTML file and the page it
creates.

Page Description Languages

PostScript, PDF, and HTML are currently the most commonly used page description languages (PDLs). PDLs are languages that allow you to specify the page
layout, fonts, and graphics of printed or displayed pages.

PostScript

PostScript, developed in 1985 by Adobe Systems, is the page description language most often used for print prepress. PostScript is the industry-standard way to represent printed pages in electronic fashion. It provides a way to describe the layout of text, vector graphics, and raster images on a printed page. (We'll describe vector and raster images in the section on "Images" below.) Text, color, black-and-white graphics, and photographic-quality images obtained from scanners or video sources can all be described using PostScript. PostScript is also (somewhat) human-readable and can be emailed.

An extension of PostScript, the Display PostScript system, allows PostScript to support screen presentations. If you have a Display PostScript capability (for example, one exists on the NeXT computer), you can use PostScript directly to present electronic documents.

For detailed information about PostScript, see the excellent Adobe language manual for PostScript listed in the Bibliography.

PDF

Acrobat PDF (Portable Document Format) is a relatively new file format which has gained wide acceptance in the market. Its use in electronic documents is described in some detail in Chapter 3, *Two Electronic Titles*, and in Chapter 6, *Authoring Systems*.

The goal of PDF is to capture page descriptions in a way that goes beyond the capabilities of PostScript. PDF files capture the text and layout features of a page, presenting the files on the screen and replacing any missing fonts with fonts that are adjusted to have the same font metrics as the originals. In this way, a PDF display maintains much of the overall graphic design of the original document. While the PDF format stores line art in the same way that PostScript does, it stores raster images with any of several image compression techniques. It then compresses the entire file with LZW compression (described later in this chapter) and translates it into one of two formats: a 7-bit format that can be moved easily over communication lines, or a more compressed binary format.

For detailed information about PDF, see the references in the Bibliography.

Documents on Networks

Documents for the World Wide Web—and for networks in general—are relative newcomers in the electronic arena. The standards for these documents are evolving rapidly. At present, HTML, Java, and VRML are emerging as standards for documents used on networks, but this whole area is very dynamic.

NOTE

Any document designed for Web standards can also be placed on a CD-ROM and used locally; in this way, you can avoid all-too-common network delays.

HTML

As we mentioned under "Text Layout" above, the original standard for Web documents was HTML. HTML has evolved through several stages, and has become a more and more capable way to prepare hypertext documents. Features such as forms handling and image maps have been added to Web documents, and individual Web browsers have added their own unique features as well.

Java

The Java programming language is a new standard for the World Wide Web which is gaining in popularity. The Java language, which in some ways is similar to C++, is used to write small applications, or *applets*, that can be downloaded from the Web and executed on your local machine. These applets can include very powerful graphics and simulations. The ability to execute Java applets is now being integrated into various Web browsers, and Java is becoming a very attractive way to add advanced functionality into Web documents. For online information about Java, check out the Java information center at *http://sdsc.edu/java/*.

VRML

Another new standard that's expected to provide tools for interactive network simulations is VRML (Virtual Reality Modeling Language). VRML supports interaction across networks with three-dimensional data and images. The VRML standard is based on visualization systems from Silicon Graphics, and it addresses complex graphics and interaction issues. We expect VRML to have applications for interactive graphical simulations on CD-ROM as well as on the World Wide Web. VRML capabilities are currently provided in the WebSpace Web browser, and we expect to see these capabilities integrated into other Web browsers in the near future. For online information about VRML, take a look at the VRML information at *http://sdsc.edu/vrml/*.

Font Standards

While there are standards for fonts in electronic prepress and in many authoring systems, there have been few, if any, standards for fonts on the Web. Recently, however, two competing Web font standards have been announced—one from Microsoft and one from Adobe, Apple, and Netscape—to allow HTML documents to add font specifications to their other tags. The use of these standards should allow your online documents to enjoy a higher level of design than is the case with the original HTML specifications. For online information about fonts, check out *ftp://jasper.ora.com/pub/comp.fonts/FAQ/*.

Image Standards

There are hundreds of different formats used for the storage of images. This large number is a result of the fact that there are so many different sources of images and that they are used in so many different ways. There are a number of different ways to categorize image formats, including the type of image (black-and-white monochrome, grayscale, or color), the type of data storage (raster, vector, or meta-file), and the type of compression that is used (symmetric vs. asymmetric, lossy vs. lossless, etc.).

The following sections provide only a brief summary of the most commonly used image standards, along with information about converting and compressing images. For detailed information, consult the articles and books listed in the Bibliography.

Converting Image Formats

With so many different image formats, you will often find that you have images in formats not supported by your own particular authoring system. In such cases, you need to use a format conversion program to translate the source format into a format you can use.

There are many format converters available for different computing platforms; some are commercial, and some other excellent tools are publicly available:

- For UNIX, the most widely-known converters are the *pbmplus* package (available via anonymous FTP from *ftp.x.org* in the *contrib* directory) and the *SDSC Image Tools* (available from the San Diego Supercomputer Center at *ftp.sdsc.edu*).

- For PCs, *pbmplus* has been ported to MS-DOS (available from *oak.oakland.edu* in the *pub/msdos/graphics* directory.) The commercial program *HiJaak* is also excellent. The *Conversion Assistant for Windows* is also a good tool for Windows.

- For the Macintosh, the *GraphicsConverter* provides a good, publicly available tool (available from *sumex-aim.stanford.edu/info-mac/grf/util*).

- The excellent commercial *DeBabelizer* program is available for all major platforms: Windows, Macintosh, and UNIX.

For information about the details of graphics file formats, see the book *Encyclopedia of Graphics File Formats*, by James Murray and William vanRyper, listed in the Bibliography; as we've mentioned, that book also includes a CD-ROM containing a number of excellent, publicly available conversion tools.

Ways of Storing Image Information

Graphics file formats are often categorized as raster (sometimes called bitmap) or vector. These terms describe the ways that image information is stored in the file. Additional categories, such as metafile, object, animation, and multimedia, have also been identified.

Most of the file formats we discuss in the sections below deal with computer images in *raster* format; that is, as an array of pixels with each having a color value. A raster file essentially contains an exact pixel-by-pixel mapping of an image, which can then be reconstructed by a rendering application. A raster image is basically an array of colors, where the color is described by either an index into a color lookup table or as a direct representation of the color level. The level may either be gray or a triple of levels of red, green, and blue colors. The former way to describe color takes up to one byte of storage for each pixel; the latter may take up to three bytes per image. As a result, the number of bytes of raw information in a full-color image may be as much as $3 \times H \times V$, where H and V are the horizontal and vertical dimensions of the image.

A single raster image the size of a modest 640×480 computer screen may use as many as $3 \times 640 \times 480 = 921,600$ bytes, almost a megabyte, while an image the size of a workstation screen may contain over 3 MB of data. Because these space requirements are so large, compression schemes for images are very important; good compression allows you to store images in less space, as we describe in the next section.

In contrast to raster (bitmap) formats, *vector* formats contain mathematical descriptions of one or more image elements, which are used by a rendering application to construct a final image. Vector files are essentially made up of descriptions of image elements, or structured graphics objects, rather than pixel values. Vector files are typically associated with graphics applications such as CAD (Computer-Aided Design), and there are many standards for them. In general, we don't describe vector formats in this chapter since they are not widely used in general-purpose electronic publications.

Color Models and Spaces

There are a number of different color models used in storing computer images. Ordinarily, images are stored using the RGB (red, green, blue) color model. With this system, varying amounts of the colors red, green, and blue are added to black to produce new colors. Graphics files that use the RGB color system represent each pixel as a color triple—three numerical values in the form (R,G,B), each representing the amount of red, green, and blue in the pixel, respectively. For example, for 24-bit color, the triplet (0,0,0) ordinarily represents black, and the triplet (255,255,255) represents white.

Because the human perceptual system does not work in precisely the same way that a computer monitor does, there are applications in which other color models can work as well as, or better than, RGB.

One of these models is the YUV model, where Y is luminance (brightness) and U and V are two axes of chrominance (colors). The human eye is much more sensitive to brightness for its detail cues, so it is possible to reduce the data in an image by reducing the spatial frequency of the two U and V color components. This reduction is frequently performed for movies, where the eye cannot dwell in detail on a single image. Thus, many of the movie formats and codecs start out by mapping images into YUV space, reducing the spatial frequency of the UV components, and then applying other compression techniques to the results.

Other color models are also used in certain applications, including CMY (cyan, magenta, yellow), HSV (hue, saturation, value), HLS (hue, lightness, saturation), and black-white-gray.

Compressing Image Data

As we've mentioned, data compression is an extremely important issue for electronic publications, particularly for images because of the very large amount of information present in a raw image. Compression is the process used to reduce the physical size of an image, and actually consists of two complementary processes: compression and decompression. The general term *codec* has been coined to describe a system for compressing and decompressing data, particularly image and digital video data.[*]

There are a number of different ways of categorizing data compression schemes, described in the sections that follow.

For online information about compression in general, take a look at the FAQ provided on the CD-ROM that accompanies this book. Check out *http://www.cis.ohio-state.edu/hypertext/faq/usenet/compression-faq/* for an updated version.

---

[*] A large part of the work on digital video has been devoted to developing appropriate codecs to cope with the very large amount of data that must be handled in real time for digital video, and this part of the story is far from finished.

Symmetric vs. asymmetric

A codec may be either symmetric or asymmetric.

A *symmetric* codec goes through essentially the same process, and performs essentially the same amount of work, for encoding and decoding an image. One good example of a symmetric scheme is the LZW compression scheme, described below.

An *asymmetric* codec, on the other hand, applies significantly different processes for encoding and for decoding. The scheme typically spends much more time and processing on encoding. The result is higher compression factors and making the decoding easy to do in real time. The Cinepak digital movie codec is an example of an asymmetric scheme. In general, the highest compression rates are associated with asymmetric codecs that dedicate a significant amount of time to compression. This time investment is made only once and pays off in allowing many users to get the benefits of the compression and the fast decoding.

Lossless vs. lossy

A number of data compression schemes are used for images and movies. All of them begin with the raster structure of images as their initial input, and then act on that structure in various ways to store the image data more efficiently.

Compression techniques are called *lossless* if the exact original data can be recovered from the compressed file. With lossless compression, when data is compressed and then decompressed, the original information contained in the data is preserved, and no data is lost or discarded.

Techniques are called *lossy* if some information is lost when the data is reconstructed. Essentially, lossy techniques throw away some of the data in an image in order to achieve better compression.

The choice between lossy and lossless compression is a tradeoff: lossless compression is obviously desirable, but the compression techniques with the highest compression rates all have some degree of loss.

RLE

RLE (run length encoding) is a relatively simple lossless technique that stores images by scanline. However, instead of storing a scanline of raw bytes, it stores a sequence of value pairs (N, C) indicating N bytes of color C. For example, using RLE, the raw string:

[93 93 93 93 255 255 255 255 255 255]

would be stored as:

[4 93 6 255]

In other words, there are four bytes containing the value 93, followed by six bytes containing the value 255. The first pair is sometimes referred to as a 4-byte run, the second as a 6-byte run.

For some kinds of images, RLE encoding can be extremely efficient, but for files containing few runs of constant value, RLE can actually expand the storage needed for an image. RLE's compression efficiency basically depends on the type of image data being encoded. For example, a black-and-white image that is mostly white, such as the page of a book, tends to encode very efficiently. An image with many colors, such as a photograph, however, tends not to encode very well.

There are a number of schemes to overcome the inefficiency caused by the simplest RLE approach described above, such as indications that a sequence of bytes is to be taken as raw data instead of run encodings. Several of these schemes are described in the references in the Bibliography.

Huffman encoding

Huffman encoding is a lossless entropy coding technique that gets its efficiency by returning different-length code words for same-length original data: more frequently occurring data tends to be encoded by shorter code words. These codes can be created by scanning a single set of data to determine the frequency of data words and then adapting the code words to this particular data, getting an optimal code length. One complexity of Huffman encoding is that it requires the "dictionary" to be transmitted along with the data, thus adding length to the encoded file.

In certain types of applications, codes may also be created by examining a large class of data, determining the general characteristics of all the data in the class, and then creating a shared dictionary for all the data in this class. This modified Huffman technique is usually employed for image data.

CCITT Group III and CCITT Group IV

CCITT Group III and *CCITT Group IV* are encoding techniques for black-and-white (sometimes called bilevel) images. These techniques were originally developed for fax transmission. There are two versions of the Group III technique:

- **One-dimensional**. The first Group III version is the simplest. It takes each separate scan line, creates an RLE encoding of the line, and then stores that line with a predetermined Huffman encoding.

- **Two-dimensional**. The second Group III technique is more common and more efficient. With this technique, a regularly spaced set of lines (typically every eighth line) is treated as a reference line and is encoded as for the one-dimensional version; however, the lines in between are stored differentially, with 0 meaning no change from the pixel above and 1 meaning that the pixel is different. This differential line is then encoded as for the one-dimensional version. This technique is more efficient because the coherence of most images means that there are significantly more 0s in the differential line than there would be otherwise.

In general, CCITT Group III has been almost entirely replaced by the more efficient CCITT Group IV encoding. Group III uses the reference lines as a means of restoring an image that has been corrupted by transmission errors in the communications system. This need for reference lines has been virtually eliminated as a consequence of using other error-handling techniques and by improved communications. Essentially, Group IV is Group III with no reference lines.

LZW

LZW (Lempel-Ziv-Welch) encoding[*] is a widely used lossless technique that has capabilities ranging well beyond image compression. The LZW technique starts with a dictionary of base symbols (for example, bytes) and expands the dictionary dynamically to include symbol sequences. The technique is both general and straightforward, and gives good file reduction because it operates on each file independently. It does not need to have its dictionary transmitted with the file, however, because it can recreate the dictionary from the incoming coded data as the file is being received.

JPEG

JPEG is a still image encoding technique that was developed by (and named for) the Joint Photographic Experts Group, a standards committee that originated within the International Standards Organization (ISO). There are several different ways images can be encoded, some of which allow lossless images, but most JPEG pictures undergo a lossy compression and suffer some quality loss. In return for this they take up much less space.

The usual lossy JPEG compression operates as follows:

1. Transform the image into a suitable color model or space, usually a luminance/chrominance space such as YUV, instead of RGB. Chrominance information may be reduced by 50 percent in each direction to begin the compression, because the eye is much more sensitive to luminance than to chrominance.

---

*The LZW coding and process are patented by Unisys.

2. Group the pixels into 8 × 8 blocks, and use a discrete cosine transformation to give a fundamental color average together with differential color changes within the block. This transformation changes absolute color information into information on color changes, essentially moving from location space into frequency space somewhat like a Fourier transform. The low indices in the result contain low-frequency information, and the higher indices contain information on higher-frequency color changes.

3. Divide the frequency coefficients by values that are larger for high-frequency image components than for low-frequency components, again because the eye pays more attention to the lower-frequency components, and the results are rounded to integers. This is usually expressed by a quantization coefficient (QC); this kind of JPEG compression gets lossy (loses information) from the chrominance reduction and when you choose a QC with value greater than one.

4. Encode the resulting coefficients with either Huffman coding or some other entropy coding.

For online information about JPEG, take a look at the FAQ provided on the CD-ROM that accompanies this book. Check out *http://www.cis.ohio-state.edu/hypertext/faq/usenet/jpeg-faq/* for an updated version.

Cinepak

The Cinepak compression system was developed by SuperMac Technologies and is a standard codec for QuickTime and Video for Windows. Cinepak uses a patented vector quantization approach that offers variable levels of compression quality depending on the video source and the data rate of the playback device. Typical compression ratios are about 20:1 compared to the original source material, and movies compressed with Cinepak require about 6 to 12 MB per minute. Factors affecting the quality are the image size and the complexity of the motion and texture in the frames. Cinepak is an asymmetric codec designed to play back video without special hardware support, but like most asymmetric schemes it requires much longer to compress a video than to replay it. On a high-speed processor, compression can typically take from 2.5 to 6 seconds per video frame, or as much as one hour of compression time per minute of 24 frames/second video.

The Cinepak encoding scheme works on 4 × 4 pixel blocks in YUV color space. During encoding it creates a lookup table of the values it sees, and during playback it simply reads encoded values and translates them with the table. Creating these tables is the (long) task of image encoding; reading them is the (quick) task of image decoding.

Grayscale Images

Grayscale images are frequently handled with no particular image format. Instead, a raster image is simply encoded with an appropriate compression scheme, such as CCITT Group IV, and the resulting file is stored or transmitted. This process requires that the system receiving the file know what original compression was used, often by assumptions based on the filename extension alone.

JBIG

JBIG encoding (named for the Joint Bilevel Imaging Experts Group that developed the method) stores grayscale information up to four bits deep (16 levels of gray). It is particularly valuable for dithered grayscale images. It operates based on two- or three-line templates, predicting the value of a pixel based on the template and a predictor pixel. The JBIG method is a relatively new lossless compression method. It takes a great deal of computation to encode and decode, and probably will require special hardware for some time to come.

Color Images

There are many types of formats for storing color images; this section briefly describes only the most common.

PCX and PackBits

PCX and PackBits are the two most common encodings of both grayscale and color images in the PC (PCX) and Macintosh (PackBits) worlds. These encodings provide a first level of image compression and storage that are widely supported in their respective environments. Both PCX and PackBits use RLE coding techniques.

PICT

PICT (Macintosh Picture) is a picture format developed by Apple that encapsulates the QuickDraw functionality. (QuickDraw is Apple's native graphics protocol for the Macintosh.) PICT is used for indexed color pictures that are one to eight bits in depth or for 24-bit direct color pictures. PICT files are structured as a file header followed by the image data. PICT files may contain not only bitmaps, but also any graphics permitted by color QuickDraw. Thus, PICT files may also contain vector-oriented graphics data

The PICT format is recognized on several platforms, but is not widely used outside the Macintosh.

TGA

TGA (Targa Image File) is a picture format developed by Truevision for use with the Targa, Vista, and NuVista graphics card family for both the PC and the Macintosh. The TGA format supports color up to 32 bits deep. Image data may be stored either raw or RLE-encoded. Because the Targa boards were one of the first sources of true-color graphics (graphics of 24 bits or higher), TGA became a widely used format, and it's still a very important one.

BMP

BMP (Microsoft Windows Bitmap) is an image format developed by Microsoft for Windows and by IBM for OS/2. There are several minor differences between these two parallel formats, but in general BMP can be considered to be a device-independent format which contains image file headers and uses a version of RLE compression. BMP files can store images of one to eight bits of color depth using color palettes, or up to 24-bit direct color.

The BMP image format is sufficiently general so that we're now seeing growing use of the format outside the PC family of computers.

GIF

GIF (Graphics Interchange Format) is an image format developed by CompuServe for images with 8-bit or less RGB color and a color lookup table. GIF files may contain more than one image, and each image is structured with an image descriptor header and color lookup table information, followed by the actual raster data. The image data in GIF files are compressed with an LZW scheme.

TIFF

TIFF (Tag Image Format File) is a format for bitmapped images developed by Aldus (now Adobe) that is widely used throughout the graphics world. TIFF may well be the most versatile and complete graphics file format currently in use. A TIFF file can store many images, and each image is stored with a list of tags that describe all the details of the image. TIFF files can store both full color and indexed color images. TIFF supports more kinds of data compression than any other format: RLE (PackBits version), CCITT Group III and Group IV, LZW, and JPEG.

JPEG and JFIF

As we've mentioned, JPEG is really more a file compression technique than it is an image format. However, after JPEG compression has been applied to a file (as described under "Compressing Image Data" above), appropriate headers may be added to identify the file, and the result may be considered to be a file in JPEG format. An example of this situation is JFIF (JPEG File Interchange Format), a file format developed originally by C-Cube Microsystems for storing JPEG images.

While JPEG is essentially a still picture format, it is also utilized by some video systems, including Avid and SuperMac; in these cases each frame is individually compressed. It is also an accepted codec for QuickTime movies.

Proprietary Formats

Besides the widely used image formats we've identified above, there are a number of proprietary file formats and compression techniques for images. These formats and techniques are tied to particular products or systems, and they're frequently very effective. Unfortunately for most of us, their creators have chosen to keep information on them from the public eye.

Digital Video Standards

Compression schemes are particularly important for digital video. A good deal of work is going on in this area in an effort to produce movies that are presented in ever-larger windows with ever-higher image quality. Some hardware features, such as higher-speed CD-ROM players and faster networks, support this work, but they require ever-larger movie files to begin with. As a consequence, the most important research in this area focuses on trying to achieve higher quality without having larger files, and this naturally requires ever-better data compression and decompression schemes. We can expect to see continued progress in this area, particularly as HDTV (High Definition TV) begins to make its presence felt in the television market.

Digital video takes some effort and experience before one can produce high-quality results within limited data transfer rates. In this section, we describe some of the current standards for digital video, but there is much more you need to know about using digital video. For detailed information, consult some of the excellent references in the Bibliography.

QuickTime

QuickTime is Apple Computer's general architecture for time-based computing, and it enables digital videos to be stored and played back on personal computers. QuickTime files can include sound, video, and animation, as well as less obvious data such as that from laboratory instruments or financial sources. These files can contain several different variations:

- Only moving pictures

- Both moving pictures and sound

- Only sound

QuickTime may also be used for synchronizing any time-dependent activities. All such data are called "movies." The spatial resolution and temporal resolution (number of frames per second) are variable, as is the choice of compression algorithm. A key feature of QuickTime technology is that it employs a real-time clock that drives the sequence of sound and frames in the movie.

QuickTime is supported on Macintosh, Windows, Silicon Graphics, and other UNIX systems. To allow a QuickTime movie to be played on a non-Macintosh system, the movie created on the Macintosh must be made self-contained, or "flattened," by moving information from the file's resource fork to its data fork; this capability is provided by most QuickTime tools. The Silicon Graphics version of QuickTime does not support the Cinepak codec, nor does the UNIX movie player, *xanim*, so QuickTime must use another technique such as the Animation codec if it is intended to be used on SGI or other UNIX systems.

A new version of the Apple architecture, QuickTime 2, allows larger frame sizes and higher frame and data rates than standard QuickTime. It also supports MIDI information for music (see the discussion of MIDI under "Sound Standards" below), as well as custom color palettes. If the computer has MPEG hardware, this version can play both embedded MPEG data and standard MPEG files.

The QuickTime toolkit allows you to manipulate movie data through standard display, edit, cut, copy, and paste techniques. QuickTime supports a number of tools to compress and decompress image data, including the use of JPEG for single images and any of several codecs, such as Cinepak, Indeo, and IVI, that have been developed by various companies. These deal with time-varying data and provide both temporal and image compression.

Creating a QuickTime movie is quite straightforward, given the tools that are available. You can capture video with any of a number of video capture boards, manipulate and compress the captured digital video, and integrate it with digital video from other sources. Alternately, you can begin with a sequence of PICT files as the original frames and create video by assembling these files. You can also capture sound, and add it to the movie.

NOTE

There are a few caveats in creating QuickTime movies: be sure that the original data is clean, and be sure that you use appropriate movie sizes and codecs to allow your movie to be played back cleanly and without jumps on the screen.

QuickTime VR

A relatively new variant on QuickTime, the QuickTime VR (Virtual Reality) system, was announced by Apple in late 1994. QuickTime VR is entirely software-based, and runs under QuickTime 2.0 for both Macintosh and Windows. It allows an author to take a series of photographs of an environment and to assemble them into a seamless panorama. Users can view the panorama from any of a number of points in the space, called *nodes*, that can be defined by the author or developer. The system automatically provides perspective correction.

Within a panorama, an author or developer can attach hot spots to allow a user to move to other areas of the title, allowing the user to experience a "home room" or "home world" instead of the more traditional "home page" of most multimedia titles. You can also create "interactive objects," objects that can be manipulated and viewed from any angle by the user. The resulting environment is much richer visually than the standard 3-D graphics modeled environment because it contains all the texture and detail of the original scene.

Video for Windows

Video for Windows is a digital video technology developed by Microsoft. Video for Windows uses the Microsoft AVI (Audio Visual Interleaved) file structure to include both video and audio information in a way that can provide adequate data for both the video and audio processors, as well as MPEG compression for video data. While QuickTime allows a full range of digital audio sampling frequencies, Video for Windows supports only full, half, and quarter rates for the standard 44.1 kHz high-fidelity CD sound; it is not possible to have an audio-only Video for Windows document.

The complete Video for Windows system includes facilities for video capture and compression, as well as for video playback. There are currently video titles on the market in this format which provide as many as 90 minutes of video on a CD-ROM. While Video for Windows was developed for Windows, there are now players for this kind of video for the Macintosh as well, and the system can legitimately be considered a multiplatform video format.

Other Codecs

Video for Windows and QuickTime have come to support much the same set of codecs (e.g., Cinepak and Indeo). In fact, the data streams for Cinepak movies for both QuickTime and Video for Windows are identical.

Among the other codecs available for digital video are Truevision-S from the Duck Corporation and Horizons Technology, and Indeo Video Interactive (IVI). Like Indeo, IVI is from Intel, with Indeo based on vector quantization and IVI based on wavelet technology. Each of these systems has its advocates. Cinepak and Indeo are generally acknowledged to give the best results for the kind of data rates available for CD-ROM. However, IVI offers some additional features, such as the ability to matte moving video onto a background during playback. In addition, its basis in wavelets means that it behaves quite differently under low data transfer rate conditions than do Cinepak or Indeo.

The whole situation with codecs is a rapidly changing one, so watch progress in this area very carefully.

MPEG

MPEG is a movie format developed by (and named for) the Moving Pictures Expert Group, a working group of the ISO. The MPEG standard is a specification for an encoded data stream which contains compressed audio and video information. Its main application is the storage of audio and video data on CD-ROM for use in multimedia systems.

MPEG uses a combination of original frames, predicted frames, and interpolated frames to produce movies without transmitting all of the data that would be needed for the original frames. The basic MPEG scheme operates in several steps.

1. The process starts with video or single frames, converted to YUV color space.

2. The U and V channels are then reduced to half their resolution.

3. Selected frames are chosen as originals (*intra frames*, or *I frames*), and motion detection and prediction algorithms are used to create *predicted frames*, or *P frames*, between the I frames.

4. Between the P frames, additional frames are created by *bidirectional interpolation,* or *B frames*. The sequence of decoded frames looks something like:

```
IBBPBBPBBPBBIBBPBBPBBPBBI...
```

   See Figure 7-2 for an example (but note that the numbers of P frames between I frames and the number of B frames between P frames or I frames may differ between systems and between individual movies). The dependencies between the various kinds of frames are shown in Figure 7-3.

   The processing we've described all occurs on 16 × 16 pixel macroblocks and includes Huffman coding as it goes along.

5. When the file is written, the first P frame must be written before the B frames that precede it so that the decoder can have the first I and P to make sense of the interpolated frames.

All in all, MPEG is a very complex system, but it offers a great deal of functionality and very good movie compression.

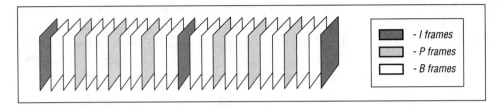

Figure 7-2.   A sequence of frames for an MPEG movie (see the color image in the center insert)

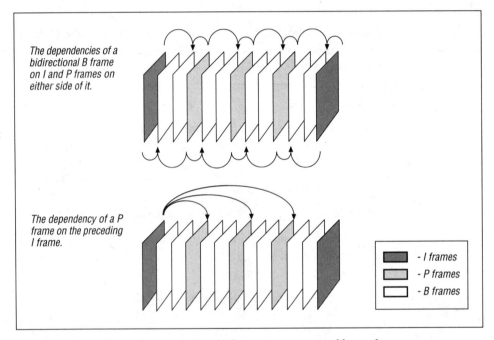

Figure 7-3.   Dependencies between I, P, and B frames in a sequence of frames for an MPEG movie

Like the usual versions of JPEG, MPEG is a lossy format. As a result, the files it compresses take up much less space that they would without compression. A key difference between JPEG and MPEG is that JPEG gives only intraframe compression (all the compression is within each frame), whereas MPEG also uses an interframe compression system (compression spans multiple frames). This distinction is important because moving picture imagery has a lot of redundancy between successive frames, and MPEG eliminates this redundancy. However, the interpolation used in the interframe compression means that it is difficult to make fully general edits in a movie once it has been encoded in MPEG format.

In general, MPEG compression is a non-realtime process, and MPEG decompression must utilize special chips or high-speed processors to get reasonable performance. One of the early questions of multimedia was whether special video hardware chips would be an integral part of every desktop computer or whether some kind of software compression would prevail. After some experience with the field, it now appears that the software approach is leading. In fact, with the current availability of high-performance desktop systems for encoding and playback, MPEG is now becoming a desktop digital video format.

MPEG is still evolving as a standard, and several additional standards are now available:

- The new MPEG-2 international standard adds a transport packet stream and a program stream. It is designed to provide for the multiplex and synchronization of multiple audio, video, and data streams and is intended to support a broad range of applications for broadcast, communications, computing, and storage.

- An MPEG-4 draft to support audio and video at very low bit rates is also underway, and this work is expected to be completed in late 1998.

Future developments in digital video are in process, but seem to be converging on some generally accepted systems, and MPEG is expected to play an important role in the systems of the future. Three examples:

1. QuickTime 2 has been extended to include MPEG data.

2. The Digital Video Disc (DVD) has chosen MPEG-2 as the basis for its digital movies.

3. It's very likely that some variation of MPEG will be adopted for consumer delivery of High Definition Television (HDTV).

Although it seems likely that MPEG will be an important standard for digital video (and may even come to dominate the field), it's also possible that the overall digital video area will probably have some surprises before it is fully settled!

For online information about MPEG, take a look at the FAQ provided on the CD-ROM that accompanies this book. Check out *http://www.powerweb.de/mpeg/mpeg-faq/* for an updated version.

Sound Standards

As electronic documents become, more and more, multimedia documents, sound becomes an increasingly important component of those publications. Sound is obviously an essential part of movie or video document components. It also has important applications for other document components, as we described in the electronic publishing examples earlier in the book.

Although most sound is based on Adaptive Differential Pulse Code Modulation (ADPCM) technology, there have been few efforts to standardize file formats for sound. Thus the sound formats we list below are very specific to particular systems; we list only the formats that seem to have wide usage, but encourage you to consult the references in the Bibliography for additional information.

AIFF

AIFF (Audio Interchange File Format) is a sound format that was developed by Apple for storing high-quality sampled sound and music instrument information. It is used mainly on the Macintosh and on Silicon Graphics (SGI) machines. The AIFF format is able to store sound files at different data rates. An extension of the format, called AIFC or AIFF-C, supports compression.

WAV

WAV (Waveform) is a sound format used as part of the Microsoft RIFF (Resource Interchange File Format) multimedia format. WAV is essentially the Microsoft/IBM equivalent of Apple's AIFF format.

MIDI

MIDI (Musical Instrument Digital Interface) is not an audio format *per se*. Unlike some sound formats, which actually store digitally sampled sounds, MIDI is an industry-standard[*] way to represent sound in binary format. Essentially, a MIDI file stores instructions for MIDI-based sound synthesizers to allow them to generate particular sounds. With MIDI, sound is stored as a series of control messages, each describing a sound event in terms of its pitch, duration, and volume. When messages are sent to a MIDI-compatible device, the information in the messages is interpreted and reproduced by the device.

MIDI is an extremely efficient technique for coding music. MIDI information can be found in many types of multimedia file formats. For example, the QuickTime movie format includes MIDI information to generate music to go with a movie.

MIDI data can be compressed, just as any other type of data can be. MIDI compression does not require any special compression algorithms.

---

[*] The MIDI specification can be obtained from the International MIDI Association (IMA).

QuickTime

QuickTime files, which we described above under "Digital Video Standards," also contain their own audio data structures. There are sound-only QuickTime movies that can be used to provide sound capabilities.

DVD

The DVD (Digital Video Disc) uses a version of five-channel Dolby sound. At the time this book was written, none of the movie formats explicitly include the DVD sound technology. However, we expect that DVD will be added as an option to MPEG-2 movies and that an appropriate digital sound format will be added to support it. (For more information about DVD, see Chapter 8.)

Looking to the Future . . .

Despite, or perhaps because of, the multiplicity of standards for electronic documents, there isn't a single set of standards that really support the kinds of capabilities needed for effective CD-ROM publishing. However, there are many developments currently going on in cross-platform authoring systems, compound document architectures, and component technology for electronic documents. The expanding market for electronic titles, and for broader kinds of communications supported by those titles, are likely to drive these developments.

A New Standard

What type of standard is needed? What capabilities must be supported? Authors must be able to create the various kinds of information that will go into electronic documents, to integrate them, and to add the user interface—all without all the detailed programming-level work that is now needed. What we would really like to see evolve is this:

• Some kind of high-level and full-function standard for multimedia documents

• A wide set of authoring systems that produce documents to this standard

• Delivery systems that present documents that conform to this standard

At present, HTML is probably the primary standard in the Internet world, but it's not yet a standard around which a full-function electronic title could be built; HTML is still too limited to create anything that could compete in the commercial market.

A genuine multimedia standard is much more complicated than any standard we've ever developed before. Why? The standards we've made before are really only two kinds.

- **Packaging standards.** The primary standards in the media world are packaging standards, such as the ASCII standard for text, the QuickTime standard for digital movies, and the PostScript page description standard. Packaging standards allow a document system to say, "Here is a file that meets the standard—now, interpret it."

- **Active standards.** The other type of standard is an active standard, and the only active standards we have today are machine instruction sets. The Intel 386 instruction set is an example of such a standard; the PDP-11 instruction set is also still an active standard. Active standards allow a document system to say, "Here is an instruction set that meets the standard—now, do it."

A true multimedia standard must include *both* packaging standards and active standards; in addition to specifying content, it must specify how an author can provide functionality in a document. Using such a standard, an author should be able to specify buttons, links, notes, and different kinds of media; in addition, a presentation system (or, indeed, a range of different presentation systems) should be able to interpret all of these components in a way that fits the platform being used and that is consistent with the design intended.

Authoring tools should also decouple presentation system from the actual contents of document. Typically, an author will want to have a series of files and use the presentation system to bring them all together. But the author also needs to be able to open up the presentation system in some kind of authoring mode, and edit the documents.

For example, suppose you are working on a scene in your electronic title and you find something wrong with an image in it. You should be able to click on the image and launch Photoshop directly to edit the picture. If you find a misspelling, you should be able to correct it without having to exit the program, open a word processor, open the document on the word processor, correct the spelling mistake, and then return to the authoring tool to continue to develop the title. Several new compound document architectures—for example, Apple's OpenDoc and Microsoft's OLE—do offer such capabilities.

Dynamic, Interactive Simulations

We consider simulations that are dynamic and interactive to be a fundamentally new medium, different from all the other media we've discussed in this book. How can we create platform-independent simulation standards in such a way that these simulations can be integrated into other documents? We believe that the eventual shape of this medium will be based on all of the following:

- Standards for data storage

- Standard ways to present information on the screen

- Standard ways to express interface abstractions

- Standard ways to save a script so the user can save his or her simulation work to share with others or to document an experiment

Some of these standards now exist, and some do not. It may take a while for all of them to emerge, but the full set of standards is likely to have significant benefits on the world of electronic documents.

That's fine for the future, but what about the present? For the time being, the best approach to supporting interactive simulations is probably to launch an external application whose output can be viewed through a screen window separate from the user's own document. This capability is offered through several products, including Acrobat's plug-ins, Gain*Momentum*'s screens, and *Dyna*Book's scripts. This solution presupposes that you have access to the appropriate applications and that you have an appropriately configured system. It is less general, and less powerful, than a genuine interaction standard would be.

Let's look at a couple of examples of current research that might result in the availability of an interaction standard in the future.

Val Watson of the NASA Ames Research Center is currently doing some work that's pointing in the direction of a genuine standard for interactive simulations. His research focuses on educational simulations for K-12 teaching. By giving students and teachers the tools for genuine interactive simulations, Watson hopes to replace preproduced movies of scientific data explorations. Using the Internet and other networks, teachers will be able to download the data for the simulation as well as a set of scripts describing some already-planned explorations. Teachers and students can then perform other explorations and record their work in scripts to be played again at a later time. Watson's work is in the early stages of development, and is now pretty limited; for example, it depends on one particular software system running on one particular platform. Currently, his system illustrates the concepts of interactive simulations and explorations, rather than the principle of a multiplatform standard for this kind of work. But his research is clearly a step in the right direction for both educational work and general electronic documents.

The VRML standard provides another example of work towards a true interaction standard. As we mentioned earlier in this chapter, VRML is designed to support interaction with three-dimensional data and images across networks. As VRML evolves, it is likely to provide an important tool for simulation.

Although the VRML work shows great promise, it's an all-in-one standard, which incorporates capabilities for both graphics and network interaction in an intermixed way. We would prefer to see a set of layered standards that addressed these two types of capabilities separately—network interaction at one level, and complex graphics issues at a higher level. In the future, as VRML evolves, it should provide an important tool for simulation.

8

CD-ROM Disc Standards

Since compact discs were first introduced in 1980, the CD-ROM industry has grown at a rapid pace. One of the major reasons that CD-ROMs have so quickly become a low-cost and reliable vehicle for information exchange is the existence of stable standards and formats. CD-ROM standards define the format in which discs are written and organized, and determine the kinds of information that can be included on a disc of a particular format. This chapter describes the main standards and formats of interest to most CD-ROM authors and publishers. It discusses in some detail the major formats—ISO 9660 and HFS—in which most CD-ROMs are written today. It also describes a new technology, the DVD (Digital Video Disc), which is expected to eventually replace today's CD-ROMs.

Standards Summary

Table 8-1 summarizes the types of CD-ROM formats and standards you'll hear about. The many-hued books mentioned here are standards documents developed by the CD industry. Some have gained the status of International Standards Organization (ISO) documents. We don't describe the details of these books in this chapter (the details aren't usually relevant to CD-ROM users and even publishers), but if you are interested in these standards, you can obtain them from:

> American National Standards Institute
> 1430 Broadway
> New York, NY 10018
> 212-642-4900

Several technical papers from Disc Manufacturing, Inc. (DMI) also provide general information on disc standards and offer a deeper view of CD-ROM technology (particularly the ISO 9660 standard) than this book can provide; in particular, see the technical report, *Compact Disc Terminology*, referenced in the Bibliography.

Table 8-1.   CD-ROM formats and standards

Book	Contents	Year
Red Book	CD-DA. Compact Disc-Digital Audio. The standard used for encoding audio data (e.g., music) onto a compact disc.	1980
Yellow Book	CD-ROM. Compact Disc Read-Only Memory. A compact disc format used for computer data storage and able to hold text, graphics, and stereo sound. The disc is built on the same technology as music CDs, but uses different tracks for data.	1984
Yellow Book, CD-XA extension	CD-XA. Compact Disc-Extended Architecture. A standard that allows sound to be played while viewing data.	1989
Green Book	CD-I. Compact Disc Interactive. A compact disc format in which computer data and compressed video are interleaved on the same track. CD-I discs must be mastered on special proprietary systems.	1990
Orange Book	CD-WO. Compact Disc Write-Once (equivalent to CD-R). A CD-ROM version of the WORM (Write-Once Read-Many) technology which can be mastered on a personal computer.	1990
White Book	CD Video. A disc format, also known as karaoke CD, that allows a combination of audio and full-motion video. It uses interleaved MPEG video and audio sectors to maximize the amount of information that can be stored on the disc.	1993
Blue Book	DVD. Digital Video Disc. A standard for a larger capacity disc.	1996

CD-ROM Layout

Compact discs are written with one single spiral track of pits and lands and are read with constant linear velocity. That is, the disc spins at a higher speed when the track is read on the inner part of the disc than it does when the track is read on the outer part of the disc; the density of the pits along the track remains constant. Each sector along the track is 1/75 second long and contains a total of 2352 bytes of data.[*] For the primary type of CD-ROM disc, Mode 1, this sector has the following:[†]

---

* Defined by the Red Book standard.
† Defined by the Yellow Book standard.

12 bytes of sync
4 bytes of header
2048 bytes of data
4 bytes of EDC
8 bytes of blank
276 bytes of ECC

This sector layout is shown in Figure 8-1. In addition, each sector contains 98 bytes of control information that contains several subcodes (although subcodes seem to be little used for standard CD-ROMs).

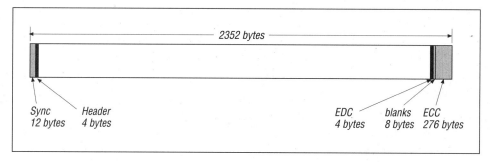

Figure 8-1.   Layout of a CD-ROM Mode I disc sector

Since CD-ROMs were first introduced as a technology, transfer rates for data from CD-ROMs have grown from the 150kb/sec of the original discs to four or more times that rate, and some disc players are claiming up to eight times the original rate. Rates of 600kb/sec to 1000kb/sec are about the best we can achieve from the current technology, however, because of limitations in the speed and balance that are feasible for the physical discs.

NOTE

For some projects, primarily those involving a great deal of digital video, the needs of true multimedia titles far exceed the storage capacity that current CD-ROMs provide. Recent work on both larger capacity discs and higher speed data transfer has led to the Digital Video Disc (DVD), announced in late 1995 and beginning production in 1996. We describe these discs at the end of this chapter, as well as the emerging ISO 13490 file system standard which will support them. Most people in the industry believe that, once players are available for the new DVD technology, the 13490 standard will probably become the standard for traditional CD-ROMs as well.

ISO 9660 Standard

ISO 9660 (sometimes called simply "9660" in this book) is the standard file system specification implemented on CD-ROMs. This specification was designed to be independent of any particular operating system. Thus, a disc formatted to the 9660 specification can be read on any system that supports 9660, including PC (DOS/Windows), Macintosh, and UNIX systems. Of all of the CD-ROM formats, 9660 is the most interoperable across platforms. You do pay a price for this interoperability, of course: a 9660 disc is the lowest common denominator for CD-ROM file systems, and may not have some functionality that you might wish to have.

If you have a PC running DOS and you want to allow access to a 9660 CD-ROM, your PC needs to run Microsoft Extensions (MSCDEX.EXE). The Macintosh and most UNIX systems have special extensions built into their operating systems that allow them to access a 9660 disc.

ISO 9660 has three interchange levels; level 1 is the most strict. Interchange level 1 is recommended for use with discs that are intended to be used on MS-DOS PCs because of limitations in the DOS file naming conventions. The following sections describe the restrictions on ISO 9660 interchange level 1 CD-ROMs.

File and Directory Names

There are a number of restrictions on the characters that may be used in file and directory names, and a number of issues arising from the ways that various platforms and applications deal with these names.

Valid names

File names and directory names on a CD-ROM must use only the characters A to Z (capitals only), the digits 0 to 9, and the underscore character '_'; these are called the *d-characters* in the ISO 9660 standard. You must also use the *8.3 format*—that is, file names must not exceed eight characters, and extensions must not exceed three characters. The file name and extension name must be separated by a period (i.e., the valid format is FFFFFFFF.EEE).

The following are all valid 8.3 names:

    DOCUMENT.NEW
    DOC.NEW
    DOCUMENT.
    DOCUMENT.1

Directory names must have no more than eight characters, and no extensions are allowed (i.e., the valid format is DDDDDDDD).

File name extensions

The extension on file names can be a source of difficulty with the ISO 9660 standard. Authoring systems and operating systems differ in how they enforce restrictions on extensions:

- Some systems allow you to create 9660 discs in which files have no extension; other systems do not.

- Some systems that allow file names without extensions still require that the file name terminate with a period (.); other systems do not. For example, on some UNIX systems, such as the RS/6000 running AIX, the period must be included even if an extension is not specified.

- Some operating systems' 9660 device drivers overlook a missing extension; other systems do not.

The only truly safe approach seems to be to include the extension on *all* file names.

Version numbers

The standard ISO 9660 file naming convention adds a semicolon separator ";" and version number (e.g., "1") to each file name on the CD-ROM. Certain mastering software and platforms are more forgiving than others in enforcing this standard. This inconsistency can lead to problems in interpreting file names later on, especially when CD-ROMs are used on multiple platforms.

For example, suppose that you have a file on your PC named FILE.EXT. When you write that file to a 9660 CD-ROM, the file now appears with the name FILE.EXT;1 on the CD-ROM. However, when you view that CD-ROM on a PC running DOS or Windows, Microsoft Extensions strips off the version information, so your file name appears again as FILE.EXT. Programs needing to use the file will recognize it under the original name, FILE.EXT.

Things don't work quite as smoothly on the Macintosh and on many UNIX systems. On these platforms, the 9660 convention effectively changes the name of the file. When you view the same CD-ROM on those platforms, you will see the version information as an intrinsic part of the file name (for example, FILE.EXT;1). Programs needing to use the file will have to recognize the file name with its version information. If your program looks for the file named FILE.EXT, it won't be able to find it.

Many applications—for example, hypermedia systems—require exact file names to be placed in the source files for electronic documents. You will find it very frustrating to carefully create 9660-compatible names and then have different systems change those names in different, and seemingly unpredictable, ways. What can you do about this problem? There are several approaches.

First, many disc mastering systems allow you to suppress file version numbers so you can make 9660 CD-ROMs without the ";1". In general, we recommend that you look for this feature in a mastering system and take advantage of this feature when you master discs. (Chapter 4, *Developing a CD-ROM*, shows an example.)

Second, if your system cannot suppress version numbers and you are able to target your application for a particular system, look carefully at how that system handles 9660 names and use that exact version of names in your application.

Third, if your application will work across different systems, you will have to keep the ";1" suffix in mind when you create a 9660 disc for in the Macintosh or UNIX world. One programming technique, which is awkward but effective, is to first try to open the file without the version number and, if that fails, try to open the file with the version number. For example, the following C code will open the file MYFILE.DAT no matter which version of the file name translation and version-number handling is used:

```
if ( !fd = open("MYFILE.DAT;1",O-RDONLY)
if ( !fd = open("MYFILE.DAT",O-RDONLY)
      if ( !fd = open("myfile.dat;1",O-RDONLY)
          if ( !fd = open("myfile.dat",O-RDONLY)
              OpenError();
```

Unfortunately, the latter approach is not always possible to implement. It poses a significant problem if you want to put HTML documents on a 9660 CD-ROM. Why? As far as we have been able to determine, it's not possible to create HTML links that can make a "second try" if the first link name fails. This would be the case if you searched for a name *with* a version number on a DOS system (since DOS strips off the version number before viewing it) or if you searched for a name *without* a version number on the Macintosh (since the Mac preserves the version number).

Your best overall approach for multiplatform CD-ROMs is probably to use only a disc mastering system that will allow you to suppress 9660 version numbers. If you are developing a CD-ROM only for the Macintosh (which always shows version numbers for 9660 discs if they are present), you can avoid the problem by including an HFS directory on the disc. (We describe this approach later, in the discussion of "Hybrid Types of CD-ROMs.")

Upper- vs. lowercase

Case conversion is another interesting side effect of different implementations of the 9660 file system. Some systems automatically downshift all the d-characters (A-Z, 0-9, and _), converting all uppercase letters into lowercase, and some systems do not. As with the version number, case conversion effectively changes the name of the file. Such a change will affect any program that needs to refer to the file.

Figure 8-2 shows the various names a file may have, depending upon how a particular disc mastering system handles version number and case conversion.

	Using version identifier	Omitting version identifier
Does not downshift name	**MYFILE.DAT;1**	**MYFILE.DAT**
Does downshift name	**myfile.dat;1**	**myfile.dat**

Figure 8-2.   File names produced by different 9660 implementations

File name sorting problems

In some cases, you may be able to get away with specifying illegal characters in file names (e.g., lowercase letters or nonalphanumerics, such as z, a, b, !, #, $, etc.). Certain software and platforms are more forgiving than others. But don't take advantage of such a situation. These illegal names will cause sorting problems later on your CD-ROM. When a sorting problem occurs, you will be able to see all of the files on your CD-ROM directory, but when you try to access some of them, the system will display the message, "file not found."

Directory Depth

The depth of the directory structure must not exceed eight levels. This often presents a problem for the CD-ROM designer, because many electronic titles, particularly those with lots of content, end up having individual files organized into very deep directories.

Unfortunately, there doesn't seem to be any way around this restriction; if you are using the ISO 9660 standard, you will have to restructure your files so they have no more than eight levels of directories.

Volume Labels

Volume labels or disc identifiers may contain as many as 32 characters, but only 11 characters are displayed in the DOS environment. The volume label is optional; you can ask the CD-ROM manufacturer to include one for you if you wish. (The volume identifier is displayed when a MS-DOS PC directory command is performed on a 9660 disc; it also shows up as the name of the generic CD-ROM icon on a disc mounted on a Macintosh.)

Number of Files

In general, it's not a good idea to put more than approximately 200 files per directory on a 9660 CD-ROM. Having too many files per directory can degrade disc performance.

To improve performance, you might consider putting files that are accessed continually or frequently at the beginning (inner) part of the CD-ROM.

Resource Forks

Another issue arises when files from the Macintosh are written onto a CD-ROM for use on other platforms. On the Macintosh, every file has two components: a data fork and a resource fork. When you process a Macintosh file on a Macintosh, there is, of course, no problem; the device driver expects to see a resource fork. But how do other platforms (or, more properly, these platforms' implementations of the 9660 device drivers) handle resource forks when they encounter them on a CD-ROM?

Most systems, such as those for DOS and Windows, and some versions of UNIX, correctly ignore the resource fork and simply use the data fork for the file. However, in the original BSD 4.2 version of UNIX and in other UNIX systems derived from it, the CD-ROM device driver ignores the data fork of a file and only provides the resource fork to a program. This isn't very helpful, because the resource fork typically does not hold the data that would be of use to non-Macintosh systems. As a consequence, such systems cannot use any file that contains a resource fork.

This situation basically means that you can't put fully-functional Macintosh files in the shared file area of a dual-directory disc. (We'll describe dual-directory discs later in this chapter.) Instead, you'll need to remove the resource fork for the version of the file being used for the 9660 file system. In addition, if you need to have full Macintosh capabilities for the file, you'll need to have a second copy of the file in the HFS directory with the resource fork intact.

Rock Ridge Interchange Protocol

The 9660 file format does not maintain the basic look and feel of the UNIX file system. The Rock Ridge Interchange Protocol was developed to help address this issue. This file system was designed to allow UNIX-like systems to retain much of the directory information in the native file system and thus maintain compatibility with the POSIX file system standards.

Compatibility with standard UNIX/POSIX is important because UNIX systems use directory entries for much more than just pointing to files. Directory entries can point to other entries (symbolic links) or to device drivers that are linked to peripheral devices such as hard disks, tape drives, and CD-ROM drives (device files). The entries also contain file permission information. The Rock Ridge Interchange Protocol retains these features. Of course, Rock Ridge discs also do not have the version number and character case problems with file names that we discussed for ISO 9660-standard CD-ROMs above. At present, there does not seem to be much use of the Rock Ridge standard outside the UNIX world.

Macintosh Hierarchical File System (HFS)

The Macintosh file system is known as the Hierarchical File System (HFS). Most CD-ROM mastering systems allow you to create a CD-ROM in either ISO 9660 or HFS format. (Some offer additional choices, which we'll describe later in this chapter).

If you are developing a CD-ROM application that is going to be used only on the Macintosh, we recommend that you create an HFS CD-ROM. Doing so will allow you to create the typical Macintosh desktop look and feel on your CD-ROM, including the ability to launch an application or file by double-clicking. With an HFS disc, all of the icons and window layouts will show up on your disc just as they appeared on the disk from which your CD-ROM was created.

By contrast, if you create a 9660 CD-ROM and read it on a Macintosh, all you will see are generic folders and files, with names under them. Because the CD-ROM does not have a desktop database, generic folders and icons are placed on the desktop by the system. You have little control over how the icons are presented in the window.

Although you may be unhappy with the look and feel of the desktop displayed by a 9660 CD-ROM on the Macintosh, the Mac nevertheless will be able to read the CD-ROM correctly. You'll have to use the 9660 format unless your application calls for a Mac-only CD-ROM or unless you are able to create a hybrid (or dual-directory) disc, as we'll describe later in this chapter.

Displaying a CD-ROM Icon

In general, when you mount a 9660 CD-ROM on the Macintosh, a generic CD-ROM icon will appear on the desktop. But there is a way that you can control the appearance of this icon. If you want a special icon to appear in place of the generic one, you can supply this icon to your CD manufacturer. When you send your product to the manufacturer, simply provide the icon with the disc image, as part of your backup media, or on a separate floppy. The name you give your CD-ROM can be any standard Macintosh name, containing up to 27 characters, with no limitations on the characters you choose.

System 6 vs. System 7

If you know that your CD-ROM is going to be used on both Macintosh System 6 and Macintosh System 7, be sure that the CD manufacturer includes both the System 6 and System 7 desktop databases on your CD-ROM. If you do not, your CD-ROM will not be able to be used on a Mac running the older System 6.

Desktop and Window Layout

When you send your data to the CD manufacturer, be sure that you arrange all of your folders, icons, windows, and files exactly the way you them to appear on the CD ROM. The exact layout is not important on a 9660 CD ROM, but it is very important on an HFS CD-ROM because this layout determines the desktop database that controls what the user sees when he opens the CD-ROM. (This is the case because the desktop database is saved to the disc.)

When you consider your layout, remember to look carefully at the location and sizes of all the windows that will ever appear on the desktop. If you don't, windows will open at random locations and their contents will be displayed randomly—neither of which instills confidence in your customers.

The usual procedure in building a CD-ROM is to have all of your windows open at the upper left-hand corner of the screen and to keep them modest in size, so none of the windows will disappear if the CD-ROM is used on a Macintosh with a small screen. It's also a good idea to offset each additional window by a tiny amount (perhaps one-eighth of an inch) when you cascade deeper into a hierarchy of displays. This way, as you open successive windows, you will continue to see a small portion of the previously opened window at the upper left corner.

NOTE

On a Windows disc, you have to create the *setup.ini* file to handle icons, window locations, and installation management. Tools such as Install Shield can help with this process.

Hybrid Types of CD-ROMs

Suppose you need to create a CD-ROM that's going to be used on both a PC and a Macintosh. If you create the CD-ROM in ISO 9660 format, you'll be able to use it both under DOS/Windows and on the Mac; however, as we've mentioned, on the Mac you won't have the familiar look and feel that would be available with an

HFS disc. Unfortunately, you can't create an HFS disc, or it won't be usable on the PC—or can you?

Actually, there is a way to get the best of both worlds, as we describe in the following sections.

Original Hybrid CD-ROMs

Many mastering systems allow you to build a *hybrid CD-ROM*—one that contains both 9660 and HFS images on the same disc. Hybrid discs have two distinct sets of components:

- An Apple partition map for the HFS file system, the HFS disc directory, and the associated HFS image

- A 9660 disc directory and the associated 9660 image

You place the Apple partition map in the first sector of the disc; this works because the 9660 disc image doesn't begin until sector 16 on the CD-ROM. The Apple partition map specifies the address of the HFS disc directory, which in turn indicates the first sector of the HFS image—the image that begins after the 9660 image ends. Figure 8-3 illustrates this layout.

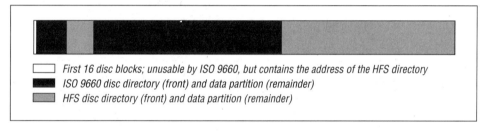

First 16 disc blocks; unusable by ISO 9660, but contains the address of the HFS directory
ISO 9660 disc directory (front) and data partition (remainder)
HFS disc directory (front) and data partition (remainder)

Figure 8-3.   Sample layout of original hybrid CD-ROM

When you put a hybrid CD-ROM into a Macintosh, it reads the first sector on the disc, finds the Apple partition map, and then goes directly to the HFS image, completely skipping over the 9660 image. On the other hand, when you put this CD-ROM into a DOS PC, the CD-ROM drive doesn't start reading until sector 16; because it skips over the Apple partition map, the system sees only the 9660 image.

The original kind of hybrid CD-ROM we've described here separates the Macintosh files from the 9660 files, so each of the HFS and 9660 directories give access to a distinct set of files. If a file is to be used by both systems, it must be included twice on the CD-ROM. The effect of this hybrid design is that each of the HFS and 9660 images can only be as large as *half* the maximum size of the CD-ROM. (On most hybrid discs, HFS and 9660 images end up being about the same size, which may cause problems if you have a substantial amount of content.)

Dual-Directory CD-ROMs

A newer type of hybrid CD-ROM has been developed to get around the space limitation of the traditional hybrid discs. With dual-directory CD-ROMs, you can indicate that certain files on the disc are common to both the 9660 and the HFS images. You do this by allowing both directories to indicate the same files. A dual-directory CD-ROM effectively allows each individual image (9660 and HFS) to be much larger than on the traditional hybrid disc. The available space for data is decreased only by the amount of the extra directory—about 15 megabytes. Figure 8-4 illustrates this layout.

Every file need not be shared. A dual-directory disc may still have individual partitions for 9660-only and HFS-only files. This is necessary because an individual file may not be appropriate on both partitions. Most disc mastering systems allow you to specify that a file is to appear in only one of the HFS or 9660 sides. (The SIGGRAPH conference proceedings CD-ROM we described in Chapter 3, *Two Electronic Titles*, is an example of such a dual-directory disc.)

Producing a dual-directory CD-ROM is not altogether straightforward, and may introduce some subtleties into your file structure. Following are some things you need to watch out for.

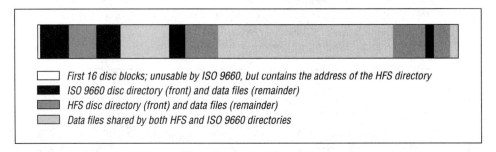

Figure 8-4.   Sample layout of dual-directory CD-ROM

Keep files in proper directories

If some files are intended for use only in the HFS partition on the disc, or only in the 9660 partition, be sure to include those files only in the directory for that partition.

Resource forks

If files are to be shared, be sure that they are readable by applications on both Macintosh and non-Macintosh systems. The main complication in this area is with the resource fork that is part of many Macintosh files. To ensure complete compatibility, you must remove this resource fork from any file that came from Macintosh sources. The resulting files will probably not have custom icons and may not support a standard double-click launch, but this is the price you must pay for the ability to share the file between the two directories.

Remember that a QuickTime movie created on a Macintosh system will have data in its resource fork. It must have this data moved to the data fork (i.e., be "flattened") before the resource fork is removed.

End-of-line characters

The PC, the Macintosh, and UNIX systems all handle end-of-line in a slightly different way:

- The PC terminates each line with both a carriage return and a line feed

- The Macintosh terminates each line with a carriage return

- UNIX systems terminate each line with a line feed

If text files, such as READ_ME files for the CD-ROM, are being shared by all of the platforms, you must take these rules into account. Often, developers include different versions of these files; for example, on the conference proceedings CD-ROM described in Chapter 4, we have three READ-ME files (one for each platform, with different extensions) every place that one is needed. Another approach is to include a browser, editor, or script on the CD-ROM that performs the necessary translation of lines.

Mixed-Mode CD-ROMs (Data and Audio)

Mixed-mode CD-ROMs contain a mixture of data and audio. Such CD-ROMS offer the benefit that the computer can be running the program and accessing the audio at what appears to be the same time. .

On mixed-mode CD-ROMs, computer-readable data resides in track 1 of the disc; audio (of the CD quality specified in the Red Book) resides in track 2 and may continue through track 99 if desired. The first track can contain any type of CD image (9660, HFS, hybrid, etc.).

Accessing audio on a mixed-mode CD-ROM

There are several different ways in which a computer program can access the audio portion of a mixed-mode CD-ROM:

1. The program could access the audio by instructing the drive to play track 2. This is one of the simpler ways to access audio on a CD-ROM.

2. The program could access the audio using the absolute time of the disc. For example, you might start playing at 20:34:45 (a given sector). There is a drawback to this method: If the starting times of the tracks are changed (for example, because of an increase to the data track), you will need to go back and reprogram your application to start at the proper point.

3. The program could access the audio using the relative timing of tracks. For example, the program might go to track 2, and then start playing at so many seconds (or sectors) in from the beginning of the track. This method is one of the better ways to access the audio portion of the CD-ROM because, even if the starting times of the tracks are changed, those changes do not affect your application.

When your disc programming needs to access audio, you must allow for some additional offset, or pause, before each audio section begins. When told to go play audio, most CD-ROM drives are only accurate to within about five sectors of the starting point they are instructed to use. Therefore, if you are programming down to the exact sector in your application you might experience some cutoff if you do not allow for so many sectors of pause or silence before your audio selection begins. (We don't recommend that you program to such a tight tolerance.)

For additional information about mixed-mode CD-ROMs, see the paper "Integrating Mixed-Mode CD-ROM," referenced in the Bibliography and available on the CD-ROM.

Other approaches

Another way to work with mixed audio and video is to use the White Book CD-ROM standard. This standard uses MPEG video and audio sectors, interleaved so that both the audio and video MPEG decoders can get information at proper rates to decode with neither starvation nor overflow conditions. For additional information, consult the White Book, referenced in the Bibliography.

There are also a number of proprietary approaches to mixing data and audio on a single CD-ROM. In general, they are much more specialized than the methods we've discussed, and as a result are beyond the scope of this book.

If you need to mix audio and data, we suggest that you contact a CD-ROM manufacturer for more information and for specific references.

Digital Video Discs (DVDs)

The Digital Video Disc (DVD) is a new format created from at least two competing laboratory developments in the early 1990s. This format is expected to be very important to the future of digital video.[*] We anticipate that we'll be seeing a full spectrum of DVD capabilities, just as we have for CD-ROM. This section looks briefly at the new DVD format.

NOTE

DVD-ROM is the data equivalent of the DVD video disc. *DVD-R* is the writable version of the DVD disc; that version is expected to have a smaller capability than molded discs.

Physical Characteristics

The DVD standard allows for four different configurations, providing four different disc capacities. The configurations are based on single or double layers on a side, and either single or double-sided discs:

- The single-layer, single-sided disc is very much like the current CD-ROM, but it achieves 4.7 GB capacity (about eight times the capacity of a CD-ROM) by using higher pit densities on the disc.

- The double-layer disc uses a semi-transmissive reflection coating on the outside layer, with a fully reflective coating on the inside layer. (See Chapter 9, *Manufacturing CD-ROMs*, for details on the reflection coating on a disc.) This configuration achieves a capacity of 8.5 GB. The double-layer disc is read by using a laser that can switch between reading the two layers, taking advantage of the fact that the two layers will have reflections at two different positions.

- The double-sided, double-layer disc will have a capacity of 17 GB, which seems enormous to us now.

With some retooling, CD manufacturers are able to manufacture DVD discs. The manufacturing cost for DVD discs are likely to settle into something in line with current manufacturing costs (taking into account the extra work of multiple layers and lamination).

---

[*] Steven Spielberg has been quoted as saying that CD-ROM is the future of the moving image; it seems clear that he's referring to DVD video.

Use for Video

When the DVD standard is used for pure video (for example, as a distribution medium for movies or broadcast television), the new discs will use MPEG-2 video encoding and Dolby Surround Sound. These technologies will provide more than two hours of video on the single-sided, single-layer disc. As a bonus, the user will be able to get multiple language tracks, multiple subtitle tracks, closed captioning, and the usual stop- and slow-motion, reverse, and search/scan options.

Use for Multimedia

When the DVD standard is used for digital data and multimedia, the new discs will allow authors to use whatever type, size, and rate of media they feel necessary, up to the standard data transfer rate of about 11 MB per second. DVD recorders and blank media are expected to be on the market fairly soon (at least for the single-layer, single-sided version), but it's not clear when the technology's prices will drop to desktop levels.

Before you become too entranced by DVD opportunities, remember the implications of larger capacity. Content has costs for licensing and development, and increasing the content by a factor of eight (or more) is likely to lead to significantly increased costs in developing electronic titles. We also question the penetration rates that some developers have projected for DVD-capable players. Real market penetration may only start to happen around the year 2000, because of the time needed for prototyping and development. We anticipate that DVD will be a fully viable market about four to five years after that date.

ISO 13490 Standard

We noted earlier in this chapter some of the inadequacies of the 9660 CD-ROM standard. These inadequacies became critical when the new DVD disc was first introduced. In response, a new standard from the ISO, known as the 13490 standard, has emerged.

We expect that the ISO 13490 standard will eventually replace the 9660 CD-ROM standard. This new standard allows such features (missing from 9660) as long file names, POSIX attributes, Unicode conventions for file names in non-Roman characters, and CD-WO and multisession discs.

III

CD-ROM Manufacturing, Marketing, and Distribution

This part of the book contains the following:

- Chapter 9, *Manufacturing CD-ROMs*, describes the process of manufacturing CD-ROMs, including production timelines, preparing data for manufacturing, and all of the production steps.

- Chapter 10, *CD-ROM Publishing Costs*, provides concrete examples of CD-ROM publishing projects and the costs of developing, licensing, producing, testing, printing, mastering, manufacturing, shipping, and marketing.

- Chapter 11, *CD-ROM Marketing and Distribution*, provides an overview of approaches to marketing titles to various audiences, and different distribution models for CD-ROMs.

9

Manufacturing CD-ROMs

Once you've finished developing the content for your CD-ROM, and have fully tested both your data and applications, you're ready to send the data to your CD-ROM manufacturing plant. The manufacturing process includes several main processes, primarily mastering and replication. *Mastering* refers to the recording of a glass master and the eventual creation of a metal stamper used to replicate your discs. *Replication* refers to the steps of manufacturing and packaging the discs for distribution to your customers.

This chapter[*] provides an overview of the mechanics of CD-ROM production. It discusses the need for an overall project timeline, includes details of many aspects of CD-ROM production (e.g., mastering, replicating, packing, labeling, and ship-ping), and describes a variety of options available to you during this process. Some CD-ROM authors are interested in understanding the mechanics of the CD-ROM manufacturing process. Others may be interested only in the content of the CD-ROM, not in the manufacturing. If you are in this second category, you may feel you don't need to read this chapter. We recommend that you do so, however, because it contains valuable information on how to get your data to the CD-ROM manufacturer and how to prepare the printed pieces that must accom-pany your disc.

NOTE

You may wonder how the emerging Digital Video Discs (DVDs) relate to the discussion in this chapter. DVDs are expected to use almost identical procedures for sending data to the manufacturer, for mastering, and for manufacturing the individual discs. For some time, it will be more difficult for developers to produce write-once masters, because DVD-density disc writers will initially be quite expensive; we expect that disc images will probably be put on tape. We also expect there to be some differences in

---

[*]Many thanks to Steve Langer and Breck Rowell of Disc Manufacturing, Inc., for providing much of the original material for this chapter.

metallizing the outer discs for laminated products, because this metallization will need to have half-silvered properties. There will also be laminat-
ing steps in manufacturing, but this should not present a problem
because disc manufacturers are already preparing for these discs.

CD-ROM Production

This section describes a number of general issues regarding CD-ROM production
scheduling and staffing.

Timelines

The overall process of producing a CD-ROM breaks down into a number of
distinct steps. Table 9-1 lists these steps, in last-to-first order, and provides estimated times for each; the result is a timeline for producing a complete disc title
(one that has already been developed).

There are some variations in the time required for some of the steps shown in the
table, and there are tradeoffs. A good example of such a tradeoff is the disc turnaround time at the duplication facility—usually, you can pay more to get quicker
turnaround, as we discuss in Chapter 10, *CD-ROM Publishing Costs*.

The "Due Date" around which we constructed Table 9-1 is the date at which you
need the disc delivered to your facility; the "Weeks From Due Date" is the date
when a specified activity must start in order for you to be able to deliver the
completed disc on time. Some of the activities, such as testing time and document
preparation time, are based on relatively straightforward technical publication
projects, and may not exactly fit your own projects. However, the discussions of
various parts of title development earlier in the book should help you know how
much time to allocate for your own tasks.

Table 9-1.   Estimated CD-ROM production schedule

Activity	Time Required	Weeks From Due Date
Ship discs from duplication	1 week	1 week
Master and duplicate discs	1-2 weeks	2-3 weeks
Print disc inserts	1-2 weeks	3-5 weeks
Test premastered discs	2 weeks	4-5 weeks
Assemble documents for disc	3 weeks or more	7-8 weeks or more

CD-ROM manufacturers can provide you with their own checklists for disc production, and you should obtain one from your own manufacturer early in the process; you'll find that most of these checklists look a good deal like the one we've provided.

Liaison

Most CD-ROM manufacturers prefer that you designate one person to act as project manager, or liaison, for disc production. This person will be the contact point for your disc development and duplication contractor, and will deal with tasks such as these:

- Providing the disc inserts and disc labels to the manufacturer

- Getting the input data to the duplicator (fully tested and in plenty of time)

- Dealing with any logistics, such as paperwork, scheduling your time for duplication, arranging credit or payment, and arranging for shipping the finished discs to you

The "Turn"

As we describe later in this chapter, there are a number of steps involved in creating the disc image, making the disc stampers, and actually pressing the discs. Because it takes extra effort to perform such steps on a rush basis, most manufacturers charge somewhat more for a rush job than for one that can be scheduled as part of their normal work.

The term for the amount of time allowed for the job is the *turn* on the project; the turn is measured in working days, and throughout this book we generally assume a relatively leisurely 10-day turn. Thus, a CD-ROM with a 10-day turn is shipped from the manufacturer two weeks from the day the master gets to the manufacturer. The turn on a project can be less than 10 days, of course, but the shorter the turn, the higher the cost.

The turn isn't the only scheduling factor. It's not always possible to schedule a disc at your convenience. At peak times, the manufacturer may be booked fully and may not be able to schedule a disc at all—no matter what the turn. For example, in the fall, when discs intended for Christmas sales are being manufactured, most manufacturers' schedules are completely full. Be sure to give your manufacturer all the notice you can so that you can get a place in their production schedule.

Sending Data to the Manufacturer

In this section, we assume that you have created your disc contents and have tested them for correctness and functionality. At this point in the process, you will usually have a hard drive with data from your DOS/Windows, Macintosh, and/or UNIX system on it.

What happens next depends on whether you have access to CD-ROM premastering software.

If You Have Premastering Software . . .

If you have access to premastering software, along with a tape drive or a CD recorder, you can generate your own CD image that can be sent directly to the CD-ROM manufacturing plant for replication. Preparing your own premastered disc is the safest way to send data to a CD-ROM manufacturing plant, and we highly recommend it. There are two reasons:

- **Assurance**. Having a CD recorder gives you the security of being able to test your application on your own disc before replicating hundreds or thousands more of them.

- **Economy**. The CD plant can master directly from the CD-R you send them. This saves you the manufacturer's charges for generating a disc image or CD-R for you.

Premastering has become fairly straightforward, thanks to the availability of software tools that do most of the work for you. These tools allow you to specify:

- What files are to go onto the disc

- How these files are to be organized into directories

- Whether these files are to be visible to the user

- If you are creating a hybrid disc (described in Chapter 8, *CD-ROM Disc Standards*), which file systems are to include each of the files

The tools then create a disc image that can be written to CD-R or other media for testing and for delivery to your manufacturer.

An example of premastering

This section contains a brief example of the premastering process. Here, we demonstrate how you specify the contents of a CD-ROM—in this case, the SIGGRAPH conference proceedings we described in Chapter 3, *Two Electronic Titles*—using the disc mastering software from Gutenberg Systems bundled with the JVC Personal ROMmaker.

Figure 9-1 shows a portion of the list of files to be included in the SIGGRAPH 94 conference proceedings disc. These specify different directories and, in some cases, that the file or directory is to be placed in either the HFS or the ISO 9660 file system.

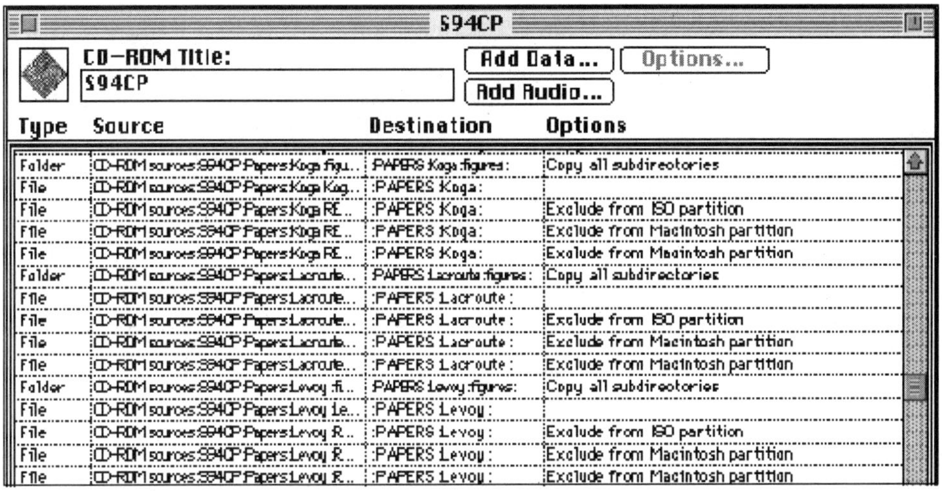

Figure 9-1.   File specification for creating a disc image

Figure 9-2 shows how you make choices from the system's dialog box, which also offers the option of making the file invisible. You might do this to protect some of the contents of your CD-ROM from being copied to a user's own system. If you make a file invisible, it's much more difficult for a user to recognize what's on the disc and copy it.

The dialog box also allows us to remove the ISO version number, which in this example we do on all files. (Chapter 8 explains why you usually want to remove this number.)

Once the files have all been specified, you can create a disc image, and then mount and execute the disc image as if it were an actual disc. Doing so allows you to test performance and general disc characteristics before creating the actual CD-R disc. The dialog box shown in Figure 9-3 gives some idea of how long the premastering operation will take on a single-speed disc writer; writing a CD-R disc takes equally long.

In fact, all testing can be done from the image, though it is more convenient to work from a CD-R disc. Once the image is finally created, it can be written to 8mm tape, DAT, or a CD-R disc to undergo additional testing and, eventually, to be sent to the manufacturer.

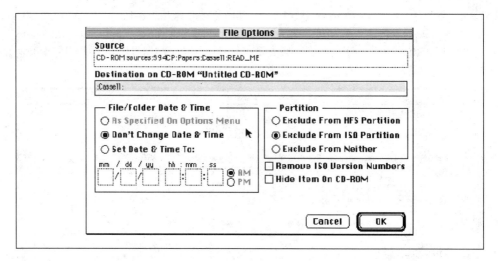

Figure 9-2.   Dialog box for selecting options for a single file

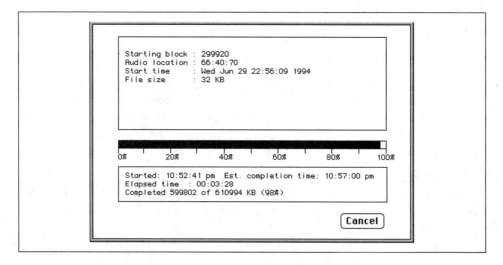

Figure 9-3.   Dialog box showing partial completion of disc image

How the CD recorder works in premastering

The CD recorder works with a special kind of disc that contains a gold reflective surface and a photosensitive dye layer. The laser writing light is driven by the premastering software and is pulsed according to the data to be recorded. When the laser light hits the dye layer, it erodes the dye and creates a surface whose reflection property matches that of a pit. The pits simulate the surface of a standard CD-ROM, and the resulting CD-R disc can be played on standard CD-ROM players.

If You Don't Have Premastering Software . . .

If you don't have CD premastering software, you will need to send the data from your PC, Macintosh, and/or UNIX system to the CD-ROM manufacturing plant on backup media—generally, some type of tape, magneto-optical (MO) disk, hard drive, or the like. Once the backup is received, the manufacturer will restore your original data and generate a CD image for you.

Although it isn't strictly necessary, at this point we strongly recommend that you have the manufacturer generate a CD-R or "proof disc" (gold disc) for you to check. (This is part of the testing process we've described above, aimed at helping you ensure that your application is performing as desired, with no bugs.) Once you've approved the proof disc, the manufacturer can master and then replicate your CD-ROMs. A proof disc usually costs around two hundred dollars, and is a very small price to pay to make sure that your application works correctly from disc before you spend several hundreds or thousands of dollars to master and replicate your image. A CD-ROM plant is like a large copy machine. If you send in a bad copy, you will not only get bad copies back, but you will have to pay for them. That is why it is so important to see a proof disc before the final copies are made.

Data Input Formats

As we've mentioned, there are two methods for sending data to a CD manufacturing plant for replication:

1. If you have premastering software, you'll send the data as a CD image, ready for mastering. You'll normally put the image file on one of the following media: CD-R, MO (magneto-optical) disc, DAT tape, or backup tape (8mm, 4mm, or 9-track).

2. If you don't have premastering software, you'll send the data in a nonimage format, putting the data on a hard disk (SCSI, IDE, etc.) backup, MO disc, SyQuest or Bernoulli, cartridge, DAT tape, or backup tape (8mm, 4mm tape, or 9-track). The data then needs to be formatted or converted to an image format.

Image format

A CD data image is a copy of the exact data that will eventually be placed on the CD-ROM, including all the directory information and all the extra information in each data sector. The best way to send your input to the CD plant to be mastered and replicated is as a complete disc image on a CD-R disc; the plant can master directly from a CD-R.

If you aren't able to put the image on a CD-R, the next best choice is probably an MO disc. A magnetic tape is also acceptable; in general, DAT or 8mm is preferred. If you send a disc image on 9-track tape, it will have to be converted to 8mm for mastering. This conversion is safe and easy, but takes time to do and there will usually be a conversion charge for the work.

When you send a tape to a CD-ROM manufacturer, follow these rules:

- Make sure that tape labels conform to the ANSI X3.27-1978 standard (recommended) or to IBM standard practice. If the labels do not conform, the tape may be unlabeled.

- Make sure that your tape has an adequate block size. For 9-track tapes, you should have a record size of 2048 bytes and a block size of 8192 bytes. A recording density of 1600 or 6250 bpi is acceptable for 9-track tapes. For 8mm tapes, you should have a record size of 2048 bytes, and your block size should be between 8192 and 16384 bytes; 16384 is recommended because it results in faster processing. These block sizes are compatible with the 2048-byte data blocks of the standard Mode 1 CD-ROMs.

- When you send a CD image on a tape, indicate what type of label is on the tape, the record and block size of the tape data, and the size of the image (number of sectors) on the tape. It is also a good idea to indicate the type of data or application on the tape. In addition, always indicate the number of 2048-byte blocks (2K sectors) that make up the image.

- When you send any type of media to a CD plant, send two copies. Having a backup copy is useful if the original copy is bad or is damaged in transit.

Nonimage format

If you don't have premastering software and aren't able to create a CD-ROM image, most CD manufacturers will accept your data in nonimage format. You can put this data on almost any media, from DOS backups on hard disks or streaming tape to PKZip files on floppies. The nonimage data will require formatting and media conversion to create a correct CD-ROM image format. The CD-ROM manufacturer usually charges a fee for formatting and conversion.

Sending Data on Various Devices

There are several ways that customers can send nonimage data, in the form of a set of directories or files, to a CD manufacturer. The following sections summarize the more common methods of sending such a backup for each platform, along with other issues, recommendations, and comments that are associated with each method.

Hard disk drive (SCSI, IDE, or other)

Sending your data on a hard drive is not a good way to get your data to a CD-ROM manufacturer. There are several reasons:

- There can be problems getting your drive configured to match the plant's PC systems

- Your drive might get damaged during transit

- You will not have the use of your drive while it is at the manufacturer

But if a hard drive is the only way you have to transport your data, it will get the job done.

It's more common for a disc duplicator to have problems with the configuration of a disc from a PC or UNIX system than from a Macintosh; there are rarely any configuration problems when you send in a SCSI drive from a Mac. On the Mac, when the drive comes up on the system, you should see one partition that has all the data in the exact layout you intend to use on the CD-ROM.

Sending in a hard drive from a DOS or Windows system can be more complicated. The most common types of DOS drives are SCSI or IDE. If you send in a SCSI drive, be sure to let the CD manufacturer know what controller you were using to run the drive (Adaptec, Future Domain, etc.). If you are not using a common controller or drivers for your drive, you might need to send your controller and/or drivers in along with the drive.

NOTE

Always call the CD-ROM manufacturer before sending in your drive to see what types of drives, controllers, and drivers they support; doing so will avoid unnecessary delays in processing your data.

If you send in an IDE drive, be sure to send the drive's documentation (setup information) and any special drivers the CD-ROM manufacturer will need to set up the drive.

Magneto-optical (MO) disc

MO discs are more problematic for PCs than for Macintosh systems. Macintosh MO discs are usually interchangeable among different Macs, and appear as ordinary hard drives to the computer. However, when you send an MO disc from a DOS or Windows system, you must let the CD manufacturer know what type of magneto-optical drive, SCSI controller, and drivers you used. If the CD-ROM manufacturer does not have compatible drives, controllers, or drivers, you might need to send yours in along with your cartridge.

SyQuest and Bernoulli cartridges

SyQuest and Bernoulli cartridges are usually interchangeable between different Macintosh systems and even between most DOS and Windows systems. However, if you are sending in DOS data, be sure to let the CD manufacturer know what type of controller and drivers were used with the disks.

Backup tapes

Backup tapes are a good solution if you need to send a large amount of data to the CD-ROM manufacturer. If you are sending Macintosh data to a manufacturer, we recommend the use of the Retrospect tape backup software writing to 4mm or 8mm tape. For DOS or Windows systems, there are several different backup programs available, including Colorado, Sytos, Novaback, and Secure.

As with other types of devices, it's a good idea to call the CD-ROM manufacturer ahead of time to find out which programs they support, and what type of tape drives they have. If the manufacturer doesn't have tape systems compatible with the one you are using, you might need to send in your software, controller, or drive so the manufacturer can successfully read and restore your data.

In the UNIX world, tar (tape archive) backups are the most popular method. Most tar backups are made on 4mm or 8mm tapes. When you send a tar tape to a CD-ROM manufacturer, be sure to indicate the block size used to create the tape; 2048-byte blocks are preferred since they are compatible with CD-ROM block sizes.

Floppy diskettes

Use floppy diskettes only to send small amounts of data to the CD manufacturer or to update files for existing CDs. Sending a large amount of data on many floppy diskettes will cost you a lot of time, and probably a lot of money, for the additional work required by the manufacturer.

Packaging and Printing

So far in this chapter, we've discussed only the CD-ROM disc itself. But a disc is not the only component of a CD-ROM product. A complete CD-ROM package includes several components:

- The disc itself

- The jewel box or other package that houses the CD

- The label that is printed on the CD (which must be prepared as graphical artwork)

- The insert—the printed cardstock or brochure that goes in the front of the case cover

- The tray card—the printed cardstock that goes in the back side of the case and includes the spine

- Shrinkwrap or polywrap

- Possibly, a box that houses the CD and displays the product on the store shelf; the box may also contain a more extensive user manual, sometimes a warranty card, and sometimes advertising for other products

All of these pieces present rather specialized design issues. Remember that your CD-ROM packaging and associated printed pieces are graphic products. You'll need a professional graphic designer to do the design and make the mechanicals for these various pieces.

Your packaging may be the main way a potential customer first encounters your product. You should view your packaging as a major marketing tool, and be willing to consider part of your packaging cost as a marketing expense. Your CD-ROM manufacturer can help you explore your options and their prices. (We provide some information on different cost options in Chapter 10.) Leave enough time—and enough money in your budget—to develop and produce appropriate designs to match your product.

Disc Inserts

The printed disc inserts for jewel box packaging—or any other printing required by your choice of packaging—are standard printed pieces. As such, they can use any traditional printing process. Your CD-ROM manufacturer will have detailed requirements for the dimensions and paper of these pieces; we've shown the requirements for one particular manufacturer in Figures 9-4 through 9-6.

NOTE

Be sure to get the exact disc insert specifications from your own CD-ROM manufacturer before you do any production. Tolerances for packaging machinery will vary between manufacturers.

Be aware that the print pieces must be produced and delivered to the production site before disc replication can begin. You may find it difficult to believe, but the printed inserts may cost more to manufacture than the discs themselves!

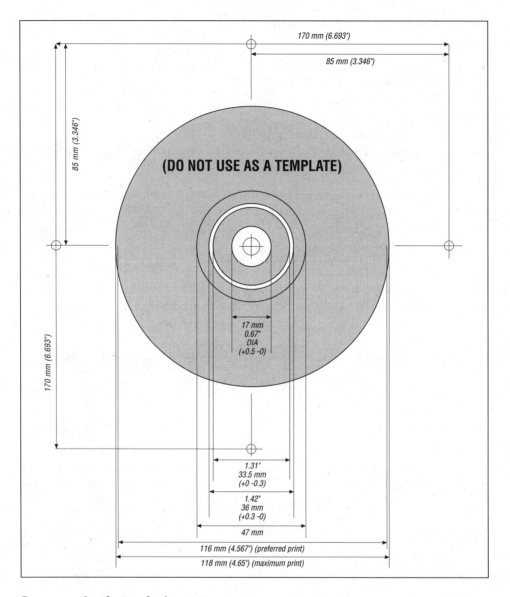

Figure 9-4.   Specifications for disc printing

Disc Printing

The image on the surface of the disc itself can be produced by either a silk-screen or offset process. Because the image is printed on plastic, not paper, this process presents special issues.

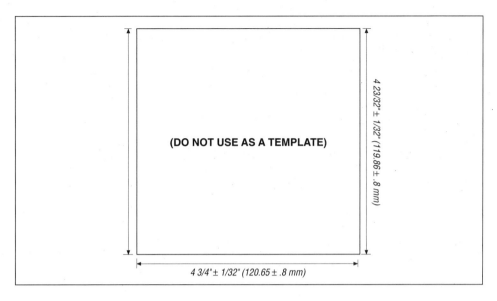

Figure 9-5.   Specifications for jewel box insert

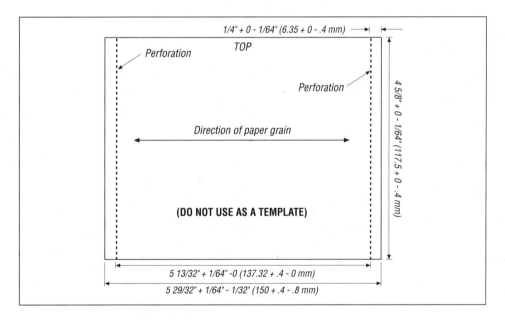

Figure 9-6.   Specifications for jewel box tray piece

You must prepare the contents of this disc graphic yourself, using guidelines provided by the replicator. Typically, you'll provide the replicator with a camera-ready film negative that is exactly what goes on the disk. The cost of replication depends heavily on the number of colors in the image. Most replicators provide a two-color disc image as part of the standard stamping price, and then charge extra for each additional color (where four colors provide a full color capability). If you want two colors, you will have to prepare two-color artwork and deliver two film separations. Remember that because the background is already a metallic silver color, you actually have silver plus two colors to work with.

The following sections briefly summarize characteristics of silk-screen and offset printing. More details on requirements and specifications for these methods of printing can be obtained from your CD manufacturer.

Silk-screen printing

Most CD-ROM manufacturers print the labels on discs using a silk-screen process. Screen printing can include any number of colors, but most discs use no more than five different colors. More colors, of course, means more cost. Different images are printed onto the disc surface, one color at a time, by placing a screen over the disc surface and pressing ink through the openings. (This process is shown in Figure 9-21, in the discussion of disc manufacturing.) The ink is cured or dried using ultraviolet light.

You will need to send the artwork used to create the screens used in printing to the CD-ROM manufacturer in the form of film positives, emulsion side up. Be sure to make the film from original art, not multigeneration copies, and check that the film is free from scratches. As with offset printing (described below), a white background is recommended for discs that use several colors; that background enhances the colors that are used.

Offset printing

A few CD-ROM manufacturing plants offer the service of offset, as well as silk-screen, printing on a disc. Offset printing allows a photographic image to be printed on the CD. It is done from a metal plate of the image you would like placed on your CD, just as it would be for offset printing on paper. The CMYK[*] primary colors can create almost any color needed for the desired image.

It's advisable to include a film positive matching the separation diameters to create a solid white background that is screen-printed onto the disc. The solid white background is highly recommended because it allows clearer color definition in the image that will be printed over the background. In addition, include a film negative, emulsion side down, for each of the separations that will be printed by this offset process on top of the white background.

---

[*]CMYK stands for cyan, magenta, yellow, black. It's often called four-color printing or process printing.

Disc Packaging

What kind of packaging do you want for your CD-ROM? You'll need to figure out how you want to present your disc to the customer. Figure 9-7 shows several different kinds of packaging. This book emphasizes the so-called "jewel box" packaging, because it is familiar from music CDs and is very common for CD-ROMs. There are several other types of available packaging options, however, as we discuss in this section. Talk with your CD-ROM manufacturer ahead of time about all of these options.

Figure 9-7. Photographs of some kinds of CD-ROM packaging (see the color version of one of these photographs in the center insert)

Jewel boxes

Many CD-ROM titles come in jewel box packaging, accompanied by shrink wrapping. This is certainly a popular option for CD-ROMs, as it is for music CDs, and is usually easy to arrange with your disc manufacturer. There are a number of types of jewel box packaging, including:

- The traditional jewel box

- The traditional jewel box, with shrink wrapping

- Double jewel boxes (for titles that need two discs)

- A double jewel box that is the same thickness as the usual single box but whose central piece is hinged so it holds one disc on each side

Jewel boxes can also be inserted in other boxes or in plastic display pieces to make them more attractive for point-of-sale display.

NOTE

Shrink-wrapping (sometimes called polywrapping) is included at no extra cost (beyond jewel box packaging) by some manufacturers; others charge a separate fee for it. Look carefully at the bids submitted by prospective manufacturers; be sure to tell them whether you want shrink-wrapping, and ask if it will add more time to the process.

Other packaging

There are other choices for CD-ROM packaging besides the jewel box. These choices range from no packaging at all to very elaborate disc presentations. For example:

- Discs can be shipped to you in a bulk package with no individual disc packaging (this package is called a spindle) so that you can add your own packaging, put the disc into a blister pack in a book, or package it with other materials.

- Discs can be inserted into several different types of envelope packages to reduce packaging volume or mailing costs.

- Some types of full packages have less plastic than jewel boxes and use cardboard enclosures; these produce less packaging waste and can include self-mailing packages. (Note, though, that the printing issues are quite different from those of jewel boxes.)

If you are going to use jewel box packaging—or any other kind of packaging for which the discs are put into the packaging at the manufacturing plant—make sure that the inserts are received at the plant before the disc duplication is scheduled to begin. If the CD-ROM will be put into your packaging at another site (as is usually the case when CD-ROMs are inserted into books), realize that the timing of disc and packaging manufacturing may well be different. Check with your vendors and/or assembly contractor to make sure that your work meets their schedules.

What Happens During Production?

When your data or premaster gets to the CD manufacturing facility, it goes through a number of steps before it becomes an actual CD-ROM for your audience. As we've mentioned, if your data is not in the form of a disc image, the CD-ROM manufacturer must first create the disc image from your sources. In this section, we'll assume that the disc image has already been created.

The CD-ROM production cycle consists of these major steps:

* Mastering

* Developing

* Creating stampers

* Injection molding

* Metallizing

* Printing

* Inspection and packaging

* Shipping

Mastering

The first step in the actual CD-ROM replication is *mastering*. During mastering, the manufacturer transfers the data from the customer's input media to a piece of optically flat glass (shown in Figure 9-8) which is coated with a photo-sensitive material called *photo-resist*. The photo-resist material is spincoated (as shown in Figure 9-9) onto the glass master to a uniform thickness of 150 nm. The photo-resist process must be performed in a cleanroom that has constantly circulated air with careful temperature and humidity control; this tight control is required to get the uniform etching necessary to produce consistent pit shapes.

The photo-resist is sensitive to blue and ultraviolet (UV) light, and is chemically altered when it's exposed to the light from a blue argon laser.

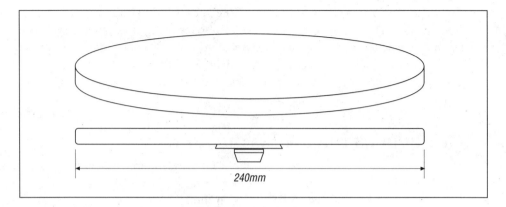

Figure 9-8.   Glass substrate on mounting hub

240mm

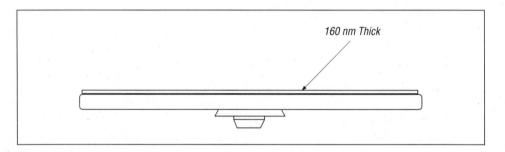

160 nm Thick

Figure 9-9.   Photoresist layer

During the mastering process, the digital data from the customer's input disc image is converted in real time into a CD format in a process called *eight-to-fourteen modulation* (EFM), shown in Figure 9-10. The function of EFM is to spread the pits in a way that increases the accuracy of the disc reading process. (This conversion is done because of the limitations of CD-ROM technology.) A 1 bit is signaled by a change in the nature of the laser reflectance signal, from a land to a pit or from a pit to a land. These changes cannot be too frequent; if they are, they can't be properly detected. The run length (the length of a sequence consisting of a 1 followed by 0s) must be at least 3 and cannot be more than 11. To accommodate this limitation for a single byte can take up to 14 bits, so that much space is allowed for each byte.

During EFM processing, *error detection codes* (EDC), *error correction codes* (ECC), and necessary *sub-codes* are added to the data stream. The data stream, including data, EDC, ECC, and subcodes, is interleaved to minimize the effects of surface defects on the CD. The output of the EFM encoder is used to modulate (turn on

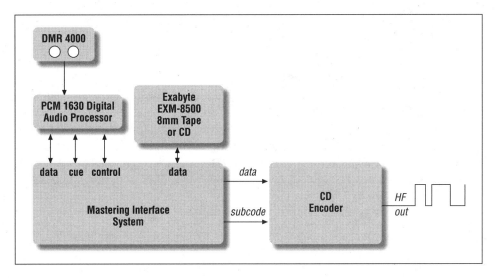

Figure 9-10.   Laser cutter signal processing

and off) the cutting laser, exposing the areas of the photo-resist where the pits will reside.

Once the laser writing (shown in Figure 9-11) is complete, the pits are present only as chemical alterations of the photo-resist. The physical pits are not created until the glass master is developed.

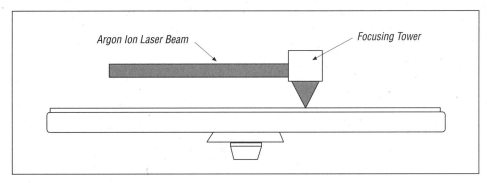

Figure 9-11.   Laser writing on the blank

Developing

A CD master is developed in much the same way that film is developed. First, a prerinse of deionized water washes off any particulate contamination prior to the actual developing process. After the prerinse, the manufacturer rinses the glass master with a sodium hydroxide developing solution, as shown in Figure 9-12;

this solution washes away the photo-resist that was altered by the cutting laser. The developing period is carefully timed because the precise size, shape, and depth of the CD pits are critical.

The developing period is followed by a postrinse, which dilutes any remaining developer solution, thus preventing any further developing. The glass master is then dried, and for the first time the image of the CD can be seen. Finally, the glass master is then visually inspected for any defects which could affect the play-ability of the disc. If a defect is found, the master will be rejected and a recut will be ordered. If the master has no visual defects, it moves on to the next step.

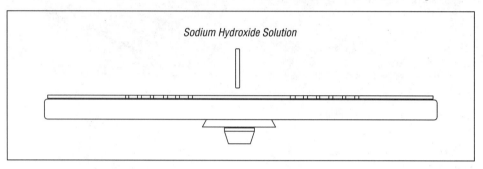

Figure 9-12.   Glass master developing

Creating Stampers

The next step in the CD-ROM manufacturing process creates the disc stampers. First, the glass master is placed in a vacuum deposition chamber, and a thin layer of vaporized silver is deposited onto the photo-resist side of the glass, as shown in Figure 9-13. As for certain other steps in manufacturing, this operation must be performed in a clean room. When this process is completed, the stamper (known as the glass master at this point) is inspected once again for visual defects.

There are three reasons for coating the glass master with silver:

- The silver makes the surface of the glass master conduct electricity for the electroplating process.

- The electrical conductivity of the disc allows electronic testing of the plating results.

- The silver makes the CD reflective, allowing it to be played on a special master player.

At this point, the master player runs an extensive inspection of the entire surface area of the CD-ROM (shown in Figure 9-14), allowing the operator to ensure the quality of the master. The master player also verifies that all the signals on the

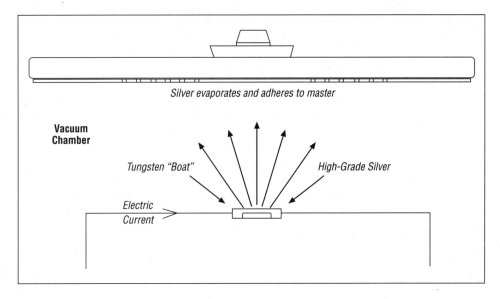

Figure 9-13.   Silver deposition

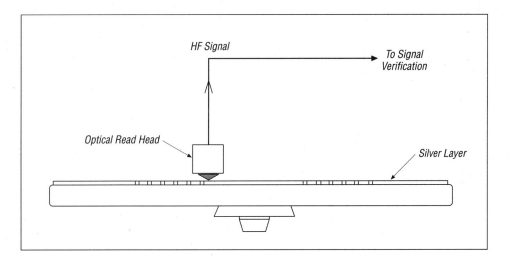

Figure 9-14.   Master player inspection

disc are within tolerance. Masters that do not meet the quality requirements are rejected, and the master is recut.

Electroplating

Once the master has successfully passed the master player, it is sent on to electroplating.

During the master electroplating process, the glass master is immersed in a plating solution, and an electrical field is created around the master. This process causes nickel particles in the plating solution to adhere to the metallized surface of the glass master, as shown in Figure 9-15.

After about two hours, the nickel layer is thick enough so that it can be peeled off of the glass master, forming a negative image of the glass master called a metal master or *father*. The structure of the metal master is shown in Figure 9-16.

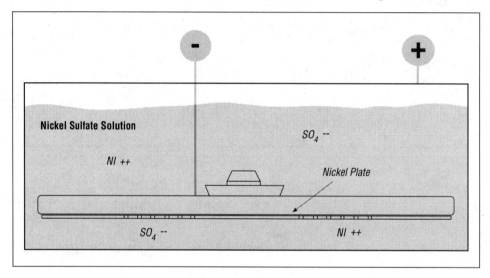

Figure 9-15.   Electroplating

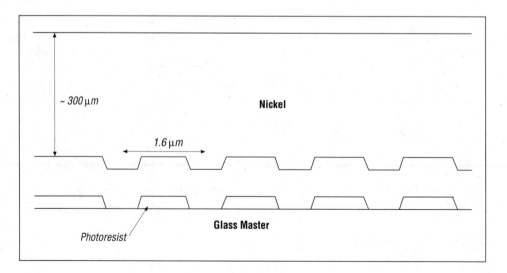

Figure 9-16.   Metal master

Because the father is a negative image of the glass master, it has bumps instead of the pits that were on the glass master. For short runs, the father can be used as the CD stamper. For larger runs, however, the manufacturer electroplates the father, and creates a negative image of the father, called the *mother*. Because the mother has pits, it is electroplated again to make stampers for the main part of the production.

After electroplating, stampers must be finished by sanding the back side and trimming them to the finished size, as shown in Figure 9-17. Upon completion, the stamper(s) are inspected for visual defects.

NOTE

Stampers wear out after a substantial amount of use; a stamper is normally good for 10,000 to 15,000 discs. Making several stampers allows the manufacturer to produce discs on several production lines at once—an important issue on long jobs with short turnaround times.

Once again, because the mother has pits and the stampers are a negative image of the mother, the stampers have bumps which will result in pits on the finished CD.

Once the stamper passes inspection, it is sent to injection molding.

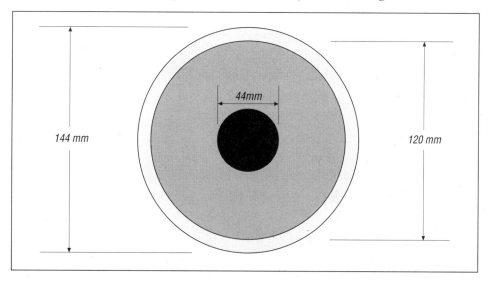

Figure 9-17.   Stamper finishing

Injection Molding

During injection molding, the stamper is loaded into the molding machine and becomes one side of the mold. The other side of the mold (called the mirror block) is flat and forms the readable side of the CD-ROM. During the molding process, the mold closes, and molten polycarbonate is injected into the mold (as shown in Figure 9-18). The polycarbonate is injected as a liquid and fills the space between the stamper and the mirror block, forming a negative image of the stamper.

At this point, the mold is cooled to solidify the polycarbonate and the disc is removed by a robotic arm. The CD-ROMs are clear at this point, so they cannot yet be played.

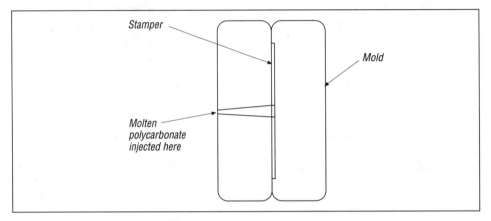

Figure 9-18.   Molding

Metallizing

To make the just-pressed disc readable, it must be made reflective. This occurs during a metallization step, shown in Figure 9-19.

Here, the transparent CDs are coated with a thin aluminum layer in a process similar to an electrostatic discharge; this layer makes the discs reflective. The manufacturer checks the first discs to be metallized, both visually and electronically, for defects in the stamper qualification process. Discs are verified, byte-for-byte, against the original customer-supplied source material, and this same testing is applied to samples from the production as it proceeds.

Next, the discs are spin-coated with an acrylic lacquer material, shown in Figure 9-20, that protects the delicate pits and prevents the aluminum from oxidizing. Some discs are made with gold metallization, since gold is not susceptible to oxidation. Although these gold discs are claimed to last longer, the gold doesn't

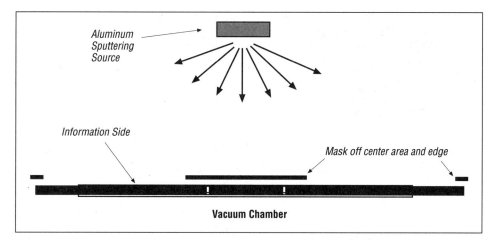

Figure 9-19.   Metallization

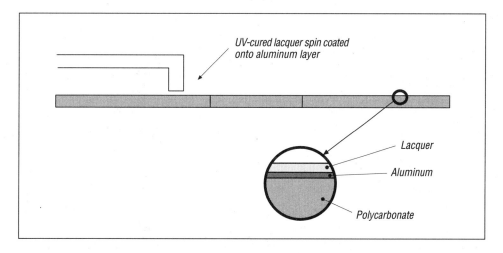

Figure 9-20.   Protective coating with cross-section of disc layers

make the data any better. Also, because gold is less reflective than aluminum, these discs are a little harder to read.

Printing

In the final step of the manufacturing process, the manufacturer prints the discs on the lacquer side, using customer-provided artwork, either by a silk-screen or an offset process, as discussed earlier in this chapter. The printing is then ultra-violet-cured to fix the image. Figure 9-21 illustrates the process of silk-screen printing.

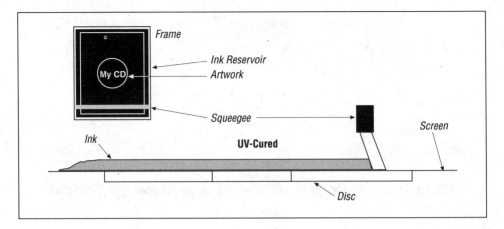

Figure 9-21.   Silk-screen printing

When disc printing is complete, the CD-ROMs can safely venture outside of the clean room for the first time.

Inspection and Packaging

During the final inspection step, the CD-ROM manufacturer inspects every disc that comes out of the clean room, visually as well as electronically, and rejects, and scraps, any disc that does not meet stringent quality standards.

The discs that do pass final inspection are packaged according to the customer's requirements.

Shipping

Once the CD-ROMs have been packaged, they're ready for shipping. The manufacturer boxes and ships the discs in whatever way the customer has specified—usually by a traditional land carrier, though they can be shipped by higher-cost courier services if your schedule demands it.

Because CD-ROMs are light in weight, they are usually relatively inexpensive to ship, so these costs will not significantly impact your budget. However, be sure to include the shipping time for the discs in your production schedule.

Shipping and scheduling details vary from one CD-ROM manufacturer and shipper to another, so contact your manufacturer early to make whatever shipping arrangements you need. And remember that if you are taking delivery of the discs yourself, you'll need some place to store them.

C H A P T E R

10

CD-ROM Publishing Costs

Calculating the costs of producing a CD-ROM is one of the most confusing parts of electronic publishing. On the one hand, some CD-ROM costs are quite low—so low that the hurdle to getting into the electronic publishing business is much lower than the hurdle that exists for the print publishing world. However, CD-ROM publishing also entails many other costs that are often not considered by enthusiastic newcomers. For example:

Development cost

> How much will it cost to produce the components of the publication? This is the cost of the content, including all licensing costs for your content assets.

Reader licensing cost

> How much will it cost for licenses for the software systems you use to create and distribute the electronic documents?

Production cost

> How much will it cost to bring together the various components into the overall publication? This includes design, integration, and programming.

Testing cost

> How much will it cost to test the disc on all appropriate platforms and with the anticipated audience?

Printing cost

> How much will it cost to create the printed pieces and packaging for the disc project?

Mastering cost

> How much will it cost to create a master from the disc components?

Manufacturing cost

> How much will it cost to create the actual discs in the quantity you need?

Shipping cost

> How much will it cost to ship the discs from the production facility to your distribution site?

Marketing and sales costs

> How much will it cost to acquire distribution if you are going through whole-salers, or to advertise if you are selling directly?

Some of these costs are fixed overheads; others are based on the number of discs you're ordering. We'll discuss each type of cost in this chapter. We'll also note, for each type of cost, what we expect the impact of distributing electronic documents on DVD (Digital Video Disc) is likely to be in the future.

Remember, though, some costs can't be specified with precision, and some depend solely on your project and production environment.

As with any other creative work, costs can vary tremendously, depending on whether you buy services or perform them yourself. Clearly, if you are a moti-vated and creative person, you can pour a great deal of yourself into the publishing project, and provide many of the most expensive tasks without the aid of outside professionals. If you do this, you may be able to publish an individual electronic title at minimal cost. Building a real CD-ROM publishing business, on the other hand, will require significant production investments.

There are many time vs. cost tradeoffs that you'll face during the publishing process, as we'll explore in this chapter.

An Example

Let's look first at an actual example of a publishing project, and its associated costs.

Consider the least expensive CD-ROM made by the Judson Rosebush Company to date. This title was a picture disc that was pressed in 1,000 copies with a total out-of-pocket expenditure of $5,380. It's not likely that many CD-ROM projects will cost less than this one. And yet, the overall experience with that disc was not a success: it was projected to cost only $2,000, and it went 250 percent over budget. This overrun was upsetting, and the project lost money. Luckily, though, the loss was only $3,500. Imagine if the project had been bid at $20,000, and suffered the same 250 percent overrun; it would have finished at a cost of $55,000!

In the picture disc project, the main item that came in on budget was the disc manufacturing. For a run of 1,000 discs at that time, the prices were good. The $5,380 overall expense for the project broke down as follows:

- $1,000 for disc manufacturing

- $800 for printing

- $1,000 to $1,500 for the graphic artist

- $1,500 in production costs (even though all that had to be done was to send slides to Kodak to have them put on PhotoCD)

- $800 for getting a disc master made

As this simple example indicates, there are a lot of costs associated with creating a CD-ROM that may not be apparent when you first look at the medium.

Cost of a CD-ROM

Bob Stein, one of the founders of Voyager, suggests that you should budget about $4 per disc for a minimal production; his estimate includes manufacturing and packaging, but not development or any other variable costs. We think this figure is about right as an overall estimate. While you might be able to beat $4 per disc for some projects, we don't believe you can beat that cost by very much. If you're going to try, your project will have to have some constraints; for example, you won't build a box for the disc, your disc will need to justify large volume production, and you'll have to fit the disc manufacturing into a slow time in the manufacturing year, and give your manufacturer plenty of time to fit the disc into its schedule.

The point is that the cost of manufacturing isn't the big cost. Although manufacturing costs do play a part, the real cost of a disc is the cost of producing the contents of the disc.

Cost of Content Creation and Licensing

The cost of content—often called the editorial cost of a disc—can range from free into the millions of dollars.

Sources of Content

The cost depends heavily on the source of the content. There are three basic sources of content: it may be free, licensed, or created, as we describe in the sections that follow.

Free content

This category includes public domain materials, donations, and (assuming that your time is valueless) anything you can make yourself. But the term "free" is something of a misnomer, because obtaining even public domain content may require hours of research, extensive travel, and high reproduction costs.

Licensed content

Content can be licensed from many sources, including books, articles, pictures, sounds, video, and film. The costs of licensing can vary widely. Although it's difficult to be specific here, we can provide some guidelines.

- A book option (that is, the right to adapt a book as an electronic publication) might cost $5,000 and up.

- Stock images (typically images from a photographer or a photographic archive) run $35 to $75 each in the current market.

- Stock video can be licensed for prices in the range of $750 to $3,000 a minute. For example, you can license video from any of the three major television networks right now in the $750 to $900 per minute range. People have licensed feature film clips in the range of $2,000 to $3,000 per minute.

- Mass entertainment content is much more. You can get a good prime license on something in the class of Garfield, Doonesbury, Oprah Winfrey, or *Married with Children* in the $25,000 to $55,000 range. But you probably can't get world-class assets, such as the Rolling Stones, Bob Dylan, or the Beatles, and lock them up for that. Such assets are extremely expensive, but usually are so attractive to the market that the expense may well be justified. For such assets, you may need to pay a royalty on each product sold, as well as an up-front licensing cost.

Created content

The costs of created content obviously will vary widely, depending on who is doing the creating. Again, some guidelines may be helpful:

- Freelance writers typically make 10 to 25 cents a word

- Professional photographers make about $500 a day

- If you need to create artwork, it will be ordinarily be done by an illustrator or an art director, who will create a background screen for about $1,500

- A video crew can be hired for $1,500 to $2,500 a day

- A sound effect might cost $25 to $50

Of course you can pay more. Consider some more startling numbers:

- Tom Clancy gets more than $1,000,000 a novel; Richard Avedon gets about $10,000 a day for his photography; Sean Connery might want $50,000 for a voice-over.

- An average half-hour television show runs on a budget of approximately $100,000 per show, while a one-hour animated television special (which is actually less than 50 minutes long) costs more than $200,000.

- A typical 30-second national TV commercial costs $75,000. One minute of a typical feature film costs $100,000.

- One second of computer animation averages $2,500.

There are several other ways to think about cost. You might consider cost in terms of the amount and unit cost of your content. For example:

- If you budget video at $1,000 per minute, and you can get 60 minutes of QuickTime video on a disc, the most you could pay is about $60,000.

- If you budget video at a higher figure of $2,500 per minute, the most you could pay is around $150,000.

- If you could put 1,000 pictures on the disc and you're paying $100 apiece for the pictures, it's a $100,000 cost for the disc content.

These costs aren't the end of it, of course. Even after the content is in hand, it must be forged into the document and into CD-ROM form. This process requires an editor, a director, and a writer who shape the content into the product. Costs for these talents are significant components of a disc's production.

Effect of DVD

What will the cost implications be if we shift from CD-ROM to DVD publishing? The greater capacity of DVD discs offers the opportunity to increase the content of a disc. Doing so will obviously tend to increase the cost of creation and licensing this content. The publisher will have to weigh possible increased content costs against possible increases in value and price in the discs.

It is too soon to draw any conclusions about how DVD will work out as a publishing medium. Some writers are claiming that multimedia publishing will all go to DVD, but we feel that such claims are over-eager and premature.

Cost of Production

Production costs are the costs of integrating the content into the form in which it's presented to the user. Like content creation costs, production costs can vary greatly. Such costs depend primarily on two variables:

- The amount of work that must be done to create a good electronic version of the document (or document components) to take to the premastering stage

- Whether the production work is done by craft professionals or by the author or volunteers

As we discussed in Chapter 5, *Designing Electronic Documents*, production work includes adapting the original content for electronic presentation, assembling the content into the disc, and putting the interface on the content to make it useful to the user.

The Volunteer Process

Let's look at a real-world example of a CD-ROM production which demonstrates one extreme of the production process.

It's difficult to imagine a less-expensive development process than the one used for the SIGGRAPH electronic conference publications (described fully in Chapter 3, *Two Electronic Titles*). That process depends totally on volunteer work, and on the ability of the contributing authors to create good PostScript versions of their papers (i.e., versions that fit the production process). The process depends further on the ability of the Adobe Acrobat product to translate authors' PostScript files into Acrobat's PDF files automatically and to add features to the electronic proceedings without a great deal of hand work. (This translation, and the extra work required to add Acrobat's features to a document, are also performed by volunteers at no cost.)

The cost of the entire SIGGRAPH proceedings production process includes only a few one-time costs: perhaps $10,000 overall in storage devices for production, a CD-R mastering system, and communication and media costs. At the time the CD-ROM was developed, SIGGRAPH already had a computer system in place to receive the final electronic materials from authors, and the production editor had a system to do the necessary translation and assembly. In fact, because of the cost reductions in hard disks and CD-R writers, these costs would be a lot lower today than they were in the early 1990s when the initial production system was assembled.

Because we tried to cut corners wherever we could (e.g., we did our own artwork), the complete manufacturing costs for the SIGGRAPH disc CD-ROM were also quite low—about $1.85 per disc.

The Professional Process

Now let's look at a development process in which programmers or media specialists are needed to translate or assemble the contents of the electronic documents being published on CD-ROM. The primary cost components for this process are salaries, equipment, space, and communications, and these costs can be very high indeed. A deluxe consumer CD-ROM, for example, might have a production budget in the range of $250,000 to $400,000.

Detailed Production Costs

Let's break down some specific production tasks and consider their costs. Assume that professional labor is valued at about $40 an hour, plus the floor space and machine for the staff person.

Text copy blocks

These blocks are about the least expensive component to install in a disc product. Including light proofreading and copyediting, a small copy block (i.e., a few paragraphs—perhaps a block that is about 15 lines long and about 3 inches wide) can be installed for about $10.

Pictures

Pictures are a little more expensive than text. We assume a production cost of about $25 to install the picture into a product, and we assume that a person can do a couple of pictures an hour. This includes getting the slides in, writing purchase orders, sending them out to get them put on the scanner, getting the scans back, reading them in, cropping, scaling, color-correcting, cleaning up the spots, and dropping the finished pictures into the product. A really skilled person, or really clean images, might even raise the rate to four images an hour. If you can install four pictures an hour, you make money at $25 per picture, but if you have problem pictures, you lose money.

Sound effects

The cost of sound effects is in the same range as pictures. You can expect it to cost about $25 to install a sound effect in a disc.

Digital video

Digital video is an area that is still in flux. The Judson Rosebush Company currently budgets video at $85 per minute in production cost to put video into a product. They know now that they are badly losing money at that rate; the actual costs are easily double that. They are going to have to bite the bullet and raise their rates.

Let's put together those individual costs and see what a professionally produced CD-ROM might cost overall.

The Judson Rosebush Company recently prepared a CD-ROM that consists of 350 photographs and about 150 text slots; these are simply files for a PC on the disc with no user interface. The budget for this disc is about $14,000, and they'll make a little money on that.

The project is an extremely simple one. We have to scan the pictures, and then color-correct, crop, and retouch them. We might also need to edit the text a bit The production run is 2,500 units. If the manufacturing costs were $2 per disc, $5,000 would go for manufacturing. That would leave $9,000 for content production. Some money must be made on that $9,000, somewhere. However, manufacturing may actually cost a bit more than $2 each because the look of the package is *extremely* important to the clients. Why? Because the CD-ROM is mainly for promotion; half, or perhaps even three-quarters, of the people who get this CD-ROM will never even put it into the machine. But they will all look at the package. It's critical to produce excellent color separations for the package—if the package doesn't sparkle, the client will never come back and do business with us again, no matter how good the disc is!

Effect of DVD

What will be the impact on production costs if the market shifts to DVD from CD-ROM? We expect this shift to have essentially the same effect on production that it has for content creation and licensing: Because of the additional cost of producing and integrating media blocks on a DVD, this technology has the potential to significantly increase production costs. The publisher will need to decide whether these additional costs are worthwhile for a particular product. As we said before, it's not possible to give any guidelines yet.

Cost of Software Purchase and Licensing

Software licensing costs can be substantial. There are two categories of tools:

- **Authoring and assembly software.** The tools you'll use to author the documents and assemble the files for building the CD-ROM at your own site.

- **Reader software.** The tools you might distribute to your customers so they can read the files on the CD-ROM.

The cost for authoring and assembly tools will likely range from several hundred to several thousand dollars. You can get exact, current prices from the vendors listed in Appendix A, *Resources*; note, though, that you'll probably be able to purchase the software through a retail or mail-order source for less than the vendors' list prices. If you're acquiring tools for many projects, you can amortize their costs; otherwise you'll have to include the total cost in the budget for your single project.

NOTE

If you are developing a product for an educational or other not-for-profit group, always be sure to check with vendors for possible donations or special pricing.

There are some cases in which you will have to put another vendor's software on the CD-ROMs you distribute to your customers. For example, with certain document systems, such as Adobe Acrobat, users won't be able to read documents unless the appropriate delivery software (Acrobat Reader) is present on the CD-ROM or on the reader's computer. Another such situation occurs when CD-ROM authors want to perform certain operations that require special fonts to be present on the delivered CD-ROM. In such cases, you need to find out exactly what the licensing situation is for the software or fonts you're considering putting on the CD-ROMs.

Different vendors have different financial requirements. For example, some vendors charge a one-time license fee for the authoring system; others may charge a fee for each disc distributed. The license fee may be a one-time charge, or it may be in the form of an annual subscription, which must be renewed. With some products, there is a charge only if the actual software is distributed on the CD-ROM; a common scenario is that the vendor charges for the authoring system, but allows you to deliver the reader for no additional charge. Some vendors charge for both the authoring system and for each copy of the delivery software. Some other software vendors—and even some commercial disc developers— charge a per-disc fee, simply for the right to distribute documents developed with their system. (Such a policy can have a chilling effect on your income from CD-ROM sales.)

Fortunately, the documents produced by many document systems don't need any runtime support, so in such cases you don't need to worry about distributing another vendor's software.

Be sure to verify exactly what the pricing will be for the tools you need before you commit to a particular software platform for your title; you may find certain vendors' policies prohibitive. Also, check on the need for any special fonts, and be sure to investigate whether public domain versions of these fonts may be available.

Because a license is a legal document, make sure to have someone with experience in licensing issues look carefully at the license agreement for you.

NOTE

If you are developing CD-ROMs within the United States and are exporting your titles, examine the license agreement with particular care. There are some tricky issues that may arise. For example, a (hard to get) government license is needed for the export of most software that contains any type of cryptography. Other countries may also have similar issues.

Cost of Premastering

As we discussed in Chapter 8, *CD-ROM Disc Standards*, there are several different approaches you can take to premastering your CD-ROM. If you have access to premastering software, you can create a disc image at your own site, and send it to the CD-ROM manufacturer for production and duplication. If you don't have access to such software, you'll have to send your manufacturer a set of files on appropriate media,* and tell the manufacturer how you want the files organized on the disc. The manufacturer will do the premastering for you for a relatively modest fee. However, as we discussed, you won't be able to test anything on your disc unless you choose to have one-off test discs created, and these cost about $200 each.

Appendix A lists a number of companies that produce premastering software systems or provide the premastering services. Premastered (CD-R) discs are essentially identical to final CD-ROM discs and are suitable for testing and for getting quality sign-offs.

There are two parts to the costs of premastering systems: the cost of the premastering software, and the cost of the CD-R writing system. These costs have been declining rapidly and should now be comfortably within the reach of most publishers.

Effect of DVD

If you are considering publishing on DVD, be aware that premastering costs may have a very different profile from those of CD-ROMs. It will probably be some time before desktop DVD-writers and their writable media are available, even for the simplest single-sided single-layer discs. When such technologies do become available, it's likely that they will be quite expensive at first. The cost of creating DVD test discs will thus be much more expensive than it is for CD-ROMs. As we point out in the next section, this expense is one of the most problematic parts of moving publishing projects to DVD.

---

* Chapter 8 lists the surprising variety of media they can usually accommodate.

Cost of Testing

Testing costs may vary widely, depending on how you organize your testing function.

- In the simplest case, you'll create a CD-ROM disc image on your hard disk, and test that image for functionality. Be aware, when you do this, that hard disk search and data transfer are faster than CD-ROM disc search and data transfer, so any tests involving speed of access will not be reliable.

- In an intermediate case, you'll make one or more CD-R discs (or have them made for you) and use these discs for testing. Although the exact file locations on the test disc may vary from those on the final CD-ROM, the performance will otherwise be that of the final version.

- In the most complex case, you'll have a "one-off" disc made by your disc duplicator and will use this disc to test all your functionality and speed.

In each of these cases, you may perform all your testing locally, or you may have it performed by a group of people in different locations.

Publisher Testing

Some publishers will perform at least some testing for you. Others will expect you to do it all yourself. On one of the projects we discussed in Chapter 3, *Isaac Asimov's The Ultimate Robot*, a good deal of the testing was done by the distributor, Microsoft. Microsoft employed a team of four people for two months for testing, while the production company employed a team of three people for six weeks. If you value each of these people and their attendant overhead at $40 per hour, or $1,600 per week, then the testing cost for this product can be calculated at approximately $80,000 for 50 person-weeks of work.

Types of Testing

In Chapter 4, *Developing a CD-ROM*, we described a number of different types of testing that are needed for a CD-ROM. Each of these has associated costs. Some testing always goes along with the disc development and can be considered part of the cost of staffing (the cost of the person installing components, for example). But other types of testing, such as environmental testing, may require outside subcontractors at substantial costs.

Test Discs

One part of testing that is sometimes overlooked is the creation of test discs. On a typical CD-ROM title, the Judson Rosebush Company goes through approximately 25 test discs in CD-R before achieving a finished product. For each of these test levels about three copies are created, resulting in a total of about 75 discs.

Including the cost of CD-R blanks and labor, and amortizing the cost of a modest-cost CD-R writer, the production of test discs adds perhaps several thousand dollars to the overall testing cost for a title.

Effect of DVD

The costs associated with testing discs are potentially dramatically different for DVD and CD-ROM. Indeed, our estimates show the current cost of testing DVDs to be prohibitive. These estimates assume that we would perform at least the same level of testing for DVD that we perform for CD-ROM, and that we would have to produce at least the same number of test discs. In fact, there is every reason to believe that adding content to a title (which would very likely happen because of the increased capacity of the DVD) will increase the number of test discs needed

At this point, it seems unlikely that we will be able to make test DVD discs for any cost that can reasonably be amortized over normal sales. In fact, we can envision scenarios where the production of test discs alone could cost as much as $100,000! This testing problem now appears to be one of the biggest potential barriers to widespread DVD publishing. Perhaps in time this issue will be less of a hurdle than it now appears.

Cost of Packaging

When you think of the cost of producing a disc, you probably think primarily of the costs of disc mastering and production. But the reality is that when you make a disc, you set up a production process to produce a whole stream of components. Not only must you make the contents of the disc, but you must also fabricate all the materials that go around it. You must create mechanical inserts and a box, pay for printing the inserts and the box, and pay for stamping the disc. As we mentioned before, in small disc runs, stamping the disc is actually cheaper than the printing!

Because the costs of disc mastering and manufacturing can be quite low, the cost of producing the printed insert pieces for the disc becomes significant. Since these are traditional printing costs, they exhibit economies of scale much more strongly than do the discs themselves.

One area where there is no particular economy of scale is the cost of the art and design for the product and packaging. You will want to hire a graphic artist to make the mechanicals. A set of separations runs about $500 for a jewel box, and much more for the box covers. A box for your disc could easily cost $12,000 to $12,500 in package design if you really want to make a splash.

Let's look at some real examples.

Jewel Box With Insert

First, consider the case of the traditional jewel box with a booklet insert in the front and a drop-in printed tray card in the back. The cost breakdowns for this type of product, shown in Table 10-1, are based on two options: a one-page insert, or an eight-page booklet with a four-color front page that is otherwise one-color (called a 4/1 job). For this package, we've shown sets of numbers over a range of production runs.

The colors assumed for this job are standard process colors; this choice allows the job to be printed with minimal press setup. Both prices include the cost of a one-color tray card, printed on one side only (called a 1/0 job), but do not include the costs for film.

NOTE

The costs we've quoted are samples only. They come from a standard quote from a printer who does a large volume of CD-ROM print work. Your own costs may vary because you can, in theory, have this work done by any printer who can handle the necessary paper stock. Be sure to get a variety of quotes from your own sources.

Table 10-1. Cost breakdown for printing jewel box booklets

Print Run	1-page booklet	8-page booklet
1,000	$230.00	$560.00
5,000	$700.00	$1,300.00
10,000	$1,100.00	$1,700.00

Point-of-Sale Display Options

There are many other kinds of packaging for CD-ROMs whose marketing is oriented to point-of-sale displays. We've listed a few possibilities below:

- **Box with artwork.** One common packaging is a box with artwork; such a package is similar to the box for a video game. The components of this package, working from the outside in, begin with the box itself. This is a complicated piece of artwork that has to fold out and that requires four-color separations that are about 30" × 15". Preparation of the art requires a designer who knows how to design boxes and to work with their special manufacturing processes. We can't quote the detailed cost of the box (designs vary too widely), but we would estimate that each box would cost about $1 for both printing and manufacturing. Of course, if you include some inserts in the box, allow some additional cost for those pieces.

- **Clear plastic package.** This is another good option for a point-of-sale display. This plastic package is similar to those used for music discs, with the booklet displayed separately from the disc.

- **Thin cardboard case.** These cases are typically the size of a magazine, with a cutout to hold the disc. They are designed to be used for discs sold at magazine stands.

The only limit on your disc packaging seems to be your (or your designer's) imagination. In general, if you are interested in packaging other than jewel boxes for your discs, contact your disc manufacturer for recommendations.

Cost of Mastering and Manufacturing

Both mastering and production costs may vary quite a lot, depending on the manufactured quantity and the turnaround time. *Turnaround time* (manufacturers use the phrase "the turn") is the number of days from the time the disc contents arrive at the production facility to the time you receive the completed disc.

Sample Cost Summary

Table 10-2 shows some sample mastering and manufacturing costs; these costs were provided by Disc Manufacturing, Inc.[*] and are based on quantities under 10,000.

Table 10-2. Sample mastering and manufacturing costs

Turnaround Time	Mastering/Setup	Replication Charge
15 days	$800	$1.40 per disc
10 days	$1,000	$1.50 per disc
5 days	$1,100	$1.50 per disc
3 days	$1,400	$1.70 per disc
2 days	$1,900	$1.90 per disc
1 day	$2,200	$2.10 per disc

Disc prices include a silk-screen printed label on the disc (provided from furnished positive film art work) in one or two colors. Assume in this cost estimate that all printed materials are to be furnished by the customer, and that prices

---

[*] Please note that these numbers were provided only as an example in a recent standard quote; they should not be considered binding in any way.

are FOB (freight on board) at the plant. The day begins with the Federal Express morning delivery. There is a $300 minimum replication charge. In addition, disc packaging in a jewel box is available at a per-disc charge of $.30 for the jewel box only, or $.35 for the jewel box with the printed booklet and tray card inserted, and shrinkwrap or polywrap (if desired). Colored plastic jewel boxes are available, but are not included in this quote.

This sample quote may or may not fit the characteristics of your particular project. Always contact your disc manufacturing firm for a precise price for each individual job.

Effect of DVD

Manufacturing is a place where the increase in costs typically associated with shifting from CD-ROM to DVD seems to be contained. Disc manufacturers are able to retool their plants to achieve the higher pit densities required by the DVD discs. In addition, the more sophisticated questions of partial silvering and disc lamination needed by the double-layer and two-sided DVD discs are within the technology that these manufacturers know well.

Costs for manufacturing DVD discs should continue to be modest compared to all the other costs of disc development and production.

Cost of Shipping

Shipping costs vary widely, depending on the location of your disc duplication firm and your distribution site, and on how quickly you must receive the discs from the duplicators. Your manufacturer no doubt has experience with shipping, and will probably have arrangements with a particular shipper. They can give you quotes based on actual locations and number of discs.

Note that shipping costs for CD-ROMs, in contrast to books, are typically quite modest because CD-ROMs are light and pack densely. Shipping costs can be reduced significantly if your schedule allows you to ship by truck or by another ground service such as UPS.

Cost of Marketing and Distribution

Chapter 11, *CD-ROM Marketing and Distribution*, describes these costs in some detail, so we won't explore them here.

NOTE

Remember that if you are selling the discs wholesale, you will only get about 50 percent of the retail dollar.

Looking at the Whole Picture

Now let's pull together the various steps and numbers we've looked at in this chapter.

Table 10-3, and its associated graphical version in Figure 10-1, presents a return-on-investment analysis for a CD-ROM with the following costs:

$100,000 for content creation and acquisition

$300,000 for production

$60,000 for testing

$40,000 for overhead and miscellaneous costs

$500,000 for total development cost

We'll assume the associated manufacturing cost to be $4 per disc, with no decline as volume increases. This is not entirely a correct assumption, as we've noted above, but the cost does includes the printing and packaging and probably provides an approximate average over a number of different kinds of projects.

This analysis also assumes a lower retail price in high volumes. The total cost we've shown equals the total development cost of $500,000 plus manufacturing and marketing costs. As you can easily observe, making money is not necessarily a trivial exercise!

Table 10-3.   Sample return-on-investment for a project with significant development costs

Quantity	Manufac-turing Cost	Marketing Cost (10% retail)	Total Cost	Retail Price	Total Retail	Wholesale (50% Retail)	Profit (Loss)
$10,000	40,000	100,000	640,000	100	1,000,000	500,000	(140,000)
$20,000	80,000	200,000	780,000	90	1,800,000	900,000	120,000
$30,000	120,000	240,000	860,000	80	2,400,000	1,200,000	340,000

It's quite important to perform this kind of break-even analysis—one in which you decide how many discs you have to sell, at what price point, in order to make the economics of a title work. This is what spreadsheets were invented for: for each different number of units you sell, your cost of goods changes a little bit as your volumes increase, whereas your fixed cost of developing the CD-ROM remains constant. In our example, we see that somewhere around a development budget of $250,000 and sales of 10,000 to 20,000 units, the economics work out to everyone's satisfaction. Clearly, this is why numbers such as these are working today.

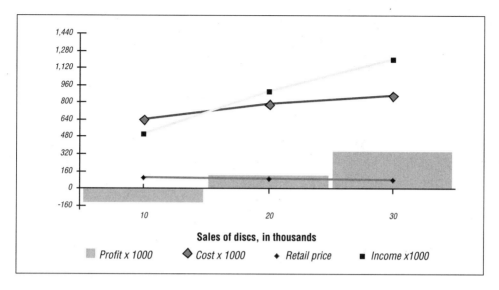

Figure 10-1.   A graphical presentation of the data in Table 10-3

NOTE

Other numbers we've seen in the trade press suggest that an average pro-
duction-only cost for consumer titles is a bit over $150,000, and for busi-
ness or education products is about $60,000. Given the production values
and content of the "average" disc, we feel a lot more comfortable with
the numbers supplied in this chapter.

Using this little economic model, you can figure out where your break-even is
and adjust accordingly. If $250,000 is too much for production, and if you think
you can sell the product for a different price point, then you must find ways to
adjust your production costs until you can find a budget that works. Perhaps the
production budget is $125,000, perhaps it's $100,000, or perhaps it's $60,000.
Many budgets are possible. The Judson Rosebush Company, for example, is
currently building discs for retail price points from $19.95 up to around $79.95,
for budgets of under $10,000 up into the mid six-figures range.

II

CD-ROM Marketing and Distribution

Marketing is the activity of promoting and selling your product. *Distribution* is the process of moving your product to the market. Marketing and distribution are closely tied together, but they are not the same thing. This chapter discusses the major CD-ROM marketing and distribution issues, and explores questions of pricing and sales quantities.

Our discussion in this chapter focuses on marketing and distribution for general-interest CD-ROM titles. We don't say a lot about the marketing and distribution of technical titles in this chapter, because these titles are most often part of an information stream oriented to a very distinct and focused audience. Examples of titles in this category include:

- The publications of a technical society (e.g., the SIGGRAPH electronic conference proceedings described in Chapter 3, *Two Electronic Titles*)

- CD-ROMs associated with a book series from a technical book publishing house (e.g., the CD-ROMs that accompany several of the books from O'Reilly & Associates and other publishers)

- The sole source of a particular body of information (e.g., the many CD-ROMs of planetary data and images from NASA)

The marketing and distribution issues for these kinds of CD-ROMs tend to be quite specialized. Nevertheless, we hope that authors, developers, and publishers of technical titles will get some benefit from reading the more general discussion in this chapter.

NOTE

A caveat: We are not experts in marketing and distributing CD-ROM publications. Much of the information we provide in this chapter represents secondhand experience, based on our watching these processes work and talking with people in the industry. We do want to share what we know with you, though, since marketing and distribution issues are very important to the overall CD-ROM business. For detailed information on marketing and distribution, we advise you to consult experts in these areas.

Nature of the CD-ROM Publishing Industry

The CD-ROM publishing industry is still very new, and it's not clear exactly what the publishing model of that industry will turn out to be. We expect that some retail model will apply in the CD-ROM business—but which model, or combination of models? Will it look like publishing models in more traditional industries? Because the industry involves aspects of the traditional book, record, movie, television, and software industries, the economic and business models from all of those industries do carry over into the CD-ROM publishing industry. But the models from those different industries are not identical to each other, and none of them can be extended exactly into CD-ROM publishing.

Looking at Publishing Models

Let's look at one particular example of the differences between industries. Consider the financial relationship of an author to her publisher. What is that relationship in different industries? Books typically pay authors royalties on the order of 10 to 20 percent of the publisher's income on the title. Videocassettes pay royalties of about 20 percent on the wholesale price. Software works on a different basis, as do records. How can we expect the royalty structure of the CD-ROM publishing industry to work?

We do think it's likely that CD-ROM publishing will incorporate the classic publishing model—one that involves distributing tangible physical property to a customer. The classical model involves a series of parties who are relatively segregated from each other. Just as a wrist is connected to a forearm, which in turn is connected to an upper arm, with joints in between, each of the parties in the publishing business—the author, developer, publisher, wholesaler, or distributor—is connected to the next one. At the beginning of this sequence of links is the party we might call the *artist*. In the record business, the artist is the musician; in the book business, the artist is the author. Further down the chain is the party we might call the *publisher*. And at the end of the chain is the *marketer* or *distrib-*

utor, who makes the connection between the product and the actual *customer* (who purchases the product through a retail store, direct mail, or some other means).

In any kind of segmented industry, we need to clearly understand how revenues are distributed. As with books, we expect the model in the CD-ROM industry to be such that the wholesaler and the retailer will together take about 50 percent of the retail dollar, and the author and publisher will take the other 50 percent of the retail dollar.[*]

Wholesaler and retailer

We're not sure what the split will end up being between the wholesaler and the retailer, but in any case, it's not something that the author, developer, or publisher can really change.

Author and publisher

The split between the author and publisher is probably of more interest because that's where the authors (and, we expect, this book's readers) are more directly involved. In the CD-ROM industry to date, authors have been getting somewhere in the range of 8 percent to perhaps 25 percent of the funds we've identified for author and publisher. One of the key factors in determining where an author falls in this range is the question of who puts up the money—the publisher or the author? (There may also be a developer, and, if so, the developer becomes another party in these arrangements.)

Comparing Books and CD-ROMs

Historically, the party who puts up the money and who finances production of a work gets the lion's share of the reward from that work. In the book business, that party is the publisher; in the record business, it's the label. It's the publisher who covers the cost of producing a book, and the label that pays for an artist's recording session. The publisher pays an advance to the author, usually in the range of $2,000 to $10,000 (the high side is actually rather rare for a typical book)—and the author usually complains that this advance is too small. What the author often fails to realize, however, is that the publisher will spend approximately $25,000 to $100,000 to get the book to press. Printing a book is an expensive endeavor; the cost of manufacturing is somewhere around $6 to $10, or

---

[*]There will likely be some variation in these percentages, of course; if you are in a powerful position because of your ability to deliver a unique product, or if you have a tremendous amount of name recognition at the time you sign, you can probably get a little extra for yourself.

even $12, to print and bind each copy of the book. Books are expensive to develop, expensive to manufacture, and expensive to store and distribute.

Most book publishers haven't yet figured out the key cost differences between books and CD-ROMs. In the CD-ROM business, the cost of development is typically quite high, whereas the cost of manufacturing and warehousing is quite low (compared with books, at least). On the other hand, in the book business, the cost of development is typically lower (all that is needed, for minimal publishing, is a graphic artist and some prepress tools), whereas the cost of manufacturing and warehousing is a good deal higher.

Publishers are often disturbed by the fact that CD-ROM development work will typically cost them somewhere around $150,000 to $300,000 (before production). They forget that, unlike books, CD-ROMs cost only about $2 apiece to manufacture once development is complete. Moreover, the economies of scale are quite different from the book business. CD-ROM publishers can go back to the manufacturer as many times as necessary to get additional discs stamped in whatever quantity is needed—at essentially that same price. In fact, CD-ROM manufacturers usually keep the stampers for some time after the initial run, which further drives manufacturing costs down.

Consider the difference between reprinting a book and restamping a CD-ROM. If a CD-ROM title is selling very well and the publisher needs availability of 5,000 copies a week, they can go to the manufacturer and get 5,000 copies a week stamped. If a title sells 5,000 copies a year, they can go back to the manufacturer a year after the initial run, and get another 5,000 stamped. If the title isn't selling as well after a year, they can ask for only 1,000 or 2,500 copies. There will be very little difference in the incremental price.

But printing books is quite a different situation. If a publisher wants to go back to the printer and get a second printing of 1,000 or 2,500 copies, their incremental expense will be considerable. First of all, they'll be quoted a much higher per-copy cost than if they'd printed the entire run the first time (possibly by a factor of two). Second, they'll end up with several tens of thousands of dollars of heavy material inventory that must be put in a warehouse, so the cost of inventory is very high.

NOTE

One conclusion we can draw from this analysis of the differences between book and CD-ROM publishing is that CD-ROMs should be much slower than books to go out of print.

We expect that, with a little experience, traditional book publishers will come to discover that the economics of the CD-ROM are quite favorable, and more and more of them will be drawn into the business. There are a number of compelling reasons that book publishers are likely to enter the CD-ROM business. The work a CD-ROM developer does to develop the ideas and presentation for a general-audience disc title is in many ways similar to the work that a literary editor performs in developing the ideas and presentation for a general-audience book. Similarly, marketing and distributing information or entertainment CD-ROMs is much like marketing books.

CD-ROM Marketing

This section describes a variety of marketing models and activities. First, some terms. As we've mentioned, *marketing* is the promotion and selling of your product. Marketing includes such activities as advertising, sales calls to distributors, market research, and often packaging. *Advertising* is the promotion of your product in mass media; it's designed to get the word out on your product, and to stimulate interest in purchasing it. *Point-of-purchase advertising* is advertising that is placed at the point of sale—for example, in the retail store.

Marketing is a nontrivial component of CD-ROM publishing. If nobody buys your CD-ROM, it doesn't matter how good it is. Marketing activities, such as getting publicity and buying advertising, are necessary components of publishing. So many titles are created today that it's very hard to get your product in front of the people who might be interested enough to pay for it. Marketing makes that connection.

Media marketing is extremely sophisticated, tedious, and expensive. Basically, to justify the cost of such marketing, you will need a critical audience mass. If you expect to sell about 5,000 copies of your CD-ROM, the finances can pay off for you (as we discuss later, in the section called "How Many Units Will You Sell?"). But that number can't justify a huge media blitz.

Even selling 5,000 copies is a lot of work. You have to find 5,000 people who want to spend their money to buy something that you've made. Fortunately, there are some good ways to reach particular audiences, and ways of taking the risk out of product marketing, as we discuss in the following sections.

Marketing Approaches

The key to successful marketing is to get your product in front of the particular audience you expect to be most interested in buying it. Suppose you decide to make a CD-ROM about Charles Babbage and Ada Lovelace. Maybe you even decide to include such unique content as a complete simulation of the Babbage

---

Branding as a Marketing Strategy

A good example of a marketing strategy was developed by Byron Preiss, owner of a small CD-ROM publishing company in New York. His brilliant idea is the idea of *branding,* that is, the idea of differential labels. There are a number of different CD-ROM labels, each with a distinct identity. A customer comes to expect a certain type of product because of its association with a particular brand.

Branding is an old idea in the book and record business, and it's also an idea that's very much part of the movie industry. For example, Touchstone Pictures is owned by Walt Disney Corporation; Buena Vista is owned by Walt Disney Corporation; Epic Records is part of what's now Sony or CBS; and Elektra, Atlantic, and Nonesuch are all owned by the same company. Despite these affiliations, each different label has a very different connotation to it.

---

analytical engine, and instructions on how to make your own copy. A pretty specialized subject! When the project is finished, and you're sitting in New York with the manufactured discs, how do you sell 5,000 of them? You could hang a little sign out on 46th Street saying "Charles Babbage CD-ROM for Sale," but we suspect you won't be able to give them away! You could send them out to every distributor in the country, and virtually all of them will think you're nuts. You can take a booth at a conference (for about $3,000), and you might succeed in selling 50 copies there. What's our point? That it's a big, hard, difficult job to market your product.

And yet, there are many good, and not too expensive, ways to get people to pay attention to your CD-ROM so they'll be receptive to purchasing it. A quick look at any CD-ROM magazine will demonstrate a number of good marketing ideas:

- You can try to get your CD-ROM featured, or even just mentioned, in a magazine article.

- You can try to get your product reviewed by the magazine—either on its own or as part of a group review.

- You can buy a display, spot, or classified advertisement.

- You can take advantage of many of the newer electronic versions of word-of-mouth advertising—for example, getting your CD-ROM mentioned on computer newsgroups or forums.

As we discuss in the distribution section later in this chapter, marketing is closely tied to distribution; it's also possible to have your distributor do part of your marketing for you.

Advertising

If you are going to publish your CD-ROMs yourself, you need to understand advertising and how to use this expensive medium to best advantage. Few CD-ROM publishing projects will justify mass media advertising. Even small ads are very expensive. Many CD-ROMs are advertised in the tiny display box ads in the back of magazines such as *CD-ROM World*. You may be surprised to learn that these tiny ads are $450 apiece—with a frequency discount, you may be able to get this cost down to $300 each.

The key to any kind of advertising is to understand your audience, to create promotional materials that will get that audience's attention, and to get these materials into the hands of that audience. Understanding the audience is vital—who they are, what they want, and what they read. If you have a tightly focused title that appeals to one particular type of audience, then taking out full-page ads in national news magazines, at perhaps $65,000 a page, is not a good way to reach that audience. Taking out ads in the trade press for your specialty, at much cheaper rates, is a far better strategy.

Advertising is its own world. Here we only touch on this area. Reading some specialized books, or taking an advertising course at a local junior college, will tell you more about what you need to know.

Mailing lists

The trouble with advertising is that it is scatter-shot; there is little guarantee that the people you want to reach will actually see your ad, never mind be receptive to it. Targeted mailing lists are often a better way to reach a specialized audience. If you buy an appropriate mailing list and do a direct mailing to that list, you'll have a much better chance of reaching the people who are most likely to be interested in buying your CD-ROM.

For example, the mailing list of a professional organization might have 60,000 names on it, identifying members and other people who have attended their conferences. Most organizations have some provision for selling, or allowing one-time use of, their lists. *National Geographic*, Time-Life Books, the National Wildlife Federation, the Smithsonian, ACM SIGGRAPH—all of them have mailing lists and marketing deals with their built-in audiences. Obviously, not all lists are interchangeable. Be sure that the people on it are representative of the audience you expect to be interested in your CD-ROM.

Catalogs

Catalogs are a good marketing tool, as the book business (and many other businesses) has discovered. Some publishers sell directly to the public through their catalogs. General catalogs like CD-ROM Warehouse are very much part of a retail marketing and distribution model: typically, the publisher sells to the catalog company; and the catalog company acts as a direct-mail retailer.

As a publisher, you may go through a wholesaler to get to the catalog company or you may not.

The section called "Direct sales" in the distribution discussion later in this chapter provides some additional information about the use of catalogs.

Trade shows

It is quite expensive to buy a booth at a trade show. Unless your CD-ROM directly matches the interests of the audience at a particular show, it's usually not worth the cost. However, you might consider showing your CD-ROM at a wholesaler's trade show.

The Internet

People are learning that Internet marketing is a very good addition to an overall marketing mix, especially if you're marketing to people who own computers and who like to do innovative things with them. In general, the Internet is an excellent place to promote your CD-ROMs. In various places there, you can put what amounts to trailers for your product online. Because people often go to the Internet to find cool stuff, it's a great place to make *your* cool stuff visible.

Advertisers, networks, and publishers don't yet get it about the Internet. They don't understand that the Internet is a bottom-up phenomenon, like the phone company—all person-to-person. The large companies want to move in with a top-down approach that is modeled on broadcasting (i.e., put the information on the Internet and then broadcast it). But that's not what the Internet culture is all about. The Internet is much more analogous to ham and CB radio than it is to Cox Broadcasting.

Marketing Models for CD-ROM Publishing

Effective marketing models for CD-ROM marketing are only beginning to emerge. As we've mentioned elsewhere, the overall model for CD-ROM publishing is similar in many ways to the publishing models for books, records, videocassettes, and so on. You'd expect the marketing models for these industries to have much in common.

There are three rules of thumb for CD-ROM publishing that you may hear quoted:

- The cost of marketing is about $4 a disc.

- The cost of marketing is 10 percent of the purchase price.

- The cost of marketing equals the cost of development.

Our experience is that the first two rules are pretty accurate; the third deserves more analysis.

The Hollywood marketing model

This last rule is really based on the Hollywood model. On an $8 million production budget for a movie, Hollywood usually spends $8 million of advertising to break the picture into the theaters. The studio spends a few hundred thousand dollars flying theater owners in from around the country to see the movie in previews. They provide various trinkets as forms of persuasion, trying to convince distributors to exhibit this picture, as opposed to somebody else's picture.

But the Hollywood-style, everything-at-once marketing and distribution model is not the only one. Some movies force themselves into the public mind by sheer excellence, some luck, and a lot of word-of-mouth. Some start in the art houses in a few major cities, get critical reviews, and then break out into the mainstream.

The record business marketing model

Consider the record business. This business is also known for breaking records from small beginnings. You and your band members can get 1,000 copies of your record pressed, take it to your local radio stations, and persuade them to give it a try. If that works, you can start working the title regionally—you break it in Akron, Ohio; you move it in Cleveland; you move it up to Detroit, down to Louisville, to Pittsburgh, and to West Virginia. That's often how a record breaks into the music stores. Records are often broken in the Midwest—in small markets where the risks are low. There, you may be able to place a few thousand copies in the record stores, because the rack jobbers may have good rapport with the store managers. Traditionally, the last place a record gets airplay is Los Angeles or New York, because they're not the places where a new record gets its first attention.

The record business marketing model deserves attention for CD-ROM titles. Few publishers can afford the Hollywood model. The economies of manufacturing CD-ROMs also plays into this model: you can produce added copies of your disc at very low cost as you slowly expand your market.

CD-ROM Distribution

Distribution is the mechanics of moving the disk to the market. Distribution is clearly of a lot more interest if you intend to publish your own title. An author or developer who works with a publisher usually needs to know only whether the publisher has good distribution channels. If the channels are there, there is a better chance that your work will reach its audience and that you will be fairly compensated for your work. If you intend to be your own publisher, however, you will quickly have to face up to the question of how best to distribute your CD-ROMs.

Looking at CD-ROM Finances

The distribution model for CD-ROM publishing, like the marketing model, is likely to evolve into one that's similar to that of other types of publishing. As with books and records, the model involves an author, a developer, and a publisher. Often, the publisher is the sole source of financing; sometimes, the publisher might have made a deal with distributors in which they promise to take a certain number of every title published, which cuts the risk somewhat. Usually, there is a retail store at the end of the chain. In some cases, the distributor will handle all of the markets—regional, national, and international. In other cases, you will work with more than one distributor to cover all the markets you expect to penetrate.

You've probably gathered, after reading Chapter 1, *Electronic Publications*, that your income from CD-ROM development is likely to be much less than you would expect. Let's look at a CD-ROM that sells 1,000 copies at $39.00 each. Unfortunately, the economics of the situation are such that you won't end up with anything like a $39,000 development budget. Let's break down the overall $39,000 revenues and see where they go.

First of all, there must be a return for the wholesaler and others in the distribution chain. This return often amounts to as much as 50 percent—or even more on a small title. After $20,000 for the wholesaler, you're now down to $19,000. If you're going to self-publish the title, you'll also have to spend about $4,000 to manufacture and package the disc and packaging—now, you're down to $15,000. On this $15,000 budget, you need to develop, market, and distribute your product.

As we've discussed in the previous section, you can expect marketing to be a significant cost. You have to get somebody to put the CD-ROM in the stores for you, to convince a wholesaler to take it, or to run ads in a magazine to sell it directly. Let's suppose that you choose to do your own magazine ads as part of your media buy. As we mentioned earlier, even tiny ads in *CD-ROM World* might run $300 each with a frequency discount. At this rate, a media buy of 10 ads will cost you $3,000. Let's also assume that you're buying at least another $2,000 on your marketing. Now you're down to a $10,000 budget. You're going to have to spend this $10,000 very, very carefully; out of that amount, you'll have to budget your development costs, all your overhead expenses, and profits.

Does this sound daunting? It's just realistic. Experience in the business shows that on a CD-ROM that has a $30 wholesale price (that is, a disc in the $59 retail range), perhaps $2 to $3 trickles back to development and profit. Because your disc has a retail price of $39, and only a $19 or $20 wholesale price, you may well fall short of those few precious dollars.

NOTE

Remember that the distributor of a CD-ROM is also the place to which customers will turn when they have problems with the product. Product support isn't something that most authors and developers pay much attention to, but it can take some real financial and personnel resources to provide. You'll need to consider these resources if you plan to distribute discs yourself.

Distribution Models

The distribution models for CD-ROM publishing are still evolving. This section looks at various models in other types of related businesses in an effort to project how CD-ROMs will be sold.

Retail outlets

There are several different approaches to retail distribution: a direct sales force, manufacturer's representatives, consignment, and association with larger publishers.

Only the largest companies employ their own sales forces to sell all of their products. More often, you'll want to take advantage of such middlemen as wholesalers and manufacturer's representatives to distribute CD-ROMs. In the retail model, the publisher sells the product in quantity to a wholesaler, who in turn distributes the product to individual retail outlets. In each industry, two or three wholesalers tend to dominate the market.

Sometimes, a publisher will sell to chain stores directly, instead of going through wholesale distributors. For example, in the book business, several large chains account for a significant amount of the retail outlets (bookstores, in this case). Most publishers sell directly to those chains, and then use wholesalers to reach the rest of the market.

A similar strategy involves the use of manufacturers' representatives. These reps typically handle several different publishing companies; they serve as a kind of substitute sales force, calling on stores on behalf of the various publishers. In the record business, such reps are called rack jobbers.

Another distribution model, known as *consignment*, might make sense for CD-ROMs, especially if you are doing your own publishing. Records and books are often consigned into retail outlets. Consignment means that you not only pay to produce and manufacture the records or books, but the store doesn't even pay you for the copies you place there. Basically, you give copies to the store, the store sells them, gives you your percentage of the copies they sell, and returns to you the ones they don't sell. Most publishers don't like the consignment model. The model isn't necessarily bad business for CD-ROMs, however, because your cost for manufacturing the product is quite small compared to the price it will command at retail.

Another variation on the retail model is appropriate for the small CD-ROM publisher. Publishers can join what is commonly called an ALP (Associate Label Program). The larger publishers in the industry, such as Brøderbund, offer ALPs. You absorb the cost of developing the CD-ROM gold master, and provide them with that master. The ALP publisher then manufactures, markets, and distributes the disc for you. Typically, they sell the product wholesale. After taking out the manufacturing and marketing costs, they pay you a certain percentage of the product. In general, you should expect to net around 20 percent of the retail selling price in this kind of ALP arrangement. That percentage might be good business or bad business for you, depending on the price point, the cost of manufacturing, and how much you value the marketing and distribution services the ALP offers.

Direct sales

Direct mail accounts for a significant portion of retail sales in America, and this channel is continuing to grow. If you are able to place your product into a direct mail catalog, the mail-order firm distributes the catalogs and processes the orders. Depending on how things are organized, they'll either fulfill the order themselves, or forward the order to you for fulfillment. In the CD-ROM business, a publisher often pays for the catalog space. Basically, this is a type of marketing cost.

You might also want to consider trying to create your own direct mail catalog, or doing other types of direct selling, such as purchasing mailing lists and soliciting customers directly.

Direct sales are very attractive financially, because they involve no wholesaler. The result is that you receive the full sales price yourself. If you sell your CD-ROM for $39.95, you get all of the $39.95 yourself—except for the 5 percent fee it takes your fulfillment house to process your transaction, the cost of your advertising, and the cost of shipping (which you may or may not be able to pass on to the customer). You will need to decide whether the extra amount of money warrants the associated costs—in money and time. Once you get into direct sales, you are now running a very different kind of business than the business of disc development. You will have to be able to deal with marketing, sales, returns, and customer support problems.

If you are seriously considering doing direct sales, you need to be sure that there is someone in your organization who can handle bookkeeping, run spreadsheets, and give you full information on your development, marketing, and fulfillment costs, and on your sales income.

Bulk sales

Sometimes you will have customers who want to buy a number of copies of your CD-ROM at the cheapest possible price. There are distribution strategies that are particularly oriented to this type of customer. For example, Sirius Publishing sells what they call a "5 Foot 10 Pak." The attractive packaging contains 10 discs in a 5-foot long foldout package at a very moderate price.

You might also be able to arrange to put your CD-ROM(s) into someone else's bulk package. You might also consider assembling your own or others' CD-ROMs into your own bulk package.

Because bulk sales involves charging minimal prices to the customer, it is only worthwhile if you'll be able to get large numbers of discs into distribution.

Subscriptions

In the subscription model, a publisher ships a new product to the customer every 30 or 60 days. The most obvious subscription model is the magazine, but subscription is also widely used for books, records, and videocassettes. With subscriptions, the product may either be prepaid (as a magazine subscription would be) or returnable (as a book club would be). This model is sure to play a role for CD-ROMs.

Premiums

With this model, a large quantity of goods are sold to a single client, usually a corporation, who gives them away for promotional purposes. For example, an insurance company might buy a large number of road atlases, and then give them away to customers or potential customers in return for filling out a questionnaire. The title might be a custom work (developed to the customer's specifications), a title altered to meet certain specifications, or simply a general title or one originally developed for another purpose.

We've seen "goodies" CD-ROMs given away in this fashion to reward customers for renewing computer magazine subscription.

Electronic distribution

Electronic distribution is a new approach to distribution. With this model, a vendor provides products on servers. A user can dial into the product directly and is charged on an access-time basis. We expect electronic distribution to be a popular area in the future, and discuss it in more detail in "Alternatives to CD-ROM Distribution," later in this chapter.

Combinations

The distribution models we've discussed can be worked in many combinations. For example, magazines are sold by subscription, but are also sold on newsstands; records are sold retail, by direct mail, and by record clubs.

Trends in CD-ROM Distribution

CD-ROM sales patterns are changing, as the content and the public perception of the medium evolve. In the early days of CD-ROMs, a large part of the content was computer software—or at least was seen as computer software. At that time, the majority of the sales were in computer stores. In 1994, for example, this was the sales picture:

- Computer stores accounted for slightly more than half of all CD-ROM sales.

- Software specialty stores accounted for just under a quarter of all sales.

- Another quarter of all sales were in all other channels combined; these included consumer electronics stores, video stores, music and book stores, and catalog sales. These "other channels" are much more typical locations for traditional consumer purchases.

In 1995, the sales picture had changed quite significantly:

- Computer store sales had shrunk to 35 percent.

- Software specialty stores accounted for only 9 percent of sales.

- The channels that represent more traditional consumer purchases now carried 56 percent of CD-ROM sales.

Naturally enough, the shift towards traditional consumer patterns parallels a corresponding shift in CD-ROM content. Now, most CD-ROMs are games, educational products, or consumer educational products. Documentary and educational television is full of advertisements for CD-ROM products whose contents are very similar to those of the broadcast programs. Retail channels are now much more like the large-scale discount chains, where discs are displayed in a way that encourages impulse purchases. The whole landscape of CD-ROM marketing has changed; the industry is moving away from the computer image to the kind of mass-market image cultivated by books and music.

This evolution may seem to be a good thing for CD-ROMs, but it has a downside. A significant limiting factor on CD-ROM sales is now the limited space available in the traditional channels for this new type of product. There is a finite amount of shelf and rack space that is available for CD-ROMs, leading to "shelf wars" for discs that are very similar to the supermarket shelf wars for detergents and cereals. In any industry, there are certain tried-and-true ways of winning such wars:

- Use distributors who are able to pull shelf space for your product.

- Use packaging that will draw the consumer's eye to your product and then intrigue him or her about the contents.

- Build name recognition for your titles and your product line; name recognition is, of course, all about promotions and publicity.

What we're talking about here is the traditional marketing taught in undergraduate marketing courses all over the world. What they teach there about cereal is just as true of CD-ROMs: all marketing, like all politics, is eventually local—you have to get the word to the individual who is going to part with the money for your product.

Alternatives to CD-ROM Distribution

Although the focus in this book is on CD-ROM publishing and distribution, be aware that there are some reasonable alternatives to CD-ROMs for distributing documents. For example:

- You could consider distributing your materials on other disk media, such as diskette.

- Some online sources allow users to download documents from the Internet or other networks or to have documents returned by an email request.

- There are a number of FTP sites that maintain documents online, and a number of places around the world that make documents available on the World Wide Web for access by a Web browser or other tools.

There are some drawbacks to each of these approaches. As we've mentioned, any other disk medium (e.g., a diskette) is less stable than CD-ROM and, for any product over almost trivial size, more expensive to manufacture. We simply do not believe that this is a viable option.

As we discussed in Chapter 2, *CD-ROM and Online Publishing*, most network distribution schemes operate with no financial return to whomever provides the documents. This model makes them an ideal vehicle for sharing public domain information, but not for more general commercial publications. In addition, documents designed originally for network distribution are usually designed to work on many different kinds of computers. Thus, they tend to have minimal functionality—they are rarely more than text files, although more and more of them are using technologies such as HTML to include standard kinds of images and other media.

There are a few examples of strongly designed documents with rich content for a single computer system that are distributed as installation packages on a network. However, taking advantage of all the functionality of software such as Web browsers may require that you prepare your documents with a lot of manual work; HTML documents, for example, require that you build all your links with markup tags and work out URL addresses for your components. Fortunately, there is a growing set of tools that can help you create your HTML documents so this is not as difficult as it was in the early days of the Web.

Suppose that you do want to avoid dealing with physical media by distributing your work on the networks. How can you get a financial return on your work? There are two common approaches:

- One approach is to distribute the documents in coded form and give the reader the key when he pays for the document (for example, by buying a subscription). If your distribution is relatively narrow, you may have some confidence that the key is adequate; if it is wide, there is inevitably a much larger chance that the key will be compromised. This may open your publication to nonpaying consumers.

- Another approach is to have some sort of validation or charge for online access. Some BBSs work by collecting your credit card payment in advance; a 900 number is another possibility. At this point, there does not seem to be a sound solution to the validation problem in the network environment.

The industry hasn't yet settled on what the best marketing and distribution models will be for selling CD-ROM content distributed via the networks. As we mentioned earlier in the book, to achieve some structured method of economic return, the models would probably have to involve some metering charges on the information—perhaps on bytes sent, files transferred, or time used. We are concerned that either the distributor or the customer would likely have to cover some significant charges for network use—we will have to wait to see how significant the network charges are to determine how much effect this will have.

NOTE

It's certainly important to have financial returns on publications that support the ongoing efforts of the publisher and to ensure that the publication enterprise can continue to function. However, it's important to ensure that the authors' intellectual property rights are respected so that authors will continue to find it worthwhile for them to publish in this way.

Financial Models

How much should you sell your CD-ROM for? And how many copies will you be able to sell? These are key questions in determining whether your publishing efforts will succeed or fail. This section looks at what your CD-ROM financial model should be.

What Should the Selling Price Be?

How do you set the price of your CD-ROM? The price of a publication is usually set by considering three major components:

- The cost of developing it

- The cost of manufacturing it

- The desired return to the author and publisher

The only price that matters to the publisher is the wholesale net (the price the wholesaler can charge the retailer).

As we discussed in Chapter 10, *CD-ROM Publishing Costs*, some CD-ROMs cost more to develop than do traditional publications, such as books, but CD-ROMs have lower manufacturing costs than print publications do. Certain other costs, such as editorial and advertising, are more or less the same, whether you're developing a book or a CD-ROM. But these are not the only price considerations for publications.

The best overall basis for a price is the value to the reader, not the cost to the publisher. The greatly increased capacity and capabilities of CD-ROM titles allow a single CD-ROM to become a very valuable resource to its audience. Of course, the price you charge for your CD-ROM must recover the cost of its development and distribution. Beyond that, however, if there are external measures of value for the information, you need not price your disc below these measures.

Here is an example. Suppose that your title is the electronic version of a book; the cost of the printed version represents an external measure. In general, you wouldn't charge less for the electronic version than the printed version, on the theory that the electronic one provides additional value. (There are some cases where this measure might not hold; for example, we priced the SIGGRAPH electronic version below the printed one to encourage sales of the new medium—and also because the manufacturing costs were lower for the electronic version.)

How Many Units Will You Sell?

The main goal of a publisher in the CD-ROM industry should be to make a good product at a price point and a budget that fits the particular product and its market. The goal is not to create products with large budgets to feed the publisher's ego! It's very important you understand this goal, because there aren't very many companies that are making products which sell a large number of copies. As the industry grows—even if it grows with the kind of inflationary madness that is projected by some market analysts—we don't believe that we'll see the average sale of a CD-ROM title dramatically increase.

Why not? The fact is that there are very few of anything that sell in the high hundreds of thousands of copies in our culture. There has been a trend in the last several years for more and more of the retail consumer dollars to be spent for a smaller and smaller number of products.

In the broadcasting world, for example, the concept of Top 40 radio is almost dead, and we now have Top 30 radio or Top 20 radio. Fewer and fewer songs are getting more and more airplay, and similarly fewer and fewer movies are generating more and more of the aggregate retail box office. There is a tendency in the culture to build hits. Madonna is a hit phenomenon that accounts for something like 20 to 33 percent of all record sales from Warner Communications, or over $200 million dollars. She even affects the stock dividends of this company!

In spite of the obsession with hits, there are many records and books that sell in modest numbers and are still solidly profitable. People like Leo Kottke or John Lee Hooker or Judy Collins do not sell hundreds of thousands of records; they sell thousands or tens of thousands of records. Similarly, in the book business, for every Stephen King, Danielle Steele, and Tom Clancy, there are many thousands of smaller sellers. A large number of books or record titles get printed or pressed in this country, but most of them are printed or pressed in fairly small quantities.

Book publishers don't print hundreds of thousands of copies for more than a handful of titles; most are printed in runs of 5,000, 7,000, or 10,000. Publishers can make money manufacturing and selling a book in 5,000 or even fewer units. You can also make money doing CD-ROMs in 5,000-unit quantities.

To make money with these quantities, however, you must approach the business conservatively. If you're thinking of entering the CD-ROM publishing business, remember that you must walk before you can run! If you're successful with a limited product, selling in limited numbers, you can always go back and make your product better. You can create new editions, or create more titles, or do many other things. But if you fail, and hemorrhage your financial resources, it's very difficult to go back and get a second shot at publishing.

Think conservatively: you may find that fewer people than you originally hoped are sufficiently interested in your special topic to spend their money to get it—even though you're sure you know what the world needs. On the other hand, there may be a dedicated cadre of people, perhaps even thousands of them, who are willing to buy your product. If you plan your title with those conservative numbers in mind, you can be successful.

CD-ROM seems to us to be an ideal niche publishing medium. As the medium matures, we expect to see a very few titles selling in the millions of units, a small number selling in the hundreds of thousands, and many titles selling in much smaller numbers. Our guess is that the titles that sell large numbers of units in a single year will probably amount to a few hundred at most.

But this isn't bad news. The key to making a success with this reality lies in shaping who your audience is, budgeting your titles carefully, holding to your budget, and finding products that go into target audiences and work economically. By all means, we want to see authors take a roll of the dice in going after the million sellers—but you don't need to have that kind of success to make a CD-ROM title worthwhile. There is more than one economic model for a title that can work for you.

We anticipate that when we look back at the industry in five years, we'll see CD-ROMs in bookstores, CD-ROMs in record stores, CD-ROMs in discount chain stores, and CD-ROM (in DVD form) probably replacing VHS as a video medium. We also expect there will be a sizeable number of CD-ROM publishers who specialize in reaching modest-sized specialized audiences, and who know how to reach these audiences through specialized marketing and distribution channels. Clearly, when there are thousands of titles, there will be a lot of horizontal growth in the industry—but remember that most of those titles will have very modest sales. There is a good business to be had in modestly selling titles, but that part of the business is going to have to be very efficient, and the developers and distributors who make their living in it will have to have very sharp pencils.

P A R T

IV

Appendixes

This part of the book contains the following:

- *Appendix A, Resources*, lists resources for organizations that provide CD-ROM hardware, software, and services.
- The *Glossary* defines the terms used in this book and in the electronic publishing business.
- The *Bibliography* provides references for further reading.

APPENDIX

A

Resources

When you start out in electronic publishing, finding out who your potential resources are can be difficult. In this appendix we list the following resources:

- Companies doing CD-ROM manufacturing

- Companies offering one-off CD-R discs or brokering disc manufacturing

- Companies making CD-ROM packaging systems

- Companies making electronic document systems

The lists of CD-ROM duplication, one-off, and packaging companies are courtesy of the Optical Publishing Association and The CD-Info Company. The Optical Publishing Association is a professional and trade association with a great deal to offer to a person or publisher who is going into CD-ROM publication, including the association newsletter, reports on the state of the industry, and professional seminars on aspects of the field. Both individual (professional) and corporate memberships are offered. For more information on the Association, contact:

Richard Bowers
Executive Director
614-442-8805
fax 614-442-8815

or by electronic mail at:

Compuserve 71333,1114
Internet *71333.1114@compuserve.com*

The Association has a Web site at:

http://www.meta-media.com/opa/home.html

The CD-Info Company is a company in Huntsville, Alabama, which publishes The CD Information Center at: *http://www.cd-info.com/*. This site contains a number of resources on the CD industry, technology, and applications. These are updated frequently and you should look there for information that is more current than that in this book. Both the Optical Publishing Association and The CD-Info Company have been gracious in supporting us in developing this chapter, and we appreciate the resources they've made available.

Be aware that there are two major limitations of the lists we publish in this chapter. First, they are compiled from various sources, both published and nonpublished, but cannot be assumed to be complete. Our searches have almost certainly missed some sources; some companies have gone out of business or changed addresses since we compiled the information; and new companies and products have started up. In all cases the information we give is based on contacts we have made personally or on direct industry listings. We believe the information is reasonably accurate, but we can't guarantee its accuracy, and we neither endorse nor guarantee the quality of products or services provided by the listed firms.

Second, many of our contacts are within North America. We do not have the resources to extend significant investigations to the rest of the world, but we have been able to find a few such listings. We are sure there are significant resources in other countries, however, and encourage anyone reading this outside North America to ask for local sources.

CD Recording Systems

These are companies that produce either hardware or software components of CD recording systems. This information is courtesy of the Optical Publishing Association and The CD-Info Company. The names of companies that are members of the Optical Publishing Association are followed by an asterisk (*).

Alea Systems
>5016 Dorsey Hall Drive, Suite 102
>Ellicott City, MD 21042
>410-995-5830; fax 410-995-1517

Astarte
>10044 Adams Avenue, Suite 331
>Huntington Beach, CA 92646
>714-963-7030; fax 714-963-0529

Astarte GmbH
> Weberstrasse 1
> 76133 Karlsruhe, Germany
> +49 (0) 721-98 55 40; fax +49 (0) 721-85 38 62
> *sales@astarte.de*
> *http://www.astarte.de*

Austin InfoScience
> 1948 South Interstate Highway 35, Building B
> Austin, TX 78704-3696
> 800-38-CDROM, 512-440-1132; fax 512-440-0531

CeQuadrat, Inc.
> 1804 Embarcadero Road, Suite 101
> Palo Alto, CA 94303
> 800-330-MPEG, 415-843-3780; fax 415-843-3799

> *CeQuadrat, Inc.*
> Dennewartstr. 27
> W-52068 Aachen, Germany
> +49 241 963 1100; fax +49 241 963 1101
> *74777.1145@compuserve.com*

CD-ROM Strategies
> 6 Venture, Suite 208
> Irvine, CA 92718
> 714-453-1702; fax 714-453-1311

Corel
> 1600 Carling Avenue
> Ottawa, ON K1Z 8R7 Canada
> 800-394-3729, 613-728-3733; fax 613-761-9176
> *info@corel.com*
> *http://www.corel.com*

Creative Digital Research
> 7291 Coronado Drive
> San Jose, CA 95129
> 408-255-0999; fax 408-255-1011
> *info@cdr1.com*
> *http://www.cdr1.com*

Crowninshield Software, Inc.
> 1050 Massachusetts Avenue
> Cambridge, MA 02138
> 617-661-4945; fax 617-661-6254

dataDisc Inc.
Rt. 3, Box 1108
Gainesville, VA 22065
800-328-2347, 703-347-2111; fax 703-347-9085

*Dataware Technologies Inc.**
5775 Flatiron Parkway, #220
Boulder, CO 80301
303-449-4157; fax 303-442-1816

Eastman Kodak Co.
Writable CD Systems
460 Buffalo Road
Rochester, NY 14652-3834
716-722-9070; fax 716-722-0838
http://www.kodak.com/

Elektroson
Elektroson USA
10 Presidential Blvd, Suite 125
Bala Cynwyd, PA 19004
610-617-0850; fax 610-617-0856

Elektroson BV
PO Box 2436
5600CK Eindhoven, The Netherlands
(+31) 40 251 5065; fax (+31) 40 514 920
sales@elektroson.com

Incat Systems
M/S 110
691 S. Milpitas Blvd.
Milpitas, CA 95035
408-957-4535; fax 408-957-4554
http://www.adaptec.com/incat
74431.2004@compuserve.com

Incat Europe
Via Carnevali, 109
20158 Milano, Italy
+39 -2- 39 31 13 41; fax +39 -2- 39 31 13 74
74431.2004@compuserve.com

Information Management Research (IMR)
5660 Greenwood Plaza Blvd, Suite 210
Englewood, CO 80111
303-689-0022; fax 303-689-0055

Jeff Arnold
125 Indian Rock Road
Merrimack, NH 03054
603-424-0269; fax 603-429-0073
jarnold@mainstream.net
http://www.mainstream.net/~jarnold/cdrom/cdrom.html

JVC Information Products
17811 Mitchell Avenue
Irvine, CA 92714
714-261-1292; fax 714-261-9690

*Meridian Data Inc.**
5615 Scotts Valley Dr.
Scotts Valley, CA 95066
800-76-SALES, 408-438-3100; fax 408-438-6816

Moniker
108 Whispering Pines Drive, Suite 110
Scotts Valley, CA 95066
408-439-0712; fax 408-439-0713

Olympus Image Systems (USA)
Two Corporate Center Drive
Melville, New York 11747
800-346-4027, 516-844-5000, fax 516-844-5339
olympus@li.net
http://www.olympusamerica.com/

*One-Off CD Shops Inc.**
304 8th Ave. SW, Suite 610
Calgary AB T2P 1C2 Canada
800-387-1633 (US & Canada), 403-263-1370; fax 403-228-6480

*Online Computer Systems**
20251 Century Blvd.
Germantown, MD 20874
800-922-9204, 301-428-3700; fax 301-428-4973

Optical Laser
315 3rd St.
Huntington Beach, CA 92648
800-776-9215, 714-536-7990; fax 714-536-0817

Optical Media International
51 E. Campbell Avenue, Suite 170
Campbell, CA 95008
408-376-3511; fax 408-376-3519
sales@optmedia.com

OptImage Interactive Services
1501 50th St., Suite 100
W. Des Moines, IA 50266-7077
515-225-7000

Philips
Philips Key Modules
2099 Gateway Place Suite 100
San Jose, CA 95110
408-453-7373; fax 408-453-6444

Pinnacle Micro
19 Technology
Irvine, CA 92718
714-789-3000; fax 714-7289-3150

Pinnacle Micro Europe
Snipweg 3
1118 DN Shiphol South
The Netherlands
+31 20 653 49 49; fax +31 20 653 02 09

Pinnacle Micro Nippon
Kagurazaka Technos
3rd Floor
4, Tsukiji-cho
Shinjuku-ku, Tokyo 162
Japan
+03 5261 7171; fax +03 3235 7621

Pioneer New Media Technologies, Inc.
2265 E. 220th Street
Long Beach, CA 90810
800-444-6784, 310-952-2111; fax 310-952-2990

Plasmon Data, Inc.
2045 Junction Avenue
San Jose, CA 95131
408-474-0100; fax 408-474-0111

Ricoh Corp.
File Products Division
5150 El Camino Real
Los Altos, CA 94022
800-955-4353, 408-432-8800; fax 408-432-9266

Script Media
221 Elizabeth Street
Utica, NY 13501
315-797-4052; fax 315-797-1850

Smart and Friendly
20520 Nordhoff Street
Chatsworth, CA 91311
818-772-8001; fax 408-772-2888
http://www.smartandfriendly.com/

Smart Storage
100 Burtt Road
Andover, MA 01810
508-623-3300; fax 508-623-3310
http://www.smartstorage.com/

Sony Electronics
3300 Zanker Road
San Jose, CA 95134
800-352-SONY, 408-432-1600; 408-955-5169
http://www.SEL.sony.com/

TMS Inc.
800 El Camino Real West, Suite 52
Mountain View, CA 94040
415-903-2252

Trace
1040 East Brokaw Road
San Jose, CA 95131-2393
408-441-8040; fax 408-441-3399

Yamaha Systems Technology Division
  100 Century Center Court
  San Jose, CA 95112
  800-543-7457, 408-437-3133; fax 408-437-8791

Young Minds Inc.
  P.O. Box 8130
  1910 Orange Tree Lane
  Redlands, CA 92374
  714-335-1350; fax 714-798-0488
  sales@ymi.com
  http://www.ymi.com/

CD-ROM Manufacturers: Mastering and Replication

These companies master and replicate discs in quantity. Most of them also offer other services, including retrieval and presentation software, premastering, printing, and packaging services. This information is courtesy of the Optical Publishing Association and The CD-Info Company. The names of companies who are members of the Optical Publishing Association are followed by an asterisk (*).

*3M Company**
  3M Optical Recording Department
  3M Center
  Bldg 223-5N-01
  St. Paul, MN 55144
  800-336-3636, 612-733-2142; fax 612-733-0158

  3M California
  2933 Bayview Dr.
  Fremont, CA 94538
  510-440-8161; fax 510-440-8162

Allied Manufacturing (WEA)
  6110 Peachtree St.
  City of Commerce, CA 90040
  213-725-6900; fax 213-725-8767

Americ Disc
  Sales Office
  7575 Trans-Canada, Suite 500
  St-Laurent, Quebec H4T 1V6 Canada
  514-745-2244; (+1) 514-337-3989 fax

Plant
2525 Canadian St.
Drummondville, QB J2B 8A9 Canada
800-263-0419, 819-474-2655; fax 819-474-2870

Americ Disc
2 Sheppard Ave. E., Suite 900
Willowdale, ON M2N 5Y7 Canada
416-512-7001

AmericUK
London Service Center
London, UK
(+44) 181 600 3900; fax (+44) 181 749 7057

Miami Plant
8455 N.W. 30th Terrace
Miami, FL 33122
305-599-3828; fax 305-599-1107

California Plant
4701 Stoddard Road
Modesto, CA 95356
209-467-2400; fax 209-467-2417

San Jose (California) Service Center
Triptych CD Corporation
1250 Aviation Avenue, Suite 155
San Jose, CA 95110-1121
408-271-7373; fax 408-271-7370

Minneapolis Service Center
2100 West 96th Street
Bloomington, MN 55431 USA
612-881-6446; fax 612-881-6476

American Multimedia
2609 Tucker Street Extended
Burlington, NC 27215
910-229-5554; fax 910-228-1409

ASR
8960 Eton Ave.
Canoga Park, CA 91304
818-341-1124; fax 818-341-9131

Astral Tech Americas, Inc.
   5400 Broken Sound Blvd.
   Boca Raton, FL 33487
   407-995-7000; fax 407-995-7001

Australian Compact Disc Manufacturers
   37 Orsmond Street
   Hindmarsh, SA 5007 Australia
   (+08) 3 46-2333; fax (+08) 3 40-9040

BQC
   146 West Olentangy Street
   Powell, Ohio 43065
   614-799-0884; fax 614-799-0885
   mward@coil.com
   http://www.concourse.com/bqc

Cassette Productions
   4910 W. Amelia Earhart Drive,
   Salt Lake City UT 84116
   801-531-7555; fax 801-531-0740

CinRAM Canada
   2255 Markham Rd.
   Scarborough ON M1B 2W3 Canada
   416-298-8190; fax 416-2298-0612

   CINRAM New York
   660 White Plains Road
   Tarrytown, NY 10591 USA
   914-631-2800; fax 914-631-9281

   CINRAM South West
   5307 La Viva Lane
   Arlington, TX 76017
   817-465-2210; fax 817-465-1074

CIS Technology USA, Inc.
   Creative Data Products, Inc.
   1005 Montague Expressway
   Milpitas, CA 95035 USA
   408-934-2455; fax 408-934-2450

(DADC) Digital Audio Disc Corporation (Sony)*
> 1800 N. Fruitridge Ave.
> Terre Haute, IN 47804
> 800-323-9741, 812-462-8100; fax 812-462-8866

Denon Digital Industries Inc.
> 1380 Monticello Rd.
> Madison, GA 30650
> 706-342-3425; fax 706-342-0637

Disc Factory
> 6525 Sunset Boulevard
> Suite 205
> Hollywood, CA 90028
> 213-465-7522; fax 213-465-2457

Disc Manufacturing Inc.*
> 1409 Foulk Rd., Suite 202
> PO Box 7469
> Wilmington DE 19803-0469
> 800-433-DISC, 302-479-2500; fax 302-479-2527
> *http://www.discmfg.com/*
>
> *DMI Anaheim*
> 1120 Cosby Way
> Anaheim, CA 92805
> 714-238-7156/7158; fax 714-630-0303
>
> *DMI Huntsville*
> 4905 Moores Mill Rd.
> Huntsville, AL 35811
> 205-851-0373/0236; fax 205-852-8354

Disctronics Texas Inc.
> 2800 Sumitt Ave.
> Plano, TX 75074
> 214-881-8800; fax 214-881-8500

EMI Manufacturing
> 1 Capitol Way
> Jacksonville, IL 62650
> 803-522-9893; fax 803-522-3242

Europa Disk Ltd.
75 Varick St.
New York, NY 10013
212-226-4401; fax 212-966-0456

Eva-Tone
4801 Ulmerton Rd.
Clearwater, FL 34622
800-EVA-TONE, 813-572-7000; fax 813-572-6214

Future Media Productions, Inc.
25136 Anza Drive
Valencia, CA 91355
800-360-2728, 805-294-5575; fax 805-294-5583
srice@fmpi.com

Harmonic Hall Limited
19th Floor, Wharf Cable Tower
9 Hoi Shing Road
Tsuen Wan, N.T., Hong Kon
(+852) 2412-1388; fax (+852) 2414-2333
harmonic@hk.super.net
http://www.hk.super.net/~harmonic

HMG
15 Gilpin Ave.
Hauppauge, NY 11788
516-234-0200; fax 516-234-0346

IBM
1001 W.T. Harris Blvd.
Charlotte, NC 28257
704-924-6300; fax 704-924-7191

IPC
9400 Jeronimo
Irvine, CA 92718
714-588-7765; fax 714-588-7763

*JVC Disc America**
9255 Sunset Blvd., Suite 717
Los Angeles, CA 90069
800-677-5518, 310-274-2221; fax 310-274-4392

JVC Disc America
2 JVC Road
Tuscaloosa, AL 35405-3598
205-556-7111; fax 205-554-5535

*KAO Infosystems - Optical Division**
1857 Colonial Village Lane
Lancaster, PA 17601
800-525-6575, 717-392-7840; fax 717-392-7897

Kao Infosystems
41444 Christy Rd.
Fremont, CA 94338
510-657-8425; fax 510-657-8427 fax

Matrics Corp.
300 Main Street
East Rochester, NY 14445
800-747-0583, 716-383-4185; fax 715-383-4188
webmaster@matrics.com
http://www.matrics.com

Matrics Corp. Georgia
6425 Lawrenceville Hwy.
Tucker, GA 30084
800-908-9920, 770-908-0426; fax 770-934-5145

Matrics Corp. North Carolina
8101 Tower Point Drive
Charlotte, NC 28227
800-747-0583, 704-845-2143; fax 704-845-3595
MATRICSNC@AOL.com

Matrics Corp. Maryland
8639 Cobbscook Harbor
Pasadena, MD 21122
800-875-7288, 410-360-2772; fax 410-360-2866
twelsh@matrics.com

Matrics Corp. Florida
2117 Dekle Avenue, Suite J1
Tampa, FL 33606
800-878-4997, 813-251-2966; fax 813-251-2846
tpisciot@matrics.com

*Metatec-Discovery Systems**
   7001 Discovery Blvd.
   Dublin, OH 43017
   614-761-2000; fax 614-766-3140
   http://www.metatec.com/

MPO
   MPO
   Paris, France
   (+33) 1 41 10 51 51; fax (+33) 1 41 10 51 52

   MPO GmbH
   Cologne, Germany
   (+49) 221 92 16 700; fax (+49) 221 92 16 703

   MPO UK Ltd.
   London, UK
   (+44) 181 600 3900; fax (+44) 181 749 7057

   MPO Replitech
   Barcelona, Spain
   (+34) 3 638 34 45; fax (+34) 3 638 15 72

   Madrid, Spain
   (+34) 1 643 12 38; fax (+34) 1 643 02 38

   MPO-Siam
   Bangkok, Thailand
   (+662) 651 91 51; fax (+662) 651 91 54

*Nimbus Information Systems, Inc.**
   Nimbus East Coast
   P.O. Box 7427
   Charlottesville, VA 22906
   800-782-0778, 201-379-2890/4883; fax 804-985-4692

   Nimbus West Coast
   4524 Tobias Avenue
   Sherman Oaks, CA 91403
   800-292-0932; fax 818-783-7475

Optical Disc Corporation
   12150 Mora Drive
   Santa Fe Springs, CA 90670
   310-946-3050; fax 310-946-6030

P&O Compact Disc GmbH
>
> Auf dem Esch 8
>
> 49356 Diepholz, Germany
>
> +49 (0) 5441 977 0, 977 175, 977 180; fax +49(0) 5441 977 177
>
> *100043.764@compuserve.com*

P & Q CD
>
> 5460 N. Peck Rd. #E
>
> Arcadia, CA 91006
>
> 818-357-4088; fax 818-359-4229

Pioneer Video Manufacturing, Inc.
>
> 1041 E. 230th Street
>
> Carson, CA 90745
>
> 310-518-0710; fax 310-522-8698
>
> *pvmi@earthlink.net*
>
> *http://www.pioneerusa.com/replication.html*

Pilz Compact Disc Inc.
>
> 54 Conchester Rd.
>
> Concordville, PA 19331
>
> 610-459-5035; fax 610-459-5958

PMDC PolyGram Manufacturing
>
> *Sales Office*
>
> 1251 Avenue of the Americas, 22nd Floor
>
> New York, NY 10020 USA
>
> 212-512-9350; fax 212-512-9358
>
> *PMDC East*
>
> P.O. Box 400
>
> Grover, NC 28073 USA
>
> 704-734-4100; fax 704-734-4180
>
> *PMDC West*
>
> 3815 West Olive Avenue, Suite 202
>
> Burbank, CA 91505
>
> 818-848-2442; fax 818-848-3090

ProtoSound
>
> 14 School Street
>
> Briston, VT 05443
>
> 802-453-3334; fax 802-453-3343
>
> *102022.537@compuserve.com*

Quebecor Integrated Media
> 4918 20th Street East
> Fife, WA 98424
> 800-451-5742, 206-922-9393; fax 206-926-0953
> *karen@quebim.com*

Rainbo Records
> 1738 Berkeley St.
> Santa Monica, CA 90404
> 310-829-3476; fax 310-828-8765

Sanyo-Verbatim CD Company
> 1767 Sheridan Street
> Richmond, IN 47374
> 800-704-7648, 317-935-7574; fax 317-935-7570

*Six Sigma-Print NW**
> (Mailing) PO Box 1418
> Tacoma, WA 98401

> (Shipping) 4101-D Industry Dr. East
> Fife, WA 98424
> 800-451-5742; 206-922-3383

Sonopress
> 108 Monticello Rd.
> Weaverville, NC 28787
> 704-658-2000; fax 704-658-6206

Technicolor
> 3233 East Mission Oaks Blvd.
> Camarillo, CA 93012
> 805-445-3000; fax 805-445-4340
> *John_Carmichael@technicolor.com*

Technidisc
> 2250 Meijer Dr.
> Troy, MI 48404
> 800-777-DISC, 810-435-7430; fax 810-435-8540

*Triptych CD**
> 1604 Tillie Lewis Dr.
> Stockton, CA 95206
> 408-271-7373; fax 408-271-7370

Ultra Media
    2048 Corporate Ct.
    San Jose, CA 95131
    408-383-9470; fax 408-383-0806

Uni Manufacturing (MCA)
    Highway 154
    Pinckneyville, IL 62274
    618-357-2167; fax 618-357-6340

US Optical Disc Inc.
    1 Eagle Drive
    Sanford, ME 04073
    207-324-1124; fax 207-490-1707

VU Video
    1420 Blake Street
    Denver, CO 80202
    800-637-4336, 303-534-5503; fax 303-595-4630
    http://thebridge.com/ibb/vuvideo/home.html

WEA Manufacturing, Inc.
    New York Office
    375 Hudson Street
    New York, NY 10014
    212-741-1404; fax 212-243-8255

    WEA Manufacturing East
    1444 E. Lackawanna Avenue
    Olyphant, PA 18447
    717-383-2471; fax 717-383-1493

    WEA Manufacturing West
    3601 West Olive Avenue
    Burbank, CA 91505
    818-953-2941

Zomax Optical Media
    5353 Nathan Lane
    Plymouth, MN 55442
    612-553-9300; fax 612-553-0826

One-Off CD-ROM Service Bureaus and Disc Brokers

These companies will provide software and services for creating one-off CD-Rs. They may also broker manufacturing, packaging, and fulfillment services. The

names of companies that are members of the Optical Publishing Association are
followed by an asterisk (*).

21st Century Media
    875 Fourth St.
    San Rafael, CA 94901
    800-520-3222

Achievers
    24318 Hemlock Avenue, Suite G-2
    Moreno Valley, CA 92557
    800-530-3583, 909-790-5953; fax 909-790-1933

Aztech Technologies International
    6 Riviera Dr.
    Concord, ON L4K 2T1 Canada
    416-738-5638; fax 416-738-1961

BetaCorp Technologies Inc.
    6770-40 Davand Dr.
    Mississauga, ON L5T 2G3 Canada
    416-564-2424; fax 416-564-2432

*The CD-Info Company**
    4800 Whitesburg Drive #30-283
    Huntsville, AL 35802-1600
    205-650-0406; fax 205-882-7393
    info@cd-info.com

CD Solutions, Inc.
    6 E. Monument St.
    PO Box 536
    Pleasant Hill, OH 45359-0536
    513-676-2376; fax 513-676-2478
    CompuServe: 71101,2221

CDROM Access Inc.
    899 Logan St.
    Denver, CO 80203
    303-894-8313

CDROM Strategies Inc.
    18 Chenile Rd.
    Irvine, CA 92714
    714-733-3378; fax 714-786-1401

CD-Works
    365 Washington St.
    Boston, MA 02108
    800-239-6757, 617-482-2759; fax 617-482-0403

Corporate Disk Company
    800-634-DISK, 708-616-0700

dataDisc Inc.
    Rt. 3, Box 1108
    Gainesville, VA 22065
    800-328-2347, 703-347-2111; fax 703-347-9085

Disc Makers
    Sales Office
    278 Fulton St.
    North Babylon, NY 11704
    516-253-0337; fax 516-253-0405

    Disc Makers
    7905 N. Route 130
    Pennsauken, NJ 08110
    800-468-9353, 609-663-9030; fax 609-661-3458

    Disc Makers
    1650 Broadway, Suite 709
    New York, NY 10036
    212-265-7505; fax 212-262-0798

    Disc Makers-Music Annex
    42650 Christy St.
    Fremont, CA 94538
    800-869-0715, 510-226-0800; fax 510-226-0455

    Disc Makers
    213 W. Alameda, Suite 101
    Burbank, CA 91502
    818-848-4180; fax 818-848-4199

    Disc Makers
    Ave. Comerio #500
    Local #6
    Bayamon, Puerto Rico 00949
    809-795-5500; fax 809-795-5554

Dolphin Computer
    239 Littleton Rd., Suite 2A
    Westford, MA 01886
    508-392-9837; fax 508-392-0458

The Gottfried Group
    507-252-0827; fax 507-252-9721
    sjgottfried@delphi.com

Grafica Multimedia, Inc.
940 Emmett Avenue, Suite 11
Belmont, CA 94002
415-595-5599; fax 415-595-4144
AppleLink: grafica

Information Technologies Corp.
1011 E. Main St.
Richmond, VA 23219
804-780-2677

Interaction: CDROM & Optical Storage
24705 US Hwy. 19N, Suite 308
Clearwater, FL 34623
800-783-3ROM

Isomedia
(formerly Archive Optical Inc.)
14808 NE 31st Circle
Redmond, WA 98052
800-468-3939, 206-869-5411; fax 206-869-9437

J&S Tech Inc.
207 Erie St.
Pomona, CA 91768
909-629-2597; fax 909-629-7084

Kinetic Technologies Inc.
1952 Gallows Rd. Suite 303
Vienna, VA 22182
703-883-1898; fax 703-883-2526

MegaSoft
819 Hwy. 33 East
Freehold, NJ 07728-8431
800-222-0490; fax 908-462-5658

New Media Solutions
335 Bryant St.
Palo Alto, CA 94301
415-617-3720; fax 415-321-3748
info@new.com

Noble House
800-260-5053 x40, 818-709-5053; fax 818-709-3503

Northeastern Digital Recording Inc.
2 Hidden Meadow Lane
Southborough, MA 01772-1700
508-481-9322

The One-Off CD Shop Salt Lake City, Inc.
4910 West Amelia Earhart Drive
Salt Lake City, UT 84116
801-531-7555; fax 801-531-0740

One-Off CD Shop Washington, Inc.*
PO Box 188, DeMarr Road
White Plains, MD 20695
800-387-1633 (US & Canada), 301-843-1800 x 339; fax 301-843-6339

OPTIM Corporation
338 Sommerset St. W.
Ottawa, ON K2P 0J9 Canada
613-23-CD-ROM; fax 613-232-8413
OPTIM - Toronto
416-360-8898; fax 416-362-6161

Ready-to-Run Software, Inc.
4 Pleasant St.
Forge Village, MA 01886
508-692-9922; fax 508-692-9990
info@rtr.com

Sabroco Interactive
114 Sansome St., Penthouse
San Francisco, CA 94104
800-544-7019

Shoestring Engineering Inc.*
584 Castro St., Suite 508
San Francisco, CA 94114
415-920-6920; fax 415-641-0520
Compuserve: 76344,1702
AppleLink: dle
AOL: dle

Tachyon Technology Corp.
74 S. Jackson St., Suite 200
PO Box 4188
Seattle, WA 98104
206-622-7805; fax 206-622-0899

Totronik
Hauptstaetterstr. 35
D-7000 Stuttgart 1 West Germany
+49 (0)711-244272; fax +49 (0)711-6406815
Fidonet: 2:244-40.17; Compuserve: 100064,1346

CD Packaging Manufacturers

These companies provide printing and manufacturing services for the physical packaging of discs. These include bubble-packs, software-style boxes, jewel boxes, and other variants that allow you to package your product shrink-wrapped and ready for shipment.

Advantage Plus Distribution Inc.
14202 Carlson Circle
Tri-County Business Park
Tampa, FL 33626

AGI
5513 W. Bay Ct.
Midlothian, VA 23112
804-739-1174

Blackbourn Inc.
10150 Crosstown Circle
Eden Prairie, MN 55344
612-949-2155

C-Case Corp.
822 Hill Grove
Western Springs, IL 60558
708-887-7000; fax 708-887-7010

Calumet Carton Co.
16920 State St.
PO Box 405
South Holland, IL 60473
708-333-6521; fax 708-333-8540

Crawford Custom Packaging
1414 Crawford Drive
P.O.Box 191
Crawfordsville, IN 47933
800-428-0840; fax 800-962-3343

Digipress
2016 Bainbridge Row Dr.
Louisville, KY 40207
502-895-0565; fax 502-893-9589

Golden Rule Printing
1864 Sparkman Dr.
Huntsville, AL 35816
800-239-9060, 205-895-9060; fax 205-722-9806

Ivy Hill
> Eastern Sales Office
> 375 Hudson St.
> New York, NY 10014
> 212-741-1404
>
> Midwestern Sales Office
> 1481 Countryside Dr.
> Buffalo Grove, IL 60089
> 708-506-9650
>
> Western Sales Office
> 4800 Santa Fe Ave.
> Los Angeles, CA 90058
> 213-587-3131

Optima Precision
> 231 Industrial Park
> Fitchburg, MA 01420
> 508-342-9626; fax 508-345-6153

Reliance Plastics & Pkg Division
> 217 Brook Ave.
> Passaic, NJ 07055
> 201-473-7200; fax 201-473-1023

Reynard CVC
> 550 Sylvan Ave.
> Englewood Cliffs, NJ 07632
> 201-567-8998

Software Packaging Associates Inc.
> 11431 Williamson Rd.
> Cincinnati, OH 45241-2234
> 800-837-4399, 513-489-2118; fax 513-489-2126

Tecval Memories SA
> c/o PTS PO Box 2471
> Acton, MA 01720
> 508-635-9863; fax 508-263-9350

Univenture Inc.
> PO Box 570
> Dublin, OH 43017
> 800-992-8262, 614-761-2669; fax 614-793-0202

Electronic Document Applications

These companies produce software that is part of various electronic document production or delivery systems. The companies listed here may or may not be particularly oriented toward multimedia documents, but most of them emphasize cross-platform electronic document translation or document delivery.

Adobe Systems
>   1565 Charleston Road
>   Mountain View, CA 94039-7900
>   415-961-4400, 800-272-3623; fax 408-562-6775
>   *http://www.adobe.com/*
>   Adobe Acrobat; Reader, Exchange, Catalog, Distiller
>   Adobe PageMill, SiteMill

AimTech
>   20 Trafalgar Square, Suite 300
>   Nashua, NH 03063
>   800-289-2884, 603-883-0220; fax 603-883-5582
>   *http://www.aimtech.com/*
>   IconAuthor multimedia software

Allegiant Technologies
>   6496 Weathers Place, Suite 100
>   San Diego, CA 92121
>   800-255-8258
>   SuperCard for Macintosh, SuperCard Runtime for Windows

Allen Communications
>   5225 Wiley Post Way
>   Salt Lake City, UT 84116
>   800-325-7850
>   Quest for DOS and Windows

APE/The Multimedia Group
>   26855 Via Grande
>   Mission Viejo, CA 92681
>   714-367-0724
>   Media Styler for Windows

Apple Developer Catalog
>   c/o Apple Computer, Inc.
>   P.O. Box 319
>   Buffalo, NY 14207
>   800-282-2732, 716-871-6555
>   *http://www.apple.com/*
>   Apple Media Kit, HyperCard

Arbortext, Inc.
> 1000 Victors Way, Suite 400
> Ann Arbor, MI 48108-2700
> 313-996-3566; fax 313-996-3566
> ADEPT authoring and delivery system based on SGML

Asymetrix Corp.
> 110-110th Ave. N.E. #700
> Bellevue, WA 98004-5840
> 800-448-6543
> *http://www.asymetrix.com/*
> Multimedia ToolBook

AT&T Multimedia Software
> 2701 Maitland Center Pkwy.
> Maitland, FL 32751
> 800-892-8550 x275
> AT&T Multimedia Designer for Windows

Auto-Graphics, Inc.
> 3201 Temple Avenue
> Pomona, CA 91768
> 909-595-7204; fax 909-595-3506
> SGML editor for Windows

Avalanche, Inc.
> 947 Walnut Street
> Boulder, CO 80302
> 303-449-5032; fax 303-449-3246
> Variety of filtering tools to convert documents to SGML, HTML, or other formats

Best Enterprises
> 118 Leroy Street Apt. N2
> Potsdam, NY 13676
> 315-265-1390
> *http://www.northnet.com/best/Web.Weaver/WW.html*
> Web Weaver HTML authoring tools for Macintosh

Cognetics
> 51 Everett Drive #103B
> P.O.Box 386
> Princeton Junction, NJ 08550
> 800-229-8437, 609-799-5005; fax 609-799-8555
> *http://www/cognetics.com/*
> *info@cognetics.com*
> Hyperties

Crosswise Corp.
  105 Locust Street, Suite 301
  Santa Cruz, CA 95060
  408-459-9060; fax 408-426-3859
  Face To Face

Data Conversion Laboratory
  184-13 Horace Harding Expressway
  Fresh Meadows, NY 11365
  718-357-8700; fax 718-357-8776
  Electronic data conversion to SGML

Electronic Book Technologies Inc.
  1 Richmond Square
  Providence, RI 02906
  401-421-9550; fax 401-421-9551
  *Dyna*Text, *Dyna*Web, *Dyna*Tag

Exoterica Corporation
  1545 Carling Avenue, Suite 404
  Ottawa, Ontario K1Z 8P9 Canada
  613-722-1700; fax 613-722-5706
  SGML tools for hyperlinks and document preparation

Farallon Computing Inc.
  2470 Mariner Square Loop
  Alameda, CA 04501-1010
  510-814-5100; fax 510-814-5023
  Replica; electronic document creator and viewer for Macintosh and Windows

FrameTechnology Corp.
  1010 Rincon Circle
  San Jose, CA 95131
  408-433-3311, 800-843-7263; fax 408-433-1928
  comments@frame.com
  FrameViewer4

Gold Disk Inc.
  3350 Scott Blvd, Bldg. 14
  Santa Clara, CA 95054
  800-465-3375
  Astound Web Publisher

Grif S.A.
>Immeuble "Le Florestan"
>2, Boulevard Vauban
>BP 266
>St. Quentin en Yvelines Cedex
>France
>+33 1 30 12 14 30; fax +33 1 30 64 06 46
>*http://www.grif.fr/*
>*grif@grif.fr*
>Symposia PRO HTML authoring system

Hal Software Systems
>3006A Longhorn Blvd.
>Austin, TX 78758
>512-834-9962; fax 512-834-9963
>OLIAS browser for SGML and WWW documents

Image North Technologies
>180 King Street S, Suite 360
>Waterloo, Ontario N2J 1P8
>Canada
>800-363-3400
>ImageQ for Windows

InContext Systems
>2 St. Clair Avenue West, 16th Floor
>Toronto, Ontario M4V 1L5
>Canada
>800-263-0127; fax 416-922-6489
>*http://www.incontext.com/*
>Spider HTML authoring system for Windows; InContext SGML authoring system

InfoAcess
>2800 156th Avenue SE
>Bellevue, WA 98007
>206-747-3203
>Guide Professional Publisher for Windows

Information Dimensions, Inc.
>5080 Tuttle Crossing Blvd
>Dublin, OH 43017
>614-761-7241; fax 614-761-7290
>BASISplus software for storage and retrieval of SGML and HTML documents

INRIA

Domaine de Voluceau-Rocquencourt

BP 105

78153 Le Chesnay Cedex

France

+33 1 39 63 55 11; fax +33 1 39 63 53 30

http://symposia.inria.fr/symposia/aboutsym.html

Symposia HTML authoring system for Windows, Macintosh, and UNIX

Interleaf Inc.

Prospect Place

9 Hillside Avenue

Waltham, MA 02154

617-290-0710; fax 617-290-4943

WorldView

JavaSoft

MS CUP01-202

2550 Garcia Avenue

Mountain View, CA 94043-1100

http://java.sun.com/

java@java.sun.com

Java programming language and HotJava Web browser

Kinetix

415-507-5000

http://www.ktx.com/

Hyperwire Web authoring tools for Java and VRML

Lighthouse Design, Ltd.

2929 Campus Drive, Suite 250

San Mateo, CA 94403

800-366-2279, 415-570-7736; fax 415-570-7787

http://www.lighthouse.com/

omniweb@lighthouse.com

OmniWeb; Internet navigation for NeXTSTeP systems

Lotus Development Corp.

55 Cambridge Parkway

Cambridge, MA 02142

800-346-1305

http://www.lotus.com/inotes/

InterNotes Web authoring tool

Macromedia
> 600 Townsend Street
> San Francisco, CA 94103-4945
> 800-326-2128, 415-595-3101
> *http://www.autodesk.com/*
> Authorware, Director, Shockwave

Mainstay
> 591-A Constitution Avenue
> Camarillo, CA 93012
> 805-484-9400; fax 805-484-9428
> *d0397@applelink.apple.com*
> MarkUp

mFactory
> 1440 Chapin Avenue, Suite 200
> Burlingame, CA 94010
> 415-548-0600; fax 415-548-9249
> *http://www.mfactory.com/*
> *info@mfactory.com*
> mTropolis

Microsoft Corp.
> 800-426-9400, 206-882-8080
> *http://www.microsoft.com/*
> Internet Assistant extension for Word 6.0; FrontPage HTML authoring;
> Visual BASIC

National Center for Supercomputing Applications
> Software Development Group
> 605 E. Springfield
> Champaign, IL 61820
> 217-244-0072
> *mosaic@ncsa.uiuc.edu*
> NCSA Mosaic Web browser

NaviSoft
> *http://www.navisoft.com/*
> NaviPress HTML authoring system for Windows, Macintosh

Nesbitt Software
> Data Transfer Group
> 2251 San Diego Avenue, Suite A-141
> San Diego, CA 92110
> 619-220-8026 Voice; 619-220-8324 Fax
> *http://www.nesbitt.com/*
> WebEdit HTML authoring system for Windows

Netscape Communications Corp.
   501 E. Middlefield Rd.
   Mountain View, CA 94043
   1-800-NETSITE
   http://www.netscape.com/
   NetScape Navigator Web browser, Netscape Gold page authoring

No Hands Software
   1301 Shoreway Road, Suite 220
   Belmont, CA 94002
   415-802-5800, 800-598-3821; fax 415-593-6868
   nohands@applelink.apple.com
   Common Ground

Optimage
   Philips Media Professional Systems
   2121 Wisconsin Ave. NW, Suite 400
   Washington, DC 20007
   800-234-5484, 515-225-7000
   Media Mogul

Pierian Spring Software
   5200 S.W. Macadam Ave. #250
   Portland, OR 97201
   800-472-8578
   Digital Chisel multimedia software for Macintosh

Quarterdeck Corp.
   13160 Mindenao Way
   Marina Del Rey, CA 90292
   310-309-3700
   http://www.qdeck.com/
   WebAuthor HTML add-on for MS Word 6.0

Sausage Software
   Suite 1
   660 Doncaster Road
   Doncaster, VIC 3108
   Australia
   http://www.sausage.com/
   HotDog HTML authoring system for Windows

Second Look Computing

> Information Technology Services
> The University of Iowa
> Iowa City, IA 52242
> 319-335-5471
> *http://www.uiowa.edu/~sec-look*
> *info@sec-look.uiowa.edu*
> Arachnid Web authoring system for Macintosh

Software Partners

> 1953 Landings Drive
> Mountain View, CA 94043
> 415-428-0160; fax 415-428-0163
> *http://www.buckaroo.com/*
> Compose and other Acrobat tools

SoftQuad Inc.

> 56 Aberfoyle Crescent, Suite 810
> Toronto, Ontario M8X 2W4 Canada
> 416-239-4801, 800-387-2777; fax 416-239-7105
> *http://www.sq.com/*
> HoTMetaL Pro and other SGML and HTML authoring and delivery systems

Spyglass Inc.

> 1800 Woodfield Drive
> Savoy, IL 61874
> 217-355-6000
> Enhanced NCSA Mosaic

Strata

> 2 West St. George Blvd., Suite 2100
> St. George, UT 84770
> 800-678-7282, 801-628-5218
> MediaForge

Sybase, Inc.

> 6475 Christie Avenue
> Emeryville, CA 94608
> 800-8SYBASE, 510-922-3500; fax 510-658-9441
> Gain*Momentum* multiplatform multimedia system

Voyager

> 578 Broadway, Suite 406
> New York, NY 10012
> 800-446-2001, 212-431-5199
> Expanded Book Toolkit, based on HyperCard

Young Minds, Inc.
 1910 Orange Tree Lane
 Redlands, CA 92374
 714-335-1350; fax 714-798-0488
 Viewtool

Glossary

This glossary covers much of the terminology that you will encounter when you work with CD-ROM discs and disc duplicators. Many of these terms are used in this book, but some additional terms are included to help you when you read further in the field. These terms are taken from a number of sources, including the publication "A Glossary of CD and CD-ROM Terms," by Disc Manufacturing, Inc., that is listed in the Bibliography. That publication is available from DMI at the address in the preface.

Acrobat

An electronic document technology from Adobe Systems that includes the PDF file format, translators for creating PDF files, and readers for displaying PDF files on the screen. Acrobat is built on PostScript and provides faithful electronic displays of fully formatted pages, along with access to other media.

Active area

An area on a screen that can respond to a mouse click or other event to produce an action.

Active region

The portion of a window in which the window's document is presented.

Active window

The window in which program input and output are occurring. In most personal computer systems this will be the topmost window, but this need not be the case.

ADPCM (Adaptive Differential Pulse Code Modulation)

A method of storing digital samples based on correlations between successive values. This is a compression technique as well.

AIFF

A sound file format primarily associated with Macintosh and Silicon Graphics computers.

Alpha

The first version of a product or title that is made available for testing or for external examination. This version will usually be incomplete or have known weaknesses, but it will have enough functionality that reviews can help shape the product.

Alt keys

Keystrokes that are formed on the PC by pressing the Alt key together with another key; these keystrokes are a primary means to execute commands from the keyboard. See *Command keys.*

AMSTEX

A particular version of a TEX macro set that is used by the American Mathematical Society to typeset their publications. See *TEX.*

Animation

A moving image created by a sequence of individually computed frames, each of which is crafted separately.

Animated cursor

A cursor that changes its form through time, often used to indicate that some processing is being done.

Animated icon

An icon that contains a sequence of images that are displayed successively, giving the illusion of motion within the icon.

Applet

An application designed to be downloaded to a user across the networks, with the implication that it is a modest-sized application intended for a special purpose.

ASCII (American Standard Code for Information Interchange)

A standardized way of representing text and control characters in one byte each.

Aspect ratio

The ratio of the height to the width of an image.

Assets

The resources an author or developer has to bring to a title. This can include things such as interface objects, images, movies, or text.

Attribute

A property of an object, such as an icon for a document, a color or shape for a button, or font or size for text. Attributes can be set in an authoring language and may be changed by a user.

Author

The person whose creative ideas shape a title and who may create significant pieces of the title's contents.

Authoring language

A system or application used to create an electronic document and define its contents, functionality, and interface.

AVI (Audio Video Interleaved)

A file format defined by Microsoft to be used by Video for Windows. This format interleaves sectors of video data and sectors of audio data so that the video player can maintain both audio and video data streams with only minimal data buffering.

Back

To return to the previous screen or state of a document.

Bandwidth

The amount of information that can be transferred in a given time over a communications line, a network, or a device connection.

Baud rate

The rate at which characters are being transmitted over character-oriented communication lines. Usually associated with modem-based communications over telephone lines.

Beta

The second level of release of a product or title before the final release to manufacturing. This level is essentially complete and has the most glaring bugs removed, but may still have minor problems, and is the final level at which testing can occur before release.

Birefringence

Double refraction (of light). Plastic materials, such as a CD substrate, demonstrate this double refringence ability due to residual stresses remaining in the plastic from the molding process. High birefringence can interfere with the laser beam of the reader and cause reading errors.

Bitmap

A two-dimensional array of pixels that is the computer's internal representation of an image.

Blister pack

A packaging technique for CD-ROM or diskettes in which a disc is placed in a transparent envelope that is attached to the binding of a book.

Block

A segment of data; on a CD-ROM, same as a sector. On CDs, data is arranged in blocks that contain header and sync, user data, error detection and correction, and control information.

BMP

A device-independent graphics file format developed by Microsoft that supports images in as few as one bit or as many as 24 bits and uses RLE compression.

Booklet

The printed material inside the front of a jewel box that includes the cover artwork and other information on the disc. The usual booklet sizes are one, two, four, or eight pages.

Bookmark

An indication of a place in a document to which the user may return directly. A bookmark can be created by the authoring system (such as a chapter title) or be created and saved by the user.

Box

A packaging technique for CD-ROMs in which a box of lightweight cardboard, printed with product identification, is used to hold the disc and additional material for an electronic title.

Browse

To look through a document without a predetermined goal in order to see what it might contain that would be of interest.

Bug

An error in the contents or functionality of a disc or of an electronic title; these must be fixed before the disc or title can ship.

Bug report

A report from testing or from a customer that there is an error in a program or title, sometimes called a maintenance request. These reports are used to ensure that the product is correct when shipped or is corrected when the next manufacturing run is made.

Bundling

Including more than one title in a package that is marketed as a unit.

Button

An area on the desktop which will respond to a mouse click. These are often represented by icons that represent a choice or an action. See *Hot Region.*

Button palette

A collection of buttons, each with a descriptive icon or other artwork, that acts as a vocabulary unit for user interaction.

Byte code

A device-independent, compressed version of a program produced by a compiler that can be interpreted on any of several platforms. The original version was probably the Pascal P-code, but byte codes are now used by Java.

Candidate RTM

A disc that is submitted as being ready to release to manufacturing, subject to final approval. See *RTM.*

Capacity (Data Capacity)

The amount of data that can be recorded and replicated on a CD. Normal capacity of a disc is 654.7 megabytes, which is 335350 2K sectors. This is equivalent to a music playing time of 74 minutes 30 seconds. The amount of data on a disc is controlled by several factors: track pitch, speed, and rotation. It is possible to record and replicate somewhat more data on the disc than the "normal" capacity and still remain within Yellow Book specifications, but some drives have trouble reading from these discs.

Cascading menus

Menus in which one or more menu items display additional menus when they are selected.

Catalog number

A number printed on the disc label that gives the publisher's catalog number for ordering or inventory.

CAV (Constant Angular Velocity)

Refers to the speed of the information track with relation to the reading head (laser). Video discs, most magnetic discs, and traditional phonograph records rotate at constant angular velocity, i.e., RPM is constant so that the tracks on the outside radii move past the reading head much faster than tracks on the inside radii. See *CLV.*

CD-I (Compact Disc Interactive)

A compact disc format in which computer data and compressed audio are interleaved on the same track. The format includes both a disc layout and an operating system, CD-RTOS, that can read the layout and play the disc contents. CD-I discs must be mastered on special proprietary systems.

CD-MO (Compact Disc Magneto-Optical)

A standard for discs that can be recorded and played by magneto-optical techniques (Orange Book, Part I).

CD-Plus

A mixed-mode disc for the music industry that allows both computer data and music to be placed on a single disc.

CD-R

Compact Disc Recordable disc (Orange Book, Part II). See *CD-WO*.

CD-ROM (Compact Disc Read Only Memory)

A compact disc format that is used to hold text, graphics, and hi-fi stereo sound. The disc is built on the same technology as the music CD, but uses different tracks for data. The music CD player cannot play CD-ROM discs, but CD-ROM players may be able to play music CD discs and have jacks for connection to an amplifier and/or earphones.

CD-ROM Mode 1

The usual mode for data-only CD-ROM (that is, discs that contain only data and applications); it has three layers of error detection and correction for computer data.

CD-ROM Mode 2

Another mode for CD-ROM use that has two layers of error detection and correction, for audio or compressed audio/video.

CD-Video

A disc format, also known as karaoke CD or the White Book standard, that allows a combination of audio and full-motion video. It uses interleaved MPEG video and audio sectors to maximize the amount of information that can be stored on the disc.

CD-WO (Compact Disc Write Once)

A CD-ROM version of the WORM (Write Once Read Many) technology. For companies wishing to do in-house preparation through premastering, this format is useful for creating test discs (one off) before sending data for mastering and replication. CD-WO discs conform to ISO 9660 standards and can be played in CD-ROM drives.

Checkbox

A box in which a click sets a value or attribute for the program or document. These are often found in a group that allows a user to set any of a group of attributes.

Cinepak

An asymmetric codec that gives good results for compressed digital video. Cinepak was developed by SuperMac Technology, Inc., and is now a Radius product as a result of the merger of SuperMac and Radius in August 1994.

CIRC (Cross-Interleaved Reed-Solomon Code)

The error detection and correction technique used by audio CDs.

Click

A pair of events, mouse-down and mouse-up, that are used to make a selection on the screen.

Clock

An object that represents time in a document and is driven from the computer system clock. This allows you to order events, such as a sequence of movie frames, to the user in real time.

Closing sequence

The sequence of screens or information that is displayed as a title is closed.

CLV (Constant Linear Velocity)

Refers to the speed of the information track with relation to the reading or recording head (laser). CD tracks pass the laser head at a constant linear velocity (1.2 to 1.4 meters per second), meaning that the speed of disc rotation when reading the inner radii must be faster than when reading the outer radii. See CAV.

Codec

A system for encoding (co) and decoding (dec) information to provide compression of a file or document.

Color depth

The number of bits used to determine the color of a pixel on the screen. The more bits used for a color, the more colors are available. Eight-bit color allows you to have 256 colors, for example; 24-bit color gives you over 16 million colors.

Color lookup table

The system used in an indexed color system to define the color used for each color index. See *Palette.*

Compound document

An electronic document that includes more than one computer medium in an integrated presentation, frequently with a user interface that allows the user to manipulate the individual document components.

Compression ratio

> The ratio of the original size of a file to the size of the compressed file. Thus a 3:1 compression ratio means that the compressed file is one-third the size of the original.

Command keys

> Keystrokes that are formed on the Macintosh by pressing the command key together with another key; these keystrokes allow the user to execute some commands from the keyboard instead of from a menu. See *Alt keys*.

Content

> All the assets of an electronic title, together with the user interface, as assembled into the final title.

Control panel

> A system extension that allows the user to set parameters for system functions. See *DLL* and *Extension*.

Copyright

> The legal rights to reproduce, publish, and sell an electronic title or the contents of a title.

Copyright notice

> A notice in the electronic title that states the appropriate copyrights for the title and, if appropriate, for individual content items.

Credits screen

> The screen of an electronic title that lists the credits for the title's development, production, and support.

Cursors

> On-screen graphic items that follow the motions of the mouse or trackball. Their shapes and actions can indicate to the user the capabilities of the area where the cursor is located or can tell the user something of the status of the system.

Cyberspace

> A large and rich virtual reality in which a user can experience a range of virtual worlds.

d-characters

> The characters that are legal to use in file names in the ISO 9660 disc standard. These are the upper-case alphabetic characters A...Z, the digits 0...9, and the underscore character _ .

DAT (Digital Audio Tape)

A digital tape format that can be used to store or communicate data, or as disk backup.

Data fork

The part of a Macintosh file that contains the data or executable code for the file. See *Resource fork*.

Data transfer rate

The speed with which data can be read from a CD-ROM drive. The standard "single-speed" rate is 150 KB/sec. Double-speed drives read at 300 KB/sec, and drives are now available that read at 800 to 1,000 KB/sec, which seems to be the top speed that is supported by the physical properties of discs.

Default

The state of a document or system as it is originally set up before the user makes any changes or customizations.

Deliverable

A component of an electronic title, such as a function or an asset, or the title itself, that is to be completed and working at a specific time in the development schedule for the title.

Derived work

Generally, a work that is created by modifying or adapting a previous work; as provided in copyright law, the right to create derived works is limited to the owner of the copyright on the original work.

Designer

The person who takes the assets of an electronic title and, using an authoring system, designs the user interface and the presentation that define the overall look and feel of the title.

Desktop metaphor

The metaphor for the computer that shows the computer's resources and activities as though they were on a desk where they can be moved around and manipulated. When mounted, a CD-ROM appears as an icon on the desktop and may open a window showing its contents.

Developer

The person or group who takes the assets and design for an electronic title, adds additional assets as needed, and assembles them all into a working document using one or more authoring systems.

Dial

> An interface component that displays a value, magnitude, or position of something and possibly allows the user to change that value. Scroll bars are an example of dials.

Dialog box

> A box on the screen that requires a response from the user in order to control the application or document that presented the box. Dialog boxes can be *modal* or *nonmodal*; see both terms.

Digital library

> A collection of material, gathered much as a traditional library would gather material, which is all in digital form and which can be accessed across the networks. Such libraries may be distributed anywhere in the world.

Direct manipulation

> A user interface style in which the user first picks the object, then indicates what is to be done with it; e.g., first selects a file, then drags the file icon to another disc icon to indicate that the file is to be copied to the other disc. This is a "subject-verb" kind of command, as opposed to a "verb-subject" command style such as COPY MYFILE.DAT C:\DATA.

Directory

> The list of all the files on a computer medium.

Directory path

> The full sequence of directory names needed to specify a file relative to the medium on which it resides. For example, this chapter's data file on one of the authors' discs has the directory path *BigDisk/EPBook/Chapters/Glossary*.

Disc real estate

> Disc storage, so called because there is a limited amount of storage available on the disc, and it must be developed carefully to get the most value from the resource.

Distributor

> The person who takes an electronic title and sees that it is placed in retail stores and other places where it can be noticed by the potential audience.

DLL (Dynamic Link Library)

> A small piece of software that adds functionality to the Windows operating system or to an application. See *Control panel*.

Documentation

Information for the user of a disc, often provided on the disc's printed pieces or in the disc's contents. This often includes fundamental program operating instructions or information on required configurations for computers to use the disc.

Drag

An action sequence of a mouse-down to select an object, moving the mouse while holding the button to indicate that the object should follow the mouse, and a mouse-up to indicate an ending position, used to move a graphical object on the screen.

Drop

An ending behavior for a drag, in which the final position of the drag is on an icon for an action; this indicates that the action should be taken on the object of the drag.

DTD (Document Type Definition)

A detailed description of the way each tag in an SGML document affects the formatting of the text covered by the tag.

Dual-directory disc

A disc with both HFS and ISO 9660 directories that may share the same files. See *Hybrid disc.*

DVD (Digital Video Disc)

A new optical disc technology that uses denser recording techniques along with layering and two-sided manufacturing to achieve very large disc capacities. Digital Video Disc readers are able to read CD-ROMs as well.

ECC (Error Correcting Code)

A code construction that facilitates reconstruction of part or all of a message received with errors. The error correction scheme for compact discs is the same CIRC that is used for music compact discs. See *CIRC.*

EDC (Error Detecting Code)

A code construction that makes it possible to detect when a message is received with errors.

EFM (Eight-to-Fourteen Modulation)

The operation of converting 8 bits of data to 14 bits for storage on the disc, to facilitate reading data from the disc.

Electroforming

A means of creating a metal master (father) disc by electroplating nickel onto the glass master until a sheet of nickel has been built up to a usable thickness. The father can then be used in the same system to create a mother, and from the mother, stampers or metal parts are made that are used in the injection molding machine to manufacture the CD.

Encapsulation

Protecting data by allowing access to the data only through a fixed set of operations whose action on the data is limited. One of the key advantages of object-oriented programming languages is that their objects encapsulate their data.

EPS (Encapsulated PostScript)

A file format for importing and exporting PostScript language files in a variety of heterogeneous environments. EPS files use a subset of the full PostScript language and may include a screen preview.

Error concealment

Techniques for recovery from disc data error with minimal notice by the user. For example, in music CDs errors are concealed by interpolating linearly between good data values.

Event

A logical entity created by a hardware condition, such as a keystroke or mouse action, or by a software action. Events are asynchronous; that is, an event may happen at any time, and a program or title must respond to each event and perform an appropriate action for each.

Event handling

Responding to an event by passing the event entity to the appropriate part of a program so it may be processed correctly.

Event queue

The collection of events that have been generated but have not yet been handled, managed as a FIFO (first-in, first-out) queue.

Extension

A small piece of software that adds functionality to the Macintosh operating system. See *Control panel.*

Fair use

Generally, the personal, noncommercial, limited use of copyrighted factual material in a way that does not damage its market potential, as provided by copyright law in the United States and many other countries.

FAQ (Frequently Asked Questions)

A posting on an Internet newsgroup that is intended to orient a user to the issues in the newsgroup and to provide fundamental background information for the reader.

Father

The first electroformed part made from a glass master. See *Metal master.*

Field

A distinct portion of a screen where a certain set of information, such as an image or a piece of text, will be displayed for the user.

File

A collection of information, either program or data, stored on a computer's secondary storage systems such as a disk or CD-ROM.

File header

Information at the beginning of a file that describes the content of the remainder of the file. This is fairly common in image files, where the file header can describe the dimensions, color depth, and palette of the image.

File server

A computer whose primary function is to manage files and provide them for other systems on a network.

Filter

A piece of software that modifies data as it is input to a program or as it moves from one stage of a program to another.

Find

To be able to move to the point in an electronic document where a user-specified item is located; this is usually a word or phrase, but it could be another kind of content.

Firewall

A facility that screens network access to a site to protect the site's contents from undesirable access.

FOB (Freight On Board)

A term indicating the point from which the customer is required to pay shipping.

Font

A typeface for displaying text on the screen or for printing text on the screen.

Frame rate

The number of frames of a (digital) movie displayed per second.

FTP (File Transfer Protocol)
>   A network technology for transferring files on the Internet.

Full color
>   A computer color system where each pixel holds its own RGB values, typically with 8 bits of precision for each color for a total of 24 bits per pixel. See *Indexed Color.*

Function
>   A unit of computer code that implements a specific piece of the functionality of a program.

Functionality
>   A behavior or activity in an electronic title such as playing a digital movie, allowing keyword searches, having hypertext links, or being able to print the document.

Ghost site
>   A site on the World Wide Web that may once have been available but that no longer can be reached.

GIF (Graphics Interchange Format)
>   A digital image format developed by CompuServe that is widely implemented on many kinds of computers. It describes images that use lookup tables of up to 8 bit depth.

Gigabyte (GB)
>   Roughly a billion, or thousand million, (actually 1,073,741,824) bytes, used as a measure of the capacity of a computer's disk system or of a medium.

Glass master
>   The medium on which manufacturers record data as the first step leading to the replication process. Consists of a glass disc larger than replicated discs, coated with a photosensitive material in which the data are recorded by a laser beam recorder (laser light).

Gold master
>   The completed electronic title ready for release to manufacturing (RTM) or candidate RTM. The name reflects the fact that this release is usually done on a CD-WO disc, and these discs are gold-colored. See *RTM.*

Green Book standard
>   The standard for Digital Video Discs.

Handler
>   The components of a program that respond to events that are passed to them by the main event loop.

HDTV (High-Definition Television)

An emerging standard for commercial television that is expected to have a large impact on computing and electronic publishing.

Hierarchical menus

Menus in which one or more menu items, when chosen, provide a submenu offering additional choices. See *Tree-structured menus*.

High Sierra standard

The first draft proposal submitted to the International Standards Organization for common file structure for CD-ROM. When it became adopted, it was changed in minor ways and became known as ISO 9660.

Highlighting

Indicating a selection or possible selection by changing the color or presentation of the selected object to indicate that the user has chosen or could choose the object.

History

A record of the sequence of actions taken by the user in working with an electronic title, often used to allow the user to retrace steps or move to anything that was previously seen.

HFS (Hierarchical file system)

The file system used by the Apple Macintosh system.

Home page

The hypermedia document that is first loaded when you start a World Wide Web browser, or the page that an individual creates to represent his or her presence on the World Wide Web.

Home screen

The main screen of an electronic title from which the significant sections of the title can be reached and to which the user should always be able to return with a single action.

Hot region

A region of the screen that can respond to a mouse event. See *Button*.

Hot text

A piece of text on the screen that can respond to a mouse event.

HTML (HyperText Markup Language)

An SGML document type that is generally used as the authoring language for creating documents on the World Wide Web. This language allows a document author to apply appropriate text styles and to create links to hypermedia components or to additional documents by interpreting URLs.

HTTP (HyperText Transfer Protocol)

An Internet document transfer protocol that is becoming the dominant protocol for sharing documents across networks based on URI references.

Huffman coding

A way of encoding data in variable-length symbols so data that occurs more frequently is represented by shorter symbols.

Hybrid disc

A disc that contains data in both HFS and ISO 9660 directories. This can be done by having separate data for each directory or by having the two directories share part or all of the data. This latter is also called a *dual-directory disc.*

Hypermedia

An extension of the concept of hypertext, in which the user chooses the sequence in which to view not only the text but also the other media components of the document. See *Hypertext.*

Hypertext

Text in which some words are hot text that provide links to other text in the same or in a different document, allowing the reader to choose the sequence in which the text will be read as he or she is reading.

Icon

A graphical representation of a system component such as a document, disc, or application.

Idle

The state of a program when it is waiting for the next user input and is neither processing a piece of a document nor processing an event.

Image

In CD-ROM, the data assembled in the exact form wanted on the replicated CDs, i.e., completely premastered or image ready. In graphics, a picture to be displayed on the computer screen.

Indemnification

A promise to secure another from penalties or liabilities resulting from one's actions.

Indeo

A digital video codec developed by Intel that is primarily used for Video for Windows, although it is also available for QuickTime.

Indexed color

Color that is specified by giving a color index for each pixel instead of giving the actual color components of the pixel. The color index is used to specify a color from a color lookup table where the actual colors are maintained. See *Full color.*

Inheritance

Obtaining properties and functionality for an object by building your own object on existing classes or objects.

Injection molding

A process for replication of CDs wherein molten plastic is injected into the cavity of a mold under pressure, cooled and removed as a solid, clear plastic disc. The data information is transferred to the plastic in this process from the "stamper."

Installer

A tool which examines the host system to determine what software the system needs to properly execute a disc title, and then installs that software along with any application software needed to run the title.

Intellectual property

Generally, the property created when an author creates an original work; protecting the author's rights in this property is the purpose of copyright law and a copyright transfer gives the rights in this property to the copyright transferee.

Interframe compression

Compression of digital movies that takes advantage of frame-to-frame coherence to provide information for a given frame in terms of other frames that precede or succeed it.

Internet

An interconnected set of networks around the world that allows computers attached to any of these networks to exchange data communications freely. One of the chief functions of the Internet is to tie together these separate networks' diverse set of underlying technologies.

Interrupt

An action that stops a computer process. In interactive computing, interrupts may be caused by events. After the interrupt has been handled, the process may or may not resume.

Intranet

A network operating entirely within an organization such as a business, allowing persons in that organization to work with network tools without exposing their work to outside access.

IP address

A number, composed of four octets (eight-bit numbers), that identifies any computer on the Internet. This is being expanded to six octets as the number of computers on the Internet grows.

ISO 13490

A file format standard for CD-ROM and DVD discs that extends ISO 9660 and corrects many of its shortcomings.

ISO 9660

A widely used file format for CD-ROM. The ISO 9660 (formerly High Sierra) standard defines a directory structure that has been accepted by the International Standards Organization. This standard allows a CD-ROM disc to be read like a write-protected hard disk. Formatting a CD-ROM to this standard will allow CD-ROM interchange on any platform that supports the standard.

Item

An entry in a list, usually one that can be used to make a menu choice or to link to another place in the document.

IVI (Indeo Video Interactive)

A wavelet-based video codec developed by Intel.

Java

An object-oriented programming language from Sun Microsystems, somewhat similar to C++, that provides the capability of creating applets for network use.

Jewel box

The thin, clear, plastic box in which audio CDs are usually sold and in which many CD-ROMs are distributed. Besides the usual jewel box, there are thinner jewel boxes as well as double-disc jewel boxes.

JPEG (Joint Photographic Experts Group)

A standard for encoding digital images using discrete cosine transformations and entropy coding. This standard can achieve part of its efficiency by data quantization, so it is usually a lossy encoding technique.

Keystroke

An event caused by the user pressing a key on the computer keyboard.

Keystroke combination

An event caused by the user pressing certain combinations of keys simultaneously on the computer keyboard, frequently used to extend the character set of the keyboard or to distinguish ordinary text keystrokes from command keystrokes.

Kilobyte (KB)

Roughly a thousand (actually 1024) bytes, used as a measure of the size of a file or the capacity of a computer's memory or of a medium.

Label

The printed area on a disc; also a brand label or imprint from a publisher.

Land (Lands)

The space between the pits on a CD disc where the photoresist on the glass master was not exposed to laser light. This space is more reflective than a pit. See *Pit*.

Launcher

A very small application whose purpose is to start up another program.

Laser

A device that creates a beam of coherent light. In a CD-ROM setting, this beam of light is reflected off the disc and the resulting reflection is measured to detect pits and lands on the disc.

LaTeX

A version of the TeX document formatting system developed by Leslie Lamport (hence the "La") and widely used in preparing technical documents. See *TeX*.

Lead in

On a CD, the area at the beginning of a disc where the Table of Contents (TOC) is recorded.

Link

A button whose function is to move the user to a different place in an electronic title.

Listener window

The window that gets the results of an event.

Load

To move a document from external memory, such as a CD-ROM, into the computer's main memory so it may be used.

Localization

Adapting the text of a program or title to a language other than the one in which the original was developed so it may be sold in additional markets.

Lossless

A technique for storing or compressing files that maintains all the information in the original file.

Lossy

A technique for storing or compressing files that does not maintain all the information in the original file. Typically, lossy techniques for video or images focus on removing information that is not perceived by the viewer. This kind of technique can be used for images or movies when it is deemed that the user will have an adequate result without needing all the original information.

LZW (Lempel-Ziv-Welch coding)

A dictionary-based coding technique that encodes variable-length data in a constant-length code word. The dictionary is not transmitted but is reconstructed from the data that is received. This technique is patented by Unisys and commercial applications that use it must do so under license from them.

Main event loop

The logical structure of any program that operates primarily by receiving and responding to events. The basic structure of a main event loop usually looks something like this:

```
Repeat
    { receive event;
      process event; }
until ProgramExit.
```

Main menu

The "top" menu from which all the contents of an electronic title may be reached.

Manual

A printed (or less often, electronic) set of instructions on how to use a program, title, or piece of equipment.

Manufacturing

The process of creating the physical discs from the gold master, consisting of creating the glass master, making stampers, molding the polycarbonate discs, electroplating the discs, printing the labels, and packaging the discs for the customer.

Master (verb)

In compact disc manufacturing, the recording of the original media (glass) in preparation for making replicates (copies).

Master (noun)

In CD-ROM, the final recording of the desired CD-ROM image to be used as a source for mastering; this may be on tape, magnetic disc, or optical disc.

Mastering

The process of encoding input data, created during premastering, to the compact disc standards and recording this information as a series of pits in a light-sensitive layer on a glass substrate.

Megabyte (MB)

Roughly a million (actually 1,048,576) bytes, used as a measure of the capacity of a computer's memory or of a medium.

Menu

A list of words that describe available actions, for which an action is selected by dragging the cursor onto one of the words and giving a mouse-up action on the word.

Menu bar

The row at the top of a screen that contains keywords for a number of pull-down menus.

Metal master

The first electroformed part from a glass master. See *Father.*

Metallizing

A process by which a thin metal coat (usually aluminum) is deposited on the clear plastic disc after it has been injection molded. The usual process is by sputtering, although vacuum vapor deposition or wet silvering can be used.

Microdollars

Very small amounts, often less than standard currency amounts, which may be charged for accessing documents online or through digital libraries. With enough uses, these amounts build up so that actual charges can be made.

MIDI (Musical Instrument Digital Interface)

A standard for representing and communicating instructions for a music synthesizer that can be used for including music in an electronic document.

Modal dialog

A dialog box that will stay on the screen and block out all other user activity until the user responds to it.

Modem

A device that connects a computer to a telephone line and allows the computer to communicate with other computers.

Moiré

An unintended visible effect in an image caused by aliasing or bitmap scaling errors.

Mosaic

An application developed at the National Center for Supercomputing Applications (NCSA) that supports viewing hypertext documents, both locally and on the World Wide Web, with embedded graphics, sound, and movies. Mosaic was the first successful Web browser.

Mother

A metal part electroformed from the father, used for making stampers.

Mouse

A device, having both positioning and clicking functions, manipulated by the user's hand to move a cursor and make selections from screen presentations.

MouseDown

An event that takes place whenever the user presses the mouse button down.

MouseEnter

An event that takes place whenever the user moves the mouse into a region that can recognize this event.

MouseIn

An event that takes place when the mouse is polled and is within a region that can recognize this event.

MouseLeave

An event that takes place whenever the user moves the mouse out of a region that can recognize this event.

MouseStillWithin

An event that takes place after a mouse-enter event, when the mouse is polled and is still within the region in question.

MouseUp

An event that takes place whenever the user releases the mouse button after it has been pressed down.

MPEG (Motion Picture Experts Group)

A standard for encoding digital movies that includes some original frames, prediction of intermediate frames from the original frames, and interpolation of additional frames between predicted and original frames.

Multisession disc

A disc format for CD-WO discs that allows a user to write beyond the section already written.

Navigable movie

A QuickTime VR movie that includes frames of a single subject shot from a number of different points of view, assembled to give the user the capability to select these individual points of view, thus navigating around the subject. See *QuickTime VR.*

Navigation

The process of selecting and viewing various parts of an electronic title by using the user interface tools of the title to select the parts to be viewed.

Netscape Navigator

A very widely used Web browser that has led to many advances in the HTML language.

Network

A connection among a set of computers that allows them to share data communication.

Next

The screen or other portion of an electronic document that has been defined as the default successor to the current document position.

Nonmodal dialog

A dialog box that can remain on the screen while the user chooses to do other things instead of responding immediately to the dialog box.

Notepad

A region of memory set aside by a document reader so that a user can create notes to himself or herself on the title being read.

Object

A software entity that has properties and can respond to messages and actions.

Object-oriented

Software that is constructed on the basis of loosely coupled objects that communicate by sending messages to each other.

OLE (Object Linking and Embedding)

A Microsoft architecture for including components from several applications in a single electronic document and linking the components to the applications that created them. This allows the components to be manipulated by their creating application, not by the application associated with the main document. See *OpenDoc.*

OpenDoc

Apple's architecture for allowing live links from a document's components to applications that can manipulate the components directly. See *OLE*.

Opening sequence

The sequence of screens or information that is displayed as a title is opened.

Orange Book standard

The Philips/Sony standard for CD-WO and CD-MO discs, named for the color of the cover of the book in which the standard was published.

Package

The container in which a CD-ROM is stored, shipped, and sold, and which identifies the disc to the consumer.

Packet

A fixed-size sequence of few hundred bytes of data that is created when a message is sent on a network and is given identification that lets the network deliver this data along appropriate paths so the receiving computer can reassemble the larger message.

Palette

The set of colors used in an image when that image uses an indexed-color scheme; typically the palette can be adjusted to fit a particular image.

PDF (Portable Document Format)

A file format developed by Adobe Systems for their Acrobat system that is becoming fairly widely used for electronic document interchange.

Pit (Pits)

Information spots on a CD (or optical disc). Pits are formed in a photosensitive layer on a glass master by exposure to laser light. Exposed material washes away in the developing process to form a pit. Pits are less reflective than lands, the space between pits. See *Land*.

Pixel

The smallest spot on the screen that can take on a discrete color; in an indexed color system, each pixel is associated with a color index, while in a full color system, each pixel has a full set of color information.

Pixmap

Another name for bitmap. See *Bitmap*.

Platform

A computer system on which an electronic title can be played.

Player

The software that displays the contents of an electronic title for the user. Often this is a small application that interprets a master source file for a specific platform.

Plug-in

Software that extends the capability of an application.

Points of contact

The persons at a publisher, distributor, or wholesaler with whom an author or developer will work directly.

Pop-up menu

A menu presented on-screen by an object in response to an event.

POSIX

A set of standards for the UNIX operating system that were established to ensure portability and security.

PostScript

A standard page-description language developed by Adobe Systems that has become one of the key standards for printing and prepress technology and for document transportation.

Premastering

Preparing the digital data to send to the CD manufacturer for mastering and replication. The data is assembled as a contiguous image the way it should appear on the CD-ROM, including the file structure (such as ISO 9660). Disc manufacturers usually have hardware and software to premaster for customers, at an additional price.

Previous

The screen or other portion of an electronic document that the user visited immediately prior to reaching the current document position.

Print

To create a copy of part or all of an electronic title on paper or another hard-copy medium.

Proof disc

A CD intended to be used for testing. This usually refers to a one-off, CD-WO, or CD-R disc, but can also refer to one or more discs from a replicated group submitted for testing. Can be used as input for disc manufacturing.

Protective coating

A coating of lacquer or polymer deposited over the metal coating on a CD to protect and seal the metal layer. The most common method is spin-coating of a UV curable polymer over the surface of the metallized disc and then passing it under ultra-violet light to polymerize or cure it.

Publisher

The person or organization who funds the development of an electronic title and arranges for its marketing.

Pull-down menu

A menu that descends from the menu bar in response to a mouse-down event in one of the menu bar words, or in response to an appropriate command keystroke.

Pull-through

Sales of a title that are created when the title is associated with a larger series of publications.

Purge memory

To free memory that a program has allocated for other uses, such as cached pages, so that the program can use that memory for other functions.

Quantization

Replacing higher-accuracy data, either digital or analog, by lower-accuracy digital data. This can lead to aliasing effects and the loss of information.

QuickTime

An architecture for time-based presentation that was developed by Apple Computer. It is the basis for the QuickTime digital movie system, as well as for sound or any other time-based control. It is said that one could automate a factory based on QuickTime.

QuickTime VR

A system for creating immersive environments from photographic panoramas. It runs under QuickTime 2.0 for Macintosh and Windows. The VR stands for Virtual Reality. See *Virtual reality* and *Navigable movie*.

Rack jobber

Someone who takes products from a wholesaler and sees that they are placed in shelf space, preferably good shelf space, in retail outlets.

Radio button

A button that is part of a button set, with the property that precisely one of the buttons in the set can be selected. These are designed to be used for choices that are mutually exclusive.

Reader

Software that displays an electronic title on the screen and that manages the user interaction in the title.

READ_ME

The name of a text file that tells a user important information about a disc, often including last-minute information that is not found in the disc's printed pieces or other documentation.

Red Book standard

The original CD standards, set by Philips and Sony, were published in a book with a red cover. These standards are the basis for later standards for other kinds of CD standards, such as those for CD-ROMs.

Registration card

A card that a purchaser of a title sends to the publisher to register himself or herself as a legal owner of that title. The registration card is often a printed piece that accompanies a CD-ROM, but it may be an online form that is filled out an printed or filled out and delivered to the publisher electronically.

Revert

A synonym for Restore. See *Restore*.

Resolution

The resolution of an image is the dimension of the bitmap that represents the image.

Resource fork

The part of a Macintosh file that contains information such as icons or text that supports the file's presentation or operations. See *Data Fork*.

Restore

To reset all the parameters of the reader for a document to the status that was last saved by a Save instruction. See *Save*.

Retail

Selling an item one unit at a time to individual customers.

RGB

A color model in which a color is determined by giving its red, green, and blue components. This color model is directly associated with the way a standard computer monitor creates color with a red, green, and blue color mask, so it is the most common color model for computer images.

RLE (Run-Length Encoding)

A system for compressing data, particularly image data.

Rock Ridge standard

> A standard for disc file systems and directories that is designed to allow users to maintain much of the directory information in a UNIX operating system. This goes beyond ISO 9660 to include longer file names with richer character sets, symbolic links for files, and the like.

ROI (Return On Investment)

> The percentage of profits in relation to the total cost of a project.

Rollover

> The act of moving the cursor over an active area on the screen. This may cause some sound or action to occur, indicating that the area is active and suggesting what will be done if the user clicks in the area.

Royalty

> The portion of the publisher's income from a title that is passed to the title's author as payment for the author's intellectual property.

RTF (Rich Text Format)

> A set of conventions developed by Microsoft to include formatting information in a text document independently of the computer system or word processing system used to generate the text.

RTM (Release to Manufacturing)

> To sign off on a gold master and certify that it is correct and ready to manufacture.

Save

> To copy the parameters of the reader on a particular document so that a user can come back to the document with precisely the current status when the *Restore* instruction is given.

Schedule

> A set of dates by which the individual tasks associated with a larger job are to be completed.

Screen real estate

> The area of the screen, so called because there is a limited amount of screen space available, and it must be developed carefully to get the most value from the resource.

Scroll bars

> Facilities in a window or field of a title that allow the user to see a larger set of information than can be displayed at once in the window or field.

SCSI (Small Computer System Interface)

A standard for connecting computers to peripheral devices such as CD-ROM players or external hard discs. This is the standard interface for peripherals on the Macintosh and is sometimes used on other computers.

SCSI-2

A newer version of the SCSI interface that is up to 5 to 10 times as fast as the original SCSI standard.

Search

The instruction to examine the contents of an electronic title in order to find an item in the title that matches the user's request.

Search engine

Online software that helps the user locate information on the Web or, more broadly, on the Internet by specifying words to be matched.

Sector

The smallest unit of a CD-ROMs file structure that may be accessed. This corresponds to 1/75 of a second of audio and contains 2352 bytes of digital data.

Selection

A user choice made by clicking on one or more objects so the user can specify what is to be done to the object. A selection must always be accompanied by highlighting the selected objects.

Set-top box

A device that processes data obtained from cable TV sources or CD-ROMs, and interacts through game-like devices to display its program output on a television screen. It may include a credit-card swipe for ordering merchandise or programming.

SGML (Standard Generalized Markup Language)

A system for marking a text document based on its structure so it may be presented according to a format defined external to the document.

Shelf space

Space in a retail outlet in which products are displayed. Since retail sales are directly linked to exposure, it is very desirable to get shelf space in outlets for your product.

SKU

A unit of piece goods sold through retail channels.

Slider

A logical screen device that is used to control a value in a computer program. This may be a linear slider or may take the form of a dial.

Specifications

A description of the contents or functionality that are to be present in an electronic title.

Spin coating

Creating an even layer of photoresist on the glass master by using centrifugal force to spread the material.

Spindle

A set of finished CD-ROMs that are not packaged or wrapped, but are delivered by the manufacturer for the customer to package. This is named for the metal rod on which the discs are stacked during manufacturing.

Splash screen

The screen that shows while the title or application is loading into the computer.

Sprite

A graphic object that is movable, clickable, and that can be animated.

Stamper

A metal part electroformed from the mother. The stamper is inserted into the mold cavity to become one side of the cavity. "Stamper" is a misnomer inherited from the phonograph record industry. CDs are not stamped, but are injection molded.

Subcodes

Codes used in the CD format to hold various kinds of information, depending on the disc type.

Substrate

The main physical body of a disc, on which other coatings or layers may be added. Compact discs are made of polycarbonate plastic, coated with metal, then coated with a UV curable polymer. A label is then printed. The polycarbonate is the substrate.

SuperDisc

An early name for Digital Video Disc. See *Digital Video Disc*.

Synchronization

The process of ensuring that simultaneous events, such as events in the video and audio parts of a digital movie, are presented to the user simultaneously. This is one of the major tasks of digital movie playback architectures.

Tag

A notation in a text file that specifies how that text is to be treated or displayed.

Tagged text

Text that includes tags for formatting or linkage purposes, such as SGML or HTML text.

tar

An acronym for tape archive, a technology for creating archive libraries that is common on UNIX systems.

Tear-off menu

A menu that either pulls down or pops up and that can then be moved to another screen position and remains on the screen until it is dismissed.

Terabyte (TB)

Roughly a million million (actually 1.0995×10^{12}) bytes, used as a measure of the capacity of a computer's disk system.

Term

The duration of a contract or agreement, after which time the agreement is no longer valid. Term may be defined as a certain period of time (e.g. five years), as perpetual, or until a condition occurs (e.g. the work goes out of print).

Termination

To cease executing a program.

TEX

A text formatting system invented by Donald Knuth in order to provide proper formatting for technical documents, particularly for mathematical expressions. It uses tagged text and often custom macros to interpret the tags.

TGA

A file format originally designed by Truevision to accompany their Targa graphics boards.

TIFF (Tag Image Format File)

A popular format widely used to store and transmit graphic images. The TIFF standard supports full-color images as well as lookup table images.

Title

An electronic document or publication that is identified and sold as a unit.

Title bar

The bar at the top of a window that gives the title of the window.

Title sequence

The sequence of screens or information that is displayed to identify the title.

TOC (Table of Contents)

This is information located in the lead-in area. The TOC contains a listing of where tracks start on the disc, as well as indications to the player as to what kind of disc it is—ROM, audio, etc.

Track

The sequence of pits that are read by the reading laser comprises a track. On a CD, a track is a spiral beginning at the inside of the disc and spiraling outward, and is about three miles long. Also, a contiguous portion of the spiral of pits and lands on a compact disc; on an audio CD each track ordinarily corresponds to a single song or piece. The tracks on a disc are identified in the disc table of contents.

Trackball

A device, having both positioning and clicking functions, manipulated by the user by moving the hand over a rolling ball to move a cursor and make selections from screen presentations. Events generated by a trackball are handled as though they were mouse events.

Track pitch

The physical distance between two rows of information pits, center to center. In CD the specification of track pitch is 1.5 to 1.7 microns. Most discs are recorded with a track pitch of 1.6 microns.

Trademark

A name indicating ownership of origin of a product that is legally reserved to the owner or creator of the product.

Tray drop-in piece

The printed piece that may be inserted in a jewel box below the plastic insert in which the disc hub holder is found. Also known as the tray insert or tray card.

Tree-structured menus

Menus for which individual menu choices have submenus. See *Hierarchical menus.*

Truevision-S

A video codec developed by The Duck Co. for both AVI and QuickTime movies.

Turn

The time required for CDs to be mastered, made, and shipped, measured from the time premastered data, artwork, and other materials are in the hands of the manufacturer. Also known as the turnaround time.

Unicode

A technique for storing characters from most languages using two bytes per character.

UNIX

An operating system widely used for workstations. There are many variations on this operating system, depending on individual vendors, but they all function in much the same way. See *POSIX*.

Up

An instruction, often attached to a button, to return to the next higher level of menu or screen in a title.

UPC (Universal Product Code)

The bar code that is placed on a product so it may be scanned by point-of-sale devices. Bookstores and other retail merchants want products to use UPCs to streamline the sales process. UPCs contain a company code and a product code, and a product manufacturer must apply for a company code.

URI (Uniform Resource Identifier)

A set of conventions for identifying any file on any system accessible on the networks so that the file can be transferred to the host and the appropriate application can be called upon to display it.

URL (Uniform Resource Locator)

A URI convention based on the network address of the file to be transferred.

URN (Uniform Resource Name)

A URI convention intended to allow access to a document by a name instead of by location.

User interface

The components of an electronic title that enable the user to navigate through a document and to execute the functionality of the document.

Vehicle simulation

To present the user with the behavior and control of a vehicle from within an electronic document by use of an interface much like that of the actual vehicle.

Video for Windows

A Microsoft design for creating and playing digital video on the Windows computing platform.

Video game box

A special set-top box for playing video games. See *Set-top box*.

Virtual reality

Real-time display of direct-manipulation interactive realistic computer graphics and digital sound with three-dimensional models, presented by a display technology that allows the user to have an experience of immersion in the model presented.

Virtual world

The synthetic model space in which a user is immersed in a virtual reality environment.

Volume descriptor

An area at the beginning of a CD-ROM reserved for the recording of information about the origination, originator, copyright, etc.

Volume name

The name of a file volume, such as a CD-ROM, that is mounted on a system.

VRML (Virtual Reality Modeling Language)

A specification for 3-dimensional models and interactivity across the networks, allowing for the creation and networked sharing of virtual worlds.

VTOC (Volume table of contents)

The list of tracks, along with their position and duration, on a CD-ROM; the list of all files in the volume (the directory) on a magnetic disc.

WAV

A digital audio format for Microsoft Windows.

Web browser

Software that allows a user to access and view documents across the computer networks and supports hypertext links through the HTML language.

Web

See *WWW*.

White Book standard

A standard developed by Philips and JVC for compact discs that supports a combination of audio and full-motion video. The video is based on MPEG video and audio that are interleaved to achieve the proper data flow rates. The standard is published in a book with a white cover.

Wholesale

Selling a product to an individual or organization that will redistribute it to individuals through one of several possible distribution channels including direct mail, catalogs, or retail outlets.

WO (Write Once)

Recordable optical disc. Can be recorded on, but not changed or erased. See *WORM.*

Work for hire

Creating a piece of work under contract to another, with the rights to that work going to the person who hired the creator. This is a legal relationship that needs to be defined by a contract between the creator and the person hiring her or him.

WORM

Write Once, Read Many. See *WO.*

WWW (World Wide Web)

A system developed at the European Particle Physics Laboratory (CERN) in Switzerland for creating and browsing distributed hypertext documents.

XCMD (External command)

A small piece of software that extends the functionality of an application.

Yellow Book standard

When the CD-ROM standards were set by Philips and Sony, they were published in a book with a yellow cover. Thus the standard for CD-ROM is sometimes called the yellow book standard.

YIQ

A color model defined for NTSC color television that takes luminance (Y) as its primary component and uses two other components, a range from orange to cyan and a range from magenta to green, to carry chrominance information. It is relatively easy to convert back and forth between YIQ and the RGB color model that is most commonly used in computing.

Bibliography

The following references cover the main technical areas that are important in electronic publishing on CD-ROM, but are far from complete; we encourage you to read widely in this emerging field.

Alber, Antone F., *Multimedia: A Management Perspective*, Integrated Media Group (Belmont, CA), 1996

Adobe Systems, *PostScript Language Reference Manual*, 2nd edition, Addison-Wesley (Reading, MA), 1990

Aldus Corp., *Tag Image File Format* - Version 6.0, Technical Memorandum, 1992

Alschuler, Liora, *ABCD...SGML*, Thomson, 1995

Ames, Andrew L., David R. Nadeau, and John R. Moreland, *The VRML Sourcebook*, John Wiley & Sons (New York, NY), 1996

Ames, Patrick, *Beyond Paper*, Adobe Press (Mountain View, CA), 1993

Apple Computer, *Apple CD-ROM Handbook*, Addison-Wesley (Reading, MA), 1992

Apple Computer, *Human Interface Guidelines: The Apple Desktop Interface*, Addison-Wesley (Reading, MA), 1987

Apple Computer, *Inside Macintosh: QuickTime*, Addison-Wesley (Reading, MA), 1993

Apple Computer, *Inside Macintosh: QuickTime Components*, Addison-Wesley (Reading, MA), 1993

Apple Computer, *OpenDoc Programmer's Guide*, Addison-Wesley (Reading, MA), 1996

Aronson, Larry, *HTML 3 Manual of Style*, Ziff-Davis Press (Emeryville, CA), 1995

Berners-Lee, Tim and Daniel Connolly, "Hypertext Markup Language," Internet draft available from *info.cern.ch*

Bienz, Tim and Richard Cohn, *Portable Document Format Reference Manual*, Addison-Wesley (Reading, MA), 1993

Bowers, Richard A., *List of Resources for CD-ROM Publishing*, Optical Publishing Association, 1996

Brockschmidt, Kraig, *Inside OLE, 2nd Edition*, Microsoft Press (Richmond, WA), 1995

Brown, Judith R. and Steve Cunningham, *User Interface Programming: Principles and Examples*, John Wiley & Sons (New York, NY), 1989

Buford, John F. Koegel, *Multimedia Systems*, SIGGRAPH Books/Addison-Wesley (Reading, MA), 1994

Bush, Vannevar, "As We May Think," *Atlantic Monthly*, July 1945, 101-108

Busk, J. Philip, Clayton Summers, C. Steven Langer, and James R. Fricks, *Compact Disc Terminology*, 2nd edition, Disc Manufacturing Inc.

CompuServe, Inc., *Graphics Interface Format*, June 1987

Cox, Brad J. and Andrew J. Novobilski, *Object-Oriented Programming: An Evolutionary Approach*, 2nd edition, Addison-Wesley (Reading, MA), 1991

Disc Manufacturing, Inc., *A Glossary of CD and CD-ROM Terms*

Disc Manufacturing Inc., *An Overview of Multimedia CD-ROM Production*

Durrett, H. John (ed.), *Color and the Computer*, Academic Press (San Diego, CA), 1987

Electronic Book Technologies, *DynaText Publisher Guide*, 1994

Flanagan, David, *Java in a Nutshell*, O'Reilly & Associates (Sebastopol, CA), 1996

Fricks, James R., *Compact Disc Terminology*, Disc Manufacturing Inc., 1992

ISO 9660 Standard, American National Standards Institute (New York, NY), 1988

ISO 10149 Standard, American National Standards Institute (New York, NY), 1989

Jackson, Jerry R. and Alan L. McClellan, *Java By Example*, SunSoft Press/Prentice-Hall Professional (Mountain View, CA), 1996

Johnson, Nels, with Fred Gault and Mark Florence, *How to Digitize Video*, John Wiley & Sons (New York, NY), 1994

Kerlow, Isaac Victor and Judson Rosebush, *Computer Graphics for Designers and Artists*, 2nd edition, Van Nostrand Reinhold (New York, NY), 1994

Murray, James D. and William vanRyper, *Encyclopedia of Graphics File Formats*, 2nd edition, O'Reilly & Associates (Sebastopol, CA), 1996

Nielsen, Jakob, *HyperText and HyperMedia*, Academic Press (San Diego, CA), 1990

Ozer, Jan, *Video Compression*, Academic Press, (San Deigo, CA), 1996

Pennebaker, William B. and Joan L. Mitchell, *JPEG Still Image Compression Standard*, Van Nostrand Reinhold (New York, NY), 1993

Phillips, Richard L., "MediaView: A general multimedia digital publication system," *Communications of the ACM*, 34(7), July 1991, 74-83

Phillips, Richard L., "Opportunities for Multimedia in Education," in *Interactive Learning Through Visualization*, S. Cunningham and R. Hubbold, eds., Springer-Verlag (Berlin, Germany), 1992, 25-35

Pohlman, Kenneth, *The Compact Disc Handbook*, 2nd edition, A-R Editions, Inc. (Madison, WI)

Pohlman, Kenneth, *The Principles of Digital Audio*, Howard W. Sams & Co. (New York, NY)

Rosebush, Judson, "My First CD-ROM," *CD-ROM Professional*, 6(6), November 1993, 226-227

Rosebush, Judson, "Digital Video: Future Predictions," *CD-ROM Professional*, 7(2), March 1994, 127-132

Samuelson, Pamela, "Copyright's Fair Use Doctrine and Digital Data," *Communications of the ACM*, 37(1), January 1994, 21-27

Smedlinghoff, Thomas J., *The Software Publishers Association Legal Guide to Multimedia*, Addison-Wesley (Reading, MA), 1994

Sosinsky, Barry, and Elisabeth Parker, *Acrobat Quick Tour*, Ventana Press (Chapel Hill, NC), 1995

Summers, Clayton, *Introduction to ISO 9660*, Disc Manufacturing Inc., 1993

Sydow, Dan Parks, *QuickTime Macintosh Multimedia*, MIS Press (New York, NY), 1994

Thompson, John and Sam Gottlieb, *Macromedia Director Lingo Workshop*, Hayden (Indianapolis, IN), 1995

Turner, Ronald C., Timothy A. Douglass, and Andrew J. Turner, *README.1ST, SGML for Writers and Editors*, Prentice-Hall (Englewood Cliffs, NJ), 1996 van Hoff, Arthur, Sami Shaio, and Orca Starbuck, *Hooked on Java*, Addison-Wesley (Reading, MA), 1996

Wallace, Gregory K., "The JPEG Still Picture Compression Standard," *Communications of the ACM* 34(4), April 1991, 30-44

Ziv, J. and A. Lempel, "A Universal Algorithm for Sequential Data Compression," *IEEE Transactions on Information Theory*, IT-24(5), September 1978, 530-536

Index

About the Authors

Steve Cunningham is a Professor of Computer Science at California State University Stanislaus. He has served as Director for Publications for ACM SIGGRAPH, where he founded SIGGRAPH's electronic publishing program, and now serves as SIGGRAPH's Chair. His other interests include computer graphics education, computer science curricula, and the use of visualization and electronic media in teaching. In recent years Steve has written and spoken widely on visualization in mathematics and on electronic publishing. He is the coauthor of *Programming the User Interface: Principles and Examples*, and coeditor of three other books on visualization in education and in computer graphics.

Steve began his academic career in mathematics, earning his Ph.D. at the University of Oregon, and switched to computer science when the computer graphics he was doing for his mathematics teaching became more interesting than the mathematics itself. He earned an M.S. in computer science at Oregon State University, and during these two periods of graduate study in Oregon became a great fan of mountains, beaches, wilderness, and birds.

Judson Rosebush is an experienced media producer and computer theorist whose companies have produced commercials (more than 1000), animations, and television (e.g., *Volume Visualization and HDTV and the Quest for Virtual Reality*). He has developed CD-ROMs for entertainment and information—for example, *Isaac Asimov's The Ultimate Robot* (published by Byron Preiss Publications and distributed by Microsoft) and *The Vietnam War* (a joint venture between CBS News and *The New York Times*, distributed by Macmillan Digital). He is the coauthor of *Computer Graphics for Designers and Artists* (Van Nostrand Reinhold) and *Computer Animation*, the author of the *Pixel Handbook*, the American editor of *Pixel Vision* magazine, and a columnist for *CD-ROM Professional* magazine.

Colophon

Hanna Dyer and Edie Freedman designed the cover of this book, using an original scan of a CD-ROM. The cover layout was produced using Quark XPress 3.3 and Adobe Photoshop. The cover font is Emigre Matrix.

The interior layout was designed by Nancy Priest and Marcia Ciro and implemented in FrameMaker 5.0 by Mike Sierra. The heading fonts are from the Matrix family and the text is set in ITC Garamond Light. The illustrations were created in Adobe Photoshop and Macromedia Freehand 5.0 by Chris Reilley.

INTERNET

Programming Books from O'Reilly & Associates, Inc.

SUMMER 1996

Internet Programming

HTML: The Definitive Guide

By Chuck Musciano & Bill Kennedy
1st Edition April 1996
410 pages, ISBN 1-56592-175-5

HTML: The Definitive Guide is a complete guide to creating documents on the World Wide Web. To become a true master of HTML, you need to develop your own style. That means knowing not only what's appropriate, but what's effective. This book describes basic syntax and semantics and goes on to show you how to create beautiful, informative Web documents you'll be proud to display.

HTML: The Definitive Guide helps you become fluent in HTML, fully versed in the language's syntax, semantics, and elements of style. It covers the most up-to-date version of the HTML standard, plus all the common extensions, especially Netscape extensions. The authors cover each and every selement of the currently accepted version of the language in detail, explaining how each element works and how it interacts with all the other elements. They've also included a style guide that helps you decide how to best use HTML to accomplish a variety of tasks, from simple online documentation to complex marketing and sales presentations.

Designing for the Web: Getting Started in a New Medium

By Jennifer Niederst with Edie Freedman
1st Edition April 1996
180 pages, ISBN 1-56592-165-8

Designing for the Web introduces you to the unique considerations of Web design and gives you the basics you need to hit the ground running. Although geared toward designers, this book covers information and techniques useful to anyone who wants to put graphics online. It explains how to work with HTML documents from a designer's point of view, outlines special problems with presenting information online, and walks through incorporating images into Web pages, with emphasis on resolution and improving efficiency.

You'll find a step-by-step tutorial on putting together a Web page from scratch, pointers on creating graphics that are optimized for the Web, tips on using background images and colors in Web pages, recommendations for reducing download times of images, and instructions for transparency and interlacing to Web graphics. This book also discusses the impact of different browsers and platforms on your design, explains how HTML tags are used for design, and offers guidelines on navigational and orientation aids, as well as on conceptualizing your Web site as a whole.

CGI Programming on the World Wide Web

By Shishir Gundavaram
1st Edition March 1996
450 pages, ISBN 1-56592-168-2

The World Wide Web is more than a place to put up clever documents and pretty pictures. With a little study and practice, you can offer interactive queries and serve instant information from databases, worked up into colorful graphics. That is what the Common Gateway Interface (CGI) offers.

This book offers a comprehensive explanation of CGI and related techniques for people who hold on to the dream of providing their own information servers on the Web. Gundavaram starts at the beginning, explaining the value of CGI and how it works, then moves swiftly into the subtle details of programming. For most of the examples, the book uses the most common platform (UNIX) and the most popular language (Perl) used for CGI programming today. However, it also introduces the essentials of making CGI work with other platforms and languages.

Programming Perl

By Larry Wall, Randal L. Schwartz, et al.
2nd Edition Fall 1996
700 pages (est.), ISBN 1-56592-149-6

Programming Perl, second edition, is the authoritative guide to Perl version 5, the scripting utility that has established itself as the programming tool of choice for the World Wide Web, UNIX system administration, and a vast range of other applications. Version 5 of Perl includes object-oriented programming facilities. The book is coauthored by Larry Wall, the creator of Perl.

Perl is a language for easily manipulating text, files, and processes. It provides a more concise and readable way to do many jobs that were formerly accomplished (with difficulty) by programming with C or one of the shells. Perl is likely to be available wherever you choose to work. And if it isn't, you can get it and install it easily and free of charge.

This heavily revised second edition of *Programming Perl* contains a full explanation of the features in Perl version 5.002. It covers version 5.002 Perl syntax, functions, library modules, references, debugging, and object-oriented programming. Also includes a Perl cookbook.

Learning Perl

By Randal L. Schwartz, Foreword by Larry Wall
1st Edition November 1993
274 pages, ISBN 1-56592-042-2

Learning Perl is ideal for system administrators, programmers, and anyone else wanting a down-to-earth introduction to this useful language. Written by a Perl trainer, its aim is to make a competent, hands-on Perl programmer out of the reader as quickly as possible. The book takes a tutorial approach and includes hundreds of short code examples, along with some lengthy ones. The relatively inexperienced programmer will find *Learning Perl* easily accessible.

Each chapter of the book includes practical programming exercises. Solutions are presented for all exercises.

For a comprehensive and detailed guide to advanced programming with Perl, read O'Reilly's companion book, *Programming Perl.*

Perl 5 Desktop Reference

By Johan Vromans
1st Edition February 1996
39 pages, ISBN 1-56592-187-9

This is the standard quick-reference guide for the Perl programming language. It provides a complete overview of the language, from variables to input and output, from flow control to regular expressions, from functions to document formats—all packed into a convenient, carry-around booklet.

World Wide Web Journal

Edited by O'Reilly & Associates and Web Consortium (W3C)

The World Wide Web Journal is a quarterly publication that provides timely, in-depth coverage of the new research and technologies, such as protocols for security, replication, and caching, HTML, SGML and content labeling from the World Wide Web Consortium and selected peer-reviewed papers. It also explores the broader issues of the web such as censorship and intellectual property rights. Call for subscription information.

Internet Security

Java Series

Exploring Java

By Pat Niemeyer & Josh Peck
1st Edition May 1996 (est.)
426 pages, ISBN 1-56592-184-4

Exploring Java introduces the basics of Java, the hot new object-oriented programming language for networked applications. The ability to create animated World Wide Web pages has sparked the rush to Java. But what has also made this new language so important is that it's truly portable. The code runs on any machine that provides a Java interpreter, whether Windows 95, Windows NT, the Macintosh, or any flavor of UNIX.

With a practical, hands-on approach characteristic of O'Reilly's Nutshell Handbooks®, *Exploring Java* shows you how to write dynamic Web pages. But that's only the beginning. This book shows you how to quickly get up to speed writing Java applets (programs executed within Web browsers) and other applications, including networking programs, content and protocol handlers, and security managers. *Exploring Java* is the first book in a new Java documentation series from O'Reilly that will keep pace with the rapid Java developments. Covers Java's latest Beta release.

Java Virtual Machine

By Troy Downing & Jon Meyer
1st Edition Fall 1996
300 pages (est.), ISBN 1-56592-194-1,

The Java Virtual Machine is the software implementation of a "CPU" designed to run compiled Java code. Using the Java Virtual Machine (JVM) unleashes the true power of Java—making it possible to develop additional syntaxes for expressing the problems you want to solve and giving you the ultimate control over the performance of your application. This book is a comprehensive programming guide for the Java Virtual Machine. It'll give you a strong overview and reference of the JVM so that you can create your own implementtations of the JVM or write your own compilers that create Java object code.

The book is divided into two sections: the first includes information on the semantics and structure of the JVM; the second is a reference of the JVM instructions, or "opcodes." The programming guide includes numerous examples written in Java assembly language. A Java assembler is provided with the book, so the examples can all be compiled and executed. The reference section offers a complete description of the instruction set of the VM, and the class file format including a description of the byte-code verifier.

Java in a Nutshell: A Desktop Quick Reference for Java Programmers

By David Flanagan
1st Edition February 1996
460 pages , ISBN 1-56592-183-6

Java in a Nutshell is a complete quick-reference guide to Java, the hot new programming language from Sun Microsystems. This comprehensive volume contains descriptions of all of the classes in the Java 1.0 API, with a definitive listing of all methods and variables. It also contains an accelerated introduction to Java for C and C++ programmers who want to learn the language fast.

Java in a Nutshell introduces the Java programming language and contains many practical examples that show programmers how to write Java applications and applets. It is also an indispensable quick reference designed to wait faithfully by the side of every Java programmer's keyboard. It puts all the information Java programmers need right at their fingertips.

JavaScript: the Definitive Guide

By David Flanagan
1st Edition Summer 1996
500 pages (est.), ISBN 1-56592-193-3

From the bestselling author of *Java in a Nutshell* comes the definitive reference manual for JavaScript, the HTML extension that allows programs to be embedded in Web pages, making them more active than ever before. In this book, David Flanagan describes how JavaScript really works (and when it doesn't).

The first eight chapters document the core JavaScript language, and the next six describe how JavaScript works on the client-side to interact with the Web browser and with the Web page. Following this detailed explanation of JavaScript features is a complete reference section that documents every object, property, method, event handler, function, and constructor used by client-side JavaScript.

This book documents the version of JavaScript shipped with Navigator 2.0, 2.0.1, and 2.0.2, and also the much-changed version of JavaScript shipped with beta versions of Navigator 3.0. The 3.0 information is current as of the 3.0b4 release. Lists known bugs and documents commonly encountered bugs on reference pages of JavaScript objects.

PGP: Pretty Good Privacy

By Simson Garfinkel
1st Edition December 1994
430 pages, ISBN 1-56592-098-8

PGP is a freely available encryption

program that protects the privacy of files and electronic mail. It uses powerful public key cryptography and works on virtually every platform. This book is both a readable technical user's guide and a fascinating behind-the-scenes look at cryptography and privacy. It describes how to use PGP and provides background on cryptography, PGP's history, battles over public key cryptography patents and U.S. government export restrictions, and public debates about privacy and free speech.

"I even learned a few things about PGP from Simson's informative book."—Phil Zimmermann, Author of PGP

"Since the release of PGP 2.0 from Europe in the fall of 1992, PGP's popularity and usage has grown to make it the de-facto standard for email encyrption. Simson's book is an excellent overview of PGP and the history of cryptography in general. It should prove a useful addition to the resource library for any computer user, from the UNIX wizard to the PC novice."
—Derek Atkins, PGP Development Team, MIT

Building Internet Firewalls

By D. Brent Chapman & Elizabeth D. Zwicky
1st Edition September 1995
544 pages, ISBN 1-56592-124-0

Everyone is jumping on the Internet bandwagon, despite the

fact that the security risks associated with connecting to the Net have never been greater. This book is a practical guide to building firewalls on the Internet. It describes a variety of firewall approaches and architectures and discusses how you can build packet filtering and proxying solutions at your site. It also contains a full discussion of how to configure Internet services (e.g., FTP, SMTP, Telnet) to work with a firewall, as well as a complete list of resources, including the location of many publicly available firewall construction tools.

Practical UNIX &Internet Security

By Simson Garfinkel & Gene Spafford
2nd Edition April 1996
1004 pages (est.), ISBN 1-56592-148-8

This second edition of the classic *Practical UNIX Security* is a complete rewrite of the original book. It's packed with twice the pages and offers even more practical information for UNIX users and administrators. In it you'll find coverage of features of many types of UNIX systems, including SunOS, Solaris, BSDI, AIX, HP-UX, Digital UNIX, Linux, and others. Contents include UNIX and security basics, system administrator tasks, network security, and appendices containing checklists and helpful summaries.

Computer Crime

By David Icove, Karl Seger & William VonStorch
1st Edition August 1995
464 pages, ISBN 1-56592-086-4

Terrorist attacks on computer centers, electronic fraud on international funds transfer networks, viruses and worms in our software, corporate espionage on business networks, and crackers breaking into systems on the Internet... Computer criminals are becoming ever more technically sophisticated, and it's an increasing challenge to keep up with their methods.

Computer Crime: A Crimefighter's Handbook is for anyone who needs to know what today's computer crimes look like, how to prevent them, and how to detect, investigate, and prosecute them if they do occur. It contains basic computer security information as well as guidelines for investigators, law enforcement, and computer system managers and administrators. The book also contains a compendium of computer-related U.S. federal statutes, the statutes of individual states, representative international laws, a resource summary, detailed papers on computer crime, and a sample search warrant for a computer crime.

Internet Administration

DNS and BIND

By Paul Albitz & Cricket Liu
1st Edition October 1992
418 pages, ISBN 1-56592-010-4

DNS and BIND contains all you need to know about the Internet's Domain Name System (DNS) and the Berkeley Internet Name Domain (BIND), its UNIX implementation. The Domain Name System is the Internet's "phone book"; it's a database that tracks important information (in particular, names and addresses) for every computer on the Internet. If you're a system administrator, this book will show you how to set up and maintain the DNS software on your network.

sendmail

By Bryan Costales, with Eric Allman & Neil Rickert
1st Edition November 1993
830 pages, ISBN 1-56592-056-2

This Nutshell Handbook® is far and away the most comprehensive book ever written on sendmail, the program that acts like a traffic cop in routing and delivering mail on UNIX-based networks. Although sendmail is used on almost every UNIX system, it's one of the last great uncharted territories—and most difficult utilities to learn—in UNIX system administration. This book provides a complete sendmail tutorial, plus extensive reference material on every aspect of the program. It covers IDA sendmail, the latest version (V8) from Berkeley, and the standard versions available on most systems.

Managing Internet Information Services

By Cricket Liu, Jerry Peek, Russ Jones, Bryan Buus & Adrian Nye
1st Edition December 1994
668 pages, ISBN 1-56592-062-7

This comprehensive guide describes how to set up information services and make them available over the Internet. It discusses why a company would want to offer Internet services, provides complete coverage of all popular services, and tells how to select which ones to provide. Most of the book describes how to set up Gopher, World Wide Web, FTP, and WAIS servers and email services.

Networking Personal Computers with TCP/IP

By Craig Hunt
1st Edition July 1995
408 pages, ISBN 1-56592-123-2

This book offers practical information as well as detailed instructions for attaching PCs to a TCP/IP network and its UNIX servers. It discusses the challenges you'll face and offers general advice on how to deal with them, provides basic TCP/IP configuration information for some of the popular PC operating systems, covers advanced configuration topics and configuration of specific applications such as email, and includes a chapter on NetWare, the most popular PC LAN system software.

TCP/IP Network Administration

By Craig Hunt
1st Edition August 1992
502 pages, ISBN 0-937175-82-X

A complete guide to setting up and running a TCP/IP network for practicing system administrators. *TCP/IP Network Administration* covers setting up your network, configuring important network applications including sendmail, and issues in troubleshooting and security. It covers both BSD and System V TCP/IP implementations.

Getting Connected: The Internet at 56K and Up

By Kevin Dowd
1st Edition June 1996
424 pages, ISBN 1-56592-154-2

A complete guide for businesses, schools, and other organizations who want to connect their computers to the Internet. This book covers everything you need to know to make informed decisions, from helping you figure out which services you really need to providing down-to-earth explanations of telecommunication options, such as frame relay, ISDN, and leased lines. Once you're online, it shows you how to set up basic Internet services, such as a World Wide Web server. Tackles issues for PC, Macintosh, and UNIX platforms.

Encyclopedia of Graphics File Formats

By James D. Murray & William vanRyper
2nd Edition May 1996
1154 pages, Includes CD-ROM , ISBN 1-56592-161-5

The Encyclopedia of Graphics File Formats is the definitive reference on graphics file formats; the first edition of the book has already become a classic for graphics programmers.

In this second edition, we have retrofitted the entire *Encyclopedia of Graphics File Formats* for display on the Internet's World Wide Web. Using the Enhanced Mosaic browser (included on the CD-ROM), you can navigate the book's contents on the CD-ROM and (if you have an Internet connection) link to the O'Reilly Web Center on the Internet where we maintain an online update service. There you'll find updates, descriptions of new formats, graphics news, and links to additional resources on the World Wide Web. On the CD-ROM, we've also included the updated printed book—still the most portable resource around.

Whether you're a graphics programmer, service bureau, or graphics designer who needs to know the low-level technical details of graphics files, this online resource/book is for you.

The CD-ROM includes a collection of hard-to-find resources (many that have never before been available outside the organizations that developed them). We've assembled original file format specification documents (covering more than 100 formats) from such vendors as Adobe, Apple, IBM, Microsoft, and Silicon Graphics, along with test images and code examples for many of the formats. The CD-ROM also contains a set of publicly available software and shareware—for Windows, MS-DOS, OS/2, the Macintosh, and UNIX—that will let you convert, view, compress, and manipulate graphics files and images.

"At last!!! No more hunting, begging, borrowing, or stealing to find that particular file format information you need—here it is...in one place. If you work with graphics files, buy this book.... The EGFFis useful to file-dissecting neophytes and veterans alike. It is a well-written resource and reference book that you will wonder how you ever did without."
—Microtimes(Product Spotlight), October 19, 1994

Understanding Japanese Information Processing

By Ken Lunde
1st Edition September 1993
470 pages, ISBN 1-56592-043-0

Understanding Japanese Information Processing provides detailed information on all aspects of handling Japanese text on computer systems. It brings all of the relevant information together in a single book and covers everything from the origins of modern- day Japanese to the latest information on specific emerging computer encoding standards. Appendices provide additional reference material, such as a code conversion table, character set tables, mapping tables, an extensive list of software sources, a glossary, and more.

Building a Successful Software Business

By Dave Radin
1st Edition April 1994
394 pages, ISBN 1-56592-064-3

The expanding global market offers many opportunities for the software industry; however, many new software companies never realize their potential. They write some great code—but they can't address the "business"side of running a profitable enterprise. Many potentially great companies have fallen by the wayside because their founders didn't understand their market, didn't understand how to get the word out, or didn't understand the mechanics of the business.

Building a Successful Software Business is a handbook for the new software entrepreneur and the old hand alike. If you're thinking of starting and building a company around some software you've developed, this book will guide you toward success. If you're an old hand in the software industry, this book will help you sharpen your skills or will provide a refresher course.

Topics covered include: marketing strategies and tactics; customer fulfillment, training, and support; getting your product out the door; using consultants effectively; understanding cash flow; and growing your staff. Also Includes a guide to other business resources.

There's no better time than the present. Let this book start you on the way to success.

Stay in touch with O'REILLY™

Visit Our Award-Winning World Wide Web Site

http://www.ora.com

VOTED
> "Top 100 Sites on the Web" —*PC Magazine*
> "Top 5% Web sites" —*Point Communications*
> "3-Star site" —*The McKinley Group*

*O*ur Web site contains a library of comprehensive product information (including book excerpts and tables of contents), downloadable software, background articles, interviews with technology leaders, links to relevant sites, book cover art, and more. File us in your Bookmarks or Hotlist!

Join Our Two Email Mailing Lists

LIST #1   **NEW PRODUCT RELEASES:** To receive automatic email with brief descriptions of all new O'Reilly products as they are released, send email to: **listproc@online.ora.com** and put the following information in the first line of your message (NOT in the *Subject:* field, which is ignored):
`subscribe ora-news "Your Name"`
`of "Your Organization"`
(for example: `subscribe ora-news`
`Kris Webber of Fine Enterprises`)

LIST #2   **O'REILLY EVENTS:** If you'd also like us to send information about trade show events, special promotions, and other O'Reilly events, send email to: **listproc@online.ora.com** and put the following information in the first line of your message (NOT in the *Subject:* field, which is ignored): `subscribe ora-events`
`"Your Name" of "Your`
`Organization"`

Visit Our Gopher Site

- Connect your Gopher to **gopher.ora.com**, or
- Point your Web browser to **gopher://gopher.ora.com/**, or
- telnet to **gopher.ora.com** (login: `gopher`)

Get Example Files from Our Books Via FTP

There are two ways to access an archive of example files from our books:

REGULAR FTP — ftp to: `ftp.ora.com` (login: `anonymous`—use your email address as the password) or point your Web browser to: **ftp://ftp.ora.com/**

FTPMAIL — Send an email message to: **ftpmail@online.ora.com** (write "help" in the message body)

Contact Us Via Email

order@ora.com — To place a book or software order online. Good for North American and international customers.

subscriptions@ora.com — To place an order for any of our newsletters or periodicals.

software@ora.com — For general questions and product information about our software.
- Check out O'Reilly Software Online at **http://software.ora.com** for software and technical support information.
- Registered O'Reilly software users send your questions to website-support@ora.com

books@ora.com — General questions about any of our books.

cs@ora.com — For answers to problems regarding your order or our product.

booktech@ora.com — For book content technical questions or corrections.

proposals@ora.com — To submit new book or software proposals to our editors and product managers.

international@ora.com — For information about our international distributors or translation queries
- For a list of our distributors outside of North America check out:
http://www.ora.com/www/order/country.html

O'Reilly & Associates, Inc.

101 Morris Street, Sebastopol, CA 95472 USA
TEL 707-829-0515 or 800-998-9938 (6 A.M. to 5 P.M. PST)
FAX 707-829-0104

TO ORDER: **800-889-8969** (CREDIT CARD ORDERS ONLY); **order@ora.com**; http://www.ora.com
OUR PRODUCTS ARE AVAILABLE AT A BOOKSTORE OR SOFTWARE STORE NEAR YOU.

O'REILLY™
Listing of Titles

INTERNET PROGRAMMING

CGI Programming on the World Wide Web
Designing for the Web
Exploring Java
HTML: The Definitive Guide
HTTP Programming with Perl
Learning Perl
Java Reference Manual
JavaScript Reference Manual
Java Virtual Machine
Programming Perl, 2nd. ed.
(Fall '96 est.)
Webmaster in a Nutshell
The World Wide Web Journal

USING THE INTERNET

Smileys
The Whole Internet User's Guide
and Catalog
The Whole Internet for Windows 95
What You Need to Know:
Using Email Effectively
What You Need to Know: Marketing
on the Internet (Summer 96)
What You Need to Know: Bandits on the
Information Superhighway

JAVA SERIES

Exploring Java
Java in a Nutshell
Java Language Reference
(Summer '96 est.)
JavaScript Reference Manual
(Summer '96 est.)
Java Virtual Machine

WINDOWS

Inside the Windows Registry

SOFTWARE

WebSite™ 1.1
WebSite Professional™
WebBoard™
Poly Form™

SYSTEM ADMINISTRATION

Building Internet Firewalls
Computer Crime:
A Crimefighter's Handbook
Computer Security Basics
DNS and BIND
Essential System Administration,
2nd ed.
Getting connected:
The Internet at 56K and up
Linux Network Administrator's Guide
Managing Internet Information Services
Managing Netnews (Fall '96)
Managing NFS and NIS
Networking Personal Computers
with TCP/IP
Practical UNIX & Internet Security
PGP: Pretty Good Privacy
sendmail
System Performance Tuning
TCP/IP Network Administration
termcap & terminfo
Using & Managing UUCP (Summer '96)
Volume 8 : X Window System
Administrator's Guide

UNIX

Exploring Expect
Learning GNU Emacs, 2nd Edition
(Summer '96)
Learning the bash Shell
Learning the Korn Shell
Learning the UNIX Operating System
Learning the vi Editor
Linux in a Nutshell (Summer '96)
Making TeX Work
Multimedia on Linux (Fall '96)
Running Linux, 2nd Edition
(Summer '96)
Running Linux Companion CD-ROM,
2nd Edition (Summer '96)
SCO UNIX in a Nutshell
sed & awk
Unix in a Nutshell: System V Edition
UNIX Power Tools
UNIX Systems Programming
(Summer '96)
Using csh and tsch
What You Need to Know:
When You Can't Find your
System Administrator

PROGRAMMING

Applying RCS and SCCS
C++: The Core Language
Checking C Programs with lint
DCE Security Programming
Distributing Applications Across
DCE and Windows NT
Encyclopedia of Graphics File
Formats, 2nd ed.
Guide to Writing DCE Applications
lex & yacc
Managing Projects with make
ORACLE Performance Tuning
ORACLE PL/SQL Programming
Porting UNIX Software
POSIX Programmer's Guide
POSIX.4: Programming for
the Real World
Power Programming with RPC
Practical C Programming
Practical C++ Programming
Programming Python (Fall '96)
Programming with curses
Programming with GNU Software
(Summer '96 est.)
Programming with Pthreads
(Fall '96 est.)
Software Portability with imake
Understanding DCE
Understanding Japanese Information
Processing
UNIX Systems Programming for SVR4

BERKELEY 4.4 SOFTWARE DISTRIBUTION

4.4BSD System Manager's Manual
4.4BSD User's Reference Manual
4.4BSD User's Supplementary Docs.
4.4BSD Programmer's Reference Man.
4.4BSD Programmer's Supp. Docs.

X PROGRAMMING

THE X WINDOW SYSTEM

Volume 0: X Protocol Reference Manual
Volume 1: Xlib Programming Manual
Volume 2: Xlib Reference Manual
Volume. 3M: X Window System
User's Guide, Motif Ed.
Volume. 4: X Toolkit Intrinsics
Programming Manual
Volume 4M: X Toolkit Intrinsics
Programming Manual, Motif Ed.
Volume 5: X Toolkit Intrinsics
Reference Manual
Volume 6A: Motif Programming Man.
Volume 6B: Motif Reference Manual
Volume 6C: Motif Tools
Volume 8 : X Window System
Administrator's Guide
Programmer's Supplement for Release 6
X User Tools (with CD-ROM)
The X Window System in a Nutshell

HEALTH, CAREER & BUSINESS

Building a Successful Software Business
The Computer User's Survival Guide
Dictionary of Computer Terms
The Future Does Not Compute
Love Your Job!
Publishing with CD-Rom (Summer '96)

TRAVEL

Travelers' Tales: Brazil (Summer '96 est.)
Travelers' Tales: Food (Summer '96)
Travelers' Tales France
Travelers' Tales Hong Kong
Travelers' Tales India
Travelers' Tales Mexico
Travelers' Tales: San Francisco
Travelers' Tales Spain
Travelers' Tales Thailand
Travelers' Tales: A Woman's World

SONGLINE GUIDES

NetLearning
Political Activism Online (Fall '96)

International Distributors

Customers outside North America can now order O'Reilly & Associates books through the following distributors. They offer our international customers faster order processing, more bookstores, increased representation at tradeshows worldwide, and the high-quality, responsive service our customers have come to expect.

EUROPE, MIDDLE EAST, AND NORTHERN AFRICA
(except Germany, Switzerland, and Austria)

INQUIRIES
International Thomson Publishing Europe
Berkshire House
168-173 High Holborn
London WC1V 7AA, United Kingdom
Telephone: 44-171-497-1422
Fax: 44-171-497-1426
Email: itpint@itps.co.uk

ORDERS
International Thomson Publishing
Services, Ltd.
Cheriton House, North Way
Andover, Hampshire SP10 5BE,
United Kingdom
Telephone: 44-264-342-832 (UK orders)
Telephone: 44-264-342-806 (outside UK)
Fax: 44-264-364418 (UK orders)
Fax: 44-264-342761 (outside UK)

GERMANY, SWITZERLAND, AND AUSTRIA

International Thomson Publishing GmbH
O'Reilly-International Thomson Verlag
Königswinterer Straße 418
53227 Bonn, Germany
Telephone: 49-228-97024 0
Fax: 49-228-441342
Email: anfragen@arade.ora.de

ASIA *(except Japan)*

INQUIRIES
International Thomson Publishing Asia
Block 211 Henderson Road
#08-03 Henderson Industrial Park
Singapore 159552
Telephone: 65-272-6496
Fax: 65-272-6498

ORDERS
Telephone: 65-268-7867
Fax: 65-268-6727

JAPAN
O'Reilly Japan, Inc.
Kiyoshige Building 2F
12-Banchi, Sanei-cho
Shinjuku-Ku
Tokyo 160 Japan
Telephone: 8-3-3356-55227
Fax: 81-3-3356-5261
Email: kenj@ora.com

AUSTRALIA
WoodsLane Pty. Ltd.
7/5 Vuko Place, Warriewood NSW 2102
P.O. Box 935, Mona Vale NSW 2103
Australia
Telephone: 61-2-9970-5111
Fax: 61-2-9970-5002
Email: woods@tmx.mhs.oz.au

NEW ZEALAND
WoodsLane New Zealand Ltd.
21 Cooks Street (P.O. Box 575)
Wanganui, New Zealand
Telephone: 64-6-347-6543
Fax: 64-6-345-4840
Email: woods@tmx.mhs.oz.au

THE AMERICAS
O'Reilly & Associates, Inc.
101 Morris Street
Sebastopol, CA 95472 U.S.A.
Telephone: 707-829-0515
Telephone: 800-998-9938 (U.S. & Canada)
Fax: 707-829-0104
Email: order@ora.com

SOUTHERN AFRICA
International Thomson Publishing Southern Africa
Building 18, Constantia Park
240 Old Pretoria Road
P.O. Box 2459
Halfway House, 1685 South Africa
Telephone: 27-11-805-4819
Fax: 27-11-805-3648

O'REILLY™

Here's a page we encourage readers to tear out...

O'REILLY WOULD LIKE TO HEAR FROM YOU

Which book did this card come from?

_____

Where did you buy this book?
- ❏ Bookstore
- ❏ Direct from O'Reilly
- ❏ Bundled with hardware/software
- ❏ Computer Store
- ❏ Class/seminar
- ❏ Other _____

What operating system do you use?
- ❏ UNIX
- ❏ Windows NT
- ❏ Other _____
- ❏ Macintosh
- ❏ PC(Windows/DOS)

What is your job description?
- ❏ System Administrator
- ❏ Network Administrator
- ❏ Web Developer
- ❏ Programmer
- ❏ Educator/Teacher
- ❏ Other _____

❏ Please send me *ora.com*, O'Reilly's catalog, containing a complete listing of O'Reilly books and software.

Name _____   Company/Organization _____

Address _____

City _____   State _____   Zip/Postal Code _____   Country _____

Telephone _____   Internet or other email address (specify network) _____

Nineteenth century wood engraving
of a mouse from the O'Reilly
& Associates Nutshell Handbook®
*CGI Programming on the
World Wide Web.*

BUSINESS REPLY MAIL

FIRST CLASS MAIL   PERMIT NO. 80   SEBASTOPOL, CA

Postage will be paid by addressee

O'Reilly & Associates, Inc.
101 Morris Street
Sebastopol, CA 95472-9902